Conflict and Com

R

Conflict and Compromise

The Political Economy of Slavery, Emancipation, and the American Civil War

ROGER L. RANSOM
University of California, Riverside

CAMBRIDGE
UNIVERSITY PRESS

the University of Cambridge
treet, Cambridge CB2 1RP
40 West 20th Street, New York, NY 10011-4211, USA
10 Stamford Road, Oakleigh, Melbourne 3166, Australia

© Cambridge University Press 1989

First published 1989
Reprinted 1990, 1993

Library of Congress Cataloging-in-Publication Data
Ransom, Roger L., 1938–
Conflict and promise: the political economy of slavery,
emancipation, and the American Civil War / Roger L. Ransom.
p.   cm.
ISBN 0-521-32343-6. – ISBN 0-521-31167-5 (pbk.)
1. Slavery – United States – History. 2. Slavery – United States –
Emancipation. 3. United States – History – Civil War, 1861-1865 –
Causes. 4. United States – History – Civil War, 1861-1865 –
Economic aspects. I. Title.
E441.R3   1990
937.7'112–dc19   88–36741
                                                              CIP

A catalogue record for this book is available from the British Library.

ISBN 0-521-32343-6 hardback
ISBN 0-521-31167-5 paperback

Transferred to digital printing 2002

FOR CONNIE

Contents

Tables and Illustrations

Tables

Figures

Maps

Preface

It is commonplace for authors introducing a book on the American Civil War to remind their readers that the war was the bloodiest in American history; that no event had a more profound impact on the course of American history; and that the scars of that war can still be found more than a century after the famous meeting of Robert E. Lee and Ulysses S. Grant at the Appomattox Courthouse, Virginia. Because the war was all of this and much more, it has continued to fascinate historians from that day to the present. That fascination has produced a huge outpouring of books – at least fifty thousand volumes according to one estimate – on the subject of the war. Why have I decided to add to that total? To answer that question, let me explain just how I became a "Civil War historian."

It was early September 1983. I was at that time a professor in the economics department at the University of California at Riverside. Carlos Cortes, chair of the history department at Riverside, and I were sitting in my office discussing what he had earlier described as an "interesting possibility." Owing to an unexpected resignation, Carlos explained, the history department had an opening for a historian of nineteenth-century America. The department had voted to explore the possibility of offering me the position. Was I interested? Taken somewhat by surprise, I replied that it seemed like an intriguing idea, and we left it at that.

Although I was surprised by the offer, the idea of having at least a part-time appointment in a department of history had crossed my mind in the past. After twenty years of living in the carefully structured theoretical world of economists, the almost limitless range of opportunities available in the world of historians seemed more and more appealing. I decided that life in the history department would be a very pleasant change in my academic environment.

So it was that in September 1984 I was sitting in a different office, contemplating my future as a historian. The move from economics to history had been very straightforward except for one minor problem: What would I teach? There is, after all, a limit to the number of economic history courses that a history department can offer. While exploring various possibilities, I mentioned that I had a modest degree of expertise and a great deal of interest in Civil War history. The offer was quickly accepted and with a stroke of a pen, I became the department's Civil War historian.

That, very briefly, is how the idea for this book was born. Coming from a different perspective than most students of the Civil War, I found myself continually reinterpreting the historical literature so that it "made sense" to someone whose background was in economics, rather than history. This book is, quite simply, the product of that effort: an economic historian's attempt to analyze and "make sense of" the economic and political factors that produced the conflict we call the Civil War.

There is more to this than explaining events that happened long ago. At a time when Americans are constantly reading and hearing reports of violent confrontations between contending parties in far-off places such as Ireland or South Africa or Nicaragua or the Middle East, it is useful, I think, to reflect upon the fact that we Americans once faced an equally bitter and intractable division. The moral and political impasse over the spread of slavery short-circuited a political system that had been designed to accommodate diversity and to seek compromise. Conflict, not compromise, prevailed in 1860. Equally sobering is the realization that the bloodiest war in American history produced only a halfhearted solution to the problem of slavery and the racism that lay beneath its surface. American blacks would have to wait more than a century before the freedoms supposedly guaranteed by the Thirteenth and Fourteenth Amendments would actually be realized. The failure of Reconstruction offers us an unpleasant lesson from the Civil War era: "Progress" on even the most basic issues — such as civil liberties for black Americans — has been painfully slow.

I am not, of course, the first person to examine the political economy of the Civil War. Almost as soon as the war broke out, the British political economist J. E. Cairnes published a treatise subtitled "An Attempt to Explain the Real Issues Involved in the American Contest." Cairnes is one of many scholars whose research efforts have provided a foundation for my own research. Whereas I trust that I have adequately acknowledged the ideas of others through the citations to their published works, a few people deserve special recognition for their generous and insightful comments on all or part of the manuscript. William Gienapp provided critical judgements and suggestions for improvements from the outset of the project to its completion, and the final draft was a far better product thanks to his efforts. Kenneth Winkle offered valuable suggestions on the penultimate draft. Louis Johnston and Debbie O'Neal each offered helpful comments and proofread the entire manuscript during final preparation. Others noteworthy for their comments and encouragement at various stages of my project include Jeremy Atack, Fred Bateman, Sue Headlee, Bruce Levine, Bob McGuire, Louis Mazur, Don Schaefer, Tom Weiss, Chuck Wetherell, and Mary Yeager. Finally, many of the insights offered in this book are the product of my long-standing collaboration with Richard Sutch. The findings reported in our book, *One Kind of Freedom*, and several of our subsequent papers provide a major part of the "economic" factor of the political economy of slavery and emancipation in the pages that follow.

In addition to this substantial intellectual support, my research efforts have benefited from two sources of financial support. The John Simon Guggenheim Foundation provided a fellowship during the 1987–8 academic year that allowed me the time to work on this project. The University of California provided sabbatical leave in the spring of 1988, and support monies for the past several years.

The editorial encouragement of Frank Smith at Cambridge University Press has been extremely valuable, and his patience in waiting for the final manuscript went well beyond the bounds of tolerance normally extended to delinquent authors. Sophia Prybylski supervised the preparation of the manuscript into final form. As one who most certainly does not have a penchant for detail, I found her willingness to look after the myriad of details associated with the organization of the manuscript into publishable form invaluable. My brother, David Ransom, provided both advice and major elements of the software and other computer operations that are now an essential part of manuscript preparation.

My largest debt, by far, is to my wife Connie. For almost three decades she has given me the most important support of all: the love of someone who cares.

1

Historical Puzzles

Four score and seven years ago, our fathers brought forth upon this continent, a new nation, conceived in Liberty, and dedicated to the proposition
that all men are created equal.

Now we are engaged in a great civil war, testing whether that nation, or
any nation so conceived, and so dedicated, can long endure. We are met on a
great battlefield of that war. We have come to dedicate a portion of that field,
as a final resting place for those who gave their lives, that that nation might
live. . . .

We here highly resolve that these dead shall not have died in vain, – that
this nation, under God, shall have a new birth of freedom – and that that
government of the people, by the people, and for the people shall not perish
from the earth.

Abraham Lincoln, November 18, 1863[1]

It was written, rumor has it, on the back of an envelope during the train
ride from Washington on the day of the speech, and it took Abraham
Lincoln less than two minutes to read the full text of his address to the
people gathered at the cemetery just outside Gettysburg on that fall day
in 1863. Intending only to say a few words to commemorate the efforts
of those who died at Gettysburg and to encourage those who were carrying on the fight, Lincoln provided history with an eloquent and succinct
statement of what the conflict between Union and Confederacy was all
about.

Lincoln's reference to the founding fathers reminds us that it is in the
creation of the Union itself that we will find the genesis of the conflict
that eventually erupted into a war between the states. The breaking of
that pact, after all, precipitated the violent struggle in which Americans
found themselves in 1863. Well before that day at Gettysburg, Lincoln
and many other Americans realized that the union created in 1789 could
not endure indefinitely. The United States of America might, as Lincoln
observed, have been "conceived in Liberty and dedicated to the proposition that all men are created equal." But the fact remained that the
government established by the Constitution of the United States sanc-

1   Cited in Allan Nevins, *Ordeal of the Union* (Charles Scribners and Sons, 1971), 7: 449.

tioned – and indeed encouraged – the continuation of one of the most pernicious systems of human bondage ever devised. The mere presence of Negro slavery in an ostensibly "free" society represented a contradiction; and the American system of slavery represented much more than a "presence." The system of chattel labor was the cornerstone of the economic and social structure for one-third of the United States.

Lincoln's Gettysburg Address also reminds us what it took to remove this contradiction: the bloodiest war in American history. Only a few months earlier, over 50,000 men had been killed or wounded near the spot where Lincoln spoke. Yet the carnage at Gettysburg was only a small fraction of the full toll of that war. By the time that Robert E. Lee's troops finally laid down their arms at Appomattox, at least 625,000 men had lost their lives fighting either to preserve the American Union or to create a new one, and almost as many endured injuries and wounds. Gettysburg was the climactic battle of that war; it has always been identified as the single event that marked when the tide unmistakably turned in favor of the Union. "The World," Lincoln claimed, "will little note, nor long remember what we say here, but it can never forget what [those who died] did here." He was only partly right. Contrary to his expectation, people remembered what Lincoln said there. His call for "a new birth of freedom" was a recognition that the time had come for the contradiction embodied in the Constitution to be finally removed. The war to preserve the Union had become a struggle to eradicate slavery in the United States.

The Changing Past: Writing and Rewriting Civil War History

The American Civil War was one of those events that inalterably changed the course of history. One out of every four soldiers who fought in the Civil War lost his life, a toll larger than the *total* number of military deaths in all other American wars from the American Revolution through the Korean War. Because it was a "civil" war, it left scars that would not heal for generations – and in places that have not yet completely healed. The efforts at "reconstruction" and eventual reunion of the rebellious southern states permanently changed the relations between black and white Americans. That this radical revolution eventually fell far short of its goals should not obscure the fact that there was one positive legacy from the Civil War: the emancipation of four million black slaves.

The history of all this has been written and rewritten many times. Although the historical events do not change, the interpretations that historians put on those events do. In the case of the Civil War, the events were so overwhelming that the scope for historical interpretation (and reinterpretation) is almost boundless. Successive generations of generals, politicians, historians, and novelists have examined in painstaking detail the causes, course, and consequences of the great conflict. The result is a vast literature that fills entire sections of every public library in the United States.

From the time when the first memoirs of generals began to appear immediately after the war, participants and historians have retraced the campaigns of the war and scrutinized the lives of the men who fought in them.[2] This fascination with "battles and leaders" continues to the present; military books on the Civil War still find a ready market in the United States today.[3] As time passed and Americans began to reflect on the events and impact of the war, various "omnibus" histories of the Civil War appeared, from highly detailed examinations of the war and its causes to much shorter volumes that sketch out a broad theme but leave out some of the details.[4] Finally, a vast collection of books, articles, and

2 The editors of *Century Magazine* paved the way for this genre of work when they published a four-volume collection of essays, "being for the most part, contributions by Union and Confederate officers." Robert U. Johnson and Clarence C. Buel, eds., *Battles and Leaders of the Civil War*, Grant-Lee edition, 4 vols. (The Century Company, 1884).

3 Recent works dealing with leaders include the following biographies: William McFeely, *Grant: A Biography* (W. W. Norton, 1981); Stephen W. Sears, *George B. McClellan: The Young Napoleon* (Ticknor and Fields, 1988); James I. Robertson, *General A. P. Hill: The Story of a Confederate Warrior* (Random House, 1987); and Emory M. Thomas, *Bold Dragoon: The Life of J. E. B. Stuart* (Harper and Row, 1986). Accounts of specific battles include Stephen W. Sears, *Landscape Turned Red: The Battle of Antietam* (Ticknor and Fields, 1983); James McDonough, *Chattanooga: A Death Grip on the Confederacy* (University of Tennessee Press, 1984); Benjamin Franklin Cooling, *Forts Henry and Donelson: The Key to the Confederate Heartland* (University of Tennessee Press, 1987). Broader analyses of the military operations of the war also abound; recent efforts worthy of note include Herman Hattaway and Archer Jones, *How the North Won: A Military History of the Civil War* (University of Illinois Press, 1983); Grady McWhiney and Perry D. Jamieson, *Attack and Die: Civil War Military Tactics and the Southern Heritage* (University of Alabama Press, 1982); and the essays in Richard Beringer, Herman Hattaway, Archer Jones, and William N. Still, Jr., *Why the South Lost the War* (University of Georgia Press, 1986).

4 The overriding work in this area is, of course, Allan Nevins's eight-volume series on *The Ordeal of the Union*. More recent examples of such omnibus works on a less ambitious scale include David H. Donald, *Liberty and Union* (D. C. Heath, 1978); Peter Batty and Peter Parrish, *The Divided Union: The Story of the Great American War, 1861–1865* (Salem House Publishers, 1987); and James M. McPherson, *Battle Cry of Freedom: The Civil War Era* (Oxford University Press, 1988). There are also many works that, although quite general in their approach, have narrowed their focus to a particular period or broad region. Examples would include David M. Potter, *The Impending Crisis: 1848–1861* (Harper Torchbooks, 1976), and Kenneth Stampp, *The Era of Reconstruction, 1865–1877* (Vintage Press, 1965). Evidence of current interest in a general approach to the coming of the war and Reconstruction can be seen in the work of William J. Cooper, Jr., *Liberty and Slavery: Southern Politics to 1860* (Alfred A. Knopf, 1983); Michael Perman, *Emancipation and Reconstruction, 1862–1879* (Harlan Davidson,

monographs have dealt with specific periods, places, or people during the Civil War era. By examining in depth some particular aspect of the times, these works provide the research findings that form the basis for the broader interpretations and reinterpretations of the Civil War and Reconstruction.

What can we add to this? One obvious possibility is to bridge the gap that exists between the general or omnibus work and the more specialized research addressed primarily to historians. We live in an age of specialization, and the academic world is no exception. The great reward to specialization is that it fosters a concentration on a specific task (or in the case of historical research, a specific topic) that permits an attention to detail that could never be attained by someone trying to do everything at once. But there is a corresponding cost. Specialization narrows the focus of historical research by imposing restrictions on the scope of study. These restrictions have several dimensions. Most obvious are those of "time and place." Historians have divided their profession into a multitude of little "boxes" delimited by the time period and the group or region to be studied. Within each of these boxes the individual historian then places his or her particular methodological imprint on the problem being studied.[5] The results of this specialization are illuminating, and they provide valuable insights toward an understanding of the larger framework of historical events. But determining how all these places fit together into a carefully crafted jigsaw puzzle requires that we step back from time to time to see if there are not some common themes to many of the specialized works.

The job of fitting various pieces into a larger picture, however, is complicated by the fact that historians are continually "revising" history. By its nature, revisionist history presents an interpretation at odds with the prevailing view, which means that a particular piece of research was not meant to fit easily into the existing historical paradigm. Still, revisionist arguments are seldom so drastically different that they represent a

1987); Eric Foner, *Reconstruction: America's Unfinished Revolution* (Harper and Row, 1988); and Richard H. Sewell, *A House Divided: Sectionalism and Civil War, 1848–1865* (Johns Hopkins University Press, 1988).

5   Two examples will illustrate the point. In *One Kind of Freedom: The Economic Consequences of Emancipation* (Cambridge University Press, 1977) by Richard Sutch and myself, we focused our analysis on the period 1859 to 1900, and we concentrated on a region that we defined as the "cotton South." Finally, we presented an analysis that stressed the "economic" consequences of emancipation. Political historians have, on occasion, carried the logic of specialization even further. In his study of the origins of the Republican party, William E. Gienapp focused on a single political party in the North, and his study covers a period of only five years; see *The Origins of the Republican Party, 1852–1856* (Oxford University Press, 1987).

total break with other interpretations. Our inability to put such pieces in place is often a result of being asked to view the piece from an unfamiliar angle. This problem can be particularly acute when methods that have not been widely employed in historical research are introduced. Specialists are preoccupied with the novelty of their methodology, whereas generalists are not familiar enough with the new techniques to see how the findings can be integrated into the larger historical framework.

Over the past three decades, the development and application of quantitative techniques – aided by the appearance of a computer technology that enables us to analyze huge bodies of data – have had a major impact on the study of American history. This use of quantitative methods has been particularly pronounced in the study of social, economic, and political developments, and the results of this research have considerably changed the way we look at the Civil War. Economic historians have pictured the antebellum South as a region full of economic vitality and growth, in contrast to the conventional view of a backward society struggling with the burdens of slavery. Extending these findings into the postwar era revealed just how profound the impact of emancipation was on southern society. Political historians found that the politics of both the antebellum period and Reconstruction were more diverse and complex than the earlier view of controversy over slavery and black equality after the war had suggested. The findings of these researchers have been largely accepted, yet the full implications of their results have not yet appeared as part of the historical explanations of the Civil War and the Reconstruction era.

This book is an attempt to step back and take a broader look at a particular part of the historical puzzle of the Civil War and Reconstruction era: the problem of slavery and emancipation in the United States. I have chosen to cover the period from 1776 to 1876 – which is slightly longer than that taken by most treatments of the Civil War – because the frustrations and anger that ultimately prompted the Civil War were the product of a long period of tension created by a problem that would not go away. Nor did the problem disappear with the outbreak of war. Emancipation was not a foregone conclusion in 1860, and when it finally came, the people in neither the North nor the South fully understood the forces that were unleashed – hence my decision to extend my analysis through the war and up to 1876. Nor do I propose to eschew the gains of academic specialization. As the term "political economy" in the subtitle suggests, my analysis will focus primarily on those economic and political factors that pertain to the way in which slavery led to the conflict in 1860. Because my arguments draw heavily on the methodology and empirical work that has been done by economic and political historians, it will be useful to review the findings of this body of quantitative research.

The Numbers Game: Economics and Politics in the Civil War Era

In 1863 the British political economist J. E. Cairnes offered the following analysis of the rupture between the American states:

> So long as [the slave power] itself was the dominant party, so long as it could employ the powers of government in propagating its peculiar institution and consolidating its strength, so long was it content to remain in the Union; but the moment when, by the constitutional triumph of the Republicans, the government passed into the hands of a party whose distinctive principle was to impose a limit on slavery, from that moment its continuance in the Union was incompatible with its essential objects, and from that moment the Slave Power resolved to break loose from Federal Ties.[6]

Cairnes's view that the Civil War was brought on by southern outrage over the triumph of the Republican president placed blame for the conflict squarely on the shoulders of a southern slavocracy determined to preserve its system of black slavery at all costs. The election of Abraham Lincoln – a man whose announced policy was the containment of the slave system – was unacceptable to slaveholders, who interpreted the Republican triumph as proof that their northern brethren were no longer willing to tolerate the presence of slavery in the United States. To threaten slavery, of course, was to threaten the very foundation of economic and social organization in the American South. Southerners – those who did not own slaves as well as those who did – took up arms to defend a way of life that depended on the continued enslavement of blacks. It was, to their way of thinking, a way of life that was incompatible with the lifestyle in other areas of the United States. Gaining independence for the South was the only way to preserve the slave system.

It is a plausible story, and like most plausible stories there is at least a grain of truth in it. A substantial majority of Southerners probably did favor dissolution of the Union if that was what it took to preserve their peculiar institution, and many Southerners doubtless felt that their system was threatened by the growing ascendancy of the northern Re-

---

6 J. E. Cairnes, *The Slave Power: It's* [sic] *Character, Career, and Probable Designs: Being an Attempt to Explain the Real Issues Involved in the American Contest* (1862; reprint, Harper and Row, 1969), p. 20.

publicans. But as an explanation of why the two regions went to war in 1860 Cairnes's story is, at best, naive and rather incomplete.

Several important questions are left unanswered. Most obvious is why the North chose to fight a war in 1861 instead of seeking – as it had on several occasions in the past – a compromise with the slave power. If the South's intransigence made compromise impossible, why not simply let the Southerners secede? The traditional answer was that Northerners wanted to be rid of slavery, yet preserve the Union. However, studies of voting patterns have revealed a far more complex interplay of forces than a simple distaste for "slave power" or a love of the Union suggests. Slavery was only one of the factors attracting the attention of voters in the free states of the North – and for most voters it may not have been the most important. By the middle of the 1840s, the arrival of large numbers of immigrants had created deep divisions in northern society. The new arrivals faced various obstacles to assimilation into the social system, and they found that rallying solidly around one or the other of the political parties offered an opportunity to mitigate these problems. The immigrants' political solidarity was matched by a strong resentment against these newcomers on the part of "native" Americans. The pressures of adjusting to economic and social change in a society that was becoming increasingly urban and industrial created additional sources of frustration for the average worker in the North. These concerns over economic conditions and ethnic rivalries overshadowed questions of slavery in shaping the political alliances of the antebellum North.[7]

Viewed in this light, the question that cries out for an answer is how were the Republicans able to forge a strong enough consensus among these disparate groups of voters to capture both the White House and the Congress by the elections of 1860? Political historians claim that the answer to this question ultimately rests on an analysis of why the political system, which had contained the problem of slavery for a long time, was suddenly unable to handle the pressures that arose in the late 1850s. The collapse of national parties was not, they argue, the result of some unifying force from the opposition to slavery gaining ascendancy in the North. On the contrary, politics in the North were becoming increasingly factionalized, as each state presented a different political agenda for the national parties to wrestle with. It was this diversity that produced political pressures that the national leadership was unable (or perhaps unwill-

---

7 Michael Holt, *The Political Crisis of the 1850's* (W. W. Norton, 1878), and Joel Silbey, ed., *The Partisan Imperative: The Dynamics of American Politics before the Civil War* (Oxford University Press, 1985), are examples of works dealing with the emergence of ethnic politics in the North.

ing) to channel effectively toward a peaceful resolution of the problem of slavery when it reappeared on the scene in the 1850s.[8]

And what about the South? Cairnes suggested that Southerners were governed by a monolithic "slave power" that hastily pushed them into secession and an unwise war. Yet, as critics of this position have pointed out, the South did not rush to war. Only six states joined South Carolina within the first four months of that state's secession; the rest waited to see what would develop when Lincoln took office. Moreover, the votes on secession were close enough in several states to suggest that there was substantial Unionist sentiment — particularly in the hill country and the "upper South." A closer look at the evidence on southern political parties confirms the suspicion that there was not a monolithic political position in the South. In fact, there were deep tensions in the slave society that frequently spilled over into the political debates of the time. As was the case in the North, these tensions were not identical in every state. Political histories of the antebellum South reveal very noticeable regional differences that were to surface with increased importance in the newly formed Confederacy.[9]

So where do we look for blame for the war? Michael Holt provides one answer when he asserts that:

> Popular grievances, no matter how intense, do not dictate party strategies. Political leaders do. . . . Much of the story of the coming of the Civil War is the story of the successful efforts of Democratic politicians in the South and Republican politicians in the North to keep the sectional conflict at the center of political debate and to defeat political rivals who hoped to exploit other issues to achieve election.[10]

According to this view, politicians in the late antebellum period were exploiting the issues for their own purposes rather than seeking to lessen

---

8 The emphasis on the problems confronting those seeking to form a Republican party can be seen in Michael Holt's study of party politics in Pittsburgh, *Forging a Majority: The Formation of the Republican Party in Pittsburgh, 1848–1860* (Yale University Press, 1969); Roland P. Formisano's study of Michigan politics, *The Birth of Mass Political Parties: Michigan, 1827–1861* (Princeton University Press, 1971); and William E. Gienapp's study of the formative years of the Republican party, *The Origins of the Republican Party.*

9 See, for example, J. Mills Thorton III, *Politics and Power in a Slave Society: Alabama, 1800–1860* (Louisiana State University Press, 1978); Steven Hahn, *The Roots of Southern Populism: Yeoman Farmers and the Transformation of the Georgia Upcountry, 1850–1860* (Oxford University Press, 1983); and Marc W. Kruman, *Parties and Politics in North Carolina, 1836–1865* (Louisiana State University Press, 1983). All of these studies stress that there were deep social and economic divisions between various groups in the South.

10 Holt, *The Political Crisis of the 1850's,* p. 184.

the level of conflict posed by the tensions of slavery: Political mismanagement, not some inexorable conflict over slavery, produced the political collapse leading to war.

Although it provides important insights into the differing political reactions of specific states or regions in the North, this contention that slavery was a problem that should have been contained by adroit political leadership contains an implicit assumption that somehow the tensions associated with it could have somehow been defused, or that perhaps slavery would simply have "gone away." Politicians, in this scheme of things, allowed the *symptoms* of the disease to get out of hand. But the symptoms were very real and represented a major political irritant so long as the disease of slavery was still there. Was the disease about to "go away"? Few people thought so in 1860. Most worried that the disease of slavery was spreading, not in some form of recession. By the middle of the century it was becoming clear that the only "cure" for the problem was to remove the contradiction of slavery. There were two options: The Union could be split into separate slave and free political entities, or slavery could be eliminated within the Union. Neither provided the basis for a political agenda leading to a national consensus.

The problem, of course, was that slavery was an institution that had insinuated itself into every facet of American life. Everyone concedes that slave labor was the cornerstone that supported the plantation economy of the antebellum period. Prior to the 1960s, most historians argued that the foundation rested on sand, not bedrock. Writing in 1918, a leading historian of American slavery claimed that:

> Because they were blinded by the abolition agitation in the North . . . , most of the later generation of ante-bellum planters could not see that slaveholding was essentially burdensome. But that which was partly hidden from their vision is clear to us today. In the great system of southern industry and commerce, working with seeming smoothness, the negro laborers were inefficient in spite of discipline, and slavery was an obstacle to all progress.[11]

What U. B. Phillips thought was "clear to us" in 1918 about the profitability of slavery remained accepted wisdom among historians for an-

---

11 Ulrich Bonnell Phillips, *Life and Labor in the Old South* (Little, Brown, 1929), p. 275. Phillips's characterization was widely accepted by critics of slavery at the time. See, for example, Frederick Law Olmsted, whose extensive travels through the South provide one of the most telling critiques of slave labor (*The Cotton Kingdom*, ed. and introd. Arthur Schlesinger [Alfred A. Knopf, 1953], originally published in 1861); Hinton R. Helper, whose view of an "impending crisis" was predicated on the economic deficiencies of slavery (*The Impending Crisis of the South: How to Meet It* [A. B. Burdick, 1860]); and J. E. Cairnes, who decried the political as well as the economic power in the hands of southern slaveholders (*The Slave Power*).

other forty years. Indeed, the proposition that slavery was "unprofit-able" was regarded as little short of historical "truth." There were, to be sure, a few who dissented.[12] But it was not until 1956, when Kenneth Stampp published his book, *The Peculiar Institution,* that the conven-tional wisdom about the economic viability of slavery was seriously chal-lenged.[13] Stampp argued that slavery was not only "profitable" but was the economic mainspring propelling economic life in the antebellum South.

Stampp's book proved to be only the opening salvo of an attack that would ultimately turn the accepted wisdom about the economic prof-itability of slavery on its head. Two years later a pair of young economic historians, Alfred Conrad and John Meyer, published an article titled "The Economics of Slavery in the Ante Bellum South."[14] Conrad and Meyer presented an economic analysis that unlocked the mysteries of how a system of chattel labor could thrive in a capitalist market setting and touched off a major revision in the way in which economic historians viewed the slave system in America. So successful were these attacks on the prevailing view that in the years following the appearance of Stampp's book and the Conrad–Meyer essay, the view of slavery upheld by Phillips has been almost totally abandoned.[15] Not only has slavery been shown to be profitable to southern planters; in 1961 Douglass North argued that the cotton economy of the South was the leading force behind the eco-nomic expansion of the American economy in the period 1790–1845.[16]

12 Lewis Cecil Gray, in his monumental study of southern agriculture, insisted that slavery was profitable, and Robert Russell also took strong exception to Phillips's view. See Gray, *History of Agriculture in the Southern United States to 1860,* 2 vols. (Carnegie Institution, 1933); Robert R. Russel, "The General Effects of Slavery upon Southern Economic Progress," *Journal of Southern History* 4 (February 1938), and idem, "The Effects of Slavery on Nonslaveholders in the Ante-Bellum South," *Agriculture History* 15 (April 1941). In 1942, Thomas Govan cautiously asserted that "the students who have stated that slavery was profitable are more nearly correct than those who deny its profitableness"; see "Was Plantation Slavery Profitable?" *Journal of Southern History* 8 (November 1942): 131.

13 Kenneth Stampp, *The Peculiar Institution: Slavery in the Antebellum South* (Alfred Knopf, 1956).

14 Alfred H. Conrad and John R. Meyer, "The Economics of Slavery in the Ante Bellum South," *Journal of Political Economy* 66 (April 1958).

15 Of course, this change in views was not accomplished without an extensive literature being published on the subject. One of the most significant consequences of the Con-rad–Meyer paper was that it brought economists into the discussion. The fruits of that discussion will be taken up in greater detail in Chapter 3.

16 Douglass C. North, *The Economic Growth of the United States, 1790–1860* (Prentice-Hall, 1961). See Richard Sutch for a discussion of the impact that North's model had on the economic history of the antebellum period ("Douglass North and the New Economic History," in *Explorations in the New Economic History: Essays in Honor of Douglass C. North,* ed. Roger L. Ransom, Richard Sutch, and Gary M. Walton (Academic Press, 1982).

This remarkable change in attitudes had rather clear implications for the interpretation of slavery as a factor in bringing on the Civil War. As Conrad and Meyer put it: "In sum, it seems doubtful that the South was forced by bad statesmanship into an unnecessary war to protect a system that must soon have disappeared because it was economically unsound. This is a romantic hypothesis, which will not stand against the facts."[17] The research on the economics of slavery suggests that, at least from the perspective of southern slaveholders, the Civil War might have made "economic" sense. In terms of the political explanations of the war, their findings suggest that the confrontations between slave and free labor would not have simply gone away; indeed, they were likely to get worse. Slavery remained a growing problem so long as the cotton economy continued to thrive.

Important though they may be, economic interests alone cannot account for the coming of the Civil War. The politics of slavery are equally important to explain why North and South were willing to fight. The political system of the United States is predicated on a balance of forces at both the state and federal levels that will produce a consensus. As the political historians remind us, the failure of the political process involved more than a simple argument for or against slavery.

Where does all this leave us? Could the Civil War have been avoided in the spring of 1861? The question has been asked many times, and if one interprets it literally, the answer is clearly and unequivocally *yes*. No war is inevitable in the sense that there exists *no* peaceful solution that might head off conflict. The American Civil War could have been avoided had the North let the South peacefully secede, or had the South been willing to accept limitations on the slave property right. In fact, there is considerable irony in the rationale provided by both sides for the war. The North fought a war whose one unequivocal result was the emancipation of slaves – even though most Northerners had only a limited commitment to the emancipation of black Americans. Southerners fought and lost a war whose avowed purpose was to break free from the American Union when, in fact, that union probably offered the most secure haven for a slave society in the world of the nineteenth century.

Although the economic historians and the political historians draw somewhat different implications from the results of their research, a common thread runs through the analysis by both groups – the role of slavery in shaping the path of economic and political development in the United States. Let us follow that thread and see where it takes us.

---

17 Conrad and Meyer, "The Economics of Slavery," p. 174.

A Century of Conflict: Slavery, War, and Emancipation

Americans had been wrestling with the question of what to do about slavery well before the revolutionary ideology of equality brought the question into stark focus in 1776 and again in 1787. In language that was as circumspect as they could manage, the founding fathers reaffirmed the right to own private property – including human property – and said as little as possible about slavery. That was probably an accurate reflection of the collective view of the American population at the time. Most Americans neither endorsed nor condemned slavery; if they had a preference, it would have been to ignore the issue.

That is not to say Americans were indifferent to changes in the status of slaves. Slaves in the United States were *black,* and any time a question dealing with slavery surfaced, it brought out the ubiquitous presence of racism in American society. The combination of a revolutionary ethic of equality on the one hand and racism on the other produced an ambivalence in the attitudes of many Americans toward slavery that was to paralyze attempts to deal with the problem for the next eighty years. Many people, in the South as well as the North, abhorred the immorality of slavery. Yet their deep-seated racial antagonisms toward blacks caused them to resist strongly any suggestion of equality for blacks. Consequently, it was extremely difficult to forge an antislave alliance that would actively resist the continuation of the slave system in the South.

Had the slave system remained quietly in the background, Americans might have lived indefinitely with the problem by ignoring it. But slavery did not remain quietly in the background. As the young republic expanded, its system of black slavery expanded with it. Ironically, in a country that had an abundance of land, competition for territory caused the frictions over slavery to erupt into bloody conflict. "The issue that drove the deepest wedge between North and South in the two decades before the Civil War," notes Michael Holt, "was not the institution of slavery itself, but the question of whether slavery should be allowed to expand westward beyond the boundaries of the slave states."[18] Holt is not alone in this view; every study of the political collapse in the 1850s stresses the dispute over the Nebraska Territory as the pivotal event that led to the collapse of compromise and eventually to war.

Economic historians also stress the importance of western land in their explanation of the economic viability of slavery. Conrad and Meyer pointed out that "the maintenance of profits in the Old South depended

18   Holt, *The Political Crisis of the 1850's,* p. 39.

upon the expansion, extensive or intensive, of slave labor into the South-west."[19] Indeed, a strong case can be made that economic growth in the South *depended* on the availability of western land in the antebellum period. Availability of land was also an important element in the plans of Northerners who were leaving the eastern states and heading west. For the most part, these two westward migrations followed parallel paths that did not intersect. The presence of the Ohio River as a natural bound-ary keeping the two groups separated made it easier to maintain an economic and political balance between the two systems of labor. On the occasions when the two streams of migrants intersected west of the Ohio – in Missouri in 1820 and Nebraska in the early 1850s – the result was a major political crisis.

To understand the role of slavery in producing conflict in the ante-bellum period, it is important to realize that it was not the *abolition* of slavery that lay at the root of the conflict between slave and free states; it was the *containment* of slavery within the original area. Controlling the expansion of slavery was not simply a moral issue: Northerners – es-pecially those in the free states in the West – increasingly opposed the extension of slavery into new territories because they did not want blacks in the areas of settlement.

The antipathy of white Americans toward blacks is a crucial element not only to an understanding of the opposition to slavery before the war, but also to the course of events during and after the war. Slavery was not abolished with the first shot fired on Fort Sumter in April 1861. Nor were the young men of the North who hurried off to war in the spring of 1861 motivated, for the most part, by thoughts of emancipation and freedom for black Americans. Nevertheless, a major issue on both sides quickly became, What to do with slavery? Northern leaders worried how to treat slaves who escaped from the Confederacy (mindful of the fact that there were still nearly 400,000 blacks enslaved in several "loyal" states). Southerners pondered how they could best use their slave labor to mobilize for a war that would keep blacks enslaved.

The answers to those questions helped determine the outcome of the war. Despite their unwillingness to accept equality for blacks, Northern-ers gradually came to recognize that emancipation was an inevitable outcome of the war. Thus, the elimination of slavery eventually provided a unifying theme that helped to overcome resistance to the war in the North. Acceptance of emancipation also meant additional manpower for the North's military effort. (By the end of the war, over 180,000 black soldiers were fighting for the Union.) In the South, by contrast, slavery

19   Conrad and Meyer, "The Economics of Slavery," p. 174.

became an increasingly divisive issue that exacerbated the social and political divisions between slaveowners and nonslaveowners within the Confederacy. The result was that the South did not use its slave resources well. One of the final ironies of the war was provided by the Confederate government's abortive effort in March 1865 to enlist blacks in the southern armies by promising them their freedom.

When, after four years of bitter fighting, slavery was finally abolished, both the victors and the vanquished accepted the finality of that outcome. Unfortunately, they could agree on little else. The institutional void left by the destruction of a system of labor that had been the cornerstone of the social and economic structure of the South since the earliest days of settlement presented a staggering challenge to those trying to "reconstruct" the South in 1865. The disagreements over Reconstruction were not limited to the differing views of Northerners and Southerners; within a few years Northerners fell to quarreling among themselves over the appropriate policy. As the excitement and idealism of the war effort gradually wore down, the antipathy of northern whites toward blacks in the South once again became the dominant factor in the effort to deal with the effects of emancipation. More interested in healing the wounds of the war and promoting economic growth than in securing equality for the freed slaves, and convinced that they had eliminated the evil of slavery simply by abolishing the institution, Northerners turned their attention to the problems of adjusting to an economic environment that was increasingly being dominated by the needs of a rapidly expanding industrial system.

The effect of the war on northern society, though less far-reaching than in the South, was still significant. The political victory of the Republican party in 1860 brought about a fundamental shift in the balance of political power in the United States. During the course of the war the Republican-controlled Congress enacted landmark legislation that included a drastic restructuring of the banking system, the creation of substantial subsidies for transportation and education, and an offer of free land in the West for anyone who would settle on it. After the war, Republican administrations implemented economic policies that provided a significant stimulus to economic growth. All of this laid the groundwork for the "Gilded Age" of industrial expansion during the last quarter of the nineteenth century.

The economic success of the postwar era has tended to gloss over the fact that the victorious North let much of what had been gained through four years of hard fighting slip through its fingers. The presidential election of 1876 marked the symbolic end of the effort to "reconstruct" the defeated South. Defiant and still unreconstructed, the last of the southern states were readmitted into the Union and the last federal troops of occupation in the South were withdrawn. The contradiction of slavery was removed, the Union was preserved, and the question of how best to deal with the "race problem" was returned to the South.

This, very briefly, is the narrative behind the analysis that is presented in the chapters that follow. For pedagogical purposes, the book follows a roughly chronological order. Chapter 2 deals with the period from the Declaration of Independence to the Missouri Compromise of 1820. Chapter 3 concerns economic aspects of the slave system from the 1820s to the Civil War. Chapters 4 and 5 retrace the same period with an eye on the political problems caused by slavery. Chapter 6 deals with the war years. Chapters 7 and 8 concern the postwar period.

My intent is to present more than just a narrative of the events of the Civil War era. Using the models and findings of the economic and political historians mentioned earlier, I propose to analyze the forces that produced the tensions and set the parameters for conflict and compromise over the slave issue. Any attempt to apply the art of "political economy" to a historical situation as complex as slavery is fraught with dangers. Clearly, no single theory or model will suffice. I have therefore approached the problem with an eclectic view of the tools available from the analytical kit of economic and political historians. Although there will be occasional analytical excursions that involve the application of specific quantitative or economic "models," the overall thrust of my analysis is driven by several broad "themes" or historical "propositions" that I regard as essential to the understanding of the period.

The underlying theme of the book is that the presence of slavery in the United States represented a contradiction that eventually could only be removed by an armed conflict between the slave South and the nonslave North. At the crux of this analysis are the *economic* aspects of capitalist slavery in the United States that made compromise increasingly difficult and eventually impossible. Understanding how economic forces operated in the context of a slave system that was uniquely capitalist provides one of the essential keys to understanding why the conflict over slavery in the United States was so bitter, and compromise so difficult.

The American political system played an equally important role by setting the parameters within which any compromise could be reached. The success of any compromise in the American political system rests with the office of the president. Because he can veto any legislation supported by less than two-thirds of the Congress, the president effectively sets the limits to any effort at resolving disputes between contending regions or parties. Because of this power, presidential elections were pivotal events in maintaining a balance of power between slave and nonslave interests. So long as the president was inclined to favor compromise, the presidency represented a stabilizing force. But if a candidate with an *un*compromising stance was elected, the presidency was potentially a very destabilizing factor that could force confrontation rather than compromise.

Slavery not only "caused" the war, it also played a major role in determining the outcome of the conflict. A second major thesis of this book is that the attempt by the southern states to create a Confederacy separate from the American Union failed because the slave society of the South was unable to sustain an effort in the face of a determined foe. The presence of slavery undermined the Confederacy's war effort by creating a divisiveness that crippled the mobilization effort. At the same time, the promise of eliminating slavery eventually provided a unifying force behind the North's efforts to hold the Union together.

The one great accomplishment of the Civil War was the emancipation of four million slaves. This action had a far more profound impact on the southern economic and social system that anyone realized at the time. The third thesis of this book is that the enormity of the changes brought about by emancipation made it impossible for people at the time to deal effectively with the problems they faced. One of the unfortunate results of this was that social and political equality for blacks was not realized in the postbellum society of the South. The legacy of war and Reconstruction was instead a stagnant system of agriculture that ultimately worked to the disadvantage of both black and white Southerners.

The war also produced some profound economic and political changes in the North. For two decades after Lincoln's election, the "Grand Old Party" dominated the postwar political scene. One of the more enduring historical debates is whether that dominance brought about a fundamental change in the economic and political structure of the United States. In the final chapter of the book, I examine the thesis that the political changes that accompanied the war brought into power a class of industrial capitalists who used their economic power to favor the rapid expansion of the industrial system.

Finally, there is the larger problem of race and slavery in the United States. The racial antagonisms produced by a system of racial slavery played a major role both in the removal of slavery, and in the shaping of society after emancipation. "Race," observes historian Barbara Fields,

> became the ideological medium through which Americans confronted questions of sovereignty and power because the enslavement of Africans and their descendants constituted a massive exception to the rules of sovereignty and power that were increasingly taken for

granted. And, despite the changes it has undergone along the way, race has remained a predominant ideological medium because the manner of slavery's unraveling had lasting consequences for the relations of whites to other whites, no less than for those of whites to blacks.[20]

Throughout the period under analysis, racial tensions and ideology exerted a profound influence on the "political economy" of slavery and emancipation.

A book must begin and end somewhere. I chose to begin in 1776 because that is the year most often identified with the formation of what was to become the United States of America. I chose to end in 1876 because that year marks, in a sense, the abandonment of the cause of black equality in the South after the Civil War. Only by viewing the process of conflict and compromise with the issues of race, slavery, and emancipation over this entire period can one see how slavery "caused" the American Civil War, determined the outcome of the titanic struggle, and left a legacy that profoundly shaped events after the war.

20 Barbara J. Fields, "Ideology and Race in American History," in *Region, Race and Reconstruction: Essays in Honor of C. Vann Woodward,* ed. J. Morgan Kousser and James M. McPherson (Oxford University Press, 1982), pp. 168–9.

2

Slavery and Freedom

[King George] has waged cruel war against human nature itself, violating its most sacred rights of life and liberty in the persons of distant people, who never offended him, captivating and carrying them into slavery in another hemisphere, or to incur miserable death in their transportation thither.

Initial draft of the Declaration of Independence by
Thomas Jefferson, July 1776[1]

In their effort to break away from the British Crown, the delegates gathered at the Continental Congress in early July 1776 had appointed a select committee to draw up a statement of their revolutionary purpose. To that end they were presented with a report, modestly titled a Declaration of Independence. Authored by the young Virginian, Thomas Jefferson, the report asserted that "We hold these truths to be self evident; that all Men are created equal; that they are endowed by their Creator with inherent & inalienable rights, that among these are life, liberty, and the pursuit of happiness."[2]

Jefferson then proceeded to enumerate a list of "injuries and usurpations" by the king of Great Britain against his colonial subjects in North America. Included in the list was a ringing indictment of the British Crown's support for the traffic in slaves between Africa and the New World.

Although they accepted – with some editorial changes – the bold rhetoric of the report, Jefferson's fellow delegates were not of a mind to endorse their young colleague's complaint about the slave trade. At the insistence of several southern delegations, the offending clause was stricken from the final draft of the declaration. Indeed, the declaration made no reference whatever to the fact that one out of five inhabitants of the newly proclaimed United States of America was, and would remain, a slave. The men who signed the Declaration were prepared to concede that the institution of slavery would be an integral part of the new republic.

1 Taken from Paul Leicester Ford, ed., *The Writings of Thomas Jefferson, 1776–1781* (G. P. Putnam's and Sons, 1893), 2: 52.
2 Ibid., p. 43.

The Great Contradiction: Slavery and Freedom

The irony posed by the self-evident fact that citizens of a "free" nation were operating a flourishing system of chattel labor was not entirely lost on the founding fathers. Jefferson's protest reveals a recognition that the slave trade was an offense against the notions of liberty expressed in the Declaration of Independence. Nor was his the only voice raised in this connection. The previous year a Massachusetts pamphleteer named John Allen had eloquently stated the problem:

> Blush ye pretended votaries for freedom! ye trifling patriots! who are making a vain parade of being advocates for liberties of mankind, who are thus making a mockery of your profession by trampling on the sacred rights and privileges of Africans; for while you are fasting, praying, nonimporting, nonexporting, remonstrating, resolving, and pleading for a restoration of your charter rights, you at the same time are continuing this lawless, cruel, inhuman and abominable practice of enslaving your fellow creatures.[3]

John Allen's sentiments can hardly be taken as a reflection of the prevailing view on the subject in 1775. Yet, as writers such as Bernard Bailyn, Winthrop Jordan, and David Brion Davis have demonstrated, antislavery advocates had considerable success in publicizing the obvious contradiction inherent in revolutionary rhetoric espousing the natural rights of man and the continued presence of slavery in America.[4] Unfortunately, simply stating the case was not enough to convince their compatriots to do something to resolve the contradiction.

Those who protested slavery faced a difficult road. However obvious the contradiction of the institution of slavery in America may have been, it was equally obvious that the slave system was so deeply ingrained in colonial America that any suggestion to change it, much less to eliminate it, would be met with strong resistance. Jefferson's slap of the king's wrist for condoning the African slave trade was too much for the delegates from South Carolina and Georgia to accept. That did not surprise Jefferson, who observed that those states "had never attempted to restrain the importation of slaves, and . . . on the contrary still wished to continue it."[5] More troubling was the fact that Northerners appeared equally

3 Attributed to John Allen of Salem, Massachusetts, 1774. Quoted in Winthrop Jordan, *White over Black: American Attitudes toward the Negro: 1550–1812* (University of North Carolina Press, 1968), p. 290.
4 Bernard Bailyn, *The Ideological Origins of the American Revolution* (Harvard University Press, 1967), chap. 6; Jordan, *White over Black*, chap. 7; David Brion Davis, *The Problem of Slavery in the Age of Revolution: 1770–1823* (Cornell University Press, 1975), chap. 6.
5 Julian P. Boyd, ed., *The Papers of Thomas Jefferson* (Princeton University Press, 1952), 1: 314.

anxious to avoid drawing attention to the presence of slavery in the United States. Jefferson went on to note that "our Northern brethren also, I believe felt a little tender under those censures; for tho' their people have very few slaves themselves yet they had been pretty considerable carriers of them to others."[6]

Jefferson's attempts to lodge a protest against the slave trade in the Declaration of Independence did not create a great stir at the time. Because the proceedings of Congress were not public, most people did not even learn of his objections until long after the fact. Yet the episode illustrates a crucial point about the slave question. From the very beginning of the American republic, the institution of slavery and the traffic in human beings that was an integral part of that institution represented an irritant that required a delicate balancing of "practical" as well as "moral" considerations. Jefferson, and others who shared his antipathy toward slavery, understood the political realities of the time. Slave interests ran very deep in the roots of colonial America, and unanimity of all thirteen colonies behind the declaration was essential. The divisiveness raised by even the mention of slavery was best avoided. The ensuing silence was deafening.

The fact that Jefferson was himself a substantial slaveholder when he drafted the clause protesting the slave trade in the first draft of the Declaration of Independence reveals another important aspect of our story: The "politics" of slavery produced conflicting pressures on those who had to deal with the issue. Jefferson clearly felt that slavery was morally degrading; it produced what he termed an "unremitting despotism" in slaveholders that corrupted the entire social system. He was particularly offended by the traffic in slaves, and consistently lobbied for an end to the "slave trade." Yet, his opposition to the institution of slavery notwithstanding, Jefferson behaved very much like other Virginia planters who used slave labor to farm their estates. By 1800 his personal holdings of slaves had increased to the point where he owned more than one hundred slaves, and Jefferson's account books reveal on a number of instances that he sold slaves to balance his accounts.[7]

Men such as Jefferson, a slaveholder who vigorously attacked the institution of which he himself was an integral part, were unusual. Most slaveholders – even those troubled by the morality of treating human beings as property – defended the system. A more common dilemma

---

6 Ibid., pp. 314–15.
7 On Jefferson's ownership of slaves at various points in his life, see Noble E. Cunningham, Jr., *In Pursuit of Reason: The Life of Thomas Jefferson* (Louisiana State University Press, 1987), pp. 9, 24, 196.

facing those who wished to see slavery end was the question of equality for blacks. If one favored the elimination of slavery, did that mean one therefore favored equal rights for free black Americans? In the minds of most Americans of the late colonial period the answer was clearly *no*.

Put very simply, most colonial Americans simply rejected the idea of racial inequality. In their eyes, black men could never be equal to free white men. Given the premise of inferiority, denial of rights for free blacks was no more difficult to defend than the equally well-entrenched canon that women should not be made equal to men. The *institution* of slavery might indeed be abominable, and because of that no man or woman – black or white – should be enslaved. But it did not therefore follow that blacks should have *equal* rights to white men. This ability to separate the issue of black equality from the issue of emancipation remained a cornerstone of political debates throughout the period from the Revolution to the Civil War. For all but a very small group of people who believed in both emancipation and equality, the two issues were quite distinct. Those in the public limelight took particular care to maintain the distinction lest they be accused of favoring black equality. This dichotomy explains why those supporting emancipation also favored schemes to transport freed blacks to Africa. Physical separation of the races resolved the dilemma of whether black Americans should have equal rights in the United States.

Racist convictions that black people were not entitled to equality with whites might assuage the conscience of those troubled by the enslavement of blacks in America. When embellished by a religious fervor to save souls, such beliefs could reconcile the enslaved status of blacks as being consistent with the "natural rights" guaranteed by the new republic. Supporters of this view believed that white Americans were "elevating" black Africans by offering them a place in Christian society, but no amount of intellectual gymnastics could eliminate the *practical* problems posed by the contradiction of slaves and free people coexisting within a political system predicated upon the proposition that "all men are created equal." And such practical problems, as we shall see, continually cropped up. When they did, the intellectual contradictions surrounding slavery and individual freedom could not be totally ignored, because they provided such fertile grounds for those attacking the immorality of slavery. Rhetoric on both sides became more heated, narrow positions were held more firmly than ever, and grounds for compromise became more difficult to find. There were no simple answers, and eventually there would ultimately be no way to compromise the contradiction of slavery and freedom in the new republic. The best that such efforts could accomplish was to buy time.

The Northwest Ordinance: Slavery Moves West

With the adoption of the Articles of Confederation in 1781, it was hoped that the divisions within and between the various states on the slave question would be quietly settled. Everyone agreed to accept the status quo. But the status quo suddenly changed. The Treaty of Paris ending the Revolutionary War in 1783 granted the United States undisputed rights to a vast area of unsettled land between the Appalachian Mountains and the Mississippi River. Even before the end of the war, settlers from Virginia and the Carolinas were spilling across the mountains into what is today Kentucky and Tennessee, and they were taking their slaves with them. Within a short time they would be pressing into the unorganized area north of the Ohio River. The question of what to do with the western lands became the burning issue as Congress prepared to meet in the spring of 1783.[8]

The problem was further complicated by the fact that, even though Britain had ceded its claim to territory between the Appalachians and the Mississippi River, the conflicting claims of various individual states to those lands remained unresolved. The obvious solution was to transfer control of the public domain to the federal government. By February 1783, that had been completed, and Congress appointed a committee headed by Thomas Jefferson to prepare "a plan for the temporary government of the Western Territory." The main thrust of the committee's report, which reached the floor of Congress in April 1784, concerned principles under which those territories could eventually become states of the union.[9] These ideas met with little opposition. Once again, however, Jefferson saw an opportunity to strike a blow against the spread of slavery beyond its present bounds. He inserted a clause stating that there should be "neither slavery nor involuntary servitude" in any of the six new states he proposed be created out of the Northwest Territory. Such a radical notion could not go unchallenged. Representative Richard Spaight of North Carolina moved to strike the language prohibiting slavery. The slave issue had once again surfaced, this time on a very specific question: Should slavery be allowed to take hold in an unsettled region?

Opponents of slavery knew that it would be impossible to eliminate the institution in the South. However, limiting the spread of slavery was a

8 For an excellent discussion of the pressures to act on the western lands question, see Peter S. Onuf, "Liberty, Development and Union: Visions of the West in the 1780s," *William and Mary Quarterly* 43 (April 1986): 179–213.

9 For a copy of the committee report, and a discussion of Jefferson's role in drafting it, see Boyd, *Papers of Thomas Jefferson*, vol. 6.

possibility that held considerable promise. The nonslave delegations strongly supported the Jefferson proposal. When the issue came to a vote, Connecticut, Massachusetts, New Hampshire, New York, Pennsylvania, and Rhode Island all voted to keep the antislave clause in the legislation. Opposed were Maryland, South Carolina, and Virginia. The North Carolina delegation was divided and did not cast a vote, and three states — Delaware, Georgia, and New Jersey — were absent.[10] Under the Articles of Confederation, states voted as a unit in Congress, and approval of seven of the thirteen states was necessary for approval. The action to retain the clause prohibiting slavery was thus defeated by a single state: six in favor, three opposed, and three not voting. It was not included in the resolution endorsing the remainder of Jefferson's report passed by Congress on April 23, 1784.

Jefferson was distraught that his efforts to control slavery should come so close and then fail. Writing from France a year and a half later (when he was the American ambassador), he eloquently described the situation:

> The voice of a single individual of the state which was divided, or of one of those which was negative, would have prevented this abominable crime from spreading over the country. Thus we see the fate of millions unborn hanging on the tongue of one man, & heaven was silent in that awful moment. But it is to be hoped that it will not always be silent & that the friends to the rights of human nature will in the end prevail.[11]

In the end, the "friends" did prevail. Encouraged by the support demonstrated for retaining the slave clause in the resolution of 1784, Rufus King of Massachusetts introduced a new resolution in March 1785 that would deny the further expansion of slavery north of the Ohio River.[12] King's motion was ordered committed to committee by a vote of eight to three. It remained there without ever getting to the floor of Congress.

The resolution was not without effect, however. Notice had been served that the opponents of slavery intended to fight the expansion of

10 The details of the debates and votes resulting in the Resolution of 1784 can be found in Thomas Donaldson, *The Public Domain: Its History, with Statistics* (U.S. Government Printing Office, 1884), pp. 147–9.
11 "Observations on the Article Etats-Unis Prepared for the Encyclopedie," June 22, 1786, in Ford, *Writings of Thomas Jefferson*, 4: 181.
12 The text of King's resolution was: "That there should be neither slavery nor involuntary servitude in any of the states described in the resolve of Congress of the 23d of April, 1784, otherwise than in the punishment of crimes, whereof the party shall have been personally guilty; and that this regulation shall be an article of compact, and remain a fundamental principle of the Constitution between the thirteen original States, and each of the States described in the resolve of the 23d of April, 1784." See Donaldson, *Public Domain*, p. 149.

slavery into new areas. Their chance to press the case once more came in July 1787, when a new "Ordinance for the Government of the Territory of the United States Northwest of the Ohio River" was reported out of a committee – still without a clause prohibiting slavery. Once debate on the ordinance began, the antislave forces decided to press for a slightly more moderate antislavery clause than that proposed by King the previous year. On July 12, King's fellow representative from Massachusetts, Nathan Dane, offered an amendment to the bill creating a Northwest Territory, which he had earlier introduced:

> Article the Sixth. There shall be neither slavery nor involuntary servitude in the said territory, . . . *provided always,* That any person escaping into the same, from whom labor or service is claimed in any of the original States, such fugitive may be lawfully reclaimed and conveyed to the person claiming his or her labor or service as aforesaid.[13]

Dane's amendment was incorporated into the law as Article 6 with one dissenting vote. The Northwest Ordinance was passed by a unanimous vote of Congress on July 13, 1787.[14]

The triumph of the antislave forces in securing the prohibition of slavery north of the Ohio was an important accomplishment at the time. The law effectively prevented the introduction of slavery into a vast area of land north of the Ohio all the way to the Mississippi River. That region eventually comprised all or part of six states: Ohio, Indiana, Michigan, Illinois, Wisconsin, and Minnesota. The fact that all of these states entered the union opposed to slavery was a crucial element in the debates that emerged later in the antebellum period.

Would the outcome have been different had the Northwest Ordinance not proscribed slavery north of the Ohio? It is tempting to argue that little would have changed, that slavery could never have flourished in the

---

13 Donaldson, *Public Domain,* p. 152; emphasis in original. Initially, Dane had not been optimistic about the chance of success for this amendment. Shortly after the ordinance was enacted, he wrote Rufus King: "When I drew up the ordinance . . . I had no idea the states would agree to the sixth article, prohibiting slavery, as only Massachusetts of the Eastern States was present, and therefore omitted it in the draft; but finding the House favorably disposed on this subject, after we completed the other parts, I moved the article, which was agreed to without opposition." See Charles R. King, ed., *The Life and Correspondence of Rufus King* (G. P. Putnam's Sons, The Knickerbocker Press, 1894; reprint, Da Capo Press, 1971), 1: 290.

14 A copy of the ordinance and discussion of its passage is in Donaldson, *Public Domain,* pp. 148–61. For a discussion of the significance of the ordinance in terms of the organization of western land policy, see J. R. T. Hughes, "The Great Land Ordinances: Colonial America's Thumbprint on History," in *Essays on the Old Northwest,* ed. David C. Klingaman and Richard C. Vedder (Ohio University Press, 1987), pp. 1–18.

Old Northwest even in the absence of legal obstacles. Such a view ignores the realities of western settlement in 1787. At that time, the areas most attractive to settlement were in the southern portions of the territory – that is, lands along the banks of the Ohio River and its tributaries. Although it offered good land and abundant resources, the region around the Great Lakes remained largely inaccessible to settlement until the completion of the Erie Canal in 1823, and the development of a canal and railroad transportation infrastructure in the 1830s and 1840s. It would be many years before the northern parts of Ohio, Indiana, and Illinois or the lands in Michigan and Wisconsin adjacent to the Great Lakes would attract large numbers of settlers. Consequently, a preponderance of the early settlers who settled here were from southern states, most notably Virginia.

Had there been no restrictions on the entry of slave labor, slaveholders almost certainly would have settled the northern as well as the southern bank of the Ohio. The topography of southern Illinois and Indiana are quite similar to the lands on the southern bank of the Ohio in Kentucky and the valleys of Virginia a bit further east. These lands could support the crops that had been popular for many years in the slave regions of the upper South. In fact, as Eugene Berwanger points out, Cairo, Illinois, is further south than Richmond, Virginia, or Lexington, Kentucky.[15] Even with the prohibition on importing slaves, the region took on a distinctively "southern" look in the first decades of the nineteenth century. For example, the southern counties in these states produced considerable quantities of pork, corn, and whiskey, which they marketed primarily in the South. Even those crops that were not sold in the South tended to travel out the "southern gateway" – that is, down the Ohio to the Mississippi and on to the Atlantic and beyond.[16]

15 Eugene Berwanger, *The Frontier against Slavery: Western Anti-Negro Prejudice and the Slavery Extension Controversy* (University of Illinois Press, 1967), p. 8. Berwanger makes a strong case that, in the absence of the prohibition of slavery provided in the Northwest Ordinance, slavery would have moved north of the Ohio River in the first decades of the nineteenth century.

16 Lloyd Mercer presents convincing evidence that in the years prior to 1840 the counties along the northern bank of the Ohio catered to the southern market; see "The Antebellum Interregional Trade Hypothesis: A Reexamination of Theory and Evidence," in *Explorations in the New Economic History: Essays in Honor of Douglass C. North*, eds. Roger L. Ransom, Richard Sutch, and Gary M. Walton (Academic Press, 1982). My own research on the Ohio Canal in the 1820s and 1830s turns up a similar pattern. See Roger L. Ransom, "Government Investment in Canals: A Study of the Ohio Canal, 1825–1860" (Ph.D. diss., University of Washington, Seattle, 1962), and idem, "Social Returns from Public Transport Investment: A Case Study of the Ohio Canal," *Journal of Political Economy* 78 (September–October 1970): 1041–60. On the importance of the southern gateway as an avenue of trade from the west before 1840, see Albert Fishlow, "Antebellum Interregional Trade Reconsidered," *American Economic Review* 54 (May 1964): 352–64.

More than just acres of land for cultivation were at stake here. The fact that it was the southern portions of these states that were settled first made the exclusion of slavery by law crucial in the formation of territorial and state governments. Had slave interests been a major force at the conventions drawing up the state constitutions for Indiana and Illinois, those states almost surely would have allowed slavery. Proslavery groups were not deterred by the terms of the Northwest Ordinance in their efforts to introduce slavery to the area. As late as 1807, attempts were made to have Congress repeal Article 6. Congress refused to do so, and the Northwest Territory remained free from slave labor. Even so, there were still protracted efforts to have slavery legalized through constitutional amendments at the state level.[17]

The Northwest Ordinance was highly significant in another way: It was the first major effort at compromise on the issue of slavery and western territories, and it was successful. The amendment offered by Dane included an important concession to the slave interests. Article 6 strongly reaffirmed the right of slaveholders to own their chattel labor, not only in the slave states, but in the new territories as well. The proviso guaranteeing that fugitive slaves must be returned to their owners set a precedent that was not lost on the Constitutional Convention meeting at Annapolis later in the same year. The issue of returning fugitive slaves to their owners was to become an increasingly volatile issue, as heated as the negotiations over slavery in the West. In another concession to the sensibilities of the South, the language of the ordinance was carefully constructed so that it could not be construed to free a single slave; it merely prohibited the entry of new slaves into the territory. This too became a pattern in future debates between the slave and nonslave factions.

For the North, the establishment by the federal government of a line that clearly delimited the boundary between free and slave territories was an important victory. Slavery was effectively shut out north of the Ohio River. The fact that the line of demarcation followed the route of a river provided a physical as well as a legal buffer between the two systems of labor. The river served as a fence separating the two groups. Consequently, as the westward settlement proceeded over the next three decades, slave and free settlers did not come directly into contact with each other. From the Appalachian Mountains to the Mississippi River, the issue of which territories would be free and which would have slaves was effectively settled by the Northwest Ordinance.

One question remains, however: Why did slaveholders acquiesce so

17 See Berwanger, *Frontier against Slavery,* chap. 1.

readily to the closing off of such a vast area of land? Several possible factors present themselves. Historian Staughton Lynd has argued that southern acquiescence to the ban of slavery in the Northwest Territory was part of a deal with delegates at the Constitutional Convention to get northern approval for the proposal to have slaves included as a basis of representation in Congress.[18] The argument that a "deal" was made is plausible; however, equally important is the fact that in 1787 there was still a great deal of unsettled land not closed to slavery. Both sides had something to offer the other. Proponents of slavery believed that the explicit prohibition of slavery north of the Ohio River implied that slavery was permissible south of the river. This interpretation was confirmed in 1790, when Congress completed the organization of the trans-Appalachian West by passing the Southwest Ordinance. That law simply stated that the inhabitants of the territory south of the Ohio River "shall enjoy all the privileges, benefits, and advantages set forth in the ordinance of the late Congress for the government of the territory of the United States northwest of the river Ohio." By omitting any mention of slavery, the Southwest Ordinance accepted the presence of slavery south of the Ohio River under the provisions by which the state of North Carolina had ceded its claims to western lands to the federal government.[19]

The first great compromise had been reached on the question of slavery and the western lands.

We the People: Slaves and the Constitution

Emotions raised by the Congressional debates on slaves in the western territories had barely settled when attention was shifted to Philadelphia and the Convention meeting in the summer of 1787 to draw up a "more perfect union" for the United States. Once again, the problem of how to deal with the contradiction of slavery in a society of free men threatened to disrupt the American union. Countless volumes have been written on the drafting of the Constitution. Because the document itself is so terse (and in several areas deliberately ambiguous), and because the official records of the proceedings of the convention contained no details of the

18 See Staughton Lynd, "The Compromise of 1787," *Political Science Quarterly* 81 (1966): 225–50; and also idem, *Class Conflict, Slavery and the United States Constitution* (Bobbs-Merrill, 1967), pp. 185–213.
19 The North Carolina cession of western territory stated that "no regulations made or to be made by Congress shall tend to emancipate slaves," and this provision was explicitly accepted in the Southwest Ordinance. See Donaldson, *The Public Domain*, pp. 161–2.

debates, scholars have struggled to discern the "true" intent of the founding fathers in phrasing this or that point in this or that fashion.[20]

For many years this effort was dominated by the influence of Charles Beard's *"Economic" Interpretation of the Constitution,* which appeared in 1913.[21] Beard insisted that the men who framed the Constitution were motivated primarily by *economic interests* – indeed, their own *individual* economic interests – in shaping the new government. His book spawned a whole school of historians who, in rejecting such a narrow focus on economic factors, stress instead a diversity of economic and social interests motivating the men at the convention. In addition to disputing the primacy of economic interests, these scholars have examined the intellectual origins of the Constitution.[22] As a consequence, the socioeconomic status and philosophical background of every delegate to the convention has been scrutinized in excruciating detail by historians of every persuasion, and each vote of the convention has been subjected to extensive analysis to determine the various interests at work. Yet this literature has largely ignored the problem of slavery and the Constitution.

There are several reasons for this omission. First, neither Beard nor his critics were able to unambiguously define the "interests" of slave and antislave groups, so that any interpretation of their actions is itself ambiguous. Second, the men at the Constitutional Convention kept their intentions well masked. We have only the impressions and recollections of leading participants such as James Madison on which to base our reconstruction of the arguments at the time. Finally, as David Brion Davis puts it, the provisions on slavery in the Constitution "were the products of an uneasy bargain and were deliberately shrouded in ambiguity. Agreement on concrete economic issues, or in blunter terms, a deal, could not resolve an unnegotiable conflict over the future of American slavery."[23]

---

20 The primary source for most of the votes and debates in the Constitutional Convention is the compilation of records by Max Farrand, ed., *The Records of the Federal Convention of 1787* (Yale University Press, 1911).

21 Charles Beard, *An "Economic" Interpretation of the Constitution of the United States* (Macmillan, 1913).

22 The most detailed criticism is by Robert Brown's *Charles Beard and the Constitution* (Princeton University Press, 1956), which provides a particularly detailed breakdown of each delegate to the convention. Also see Forrest McDonald, *We the People: The Economic Origins of the Constitution* (University of Chicago Press, 1958), and idem, *E Pluribus Unum: The Formulation of the American Republic, 1776–1790* (Houghton-Mifflin, 1965). Beard is not without his defenders; see the essays in part 3 of Lee Bensen, ed., *Turner and Beard: American Historical Writing Reconsidered* (Free Press, 1969). Robert McGuire and Robert Ohsfeldt present a quantitative analysis that disputes McDonald and tends to support at least a weak version of the Beard thesis; see "Economic Interests and the American Constitution: A Quantitative Rehabilitation of Charles A. Beard," *Journal of Economic History* 44 (June 1984).

23 Davis, *Problem of Slavery,* p. 130.

On one issue, however, there was widespread consensus among the delegates: The rights of slaveholders in the present slave states could not be threatened by the federal government created by the Constitution. Although some voiced dismay or moral indignation that such assurances were necessary, no one seriously believed that a union of states that did not recognize the property rights of slaveholders could be created and maintained. The problem was how to do this with sufficient firmness to reassure the Southerners and at the same time not offend the sensibilities of those strongly opposed to slavery. This was not an easy task. Nothing short of ironclad assurances that the federal government would actively enforce the rights of slaveholders to own their slaves would allay the fears of slaveholders. A particular demand of Southerners was the explicit recognition that slaves who escaped to "free" states be returned to their masters. Opponents of slavery argued with equal fervor that the assurances of property should be kept as vague as possible. These people found the "fugitive slave" issue highly offensive, and they were adamant that the most objectionable aspect of slavery – the African slave trade – must be abolished.

One way of keeping the peace while these problems were being hammered out was to see that the issue of slavery itself did not surface in a straightforward fashion during debates on various points. This obliqueness is reflected in the carefully crafted language of the final document: Nowhere in the Constitution of the United States do the words *slave* or *involuntary servitude* appear; even the sections that deal directly with the institution of slavery avoid referring to it by name. Not until the Thirteenth Amendment, ratified in 1865, can one find any direct reference to such concepts. That reference, of course, came with the abolishment of an institution that had existed for two and a half centuries.

How did the founding fathers provide the necessary guarantees for the slaveholders with such innocuous language? In three ways. First, they saw to it that private property rights were inviolate. Second, the slave states were given exaggerated political power through a process of representation that overrepresented slaveholders in Congress. Finally, Congress was enjoined from any interference in the slave trade for twenty years. Or, put another way, in twenty years Congress could, if it chose, abolish the slave trade.

The right to own slaves was never explicitly defined. Rather, the right to own someone's labor was conveniently subsumed under the more general right to enforce contracts contained in Article 1, Section 10. That article included a clause stating that "No state . . . shall . . . pass any bill of attainder, ex post facto law, or law impairing the obligations of contracts." The relation of a black slave to his or her master was a labor contract for life; hence, slaves could be held indefinitely in such service by their masters. Lest there be any question whether that obligation extended outside the state where the slaveowner resided, Article 4, Section 2, states: "No person held to service or labor in one State, under the laws thereof, escaping into another, shall in consequence of any law or regulation therein, be discharged from such service or labor, but shall be delivered up on claims of the party to whom such service may be due." On this point there was no ambiguity. It was the responsibility of the government to see that persons "held to service of labor" in another state were to be returned to their masters.

The problem of determining how representation in the national legislature should be apportioned among the states very nearly destroyed the efforts to write a new constitution. The stalemate is usually described as a situation in which "small" states feared domination by "large" states in a legislature apportioned solely on the basis of population, whereas large states were hesitant to enter a union where their greater size meant nothing. Undoubtedly these concerns did affect the voting on representation, and this is the picture the delegates provided after the fact. But population was by no means the only important factor creating this stalemate. James Madison pointed to another possibility: "It seemed now to be pretty well understood that the real differences of interests lay, not between the large and small but between the N. and Southn. States. The institution of slavery and its consequences formed the line of discrimination. There were 5 states on the South, 8 on the Northn. side of this line."[24]

The solution, which was to create a Senate (with two members from each state) and a House of Representatives (with membership based on population), not only resolved the stalemate over size; it also quelled the fears of slave states that, with their substantially smaller free population, they would be at the mercy of northern (and potentially antislave) majorities in Congress. A senate with fixed representation from each state made it far easier to maintain a balance of power between slave and nonslave interests in the legislature.

In the House of Representatives, however, there remained the issue of how seats would be apportioned, and an integral part of this problem was how to deal with the slave population. A plan first circulated by Charles Pinckney of South Carolina proposed a simple solution: Representation in the lower house would be based on population, with some fraction of the slave population (he suggested three-fifths) counted as a basis for apportionment of seats. The idea was not entirely new; apportionment of taxes among states using a formula based on wealth had

24   Cited in Winthrop Jordan, *White over Black*, p. 324.

been employed in the Articles of Confederation, and Pinckney's plan simply extended the logic to the question of representation.[25] As it was finally adopted, Article 1, Section 2, says: "Representatives and direct taxes shall be apportioned among the several states . . . according to their respective numbers, which shall be determined by adding to the whole number of free persons, including those bound to service for a term of years, and excluding indians not taxed, *three fifths of all other persons*" (emphasis added).

Historians offer widely diverging explanations for the adoption of a clause that so clearly favored the slave states. The simplest explanation, and one that is particularly appealing in the context of our argument, is that put forward by Alfred Simpson in 1941. "The South demanded the counting of at least three-fifths of its slaves in the apportionment of representation as its price for uniting with the North under a strong, centralized government."[26] More recent interpretations have argued that the facts are not so simple. Howard Ohline insists that "whatever the three-fifths clause meant to Americans after 1787, in the Philadelphia Convention it was not primarily the product of a sectional struggle for power or a rejection of Revolutionary ideals." It was, he claims, a part of an effort to bring about "a national union in which representation was related to the changing distribution of the population."[27]

Ohline's point that the divisions on the question of representation were not merely sectional is well taken. But his argument also underscores the willingness of "Republicans" at this time to accept simultaneously the notion of slaves as property as well as persons. James Madison took particular note of this curious fact, pointing out that the Constitution "decides with great propriety on the case of our slaves, when it views them in the mixed character of persons and of property. This is in fact their true character."[28] Ohline is probably correct when he says that northern as well as southern men accepted the three-fifths rule on Republican principles in 1787. But as he also notes, "the paradox in the eighteenth century was that a national legislature accurately reflecting

25 The origins of Pinckney's plan is somewhat unclear, and the plan itself has not survived. Howard A. Ohline makes a convincing case that Pinckney circulated his plan among a wide circle of delegates, and that his memorandum was the genesis of the idea as it emerged for debate; see "Republicanism and Slavery: Origins of the Three-Fifths Clause in the United States Constitution," *William and Mary Quarterly* 28 (October 1971).

26 Albert F. Simpson, "The Political Significance of Slave Representation, 1787–1821," *Journal of Southern History* 7 (August 1941): 319. Glover B. Moore, *The Missouri Controversy, 1819–1821* (University of Kentucky Press, 1953), reiterates and supports Simpson's position.

27 Ohline, "Republicanism and Slavery," p. 568.

28 Madison, *Federalist Paper* no. 54.

eighteenth-century American society would also have to reflect the institution of slavery."[29] Views of historians such as Simpson, who insists that the clause became a major irritant in the subsequent debates, do not really conflict with Ohline's argument. Certainly the added representation that the rule provided slave states was a potential political weapon in the struggles that eventually surfaced in 1819 with the Missouri crisis. With the added representation given by counting three out of five slaves, the South entered the union in 1790 on almost an equal basis with the North; without it, Southerners would have experienced an initial disadvantage that would have worsened over the years.

These provisions would seem to offer strong guarantees to slaveowners fearful of their property rights under the new arrangement. Yet at least one recent study of the votes taken at both the Philadelphia Convention and at the various state conventions that ratified the document suggests that slaveholders consistently opposed the Constitution. Robert McGuire and Robert Ohsfeldt argue that slaveholders remained fearful of the power of the federal government proposed under the Constitution.[30] The reluctance of slaveholders to support the Constitution is understandable. Their first preference would almost surely have been to create a weak central government that would leave control of slave property in the hands of the states. Yet this plan had drawbacks: A weak central government would lack the power to protect slave interests against the interferences of other states in the smooth operation of the slave system – most notably in the return of slaves who ran away to free territories.

The final element in the constitutional debates over slavery involved the closing of the infamous slave trade. Here the founding fathers resorted to what seem today incredible lengths to avoid saying what they meant. Article 1, Section 8, reads: "The migration or importation of such persons as any of the States now existing shall think it proper to admit shall not be prohibited by the Congress prior to the year one thousand eight hundred and eight, but a tax or duty may be imposed on such importation, not exceeding ten dollars for each person." The "importation of persons" referred, of course, to the slave trade. But the clause also left open the regulation of all migration to the United States. Nor did it actually prohibit the slave trade, it merely prohibited Congress from

---

29 Ohline, "Republicanism and Slavery," p. 568.
30 McGuire and Ohsfeldt present a summary of their findings in "Economic Interests and the American Constitution." For a more detailed quantitative analysis of the votes at the various conventions, see Robert A. McGuire and Robert L. Ohsfeldt, "An Economic Model of Voting Behavior over Specific Issues at the Constitutional Convention of 1787," *Journal of Economic History* 66 (March 1986); and Robert A. McGuire, "Constitution Making: A Rational Choice Model of the Federal Convention of 1787," *American Journal of Political Science* 32 (May 1988).

acting to interfere in this matter for a period of twenty years. Those who went back to their constituents in either the North or the South could argue, as David Brion Davis claims, that on the question of the slave trade "slavery had been given a mortal wound or the most secure protection." Actually, he points out, "both sections had agreed to defer the question to the future."[31]

That, indeed, characterizes the approach taken by the Constitutional Convention to the entire question of slavery. Whenever possible, the delegates chose to finesse the issue rather than to tackle the problem head-on. For quite a time the finesse worked. But eventually the issue could be avoided no longer.

Western Land Again: The Missouri Crisis of 1819

The issue of slavery remained relatively quiet for the three decades following the ratification of the Constitution. The slave trade was banned in 1809 with relatively little opposition from North or South. As Jefferson had observed in 1776, only two states — South Carolina and Georgia — really favored a continuance of the trade at that time; in the rest of the South, a growing number of slaveholders favored putting an end to the flow of slaves from abroad. The question of allowing importation of slaves had always produced some ambivalence among slaveholders. Although imported slaves obviously represented a cheap source of labor for those wishing to purchase slaves, their presence also depressed the price of slaves. Those owning slaves realized that the value of their investment would be depressed by continuing imports. On balance, the slave interests were content to let the external slave trade disappear.

With the arrival of what promised to be a lasting peace in Europe and the settlement of our quarrel with England, the United States turned its attention with renewed vigor toward economic expansion. That meant western settlement. The years immediately following 1815 witnessed the first great land boom in the United States. Settlers pushed westward into both the Northwest Territory and the Southwest Territory. With the admission of Alabama in December 1819, nine new states had been formed and admitted into the Union. That brought the total to twenty-two states, evenly balanced between eleven slave and eleven nonslave.[32] All this was in accordance with the guidelines of the Ordinance of 1787;

31 Davis, *The Problem of Slavery*, p. 131.
32 Between 1790 and 1819 five slave states were admitted: Kentucky (1792), Tennessee (1796), Louisiana (1812), Mississippi (1818), and Alabama (1819). Over the same period four free states were admitted: Vermont (1791), Ohio (1803), Indiana (1816), and Illinois (1818).

each of the slave states had been south of the Ohio River, and each had been regarded as a slave territory from the outset of settlement. Thanks to the agreement of 1787, the process of settlement and organization had proceeded peacefully. That was about to change. As the Sixteenth Congress of the United States convened in the spring of 1820, the question of slavery and the western territory had suddenly been thrust to the forefront of national politics once again.

The immediate source of the problem was a difficulty in Congress over the request of Missouri to be admitted as a slave state. The roots of controversy went back to 1803, when President Thomas Jefferson obtained the Louisiana Purchase. At the time, it seemed a masterful stroke. For a mere $15 million, the nation's land area was almost doubled and the use of the Mississippi was secured for Americans. The issue of settling the new land (with or without slavery) was hardly on anyone's mind. Apart from New Orleans, most of the Louisiana Purchase was far beyond the limits of settlement in 1803. But as people began to think more seriously about settling in the new territory, they realized that most of that land lay north of the area defined in the Northwest Ordinance as being free from slavery. Of the land west of the Mississippi River, only Louisiana (admitted as a state in 1812) and the Arkansas Territory were clearly marked as territories that would have slavery if the boundaries implicitly laid down by the compromise of 1787 were to be applied to the Louisiana Purchase.

The problem that arose in 1819 began in 1817 with the establishment in Missouri of a territorial government in preparation for statehood. The situation is evident in Map 2.1. The proposed state of Missouri lay only slightly south of Illinois; the Ohio River joins the Mississippi River in the southeastern corner of the territory. By the terms of the compromise of 1787, the new state would clearly be free territory. Slaveholders, however, were determined that Missouri would have slaves, and a substantial number of settlers pushed north into the territory bringing their slaves with them. In November 1818, the Legislative Council and the House of Representatives of Missouri petitioned Congress for statehood. Speaker of the House Henry Clay presented the memorial from the citizens of Missouri to the House on December 18, 1818. There was no question but that Missouri would eventually enter as a slave state under the arrangements existing in 1818.

Just prior to the Missouri request, Illinois and Alabama had each petitioned Congress for statehood. Although there was little controversy over the admission of these two states, Representative James Talmadge of New York created a minor crisis when he argued that the petition of Illinois to form a government should be rejected on the grounds that the

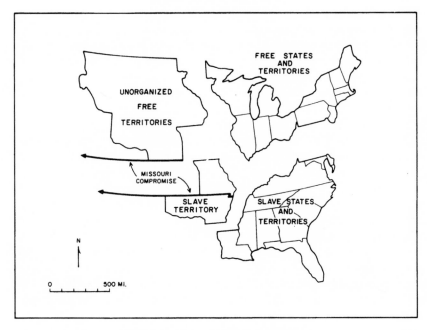

Map 2.1. The Missouri Compromise

proposed constitution of that state did not explicitly prohibit slavery. Talmadge's opposition did not carry the day, but his efforts signaled a warning that the case of Missouri might not be so simple.[33]

Missouri's petition for statehood represented the first attempt to allow slavery in a state that lay north of the implicit line of the Ohio River established by the Land Ordinances of 1787 and 1790. On February 13, 1819, as the House took up the bill for Missouri statehood, Talmadge renewed his efforts to exclude slavery north of the Ohio. He offered the following amendment to the bill admitting Missouri to the Union: "That the further introduction of slavery or involuntary servitude be prohibited . . . and that all children of slaves, born within the said state, after the admission thereof into the Union, shall be free, but may be held to service until the age of twenty-five years."[34]

The House split Talmadge's amendment into two parts. The clause dealing with prohibition of slavery passed by a vote of 87 to 76; the

33 Talmadge and his allies managed to get 34 votes opposing the resolution giving Illinois permission to form a government. See Moore, *The Missouri Controversy*, p. 34.
34 Cited in ibid., p. 35.

clause for gradual emancipation passed by 82 to 78. The amended bill was then sent to the Senate. By a rather substantial margin, that body refused to accept Talmadge's clause and passed a bill admitting Missouri with no restrictions regarding slavery.[35] Efforts to resolve differences between the bills passed by the House and the Senate failed, and the Fifteenth Congress adjourned without acting on Missouri's application for statehood. Talmadge had created a crisis in Congress that reached a critical juncture just as Congress adjourned.

The votes on the Talmadge amendments made it clear that opponents of slavery in the House of Representatives had enough votes in the House to hold up statehood for Missouri indefinitely. Encouraged by their success, antislavery forces redoubled their efforts during the Congressional recess to solidify the opposition to the admission of Missouri with slavery. Two issues were at stake here. The first was the importance of maintaining a balance between slave and nonslave states. This was largely a problem of timing and was clearly of greater concern to the South than to the North. Everyone could see that at least two more free states were going to be formed from existing territories in the Old Northwest, and there was the added possibility that Congress would act on the application of the newly formed territory of Maine for statehood.[36] The second issue was more difficult: How could the territories of the Louisiana Purchase be kept free from slavery in the future?

As the Sixteenth Congress began debate on the Missouri question, it became apparent that the Senate would continue to oppose the Talmadge amendment adamantly and that the House was equally determined to force the issue of eliminating slavery in Missouri. The resolution of this stalemate is known as the Compromise of 1820. It was ultimately fashioned by tying together three related actions:

1. Admit Missouri as a slave state in accordance with the initial request for statehood.
2. Approve the application for statehood of Maine as a free state.
3. Define the territories in the Louisiana Purchase, which henceforth would be free and slave.

The first two parts of the compromise "package" were obvious enough;

---

35 As with debates in the House, the Senate had separate votes on motions to remove the amendment. The votes were 22 to 16 to remove the clause on the introduction of slavery, and 31 to 7 to remove the clause dealing with emancipation of slaves already in the territory. For a discussion of the debates and votes on these issues, see Moore, *The Missouri Controversy*, p. 55.
36 Michigan and Wisconsin remained prime candidates in the Old Northwest Territory. In June 1819, Maine had been granted permission by the Commonwealth of Massachusetts to form a separate territory and petition Congress for statehood.

the applications for statehood from Maine and Missouri were combined into an omnibus bill. The third part of the bargain was the crucial element to get passage in the House. The solution, offered by Senator Jesse Thomas of Illinois, was to take the language used in the Northwest Ordinance of 1787 and apply it to the Louisiana Territory. What became known as the Thomas Proviso was attached to the bill approving statehood for Missouri and Maine:

> That, in all that territory ceded by France to the United States, under the name of Louisiana, which lies north of thirty-six degrees and thirty minutes north latitude, excepting only such part thereof as is included within the limits of the State contemplated by this act, slavery and involuntary servitude . . . shall be and is hereby forever prohibited: *Provided always,* That any person escaping into the same, from whom labor service is lawfully claimed in any State or Territory of the United States, such fugitive may be lawfully reclaimed and conveyed to the person claiming his or her labor or service as aforesaid.[37]

In the Senate there was little problem putting the pieces together, although the vote on the omnibus Missouri–Maine bill with the Thomas Proviso was uncomfortably close: 24 in favor and 20 opposed. In the House the task was not so easy. As Glover Moore observes, "One of the noticeable things about the passage of the Missouri Compromise was that the House never voted yea or nay on the compromise as a whole."[38] Instead, Speaker Henry Clay masterfully guided the various parts of the package through the legislature piece by piece. The closest call came on the vote to eliminate the Talmadge clause from the Missouri bill and allow slavery in the new state, an action that passed by only 3 votes. The Thomas Proviso was then approved by an overwhelming majority, 134 to 42. The result of the compromise can be seen in Map 6.1, which shows the demarcation line established by the Thomas Proviso.

Although it has received relatively little attention from historians in recent years, the Missouri Compromise was a pathbreaking achievement on the part of those who fashioned it.[39] The narrowness with which it

---

37 Cited in Moore, *The Missouri Controversy*, pp. 88–9; emphasis in the original.
38 Ibid., p. 102.
39 The best source for a description of the legislative battle is Glover Moore, *The Missouri Controversy*, and my description has drawn heavily from the information on votes and procedure that he provides. Moore's overall thesis, however, is flawed by the very narrow sectional interpretation in which the South magnanimously gives way to selfish pressures from the northern interests that consistently oppose efforts at compromise. This view, which is echoed by Simpson ("The Political Significance of Slave Representation"), has been challenged by Howard Ohline ("Republicanism and Slavery"). Richard Brown presents an excellent analysis of the impact of the Missouri

passed suggests a fragility that belies the robustness of the contract once it was struck. In fact, for the next three decades, the line defined in the Missouri Compromise clearly established the limits of slavery in the United States. One reason it worked so well was that it was based on the precedent established by the Northwest Ordinance in 1787. A majority of Southerners actually favored the Thomas Proviso when it came to a vote in the House.[40] Although Northerners were more truculent in agreeing to the admission of Missouri as a slave state, it is easy to exaggerate the force of their opposition. Slavery, after all, was firmly established in Missouri by the time the issue came to a head in Congress. However distasteful opponents of slavery might find this fact, they could not reverse the pattern of settlement. Moreover, by the time the issue came to a vote, the outcome was assured.[41] This meant that those strongly opposed could vote negatively so long as their vote did not jeopardize the agreed-upon outcome. They then overwhelmingly approved the Thomas Proviso. This was a compromise in the classic sense of the term: Each side got something and each side gave up something they deemed important. The slave interests got approval of Missouri as a slave state; opponents succeeded in permanently extending the ban on slavery in the Louisiana Territory north of the line thirty-six degrees thirty minutes.

Over the long term, the most important development of the Missouri Compromise turned out to be even more basic than the details of the bargain itself. The Missouri Compromise established the right of Congress to pass legislation allowing or prohibiting slavery in the western territories. This was not universally applauded; indeed a few people saw in the Thomas Proviso a threat to their long-term interests. Nathaniel Macon of North Carolina was one of only two southern senators to vote against the omnibus bill in the Senate. "To compromise," he wrote a friend shortly before the vote, "is to acknowledge the right of Congress to interfere and to legislate on the subject, this would be acknowledging too much."[42] Future generations of southern representatives in Washington would tend to agree with Macon's assessment, while Northerners,

---

Crisis and subsequent debates on the slave issue on the party structure of the early 1820s and after. He is quiet, however, on the territorial aspects of the compromise ("The Missouri Crisis, Slavery, and the Politics of Jacksonian Democracy," *South Atlantic Quarterly* 65 [Winter 1965]).

40 Representatives from southern states voted 39 in favor, 37 opposed (Moore, *The Missouri Controversy*, p. 111). Because the Senate did not vote on the separate aspects of the bill, we have no comparable test of senatorial support in the South.

41 In addition to several changes of votes, a number of representatives opposed to Missouri as a slave state absented themselves from the House to ensure the outcome.

42 Natnaniel Macon to Bolling Hall, February 13, 1820, cited in Moore, *The Missouri Controversy*, p. 108.

many of whom resisted the compromise, gradually came to see the limitations to slavery contained in the Thomas Proviso as the cornerstone upon which a resistance to expansion of slavery could be built.

Emotions ran high during the debates over slavery in Missouri and the Louisiana Territory. Yet almost as quickly as it arose, the tension subsided. The country, as it were, heaved a collective sigh of relief and went back to work. Why was the compromise so successful? In part, because it reflected the fact that both sides could point to tangible gains from the legislation. But in a larger sense it was because, despite the rhetoric that proclaimed a willingness to fight for the principles at stake, the fact remained that most Americans were not prepared to "go to the wall" on the slavery issue in 1820. The specter of a slave system that was a genuine threat to northern interests had not yet appeared on the political scene. Slavery was a moral indignity; and some Southerners had pressed a step too far in allowing slavery to take hold in Missouri. But for most people living outside the south in 1820, slavery was a distant and relatively quiescent institution. Patience, not force, was needed to deal with the problem. The slave trade had been eliminated and a clear line of demarcation between slave and free territory had been established by the terms of the Thomas Proviso. Even if it could not be eradicated, slavery had been contained.

The political situation added to the sense of consensus rather than sectionalism. "Republicanism," the political movement launched by Thomas Jefferson with his presidential victory in 1800, was just reaching its zenith at this point. There was, for all practical purposes, only one effective political party. In the elections of 1820 the Federalists captured only 7 of 42 seats in the Senate, and 27 of 183 seats in the House. The absence of party rivalries made the quest for a compromise much easier. The other side of that coin was that the crisis over slavery between 1819 and 1821 had a profound effect on the development of the two-party system that was to emerge a decade later.[43]

That was all in the future. For the time being, the deal that had worked in 1787 had worked again in 1820. Both sides had been given some territory; both sides had some assurances about the future. A few could look ahead to see that a troubling question remained: What would happen when there was no longer any land to give away? The issue of slavery and territories was put to rest for the time being, but for how long? The

43 On this point, see in particular Richard Brown, "The Missouri Crisis and the Politics of Jacksonianism"; Robert E. Shalhope, "Race, Class, Slavery and the Antebellum Southern Mind," *Journal of Southern History* 37 (November 1971); and James Oakes, "From Republicanism to Liberalism: Ideological Change and the Crisis in the Old South," *American Quarterly* 37 (Fall 1985).

man who drafted Article 6 of the Northwest Ordinance thirty-four years earlier was uneasy over the solution of 1820:

> But this momentous question, like a fire bell in the night, awakened and filled me with terror. I considered it at once as the knell of the Union. It is hushed, indeed for the moment. But this is a reprieve only, not a final sentence. A geographical line, coinciding with a marked principle, moral and political, once conceived and held up to the angry passions of men, will never be obliterated; and every new irritation will mark it deeper and deeper.[44]

The passage has been quoted often, perhaps because no one since has said it any better. Jefferson understood where the crux of the conflict lay. The line that had resolved the dispute of 1820 would become the basis of an even more bitter fight thirty years later.

44 Ford, *Writings of Thomas Jefferson*, 10: 157.

3

The Economics of Slavery

We got up early, you betcha. You would be out there by time you could see and quit when it was dark. They tasked us. They would give us 200 or 300 pounds of cotton to bring in and you would git it, and if you didn't git it, you better, or you would git it tomorrow or your back would git it. Or you would git it from someone else, maybe steal it from their sacks.

Austin Grant, A slave in Mississippi and Texas[1]

The first black laborers arrived in British North America in the fall of 1619. They were brought to Virginia – as were many whites – to work either as servants or as laborers in the field. Laborers, particularly those willing to toil in the hot Virginia sun, were in great demand at this point, as colonists scrambled to cash in on the discovery that tobacco leaves grown in Virginia had a ready market back home in England. Although Negro slavery was common in the Spanish part of the New World, there was no legal basis for slavery in the British colonies at this time. Consequently, these first arrivals from Africa were not regarded as slaves, but as indentured servants, and were granted rights similar to those of white indentured servants. The status of black indentured servants as free laborers was short-lived. As the number of blacks began to increase in the 1630s and 1640s, the normal contracting arrangements for indentured labor were viewed as unsatisfactory. The practice of indenturing black "servants" for life was introduced. This, of course, was virtually the same as slavery. By 1640 it had already become common to refer to blacks as "slaves" rather than servants, and evidence from probates on the value of black "servants" reveals that they were quite valuable.[2] In 1662 the first legal statutes defining the status of blacks as chattel labor were in place. These laws became the model for instituting legal slavery in each of the British colonies in the years ahead.[3] By the end of the

1 Recollections of Austin Grant, quoted in Leon F. Litwack, *Been in the Storm So Long: The Aftermath of Slavery* (Vintage Books, 1979), p. 298.
2 Herbert S. Klein notes that in the estate of William Burdett, recorded in 1643, Negro servants were valued three or four times more highly than white indentured children; see *Slavery in the Americas: A Comparative Study of Virginia and Cuba* (University of Chicago Press, 1967), p. 43.
3 On the early history of slavery and indentured servitude in Virginia and the other British

colonial period the legal position of black slaves had been defined to exclude the rights afforded whites, and the use of black slave labor had become the cornerstone of commercial agriculture in the South.

The absence of any "slave code" in British common law meant that the legal basis for slavery evolved as the use of slave labor in the colony expanded over time. This resulted in a situation where, as historian Herbert Klein notes, "it was economic considerations, to the exclusion of all others, that operated most decisively upon the entire structure of statutory law and custom that made up the slave regime."[4] Moreover, these "economic considerations" were dominated by a market-oriented plantation agriculture that demanded an increasing supply of labor. Slave labor was brought to the British colonies because of a demand for labor and the willingness of the planters to pay for that labor by purchasing what amounted to a lifetime contract for the labor of a slave. For this system of chattel labor to work, not only was there need for a legal code that defined the slave as a piece of property; there must also be a fairly sophisticated set of market arrangements to provide slave labor at a price that reflected the value of slaves in the vicinity. By the time of the American Revolution, slave markets had developed to the point where the sale or purchase of a slave was a transaction no more difficult or unusual than the sale or purchase of land at auction.

Did Slavery Pay? The Slave as an Economic Asset

The fact that slavery in the United States has always been so closely associated with markets and economic considerations raises the obvious question: Was slavery a "profitable" enterprise for the thousands of slaveowners in the United States? In one sense, the question is almost trivial; slavery must have been profitable in the antebellum South – at least to the owners of the slaves. How else could the institution have survived the pressures of an expanding market system for two and a half centuries? Moreover, it is instinctive to note that, once the United States gained its independence, slavery did not merely *survive*; it clearly *thrived* in the new environment of a "free" nation. Whatever the deleterious effects of slavery on economic growth in the slave South, they are not evident in the rapid expansion of the cotton economy from 1790 to 1860.

colonies, see Klein, *Slavery in the Americas*; and Winthrop Jordan, *White over Black: American Attitudes toward the Negro: 1550–1812* (University of North Carolina Press, 1968). Sharon V. Salinger provides an excellent summary of the arguments as to why slavery, rather than indentured servitude became the dominant form of labor contract in the South; see *"To Serve Well and Faithfully": Labor and Indentured Servants in Pennsylvania, 1682–1800* (Cambridge University Press, 1987).
4 Klein, *Slavery in the Americas*, p. 164.

How is it that the arrangement that produced one of the great examples of a reasonably free market system also produced one of the most pernicious examples of a slave labor system? The key to understanding this paradox turns out to be blindingly simple. Under the Constitution, as we have seen, slaves were property as well as persons. If slaves were property, they would be treated by their owners just like any other piece of property that can be used to earn income. Slaves, in short, were *economic assets,* whose value was governed by the same factors that determined the price of other assets in the capital market. Economic historians have used this insight to develop an economic model that we shall call the *asset-pricing model* of slavery.[5] Put very succinctly, the asset-pricing model asserts that the value of any slave will depend on the discounted present value of the annual net income plus any capital appreciation (or depreciation) expected over the life of the slave.

The most obvious return from owning a slave was the income gained each year from the slave as a productive laborer. This included:

The Physical Output Produced by the Slave (what economists term the marginal physical product of the slave).

The Value of the Slave's Output – In other words, the price of the output times the marginal physical product.

The Cost of Maintaining the Slave, including food, shelter, and any tools that were necessary for the slave to be a productive worker.

Two observations are pertinent at this point. First, note that it is the expected stream of income over the lifetime of the slave that is relevant to the calculation of the slave's market value. This accounts for the fact that even newborn slave babies had a positive price even though net annual income from infants was clearly negative. Second, so long as the anticipated annual value of output of the slave at least covered the expected maintenance costs over his or her lifetime, the price of a slave would be positive.[6] This was the minimal condition for slavery to be "profitable"

5   The first complete statement of the asset-pricing model was by Alfred H. Conrad and John R. Meyer, "The Economics of Slavery in the Ante Bellum South," *Journal of Political Economy* 66 (April 1958). As noted in Chapter 1, their article touched off a major debate on the "profitability" of slavery. For an assessment of the economic insights that this approach contributed to the historical debates on slavery, see Gavin Wright, "New and Old Views on the Economics of Slavery," *Journal of Economic History* 33 (June 1973). Two other useful sources are Robert W. Fogel and Stanley L. Engerman, "The Economics of Slavery," in *The Reinterpretation of American Economic History,* ed. Robert W. Fogel and Stanley L. Engerman (Harper and Row, 1971); and Roger L. Ransom and Richard Sutch, *One Kind of Freedom: The Economic Consequences of Emancipation* (Cambridge University Press, 1977), chap. 1 and appendix A.

6   Because we are talking about *discounted* streams of income, the level of interest rates could have an important bearing on the price of slaves. We ignore the effects of interest rates here largely for simplicity. In the period under examination, the "real" interest

in a capitalist system, and there was no period of American history when slaves were not able to produce at least a small surplus of output over their lifetime.

The annual production of the slave on the farm was the most obvious source of income from the investment in a slave, but there was another very significant source of return to slave assets. The slaveholder would benefit from any appreciation in price of slaves owned, and also any natural increase in the number of slaves. Under American custom, the child belonged to the owner of the mother. Thus, the owner of female slaves stood to gain from the birth of children, and this was reflected in the value of women of child-bearing age.

The asset-pricing model predicates a world where slave ownership brings financial returns to the slaveholder, and where the price of a slave reflects those returns over time. In a well-functioning marketplace, the "rate of profit" from ownership of a slave should just equal that of alternative assets available to the slaveholder. Is this a world that mirrors the reality of the antebellum South? Extensive studies have demonstrated rather convincingly that, at least for the last twenty to thirty years of the slave regime, the model mirrors reality rather closely.[7] The world of the southern slaveholder was one where slaves were bought and sold just like any other asset. Madison was right when he noted that the founding fathers defined slaves as both men and property; by the middle of the nineteenth century there was little doubt that property was the characteristic that dominated the lives of both slaves and their masters.

What is of more interest to us here than the details of the asset-pricing model are the implications one can draw from that model about the nature of slavery in the South. Given that slavery was "profitable," what else does the model tell us about the role of slavery in exacerbating the tensions between North and South?

---

rate was relatively stable. The role of interest rates would be minimal, therefore, in explaining *changes* in the price of slaves.

7 Empirical studies on the "profitability" of slavery abound in the literature. Virtually all of them find the rate of return on slaves to be roughly equal to that on other assets. Three particularly important contributions are: Robert Evans, Jr., "The Economics of American Negro Slavery," in Universities-National Bureau Committee for Economic Research, *Aspects of Labor Economics* (Princeton University Press, 1962); Richard Sutch, "The Profitability of Slavery – Revisited," *Southern Economic Journal* 31 (April 1965); and James Foust and Dale Swan, "Productivity and Profitability of Antebellum Slave Labor: A Micro Approach," *Agricultural History* 44 (January 1970). Evans used the differences in hire rates of male and female slaves to demonstrate that there was indeed a premium in the price of female slaves to reflect their childbearing capabilities. Sutch was the first to incorporate the returns to growth in the slave population into a single calculation of profitability. Foust and Swan provide the most detailed estimates of returns to slavery based on microeconomic data. In addition to a breakdown of returns by region, they also examine the effects of "breeding" on the returns to slaveholders.

First we can conclude that, contrary to views espoused by critics of the system at the time, *slave labor was productive*. Slaveholders in the South extracted sufficient labor from their slaves to produce a considerable surplus each year. They did this with a combination of coercion and incentives that implies a very close control of labor by the master. Even the smallest task was organized and supervised by the master or his "driver," and little regard was given to the desires of the slave for leisure time.

Next, it seems safe to assert that *the capital invested by planters in chattel labor was employed where it would be most productive*. This was no accident; there were powerful market pressures on slaveholders to see that their slave capital was efficiently allocated.[8] Those market pressures produced one of the most invidious features of American slavery – the internal trade in slaves. Slaves had no choice as to where they worked and lived. If slaveowners moved, their slaves moved with them. By the same token, if market conditions dictated the sale of a slave, that slave moved to his or her new home without regard to family or personal ties. Such moves were common, and they entailed great distances. The settlement of western lands created a demand for slaves in the newly settled areas. While some slaves moved west with their white masters, many more were sold to slave traders who took them west and then resold them to a new master. The exact numbers involved in this trade will never be known, but from the demographic characteristics of the population alone, we know that it was substantial.[9]

The market pressures for economic efficiency produced another important characteristic of the slave system. The *output per slave was markedly higher on the more fertile lands of the West*. Indeed, according to most observers at the time, as well as many economic historians in subsequent years, it was the high returns from slave labor on these fertile

8 Some writers have argued that the plantation system may have tended to reduce overall efficiency of the southern economy by limiting the transfer of slave labor into high-productivity, nonagricultural enterprises. See in particular, Fred Bateman and Thomas Weiss, *A Deplorable Scarcity: The Failure of Industrialization in the Slave Economy* (University of North Carolina Press, 1981). The very small scale of manufacturing in the South makes overall assessment of this point difficult, and Bateman and Weiss do not contest the finding that slavery was highly profitable in the agricultural sector.

9 With the closing of the slave trade in 1809, the black population of the United States was, for all practical purposes, a "closed" population from that point on. This allows us to infer migration from evidence in the decennial census on the age of the black population in each state. See Richard Sutch, "The Breeding of Slaves for Sale and the Westward Expansion of Slavery, 1850–1860," in *Race and Slavery in the Western Hemisphere: Quantitative Studies*, eds. Stanley Engerman and Eugene Genovese (Princeton University Press, 1975). Sutch presents detailed estimates of black migration for the period 1840–60 that suggest that a substantial slave trade flourished between the seaboard states and the western interior.

areas that sustained the value of slaves in the older regions.[10] Whether this pressure was sufficient to explain the territorial aggressiveness of the South is a point we shall examine later; for now it is sufficient to note that the *observed* rates of return on slave investment were associated with the higher productivity obtained by moving slaves to western lands.[11]

All of which brings us back to our original proposition: *Slavery in the antebellum South was not on the verge of economic destruction in 1860.* Indeed, it is hard to argue that slavery had ever been in any serious jeopardy from economic factors in the United States. One of the most penetrating insights of the asset-pricing model is that, so long as the price of slaves adjusts to changes in the marketplace, profitability can be maintained. And prices of slaves clearly did adjust to changing market conditions throughout the antebellum period. Figure 3.1 plots a three-year moving average for two series of slave prices from 1805 to 1860. The top series is the price of a "prime" field hand in New Orleans; the lower series is the "average price" of all slaves in the South. It is immediately evident that slaves were very valuable assets throughout the antebellum period. The average price never fell below two hundred dollars, and in 1859 it had reached eight hundred dollars. A prime field hand in that year was worth over fifteen hundred dollars. The chart clearly shows that slave prices were subject to changes from year to year. The distinct cyclical pattern of prices corresponds to the major swings in economic activity – particularly the cotton booms after the War of 1812, in the 1830s, and in the 1850s. Nothing in the data suggests that the market price of a slave was rigid or divorced from the underlying forces stimulating the expansion of the southern economy.

Slaves, in short, were valuable assets in 1805, and they were even more valuable in 1860. In addition, there was a well-established market for slaves, which meant that the slave was a highly "liquid" asset that could easily be converted to cash if the owners wished to sell the slave for any reason. Southerners investing in their "peculiar institution" in 1860 certainly had little basis for fears about the economic viability of their

10 Conrad and Meyer, "The Economics of Slavery," p. 174. Foust and Swan present detailed estimates of returns by region that make it clear that the productivity of western land was crucial to the level of slave returns throughout the South in the 1850s ("Productivity and Profitability of Antebellum Slavery").

11 This is not to say that profitability of slavery in the South as a whole depended upon the availability of western land. In the absence of western land there could have been a very different pattern of slave prices that could have maintained a profitable rate of return on the investment in slaves. That is a counterfactual world that exists only in the theoretical models of slavery. The point made here is simply that the observed pattern of returns to slave investments was a consequence of movement to better land in the West.

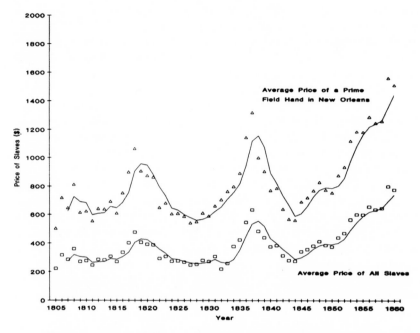

Figure 3.1. Price of slaves, 1805–60 (three-year moving average)

investments. Quite the opposite – on the eve of the Civil War, American slaveholders were coming off a decade and a half of exuberant growth and expansion.

A Growing Problem: Economic Growth in the Antebellum South

The asset-pricing model of slavery seems to fit contemporary descriptions of the slave system in the South rather well. The need for close supervision to maintain productivity, the callous attitude toward the preferences of slaves in the determination of their working conditions, and the willingness to break up families if necessary, when selling slaves in response to economic factors are all attributes of the profit-seeking slaveowner. Another trait of slave agriculture often pointed out by observers was the heavy emphasis on a cash crop. This was also consistent with a world in which options are governed by demands for cash payments.

From the outset of the antebellum period, southern planters believed that "King Cotton" was the driving force behind economic growth not only for the South, but for the rest of the United States as well. In the mid-twentieth century, a growing number of economic historians provided quantitative support for such a claim. Douglass North's picture of the South in the period after 1790 documents the importance of staple crops: "Cotton was the most important influence in the growth of market size and the consequent expansion of the economy."[12] The South's cash crop, North points out, accounted for one-half of the total exports from the United States at this time. Significantly, the stimulus from cotton production was not confined to the South. Cotton producers relied, for the most part, on outside suppliers for the transportation and handling of the crop as it went to market. This arrangement not only provided employment for the northeastern interests in commerce but also stimulated the demand for foodstuffs produced in the Ohio Valley. In the period between the end of the War of 1812 and the depression of the early 1840s, the cotton production of the South was a major factor driving the economic expansion of the United States.

North's argument that the South's stimulus to interregional trade made it a "leading sector" of the antebellum economy is supported by research on the level of income in the United States. Figure 3.2 presents estimates of per capita income for the free population of the United States by regions in 1840 and 1860.[13] The figures suggest that the South was more than keeping pace with the rest of the economy in the interval 1840 to 1860. In fact, if one compares the annual growth rates for each region, the South was growing faster than the country as a whole. If only free persons are considered as receiving "income" in the South, then the southern states appear to be relatively well-off. Although this measure overstates the productivity of free whites in the South (by attributing all income to white labor), it is a valid measure of the income enjoyed by whites.[14] The evidence on per capita income levels reinforces the finding

---

12 Douglass C. North, *The Economic Growth of the United States, 1790–1860* (Prentice-Hall, 1961), p. 68. For an excellent summary of the "North thesis," and its implications for American economic development, see the essay by Richard Sutch, "Douglass North and the New Economic History," in *Explorations in Economic History: Essays in Honor of Douglass C. North*, eds. Roger L. Ransom, Richard Sutch, and Gary M. Walton (Academic Press, 1982), pp. 15–21.

13 The data presented in Figure 3.2 were developed by Stanley L. Engerman from the work by Richard Easterlin. The per capita income for the free population is estimated by assuming that slaves received no income, but received a "maintenance allowance" of twenty dollars per slave. See Engerman, "Some Economic Factors in Southern Backwardness in the Nineteenth Century," in *Essays in Regional Economics*, eds. John F. Kain and John R. Meyer (Harvard University Press, 1971).

14 If the slaves are included as income earners, the level of per capita income in the South would be 25 to 35 percent less than the numbers in Figure 3.2. Slaves received only a subsistence allowance as income, which is taken to be worth twenty dollars per year in

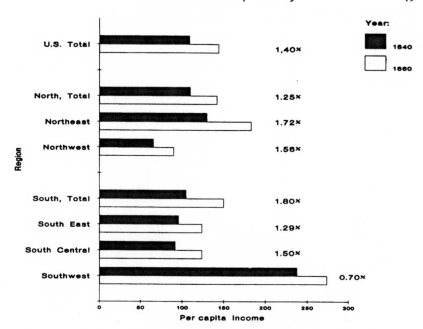

Figure 3.2. Per capita income by region, free population,
1840 and 1860 (1860 dollars)

that slavery was profitable. The obvious conclusion to draw from these findings is that the South in 1860 was not an economy teetering on the brink of economic disaster. Put another way, the South – or more accurately, the slaveholders of the South – had a great deal at stake in the continuation of their peculiar institution.[15]

Although the implications of the asset-pricing model of slavery fit the traditional views of the slave South rather well, the same cannot be said of a view that pictures the South as a vibrant and rapidly growing agricultural region. Observers traveling in the slave states were uniformly negative in their comparison of conditions in the southern and northern

the estimates of Figure 3.2. If we allow for this subsistence, the difference in the two measures of per capita income gives some idea of the magnitude of exploitation of slaves by their white masters. Even if slaves are included in the denominator of the per capita income measures, the rate of growth in per capita income in the southern states still kept pace with the rest of the nation.

15 The interest of the slaveholders is, of course, greatly understated by the use of per capita estimates of income that make no allowance for the highly skewed distribution of income in the South.

states. One of the most astute northern visitors to the South was Frederick Law Olmsted, whose book, *The Cotton Kingdom,* was compiled from three earlier books describing his journeys through the South from 1857 through 1860.[16] Responding to the comment of a friend who claimed that the South "must be rich," because "their last cotton crop alone was worth two hundred million," Olmsted noted that "my own impression of the real condition of the People of our Slave States gave me, on the contrary, an impression that the cotton monopoly in some way did more harm than good; . . . and I find that the impression has become a conviction."[17] Olmsted was particularly struck by the contrast between slave farms in Virginia and free farms in the North:

> Coming directly from my farm in New York to Eastern Virginia, I was satisfied, after a few weeks' observation, that most of the people lived very poorly; that the proportion of men improving their condition was much less than any northern Community; and that the natural resources of the land were strangely unused or were used with poor economy.[18]

As he progressed further into the South, the contrast between slave farms and free farms in the South became equally strong:

> I went on my way into the so-called cotton states, within which I travelled over, first and last, at least three thousand miles of roads, from which not a cotton plant was seen, and the people living by the side of which certainly had not been made rich by cotton or anything else. And for every mile of road-side upon which I saw any evidence of cotton production, I am sure that I saw a hundred of forest or waste land, with only now and then an acre or two of poor corn half smothered in weeds; for every rich man's house, I am sure I passed a dozen shabby and half-furnished cottages and at least a hundred cabins – mere hovels, such as none but a poor farmer would house his cattle in at the North.[19]

16 Frederick Law Olmsted, *A Journey in the Seaboard Slave States* (Dix and Edwards, 1856); idem, *A Journey through Texas* (Dix, Edwards, and Company, 1857); idem, *A Journey in the Back Country* (Mason Brothers, 1860); and idem, *The Cotton Kingdom,* ed. and introd. Arthur M. Schlesinger, Jr. (Alfred A. Knopf, 1953; originally published in 1861). Although he was astute and meticulous in writing what he saw, Olmsted was by no means free from bias in his observations of the slave society. He was an ardent abolitionist, and some historians have questioned his picture of the South. See, for example, the comments of Robert W. Fogel and Stanley L. Engerman in their study, *Time on the Cross* (Little, Brown, 1974), 1: 170–81. Schlesinger provides a more balanced assessment in his introduction to *The Cotton Kingdom.*
17 Olmsted, *The Cotton Kingdom,* p. 8.
18 Ibid.
19 Ibid., p. 11.

Historians have tended to echo Olmsted's observations, characterizing the South as economically "backward," and attributing that lack of progress to the presence of slavery.[20] Such a view seems very much at odds with the historical picture of a South with efficient slave labor and growing per capita incomes.

Can the two views be reconciled? Perhaps they can. We can begin by noting that both views of southern development accept one incontrovertible fact: The production of cotton expanded enormously in the South in the years after 1790, and this generated very sizable incomes for cotton producers of the South. But what were the implications of this cotton crop for the South as a whole? The dominating presence of this "cash crop," together with the concentration of production on slave plantations, tends to distort the regional comparisons of income in several respects.

We have already noted one of the most obvious possible distortions in the slave system: the allocation of all surplus produced by slaves to their masters. If slaves were owned by a broad spectrum of the southern population, this distortion would be relatively unimportant. But, as Olmsted observed and census data confirm, only a minority of southern households owned slaves.[21] Yet this group received all of the income produced by their chattel labor. This did more than simply produce a skewed income distribution favoring slaveholders. Although the South as a region experienced substantial economic growth in the antebellum period, this expansion was largely the result of production on large slave plantations. Southerners who did not own slaves produced only a marginal crop of cotton for the market. These farms were, for the most part, outside the marketing infrastructure that sprang up around the cotton trade. There were, in other words, two "Souths" in the antebellum period; a slave South that experienced growth and expansion and a nonslave South that was far less prosperous. Because the nonslave farms were far more numerous than the plantations, Olmsted's report of a few plantations interspersed among a mass of poorer farms is consistent with the cliometric view that has tended to focus primarily on the plantation

20 See, for example, Douglas Dowd, "A Comparative Analysis of Economic Development in the American West and South," *Journal of Economic History* 16 (December 1956); and Eugene D. Genovese, *The Political Economy of Slavery: Studies in the Economy and Society of the Slave South* (Vintage Books, 1965).

21 According to the 1860 census, there were 384,884 slaveholders in the United States, out of a population of 7.1 million free whites in the South (U.S. Census Office, Eighth Census, *Population of the United States in 1860* [U.S. Government Printing Office, 1864], p. 247). If we conservatively estimate that each slaveholder represents a head of household, and that the average household had six individuals, this would mean that roughly one in three households in the South owned at least one slave.

economy. Several additional factors also tend to bias measures of per capita income such as those in Figure 3.2 in favor of the South. The presence of a cash crop such as cotton can exaggerate the difference in income between regions because northern farms took a higher fraction of their farm income in nonmarketed outputs that are difficult to value. Moreover, slavery makes it extremely difficult to compare labor inputs in the two cases, because slaves operate under a completely different set of constraints in determining their labor services.[22]

A look behind the estimates presented in Figure 3.2 reveals further evidence that, despite the apparent prosperity of the cotton sector, the South remained a relatively undeveloped region. The estimates of per capita income imply that the growth of per capita income for the South as a whole actually exceeded the rate of growth in any of the subregions of the South. This means that incomes rose not because of increased agricultural productivity, but because Southerners were migrating away from low-income regions in the East to high-income regions in the West. In *One Kind of Freedom*, Richard Sutch and I pointed out that:

> To argue from these figures that the South grew more rapidly than the North, however, is highly misleading. Viewed in this way, southern growth occurred primarily because of a continuous migration to more productive soils of the West. Yet within each geographic division southern growth was slow (and slower on the good lands of the West South central than on the poorer soils of the South Atlantic region). Rather than refuting the arguments that the southern slave economy was moribund, [these figures] support the notions that the South was indeed stagnating with respect to the North and that the only recourse left to white Southerners who wished to better their positions was to move westward.[23]

Evidence on levels of crop output provides further support for the contention that agriculture in the South was not growing rapidly over this period. In the cotton-growing regions of the South, crop productivity

22 These points are developed further in Ransom and Sutch, *One Kind of Freedom*, chap. 1 and appendix A; and Gavin Wright, *The Political Economy of the Cotton South: Households, Markets, and Wealth in the Nineteenth Century* (W. W. Norton, 1978).

23 Ransom and Sutch, *One Kind of Freedom*, p. 268. We also noted that the Engerman estimates are exceedingly sensitive to the regional definitions used. Others have cast some doubt on the strength of these estimates by questioning the very high levels of per capita income shown for the Southwest; see Gerald Gunderson, "Southern Ante-Bellum Income Reconsidered," *Explorations in Economic History* 10 (Winter 1973); and idem, "Southern Income Reconsidered: A Reply," *Explorations in Economic History* 12 (January 1975).

rose by less than 1 percent from 1839 to 1859 – hardly an impressive figure.[24]

Two conclusions emerge from the quantitative studies of the slave South. First is the fact that, however one wants to measure "profits" to slave ownership, plantation agriculture was prospering in the late ante-bellum period. Whether the prosperity of the slaveowners "trickled down" to the other farmers in the South is a matter of some debate, but it seems likely that a significant fraction of the smaller landholders may not have been doing so well, particularly those working in areas outside the staple agriculture. The second fact is that the returns to staple agriculture in the South were closely tied not only to the demand for those staples abroad, but to the availability of more fertile soil in the western United States. This brings us to the issue of whether that quest for profitable land to the west was a driving force behind the territorial demands of the South in the late antebellum period.

The Territorial Imperative: The South and Western Land

Among the various perceptions of the South that have raised the most controversy, few are more hotly disputed than the question of whether slavery produced a voracious appetite for western land on the part of the slave South. Contemporary writers such as J. E. Cairnes and Hinton Helper asserted that an ever-increasing supply of land was a prerequisite for southern slaveholders. "Slavery," Cairnes wrote, "cannot be con-fined within certain specified limits without producing the destruction of both master and slave; it requires fresh lands."[25] To Cairnes this was a "fundamental principle" of the political economy of slavery. There is a plausibility about this argument that fits well with the well-known fact that soil in the Southeast was being depleted by the plantation economy and with the highly publicized rhetoric of southern politicians demand-ing territory for the South. Not surprisingly, the view that the South "needed" land has attracted a great deal of support through the years.[26]

---

24 Roger L. Ransom and Richard Sutch, "Growth and Welfare in the American South in the Nineteenth Century," *Explorations in Economic History* 16 (April 1979): 212–18. Gavin Wright also argues that the appearance of economic vitality in the ante-bellum South was misleading and that, in fact, the economic foundations of the slave economy were not conducive to long-term growth. See Wright, *Old South, New South: Revolutions in the Southern Economy since the Civil War* (Basic Books, 1986), chap. 2.

25 J. E. Cairnes, *The Slave Power: It's* [sic] *Character, Career, and Probable Designs: Being an Attempt to Explain the Real Issues Involved in the American Contest* (1862; reprint, Harper and Row, 1969), p. 181.

26 One of the best statements of the expansionist argument is by Eugene D. Genovese,

Appealing though it is, the land-expansionist thesis ran into a storm of criticism from quantitative economic historians. According to Gavin Wright, "the land-expansion hypothesis as argued by Cairnes and his followers is an economic *Hamlet* without the prince. At most, it could explain the emergence of sectional conflict over a much longer period of time, but not the intensification of these conflicts during the 1850s."[27] On one point there seems no question: There was ample land available for settlement in the South throughout the antebellum period. The idea that the southern planters were facing a "land squeeze" simply makes no sense. In Alabama, Mississippi, and Louisiana extensive sales of public lands continued through the 1850s.[28] Moreover, those claiming that new land was necessary to sustain the level of slave profits fail to see that, even if there were no more land to settle, the result would not necessarily be a disaster for slaveholders. So long as the demand continued to grow, any factors limiting the expansion of cotton production would produce pressures that would increase the price of cotton. Higher prices for cotton would be reflected in the return to slave labor. Neither the profitability nor the viability of slavery was threatened by a shortage of land in the cotton regions.[29] The argument that market pressures forced southern farmers to seek new land in the Southwest cannot be supported on the basis of a squeeze on the returns to slave labor in the Southeast.

In fact, the problem facing slaveholders may have been precisely the opposite of what writers such as Cairnes suggested. It was the opening of new lands to settlement, not the depletion of existing cotton land, that

"The Origins of Slavery Expansionism," in Genovese, *The Political Economy of Slavery.*

27 Wright, *The Political Economy of the Cotton South*, p. 133; also see idem, "Capitalism and Slavery on the Islands: A Lesson from the Mainland," *Journal of Interdisciplinary History* 17 (Spring 1987). The empirical basis for the argument can be found in Peter Passell and Gavin Wright, "The Effects of Pre-Civil War Territorial Expansion on the Price of Slaves," *Journal of Political Economy* 80 (November–December 1972); Susan Previant Lee, *The Westward Movement of the Cotton Economy, 1840–1860; Perceived Interests and Economic Interests* (Ph.D. diss., Columbia University, 1975; reprint Arno Press, 1977); and idem, "Antebellum Land Expansion," *Agricultural History* 52 (October 1978).

28 Statistics for the sale of public land in each state from 1815 to 1860 are given in Arthur H. Cole, "Cyclical and Sectional Variations in the Sale of Public Lands, 1816–60," *Review of Economic Statistics* 9 (January 1927). According to Cole's figures (which do not include sales of land in Texas), land sales in these states and Arkansas account for half the total federal receipts in the early 1850s.

29 This criticism is a particularly telling argument against Charles W. Ramsdell's contention that slavery had reached a "natural frontier" by 1860 beyond which it could not extend; see "The Natural Limits of Slavery Expansion," *Mississippi Valley Historical Review* 16 (September 1929). Fogel and Engerman go to some pains to argue that, because the price of cotton and slaves would adjust to market conditions, the profitability of slavery could be sustained in the face of a closing off of new lands ("The Economics of Slavery," pp. 314–18).

threatened the returns to slaveholders.[30] We have already noted that slave labor on the more fertile lands in the West had higher productivity than slave labor working on eastern land. But this does not insure that the net effect of moving slave labor to the West will be to increase the value of slaves. As Susan Lee points out:

> Land expansion was potentially a two-edged sword. Every increase in land for cotton production carried with it two effects – an increase in the marginal physical product of slaves and an increase in the supply of cotton. An increase in marginal physical productivity made slaves more valuable, but an increase in the supply of cotton drove down the price of cotton and tended to depress the value of slaves. . . . Hence the effect of land expansion on slave values is neither obvious nor simple.[31]

In other words, Lee and others claim that the increase in slave productivity was more than offset by a fall in the price of cotton. She concludes that, "far from being an economic necessity, expansion appears to have had a negative impact on southern wealth."[32]

Lee's point can be clearly seen in Figure 3.3, which presents indexes of the value of cotton output per slave, the average price of a slave, and the export price of cotton for the period 1805 to 1860. On the one hand, output of cotton per slave rose by a factor of 2.5 times, with a particularly pronounced increase in the late 1840s and the decade of the 1850s. The price of cotton, on the other hand, failed to maintain the levels of the early antebellum years; by the 1840s the price was only half what it had been at the time of the Missouri Compromise. The econometrics of Lee, Passell, and Wright all show that, had there been no western land, the price of cotton would not have fallen, and the value of slaves might have been greater. Despite a continued increase in the supply of land, however, the price of cotton remained relatively stable after the collapse of 1837–

---

30 The argument is that continued expansion of cotton land would increase production to the point where the price of cotton would decline and threaten the return to owning slaves. Passell and Wright ("The Effects of Pre-Civil War Territorial Expansion on the Price of Slaves") and Lee (*Westward Movement of the Cotton Economy*) provide the econometric basis for the argument. Of course, slave prices did not actually fall; they simply did not rise as much as they would have in the absence of westward expansion. Several writers have pointed out that these results depend crucially on the responsiveness of cotton prices to changes in demand, and they question the robustness of the Passell–Wright–Lee hypothesis. See Laurence J. Kotlikoff and Sebastian E. Pinera, "The Old South's Stake in the Inter-Regional Movement of Slaves," *Journal of Economic History* 37 (June 1977); and Mark Schmitz and Donald Schaefer, "Paradox Lost: Westward Expansion and Slave Prices before the Civil War," *Journal of Economic History* 41 (June 1981).

31 Lee, *Westward Movement of the Cotton Economy*, p. 49.

32 Ibid., p. 120.

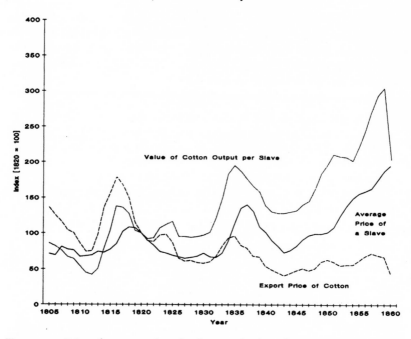

Figure 3.3. Price of cotton, price of a slave, and value of cotton output per slave, 1805–60

43. Accordingly, the price of slaves, which had experienced wide swings and only a mild upward trend overall prior to 1843, moved rapidly upward during the last fifteen years of our period. With a constant price of cotton, the increased productivity of slave labor on western lands caused slave prices to double. This suggests that slaveowners might have been far less concerned about the impact of more land in cotton production on the value of their slave investment during the 1850s than they were in the 1820s or 1830s. At the very time when the debates over slavery in the territories of Kansas and Nebraska were reaching their peak, the price of slaves was in the midst of a dramatic increase – an increase that was to continue to the outbreak of the Civil War.

The logic employed by those arguing that the South did not need more cotton land is impeccable. Yet the picture of a South content with the territory reserved for slavery at the time of the Louisiana Purchase is difficult to reconcile with the observed behavior of southern politicians in the years after 1815. The problem, perhaps, is that the cliometricians have not fully addressed the question of why Southerners wanted land.

There seems little doubt that slaveholders were interested in maintaining the value of their slaves, and that in an effort to accomplish this, planters engaged in what political economists call "rent-seeking" behavior. (That is, planters used the political process to increase the return to a factor of production that they controlled – slaves.) In support of this point, Gavin Wright notes that after 1809 southern slaveholders consistently rejected attempts to reopen the importation of slaves, an action that protected their existing interests.[33] In fact, this position was so firmly held that the prohibition of the slave trade was written into the Confederate Constitution.

But if southern planters were equally determined to close off western settlement in order to protect the value of their slaves, they failed miserably; land settlement continued unabated in both North and South. Why? Perhaps because planters could afford to favor territorial expansion for both political and economic reasons. The simple fact of the matter is that antebellum slaveowners could have their cake and eat it too. Cotton production, the income from cotton production, the price of slaves, and the value of the slave stock all increased throughout the antebellum period, and the increase was especially dramatic over the period 1843– 60. Figure 3.4 presents indexes of growth for each of these variables, keyed to a base year of 1820. The predicted effect of territorial expansion on the price of cotton is at once evident here as it was in Figure 3.3. Although the quantity of cotton increased by a factor of 12, the value of cotton increased by a factor of only about 7.5. Still, slaveowners hardly had cause to worry. The price of slaves, their most important asset, had doubled since 1820; the total value of their investment in slaves over that period had quintupled, and the annual return on slave assets was still equal to that of other assets.

Restricting settlement of western lands would have increased rents for slaveholders, and the political debates and votes on homesteading and the Graduation Act in the 1840s and 1850s suggest that both slaveowners and landowners in the South realized this.[34] What the opponents of the land-expansion hypothesis claim is that, because the American South was the most important producer of cotton in the world at this time, "King Cotton" had the economic clout to affect prices. But this claim has not gone uncontested; several writers claim that, in fact, the

---

33 Wright, *Political Economy of the Cotton South*, pp. 150–4.
34 As Lee points out, the *distribution* of gains from restricting land in cotton was not even throughout the South, a factor that greatly complicates our ability to draw unequivocal conclusions about support for new land in all parts of the South (*Westward Movement of the Cotton Economy*, chap. 11).

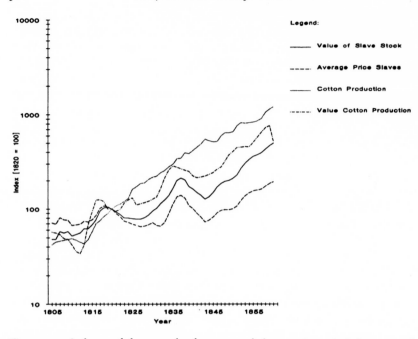

Figure 3.4. Indexes of the growth of cotton and slaves, 1805–60 (1820 = 100)

international demand for cotton was such that an increase in supply would *increase* total returns to cotton producers.[35]

Econometrics aside, the fact remains that individual cotton producers lacked any effective mechanism for controlling either the supply of land or the level of cotton production in the South. Competitive pressures in the agricultural marketplace made any attempts to control production impossible, and the same was true with regard to attempts at imposing restrictions of land. Closing the slave trade in order to maintain rents on slaves had little effect on nonslaveholders. By contrast, closing the West to new settlement would not only increase the rents to slaveholders; it would also increase the price of land. This would bring the interests of a much larger, and much more diverse, portion of the electorate into the

35 In economists' terms, what is disputed here is whether the demand for cotton was *inelastic*, in which case an expansion of supply would decrease gross revenue. The studies by Wright and Passell and Lee cited earlier argue that this was the case. Kotlikoff and Pinera claim that the elasticity of demand was greater than one. Neither camp has sufficient data to establish the point firmly – my own "guesstimate" is that the elasticity of demand of cotton was about unity.

issue. Rent-seeking behavior of the sort we are considering works primarily to the advantage of the current owners of the scarce input – in this case, owners of slaves and land. People seeking entry into agriculture, whether as slaveholder or free farmer, would strongly oppose restrictions on land because this would increase the costs of entering agriculture.

Observers outside the South uniformly viewed the cotton kingdom as eagerly seeking new land. By the 1850s this view had become an obsessive fear. While these contemporary observers tended to identify the depletion of soil in the Tidewater as the underlying force pushing slavery west, the economic forces were actually more subtle and more complex. Nevertheless, there is more than a grain of truth in the traditional story. Planters in the Tidewater were being pressed by low returns to use slave labor on their increasingly depleted soil. Western land was there for the taking. The gains from moving to more fertile land were far more evident to the average planter than was the possibility that returns to his farming venture would be reduced because of an increase in world supply. Some adjustment had to be made; often a move west was seen as the easiest alternative.

An additional factor often tipped the scale in favor of moving rather than staying. Slave labor was not only very valuable, it was highly mobile; the slaveholder was guaranteed a supply of labor wherever he went. The mobility of slave capital was an important element fostering the westward expansion of American slavery. As Gavin Wright explains:

> There is a basic difference between investment in slaves on the one hand, and investment in land and industrial capital on the other: slaves are moveable, most other investments are not. . . . This characteristic is the economic essence of the distinction between real and personal property, slaves almost always being clearly classified as the latter. Whereas free markets were often localized and imperfect, constrained by geographic, ethnic, and family loyalties and by social norms, slave markets were bounded only by profit calculations and legal barriers.[36]

All of this made the lure of fertile land to the west as irresistible to southern planters as it was to other Americans.

The territorial expansionism of the South that so alarmed many of its northern neighbors involved more than the economic variables on which we have been focusing. There is a difference between *territory* and *land*. When economists talk of land, they deal with it as a factor of production. Our discussion of the land-expansion thesis has focused on the economic effects of placing more land in cotton production, not on the importance

36 Wright, "Capitalism and Slavery," p. 852.

of territory that may some day be settled by free rather than slave labor. Slaveholding states were not running out of land as a factor of production in 1860, but they were running out of territory to maintain the political status quo. The Compromise of 1820, the annexation of Texas in 1845, and southern support for the acquisition of the Mexican Territories in 1848 were all viewed as extending the political as well as the economic influence of slavery to the west. But by 1850 the prospect of new territorial areas open to settlement by slaveholders was becoming increasingly limited.

One element that worked against the political interests of the South in the race to settle the West was the population explosion in the North. In 1790 the two regions each had just under two million people. By 1860, the population of the North had grown to just over twenty million, while the South had only eleven million people – four million of whom were slaves. But did this slower population growth lessen the political pressure for added territory? Much of the rhetoric at the time suggested that it did not; indeed, it seems to have increased the perceived need to "reserve" some areas for future settlement by slaveholders. Southern population growth was slow compared with that of their northern neighbors, but this should not obscure the fact that it was increasing at a rate sufficient to create a considerable appetite for new territory. The population growth in the North was further cause for concern to southern politicians.

A Contrast in Style: Slave and Free Farms

Through most of the antebellum period, the westward push of slave and free-labor settlers followed parallel courses that avoided competition for the same land. Prior to the 1850s, only the settlement of Missouri had brought the two styles of farming into direct competition. That collision, as we saw, produced the major political crisis in 1820, which was resolved by allowing slave interests to predominate in Missouri. In the 1850s the two sides were again looking to settle in the same area: This time it was the Kansas–Nebraska Territory. Again there was a conflict of slave and free settlers, and this time the attempt at compromise failed. "Bloody Kansas" was a prelude to the Civil War.

The sectional rivalry that had emerged by the middle of the nineteenth century in America was rooted in the perceptions that various regions of the nation had of each other. Economic differences played a significant role in shaping these perceptions. The gulf created by the emergence of an industrial system in the northeastern states is evident enough. But, although many Southerners decried the commercialism of "yankee" industry, industrialization did not pose the greatest economic threat to the South. In fact, the industrial Northeast with its cotton mills, and the agricultural South with its black slaves in the cotton fields, shared a mutual economic interest: the cotton trade and manufactures. The cause of the greatest antagonism was the vastly different forms of agriculture in the northern and southern states.

Northerners who observed southern agriculture came away convinced that slavery was a pernicious system that not only degraded black labor but stifled free labor as well. As historian Eric Foner has noted, these perceptions were based on more than abolitionist rhetoric. He cites the reaction of Henry Seward, who made several trips to the slave states between 1835 and 1857, as one example of a view widely held: "An exhausted soil, old and decaying towns, wretchedly-neglected roads, and, in every respect, an absence of enterprise and improvement, distinguish the region through which we have come, in contrast to that in which we live. Such has been the effect of slavery."[37]

The South, in the view of these observers, was not only a morally corrupt society holding human beings in bondage; it was a backward economic system as well. At the root of this problem was the concentration of wealth and power in the hands of the slaveholders, which allowed them to dominate the economic and social environment in which they lived. "The trouble is," observed an Illinois farmer cited by Olmsted,

> the large slaveholders have got all the good land. There can be no schools, and if the son of a poor man rises above his condition there is no earthly chance for him. He can only hope to be a slave-driver, for an office is not his, or he must leave and go to a Free State. *Were there no Free States, the white people of the South would today be slaves.*[38]

Were such fears about the economic power of the southern slave-holders justified? The evidence at hand suggests that there were considerable differences between these two major agricultural regions of the United States, and that these differences were, in fact, rooted in the economic power amassed by the slaveholding class of the South. It is difficult to appreciate today the enormous wealth embodied in the ownership of slaves. As Gavin Wright notes, "a man who owned two

37 Cited in Eric Foner, *Free Soil, Free Labor and Free Men: The Ideology of the Republican Party before the Civil War* (Oxford University Press, 1970), p. 41. Other travelers agreed; recall the quotation from Frederick Olmsted.
38 Olmsted, *Cotton Kingdom*, p. 541; emphasis in original. Olmsted identified it as a letter published in the *New York Times* on June 7, 1861, "written by a worthy farmer of Illinois . . . who is deemed by those who have known him for many years a sound and trust worthy man" (p. 539).

slaves and nothing else was as rich as the average man in the North."[39]
Put another way, the average value of a single slave exceeded the annual
income of most families in the late antebellum period.

The data from the 1850 and 1860 censuses provide a clear picture of
agriculture in both the Cotton South and in the northern states on the eve
of the Civil War.[40] Table 3.1 presents some summary statistics on wealth
holdings of farmers in four broad regions: the Northeast, the Old Northwest, the West, and the South. Data for the South are broken into farms
with and without slaves.

The planters' wealth was so overwhelming that the average level of
wealth reported by all southern farmers was almost six times the level of
wealth reported by farmers in the northern states. Farmers owning slaves
reported an average of $33,906 of real and personal estate in 1860,
whereas northern farmers reported an average of only $3,858. But this
aggregate figure is clearly misleading. Southern farmers who owned no
slaves reported an average wealth of only $2,362 — substantially below
the level reported by northern farms. One reason for this disparity can be
seen in the average value of farms. Free southern farms were worth only
about one-half the value of northern farms.

Southern farms, particularly slave plantations, were much larger than
family farms in the North, and that alone would account for a higher
level of wealth. But the greatest disparity in wealth was not in real estate
or the value of the farm but in the personal estate reported by farmers in
the four regions. Southern farmers in our sample reported $13,277 in
personal estate, compared with an average of only $834 in personal
estate for northern farmers. The great difference lay in the value of the
slaves, treated by the census office as "personal estate." What we see here
is the enormous investment in slave capital; farms with slaves report an
average of $19,828 in personal estate.

Finally, we should note that within the South itself there was an even
greater inequality of wealth than that which existed between the two
regions of the country. Slaveholders clearly held the preponderance of
wealth. In fact, the distribution of wealth in the South was even more
concentrated than these figures suggest, because large slaveholdings accounted for a disproportionate share of wealth within the slaveholding
class. The most common measure of wealth concentration is a Lorenz
curve, which compares the actual distribution of wealth in a population to
an "ideal" distribution of complete equality. The Lorenz curve does this

---

39 Wright, *Political Economy of the Cotton South*, p. 35.
40 The evidence summarized in this section is drawn primarily from the data sets de-
     scribed in the appendix to this chapter. Note that the samples of farms in the southern
     states are drawn from the areas specializing in cash crops.

Table 3.1. *Wealth of farmers by region, 1860*

Region	Farms sampled	Total reported wealth ($)	Personal estate ($)	Value of farm ($)	Age of farmer (yrs.)
North	1,050	3,858	834	2,909	44.2
Northeast	3,599	4,620	1,104	3,694	46.9
Old Northwest	5,349	3,176	682	2,524	42.8
West	846	2,212	532	1,672	39.9
South	643	22,819	13,277	8,186	44.0
Slave farms	417	33,906	19,828	11,817	45.2
Free farms	226	2,362	1,188	1,568	41.8

Note: Northeast: Connecticut, Maine, New Hampshire, New Jersey, New York, Pennsylvania, Rhode Island, and Vermont; Old Northwest: Illinois, Indiana, Michigan, Ohio, and Wisconsin; West: Iowa, Kansas, and Minnesota; South: Alabama, Georgia, Louisiana, Mississippi, South Carolina, and Texas.
Source: Samples drawn from the 1860 manuscript census: see appendix to Chapter 3 for details.

by plotting the share of wealth held by each percentile of farmers in the sample, from the poorest farmers to the most wealthy. If the wealth were evenly distributed, the curve would be a forty-five-degree line through the origin. Any inequality in wealth will cause the Lorenz curve to bow away from the forty-five-degree line, and the more it bows, the more unequal is the distribution of wealth. Figure 3.5 compares the Lorenz curves for our samples of northern and southern farms. The conclusion is evident: Agricultural wealth in the slave South was far more concentrated than was agricultural wealth in the North. By how much? One method of measuring inequality is to compute what is known as a gini coefficient.[41] The wealth distributions depicted in Figure 3.5 produce a gini coefficient of 0.486 for northern farms, and a value of 0.716 for southern farms. Put another way, the Lorenz curves in Figure 3.5 show that the wealthiest 10 percent of southern farmers owned just under 60 percent of all agricultural wealth, whereas the same group in the North accounted for 36 percent of all wealth. In the South, the richest 2 percent of the farmers accounted for 24 percent of all wealth. However you measure it, the economic power of slaveholders in the South was very real.

41 The gini coefficient is defined as the ratio of the area between the line of complete equality and the Lorenz curve(s) in Figure 3.5 and the total area under the forty-five degree line. Thus, with complete equality the gini coefficient would be 0; with extreme inequality (i.e., all wealth owned by a single individual) the gini coefficient would approach a value of 1.

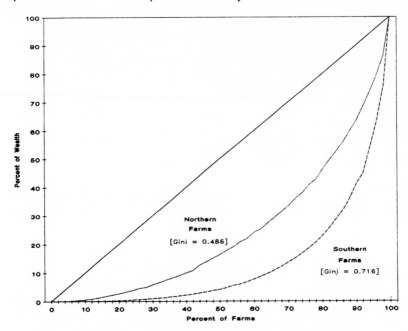

Figure 3.5. The distribution of personal wealth among northern and southern farmers in 1860

Why was this economic inequality so offensive to Northerners? After all, cities in the North had concentrations of wealth that were surely just as unequal as that of the slave South.[42] The answer is that, particularly in the West, where slave and free settlers occasionally competed for the same land, the raw power of the plantation system came into stark focus. Again we come back to the question of access to land. The description of the activities undertaken by a planter in Mississippi provided by one of Olmsted's correspondents reflected a perception of planter behavior widely held in the North:

> [J. B.] has bought out, one after another, and mainly since 1850, more than twenty small landowners, some of them small slave-

42 Robert E. Gallman has estimated the wealth controlled by the richest 5 percent of the population in several cities to be: Baltimore, 71.7 percent; St. Louis, 67.6 percent; and New Orleans, 71.6 percent. See Gallman, "Trends in the Size Distribution of Wealth in the Nineteenth Century: Some Speculations," in National Bureau of Economic Research, *Six Papers on the Size Distribution of Wealth and Income: Studies in Income and Wealth,* vol. 33 (Princeton University Press, 1969). This would roughly correspond to the Lorenz curve for the South in Figure 3.5. It is unlikely that the more industrialized cities of the North would have more equal distributions of wealth.

holders, and they have moved away from the vicinity. . . . It is a common thing to hear a man say, "J. B. has bought up next to me, and I shall have to quit soon." He never gets the land alongside of a man that within two years he does not buy him out. In the last ten years I know of but one exception. . . . There are two other men in the county who are constantly buying up the land around there. The white population of the county is diminishing and the trade of the place [the county town] is not so good as it was ten years ago.[43]

There are several possible explanations for this phenomenon. One is that, as slaveholders became more prevalent in an area, nonslaveowning white farmers left due to their objections to the presence of black slaves. Certainly there is ample evidence that "poor whites" strongly resented the presence of blacks. A second possibility is that slavery produced a dominating plantation structure that stifled the opportunities for free family farms. Is there statistical evidence in support of such a view? An examination of the data presented in Table 3.2, which considers the size and value of farms in the Southwest and the Cotton South, suggests that the answer to our question is yes and no.

On the affirmative side, we see that by comparison with free farms, slave farms were five and a half times as large in terms of total acres, and they tilled over four times the acreage of farms to the North. Slave farms may also have had the best land. Table 3.2 presents a very crude estimate of the value of improved acreage.[44] The value of an improved acre of land on slave farms was \$46.74, that on nonslave farms only \$13.47. This differential might be interpreted not only as evidence that slave farms had better land; it is also consistent with the contention of northern critics that nonslave farms in the South were backward in comparison with both plantations and farms in the West.[45] Western farms, although substantially smaller in total size than nonslave farms of the South, reported an average value of the farm substantially greater than in the South, and our estimate of the value of improved acreage for southern nonslave farms was barely half that for the western regions. Finally, we should note that the cotton regions were the most prosperous part of the South. If the back-country and hill regions of the South had been included in our sample, nonslave farms in the South as a whole would probably look even more backward than the picture portrayed by the data of Table 3.2.

43 Olmsted, *Cotton Kingdom*, p. 539.
44 The value of an acre of improved land for each of the regions in Table 3.2 was estimated by regressing the value of farm per acre against the fraction of total acreage that was unimproved. The estimating procedure is described in greater detail in the appendix.
45 The higher value for slave farms might also have reflected greater productivity of slave labor. It seems unlikely, however, that a difference of the magnitude reported in Table 3.2 could be accounted for solely on the basis of labor productivity.

Table 3.2. *Statistics of farms by region, 1860*

Region	Farms	Total acres	Improved acres	Value of farm ($)	Estimated price of improved acre ($)
Western farms	5,891	134.5	65.8	2,507	25.99
Old Northwest	5,128	128.4	67.1	2,574	27.06
West	763	162.5	47.3	1,719	21.17
Missouri	743	202.8	82.8	2,031	14.63
Cotton South	376	484.2	180.6	8,588	39.77
Slave farms	250	637.3	295.1	12,181	46.74
Nonslave farms	126	180.6	217.1	1,658	13.47

Note: Northeast: Connecticut, Maine, New Hampshire, New Jersey, New York, Pennsylvania, Rhode Island, and Vermont; Old Northwest: Illinois, Indiana, Michigan, Ohio, and Wisconsin; West: Iowa, Kansas, and Minnesota; South: Alabama, Georgia, Louisiana, Mississippi, South Carolina, and Texas.
Source: Samples drawn from the 1860 manuscript census: see appendix to Chapter 3 for details.

Critics of the South were quick to use evidence such as the data presented in Tables 3.1 and 3.2 to argue their point that the South's peculiar institution led to the dominance of the plantations; however, there is reason to pause before accepting the argument that slavery completely stifled opportunities for economic advancement by free farmers. The inferences being drawn here refer specifically to the plantation economy of the cotton-producing areas of the South. Even if we acknowledge the pernicious impact of plantation slavery in the cotton areas, does this necessarily imply that the extension of slavery into noncotton areas will result in an equally pernicious situation for free farms?

The question is important because, as we argued previously, the territorial aggressiveness of the slave economy brought it into competition with free settlers along the boundary defined first by the Northwest Ordinance and then by the Missouri Compromise. What about Missouri, the state that had caused such a fuss in 1820? Were the floodgates thrown open to a wave of slaveholders to gobble up land and establish their plantation economy? The evidence of Table 3.2 suggests that this was hardly the case. Forty years after the compromise, farms in this "slave state" were not vastly different from those in nearby western "free states." Although we do not know what fraction of the farmers in the sample owned slaves, we do know that only 10 percent of the state's population in 1860 was black.[46] At the time of admission, 16 percent of the state's population was black, which suggests that the influence of slavery was declining, not increasing.

Yet the agricultural background of the farmers in Missouri was overwhelmingly southern; 73 percent of the farmers in the 1860 sample of farms were born in either the South or another border state, whereas only 11 percent came from the North or were immigrants from abroad.[47] Like the early settlers along the northern banks of the Ohio River, these Southerners brought with them a tradition of slave agriculture. The pattern of farming that had emerged by 1860 resembled the diversified farming of the Midwest more than the cash-crop economy of the Cotton South. Despite the fears of slave dominance, the fact remains that family farms, not large slave plantations, were the common mode of production outside the cotton regions of the Southwest.

Where does all this leave us? There is no question that the presence of slavery produced an enormous concentration of wealth and economic power in the hands of the very wealthy planters, and that this situation was in sharp contrast to the situation existing in the free territories of the West and North.[48] Nor can there be any doubt that this concentration of wealth led to a concentration of agricultural production. Ninety percent of the cotton crop grown in the South was grown on slave farms, with the bulk of that produced by a relatively small number of very large plantations.[49] But can we leap from these "facts," which were well known at the time, to a conclusion that slavery and free farms were "economically" incompatible? Hardly. Only in the staple-producing regions of the South, where plantation agriculture became the dominant mode of production, does this conclusion appear to have much force, and there are some who claim that nonslave farms may have actually benefited from

---

46 Unfortunately, ownership of slaves was reported on separate schedules from the free population, and this information was not collated for the states in the Bateman–Atack sample of northern farms. The farms were not located in a cotton-growing region, and based on the data for personal estate, there appear to be few if any "plantations" among the farms in the sample.

47 The largest group (69.9 percent) came from the Upper South, defined here as Virginia, North Carolina, and Tennessee; another 1.3 percent came from the Cotton South; 1.8 percent came from border states, primarily Kentucky; and 17 percent were born in Missouri.

48 Our discussion of farms in the North has centered only on a few of the more prominent statistical features; for a more complete examination of this data and the development of agriculture in the North, see Jeremy Atack and Fred Bateman, *To Their Own Soil: Agriculture in the Antebellum North* (Iowa State University Press, 1987).

49 See the evidence of concentration in Wright, *Political Economy of the Cotton South*, pp. 79–81; and idem, "'Economic Democracy' and the Concentration of Agricultural Wealth in the Cotton South," *Agricultural History* 44 (January 1970).

the slave–cotton economy.[50] Elsewhere, plantation slavery did not flour-ish, and the interspersing of small or medium-sized slave farms did not seem to dramatically change the pattern of farming from that which was common to family farms throughout the West and Midwest.

A final observation about southern and northern farms pertains once again to the issue of western settlement. In the eyes of most Southerners, the prosperity of the cotton economy was tied to the ownership of slaves. And ownership of slaves was open to anyone who could raise the capital to purchase them. The opportunity to become a slaveholder was an important element in the thinking of nonslaveholding farmers of the South, many of whom aspired to be slaveholders themselves someday. Once again we see the importance of the West in the struggle over con-taining or extending slavery. The West offered cheap land, which the aspiring slave farmers needed; all that remained was to obtain the capital for slaves.

The pattern for western settlement in the United States at this time is well known, and is evident in Table 3.1. Farms in the West had far more acres than those in the East, but tilled a much smaller fraction of those acres. Western farmers were younger and less wealthy than their counter-parts in the East, supporting the common view that it was the younger generation that went west in search of opportunity. The data for the two Texas counties in our 1860 sample suggest a similar pattern except for the farmer's age. Texas farms were very large (760 acres) and the fraction of tilled land was quite small (less than 10 percent). And although Texas farmers – free as well as slave – were noticeably older than their counter-parts in the eastern regions of the cotton belt (45.1 years versus 41.9 years), their wealth ($10,934) is only about half the average elsewhere.[51] Here again the pattern was one of people searching for opportunity, although the search was delayed by the need to acquire sufficient capital to buy a few slaves. Interestingly, Robertson County, Texas, had no farm in 1850 that might reasonably be termed a "plantation."

Who Will Pay? The Economics of Emancipation

The picture emerging from our examination of the "economics" of slav-ery is that of a robust economic system that, far from being on the brink

---

50 See, for example, Robert R. Russel, "The Effects of Slavery on Nonslaveholders in the Ante-Bellum South," *Agricultural History* 15 (April 1941). Russel argued that those who did not own slaves gained some advantages of slave plantations, and that "to many nonslaveholding whites, (slavery) was a matter of economic indifference. It is impossible to strike a balance in which confidence can be placed. It is certain that the net injury, if there was any, has been commonly greatly exaggerated" (p. 127).

51 The figures cited for Texas in this section are based on averages for the 101 farms with ten or more improved acres in Red River and Robertson counties.

of collapse in 1859, was coming off a decade of almost explosive economic growth. The cotton economy had never had it so good and slaveholders confidently expected things to get better. This optimism over the economic future of "King Cotton" was a crucial element in the disputes over controlling the extension of slavery.

The statistics on slave profitability presented earlier emphasize that choosing to be a slaveholder in the 1850s could be quite lucrative. What is often forgotten is that nonslaveholders in the cotton areas also prospered in the 1850s. Figure 3.6 presents evidence on the increase in farm value and the value of improved land in the Cotton South between 1850 and 1860. The prosperity of the slave farms is readily apparent: The value of slave farms tripled and the value of an acre of improved land on these farms quadrupled over the course of the decade. Free farms did not do as well, but they did not fare too badly either; the average value of free farms rose by a factor of more than 2, and the value of an acre of improved land on these farms increased by a factor of 1.83. What these figures underscore is that slaveholders and free farmers in the cotton belt both had a strong economic interest in keeping the cotton economy moving along. To the extent that slave labor was the cornerstone on

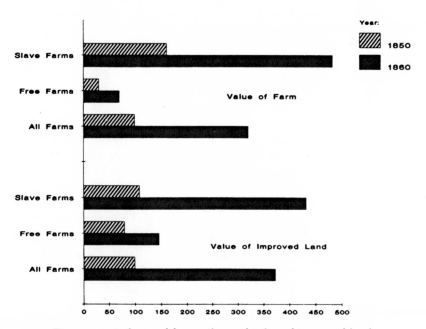

Figure 3.6. Indexes of farm value and value of improved land, samples of southern farms in 1850 and 1860 (value for all farms in 1850 = 100)

which the southern economy rested, everyone shared a common interest in protecting their "peculiar institution."

Of course, it goes without saying that Southerners had a great deal at stake in the preservation of slave property. The asset-pricing model of slavery illustrates how capitalist slavery insinuated itself into every aspect of economic life in the South. It also provides some insights into why peaceful emancipation was unlikely to offer a viable alternative to those seeking some way to check and eventually to eliminate slavery from the United States. To free the slaves would have required the transfer of $3 billion of assets from slaveowners to slave. This was a huge sum of money in an economy where the gross national product was only about $4 million per year. The question was: Who would pay for the transfer of ownership of slave property from slaveholders to freed blacks?

Slaveholders would obviously not accept an uncompensated emancipation that placed the full costs on them. Slaves would be willing to purchase their own freedom, but because the market price for their freedom included all the potential exploitation of remaining a slave, they would have to work "like slaves" for the remainder of their lives. In the case of women, whose value as slaves included the expected returns from children, the task would be greater still. The cost of emancipation, therefore, would have to be borne by the nonslaveholding free population. No one seriously expected that such a sum would be levied as a "lump-sum" in a given year. The few people who did think about emancipation talked of having the government issue bonds that would be given to the slaveholders in lieu of their rights to chattel labor. Although this would amortize the costs of emancipation over a longer period of time, it should be noted that the costs of supporting such a bond issue would not be trivial. Ignoring the costs of amortization, a rough calculation would put it in the neighborhood of $6.75 per capita, or just under 5 percent of the total per capita income in 1859.[52] This figure may seem small when compared to the costs of a bloody war, but it must have seemed a forbidding figure to constituents looking at the increase in their taxes any such scheme would have entailed. Annual federal outlays would have been tripled by the costs of a compensation scheme financed by the issuance of bonds.[53]

52 The calculation is made assuming the value of the slave stock was $3.058 billion, a free nonslaveowning population of 27.2 million in 1859, and a per capita income of $149. A more complete discussion is in Roger L. Ransom and Richard Sutch, "Capitalists without Capital: The Burden of Slavery and the Impact of Emancipation," *Agricultural History* (Fall 1988). Claudia Dale Goldin provides estimates that are the same order of magnitude; see "The Economics of Emancipation," *Journal of Economic History* 33 (March 1973).

53 The total level of federal government spending at this time was about two dollars per capita. See Lance E. Davis and John Legler, "The Government in the American Economy, 1815–1902: A Quantitative Study," *Journal of Economic History* 26 (December 1966), tables 1 and 2, pp. 529–31, and table 8, pp. 548–9.

Moreover, to many, compensated emancipation was not only expensive, it was immoral. The defense of property and the economic logic of the asset-pricing model implied a policy recommendation that rewarded the one group who, in the eyes of those paying the bill, was least deserving of any payment: the slaveowners.

Who, then, would pay the bill for emancipation? Those most able, slaveholders, would resist; those most willing, slaves, lacked the means. For the rest of the electorate, both in the North and in the South, there was little enthusiasm for a scheme that promised little or no economic gain and would impose large and very direct costs. There were, of course, forces much greater than the economic costs that made peaceful emancipation in the United States unfeasible. But it is interesting to note that the only scheme that might have been seriously considered as a means of emancipating slaves was well beyond reach in the middle of the nineteenth century. Most politicians, in the North and the South, realized this. Apart from a minority of abolitionists, emancipation was not high on anyone's political agenda. But controlling the expansion of slavery was an increasingly appealing idea to the electorate in the northern states. As the balance of political power gradually swung to those areas, the debate over slavery heated up to the point where compromise was no longer possible.

An economic analysis based on the possibility of trade-offs at the margin can never satisfactorily explain a war as devastating as the American Civil War. Putting aside the bloodshed, the financial costs of the war alone far exceeded even the most generous estimates of the costs of emancipation. Viewed in this light, there *must* have been a better alternative to war.[54] Does this mean that Claudia Goldin was correct when she concluded that:

> Although the Union was able to view in historical perspective emancipation schemes of all types, none were seriously considered before 1861. After that date abolition plans were discussed only as a part of the Union's war effort. It appears . . . that the Union erred. It did not look to other slaveocracies for advice in solving its slave problem, for the realized costs of the Civil War were far greater than those of various emancipation schemes.[55]

---

54 For quantitative estimates of the costs of the war compared with the alternatives that clearly show this point, see Goldin, "The Economics of Emancipation"; Claudia Dale Goldin and Frank Lewis, "The Economic Costs of the American Civil War: Estimates and Implications," *Journal of Economic History* 35 (June 1975); and Gerald Gunderson, "The Origin of the American Civil War," *Journal of Economic History* 34 (1974).

55 Goldin, "The Economics of Emancipation," p. 84.

Before we accept this conclusion, we must look at the politics of slavery in the United States before the Civil War.

Appendix: Samples of Farms

The analysis presented in this chapter, and in several subsequent chapters, draws heavily on two samples of farms that have been drawn from the manuscript censuses. Because these samples collect matching data from the population schedules and the agricultural schedules (and for the southern states, the slave schedules), they provide a micro detail of data not available from published sources.

For the northern farms the sample of 21,118 "Agricultural and Demographic Records for Rural Households in the North, 1860," collected by Fred Bateman and James Foust, was used.[56] Only the 10,050 "Farm" households in the sample were included for this analysis. The Bateman–Foust sample was collected by identifying target counties in sixteen northern and western states. The distribution of farms by state is given in Table A.3.1. For the South I employed a sample of 2,206 farms from eight counties in the census years of 1850, 1860, and 1870, which Richard Sutch and I collected as a part of the *Southern Economic History Project*. The distribution of the farms actually used in the analysis is given in Table A.3.2 for each county and year. The basis on which counties were selected to be sampled, together with a detailed description of the procedures used to match data taken from the population and farm census schedules, is described in Ransom and Sutch (1977, appendix G).[57]

Except where noted, the values reported in Tables 3.1 and 3.2 are averages of the variables reported by the head of the farm household. The census did not report the value of improved land. This was estimated from data on the value of the farm and the ratio of unimproved acreage to total acreage using regression analysis. The equation was:

$$V_i = P - C \frac{U_i}{T_i}$$

Where V_i is the value of the farm per acre; P is the price of an acre of improved land; C is the cost of improving an acre of land; and U_i/T_i is

56 I am indebted to the Inter-University Consortium for Political and Social Research for access to these data. The codebook for the sample is ICPSR 740, 1st ed., 1976. For an analysis that makes a much more extensive application of these data, see Atack and Bateman, *To Their Own Soil*.

57 The analysis here used only those farms where the farm operator was at least twenty years of age. Consequently, the numbers reported in Table 3.4 differ slightly from those reported in Ransom and Sutch, *One Kind of Freedom*, appendix G.

Table A.3.1. *Sample of northern farms, 1860*

Region	Over ten tilled acres	All sample farms
East	3,867	3,955
New Hampshire	446	446
New Jersey	134	142
New York	1,994	2,025
Pennsylvania	1,116	1,159
Vermont	80	82
Connecticut	97	101
Midwest	5,226	5,349
Illinois	878	894
Indiana	2,981	3,029
Michigan	561	604
Ohio	455	466
Wisconsin	351	356
West	812	846
Iowa	350	354
Kansas	275	287
Minnesota	187	205
Total	9,905	10,150

Source: Appendix to Chapter 3.

the ratio of unimproved to total acres.[58] To account for differences within the various regions, the estimation equation included dummy variables for each county (in the South) or state (in the North). These dummy variables were the basis for adjusting the price of land in each state/county. The averages reported in Table 3.2 are the estimated price for each state/county weighted by the total improved acreage in that state/county.

A third sample of southern farms that has been widely used by investigators of the antebellum Cotton South is the Parker/Gallman sample of

[58] The equation to estimate value of improved land was derived from a model of land values that assumes that within each region there is some fixed cost, C, for clearing land. The value of the farm is then given as:

$$FV_i = P_i I_i + (P_i - C)U_i$$

Dividing through by the total acreage and rearranging terms gives the equation in the text. See Roger L. Ransom and Richard Sutch, "Tenancy, Farm Size, Self-Sufficiency, and Racism: Four Problems in the Economic History of Southern Agriculture, 1865–1880," in *Southern Economic History Project Working Paper Series*, no. 8, (Institute for Business and Economic Research, University of California, Berkeley, April 1970) pp. 85–9.

Table A.3.2. *Sample of southern farms,*
1850, 1860, and 1870

County by year	Over ten tilled acres	All sample farms
1850		
Attala, Mississippi	157	157
Georgetown, South Carolina	31	36
Dallas, Alabama	75	76
Madison, Louisiana	24	24
Coweta, Georgia	109	110
Halifax, Virginia	164	164
Red River, Texas	29	29
Robertson, Texas	10	12
Total	599	608
1860		
Attala, Mississippi	154	157
Georgetown, South Carolina	27	29
Dallas, Alabama	89	95
Madison, Louisiana	20	20
Coweta, Georgia	104	104
Halifax, Virginia	136	137
Red River, Texas	67	68
Robertson, Texas	33	33
Total	630	643
1870		
Attala, Mississippi	292	206
Georgetown, South Carolina	19	23
Dallas, Alabama	107	107
Madison, Louisiana	178	199
Coweta, Georgia	84	84
Halifax, Virginia	142	148
Red River, Texas	157	158
Robertson, Texas	22	22
Total	911	947
Total farms sampled	2,148	2,206

Source: Appendix to Chapter 3.

farms for 1860. This sample has provided the basis for the research carried on by a number of investigators who were examining the workings of the slave economy.

All of these samples suffer from a common drawback; they focus on the Cotton South and touch only marginally the backcountry areas of the South. They also exclude, for the most part, the tobacco areas of Virginia and the Upper South. In assessing the results reported from these samples, therefore, it is important to bear in mind that what we are describing is the heartland of the cotton-producing regions.

Table A.3.3. *The price of slaves, 1805–60*

Year	Slaves (millions)	Average price ($)	
		All slaves in South	Prime hand in New Orleans
1805	1,032	222	504
1806	1,062	317	719
1807	1,093	286	647
1808	1,125	360	813
1809	1,158	272	615
1020	1,191	277	624
1811	1,222	246	555
1812	1,254	286	642
1813	1,286	284	638
1814	1,320	309	694
1815	1,354	272	610
1816	1,389	337	753
1817	1,425	403	900
1818	1,461	477	1,065
1819	1,499	407	908
1820	1,538	393	875
1821	1,580	389	864
1822	1,622	294	650
1823	1,666	309	683
1824	1,711	275	606
1825	1,758	277	608
1826	1,805	268	588
1827	1,854	248	542
1828	1,905	253	551
1829	1,956	281	611
1830	2,009	273	591
1831	2,052	308	662
1832	2,097	220	707
1833	2,142	259	765
1834	2,188	378	800
1835	2,235	424	893
1836	2,284	547	1,146
1837	2,333	634	1,322
1838	2,383	484	1,002
1839	2,435	440	906
1840	2,487	377	773
1841	2,551	385	788
1842	2,617	314	640
1843	2,684	280	569
1844	2,753	276	561
1845	2,823	342	692
1846	2,896	358	723
1847	2,970	382	771
1848	3,046	413	830
1849	3,124	378	776
1850	3,204	377	756
1851	3,272	440	878
1852	3,342	471	937
1853	3,413	565	1,122
1854	3,485	601	1,189
1855	3,559	600	1,185
1856	3,635	656	1,291
1857	3,712	636	1,249
1858	3,791	645	1,262
1859	3,872	801	1,564
1860	3,954	778	4,513

Source: Roger L. Ransom and Richard Sutch, "Capitalists without Capital: The Burden of Slavery and the Impact of Emancipation," *Agricultural History* (Fall 1988), table A.1.

Table A.3.4. *Per capita income in different regions for total and free populations, 1840 and 1860 (1860 dollars)*

	Total population's income			Free population's income		
	1840	1860	Annual growth rate	1840	1860	Annual growth rate
National average	96	128	1.45	109	144	1.40
North	109	141	1.30	110	142	1.28
Northeast	129	181	1.71	130	183	1.72
North Central	65	89	1.58	66	90	1.56
South	74	103	1.67	105	150	1.80
South Atlantic	66	84	1.21	96	124	1.29
East South Central	69	89	1.28	92	124	1.50
West South Central	151	184	0.99	238	274	0.71

Notes: Free population excludes slaves as income earners and allocates a "maintenance allowance" of twenty dollars per slave.
Source: Stanley L. Engerman, "Some Economic Factors in Southern Backwardness in the Nineteenth Century," in *Essays in Regional Economics*, ed. John F. Kain and John R. Meyer (Harvard University Press, 1971), table 2, p. 287.

Table A.3.5. *Index of slave profitability,*
1805–60 (1820 = 100)

Year	Average price of slaves	Export price of cotton	Average value of cotton per slave
1805	71	136	86
1806	69	125	82
1807	81	116	76
1808	77	104	67
1809	76	100	64
1810	67	86	54
1811	68	74	45
1812	69	75	42
1813	74	98	50
1814	73	136	78
1815	77	156	104
1816	85	179	138
1817	102	168	136
1818	108	149	127
1819	107	115	103
1820	100	100	100
1821	90	89	92
1822	83	88	93
1823	74	97	107

Table A.3.5. (*cont.*)

Year	Average price of slaves	Export price of cotton	Average value of cotton per slave
1824	72	98	112
1825	69	87	116
1826	67	65	95
1827	65	61	95
1828	66	62	94
1829	68	59	95
1830	72	58	97
1831	67	60	101
1832	66	68	120
1833	72	82	151
1834	89	93	183
1835	113	96	195
1836	135	83	187
1837	140	79	176
1838	131	68	166
1839	109	67	158
1840	101	54	139
1841	90	49	130
1842	82	45	128
1843	73	41	128
1844	76	44	130
1845	82	48	132
1846	91	51	140
1847	97	48	145
1848	99	51	162
1849	99	60	184
1850	101	63	196
1851	108	60	211
1852	124	55	208
1853	138	56	207
1854	149	56	202
1855	156	62	221
1856	159	68	245
1857	163	72	271
1858	175	69	294
1859	187	67	305
1860	195	44	204

Sources: Price of slaves, and export price of cotton and value of cotton per slave: Computed from Roger L. Ransom and Richard Sutch, "Capitalists without Capital: The Burden of Slavery and the Impact of Emancipation," *Agricultural History* (Fall 1988), tables A.1 and A.3, respectively.

Table A.3.6. Statistics on the growth of cotton and slaves, 1805–60 (three-year moving average)

Year	Value of all slaves (mill. $)	Quantity cotton output (mill. lbs.)	Value of cotton output (mill. $)	Implicit export price (cents)	Index (1820 = 100)			
					Value of slave	Price of slave	Quantity cotton output	Value of cotton output
1805	291	59.9	13.5	22.59	48	71	42	57
1806	292	64.0	13.2	20.76	48	69	45	56
1807	351	65.5	12.6	19.23	58	81	46	54
1808	344	66.1	11.4	17.32	56	77	47	49
1809	351	67.6	11.2	16.64	58	76	48	48
1810	316	68.9	9.8	14.20	52	67	49	42
1811	330	66.9	8.3	12.33	54	68	47	36
1812	341	64.1	8.0	12.51	56	69	45	34
1813	377	61.3	9.9	16.29	62	74	43	42
1814	381	68.3	15.9	22.54	62	73	48	68
1815	414	81.9	21.6	25.90	68	77	58	92
1816	468	98.7	29.4	29.66	77	85	70	125
1817	578	105.7	29.5	27.86	95	102	75	126
1818	627	117.7	28.3	24.68	103	108	83	121
1819	638	126.1	23.5	19.02	105	107	89	100
1820	610	141.5	23.5	16.58	100	100	100	100
1821	566	153.5	22.2	14.68	93	90	108	95
1822	536	160.4	23.0	14.51	88	83	113	98
1823	488	170.1	27.3	16.00	80	74	120	116
1824	491	182.7	29.3	16.24	80	72	129	125

1825	481	228.7	30.9	14.36	79	69	162	132
1826	477	244.0	26.1	10.83	78	67	172	111
1827	476	263.6	26.7	10.16	78	65	186	114
1828	497	267.9	27.3	10.23	81	66	189	117
1829	526	290.1	28.3	9.76	86	68	205	121
1830	577	306.8	29.7	9.68	95	72	217	127
1831	623	313.7	31.5	10.01	102	67	222	134
1832	697	340.3	38.5	11.25	114	66	241	164
1833	762	361.2	49.4	13.53	125	72	255	211
1834	847	394.0	61.1	15.42	139	89	279	260
1835	1,005	420.4	66.6	15.91	165	113	297	284
1836	1,222	482.5	64.9	13.78	200	135	341	276
1837	1,295	486.7	62.6	13.11	212	140	344	267
1838	1,237	556.7	60.3	11.25	203	131	393	257
1839	1,055	546.0	58.8	11.18	173	109	386	250
1840	997	586.7	52.6	9.00	163	101	415	
1841	915	637.5	50.4	8.19	150	90	451	224
1842	853	691.1	51.1	7.51	140	82	489	215
1843	778	781.9	52.3	6.76	128	73	553	218
1844	823	751.3	54.4	7.31	135	76	531	223
1845	918	731.9	56.9	7.95	150	82	517	232
1846	1,044	738.4	62.0	8.51	171	91	522	243
1847	1,141	846.3	65.5	8.03	187	97	598	279
1848	1,200	907.9	75.3	8.46	197	99	642	321
1849	1,225	908.9	88.1	9.95	201	99	643	375
1850	1,286	933.5	95.7	10.49	211	101	660	408

(continued)

Table A.3.6. (cont.)

Year	Value of all slaves (mill. $)	Quantity cotton output (mill. lbs.)	Value of cotton output (mill. $)	Implicit export price (cents)	Index (1820 = 100)			
					Value of slave	Price of slave	Quantity cotton output	Value of cotton output
1851	1,405	1,075.3	105.4	9.98	230	108	760	449
1852	1,644	1,159.3	106.0	9.12	270	124	820	452
1853	1,862	1,147.2	107.5	9.35	305	138	811	458
1854	2,052	1,159.3	107.3	9.24	336	149	820	457
1855	2,203	1,173.7	120.5	10.27	361	156	830	513
1856	2,293	1,214.3	136.0	11.26	376	159	858	579
1857	2,397	1,285.9	153.5	11.97	393	163	909	654
1858	2,632	1,503.7	170.5	11.39	431	175	1,063	727
1859	2,870	1,614.3	180.0	11.17	470	187	1,141	767
1860	3,059	1,712.0	121.8	7.30	501	195	1,210	519

Note: Value of cotton is the quantity of cotton (col. 2) multiplied by the export price of cotton (col. 4). The export cotton price is computed by dividing the value of cotton exports (series U-275) by the quantity of cotton exports (series U-276) reported in *Historical Statistics*, part 2, p. 899. The index of growth are computed using the value of 1820 as the base year.

Sources: Value of slaves: Roger L. Ransom and Richard Sutch, "Capitalists without Capital: The Burden of Slavery and the Impact of Emancipation," *Agricultural History* (Fall, 1988), table A.1. Quantity of cotton: U.S. Census Bureau, *Historical Statistics of the United States, Colonial Times to 1970*, part 1 (U.S. Census Bureau, 1976), series K-551, p. 517. The series was converted to pounds by assuming a 400-pound weight for bales of cotton.

Table A.3.7. *Index of the value of farm and the value of an improved acre of land, sample of southern farms, 1850 and 1860*

	Dollars		Index number		Ratio 1850 to 1860
	1850	1860	1850	1860	
Value of farm					
Slave farms	3,912	11,704	161.6	483.4	2.99
Free farms	748	1,703	30.9	70.3	2.28
All farms	2,421	7,778	100.0	321.3	3.21
Value of improved acre					
Slave farms	11.39	45.19	109.1	432.9	3.97
Free farms	8.35	15.28	80.0	146.4	1.83
All farms	10.44	38.97	100.0	373.3	3.73

Note: Value for all farms in 1850 = 100.
Sources: Computed from sample of farms in eight southern counties; see appendix to Chapter 3.

4

The Politics of Slavery

There is a new spirit abroad in the land, young, restless, vigorous and om-
nipotent. . . . It demands the immediate annexation of Texas at any hazard. It
will plant its right foot upon the northern verge of Oregon, and waving the
stars and stripes in the face of the once proud Mistress of the Ocean, bid her,
if she dare, "Cry havoc, and let slip the dogs of war."

Theophilus Fisk, May 3, 1843[1]

In March 1825, James Monroe stepped down from the presidency. With
his retirement, the last of the founding fathers left the political scene, and
leadership passed to a new generation. On balance, the first quarter of
the nineteenth century had been a good one for the United States. The
young nation's territory had doubled with the acquisition of Louisiana
and Florida. The threat to American independence from European interferences had been removed by a second war with England, which had
culminated with a brilliant victory at the Battle of New Orleans. Americans were bristling with confidence. In his final message to Congress,
President Monroe went out of his way to warn European nations that
this new generation of Americans would brook no interferences from
Europe in American affairs. "We owe it to candor and to the amicable
relations existing between the United States and those powers," he told
Congress, "to declare that we should consider any attempt on their part
to extend their system to any portion of this hemisphere as dangerous to
our peace and safety." The Monroe Doctrine was hardly noticed in
European capitals, but it generated a great deal of enthusiasm at home.

Monroe's message was more than just a warning that European
powers should not interfere with the efforts of former Spanish colonies to
break free from Spain. It was also a statement that the United States
regarded the huge areas of western North America that were still unsettled as an American province. In the 1820s, the stream of people pouring
over the Appalachian Mountains continued to grow both north and
south of the Ohio. Settlement of the western lands was becoming an
American obsession. At its peak in the 1840s, when men like Theophilus

---

1 Cited in Frederick Merk, *Manifest Destiny and Mission in American History* (Vintage
Press, 1963), p. 54.

Fisk were considering the possibility of a third war with Great Britain, the editor of *The United States Magazine and Democratic Review* gave this American preoccupation with western settlement a name. Controlling the whole of the North American continent was, according to John L. O'Sullivan, our Manifest Destiny.[2]

The compromise reached in 1820 over the extension of slavery to the Louisiana Purchase had cleared away a far more dangerous obstacle to the realization of manifest destiny than European intervention. For nearly two decades the regional differences over slavery took a back seat to other, more pressing concerns on the political scene. "Americans," as one political historian of the period notes, "were preoccupied by the need to deal with the forces of internal development and rapid economic growth."[3] The forces of growth that manifested themselves in the 1820s and 1830s were not entirely new, but the pace of economic change had clearly accelerated. American farmers found themselves dealing more and more with markets that were further and further away. The development of short-staple cotton in the South transformed that region into a bustling center of commercial agriculture in the space of two decades. Agriculture expansion in the northern states stayed in the more traditional area of grains and foodstuffs. As early as 1794, Tench Coxe had observed that "it is manifest that the great increase in our population has been attended with a very considerable addition to our export of staples. . . . But it is not to be forgotten, that considerable quantities are consumed by our *manufactures*, who are rapidly increasing."[4] The growing internal demand for foodstuffs pointed to a development that was to have a profound effect on the economic relationships between the states. By the 1820s, the "industrial revolution" in England was beginning to find its way across the Atlantic. Manufacturers in New England began a period of expansion that was to continue, with some cyclical interruptions, up to the eve of the Civil War. In addition to the farmers, planters, and merchants who had formed the core of the body politic in Jefferson's day, politicians found themselves having to deal also with the demands of industrialists and their working-class employees.

Monroe's departure is noteworthy because it marked the end of what is often termed the "Virginia Dynasty," a period of political hegemony when the presidency and national politics were dominated by leaders

---

2 On O'Sullivan and the origins of Manifest Destiny, see Merk, *Manifest Destiny*, pp. 46–60.
3 Joel H. Silbey, ed., *The Partisan Imperative: The Dynamics of American Politics before the Civil War* (Oxford University Press, 1985), p. xi.
4 Tench Coxe, *A View of the United States of America* (William Hall and Wrigley and Berriman, 1794; reprint, Augustus Kelly, 1965), pp. 227–8.

from Virginia. Following Jefferson's election in 1800, a succession of patrician Virginians became president, each serving two terms in office before passing the baton along to his successor. In 1824 the heir apparent to the office was not a Virginian, but his credentials were impressive. John Quincy Adams was the son of a president and could point to a long and distinguished career of service under the administrations of Madison and Monroe. As secretary of state for Monroe, he was the man who actually wrote the text for Monroe's doctrine. Still, John Quincy Adams did not have the aura of a Jefferson or Monroe or Madison. No fewer than four challengers stepped forward to contest Adams's candidacy in 1824. This produced a deadlock in the electoral college between Adams and Andrew Jackson of Tennessee. The contest was resolved in the House of Representatives, where Adams received the votes of thirteen states, Jackson four states, and William Crawford of Georgia received support from four states. Jackson, who had received a substantial plurality of votes both in the popular vote and in the electoral college, was distressed by the outcome, but did not give up his quest for the presidency. From that point on he began a campaign that was to carry him to victory in the 1828 presidential election.[5]

Jacksonian Democracy: The Genesis of the "Second-Party System"

Andrew Jackson's election did more than simply break the succession of Jeffersonian Republicans to the presidency. Jackson brought to the White House an entirely new set of ideas and perspectives on how the power of the presidency should be exercised. He was a man who had grown up on the western frontier, and he delighted in referring to that background when he called himself the champion of the "common man." Jackson was immensely popular and did not hesitate to use his personal popularity as president to form a political coalition that eventually became the Democratic party. In his two terms as president, Jackson not only laid the basis for a political party; he also expanded the influence of the president by forcefully demonstrating the power that could be wielded by a determined chief executive.

He was not without his critics. Angered and frustrated by his success, Jackson's opponents tried to band together and form a party to challenge the Jacksonians. Although they were unable to challenge seriously Jackson's presidency, they were able to form a political coalition that became

---

5 Jackson defeated Adams, 152,901 votes to 114,023, and he carried the electoral votes of eleven states totaling 99 electoral votes to seven states with 84 electoral votes for Adams.

known as the Whig party. By the time he retired from office in 1836, Jackson left a legacy of not one, but two, national political parties. The Whigs and the Democrats formed what historians have termed the second-party system, an arrangement that dominated the American political scene throughout the 1830s and 1840s.[6]

The emergence of national political parties should not obscure the fact that the bread and butter of party politics in this period were local, not national, concerns. Men might call themselves "Democrats" or "Whigs," but in so doing they were identifying more with a group of friends near their home than to some far-flung political organization headquartered in Washington, D.C. Political parties in this period frequently referred to themselves as "clubs," and the term club certainly conveys a much better sense of what political affiliation meant to the average voter's life in the 1830s than does our modern notion of a "political party." This meant that the focus of political parties was on their own neighborhood. The matters that gave local party organizations their solidarity and stability were those bearing most directly on items such as the appointment of a postmaster or county judge; the election of an alderman or city councilman or representative to the state legislature; the setting of levies for roads or schools. Political clubs also played an important social function for their members. The ties that linked voters to their party were therefore highly personal.

The emphasis of political organization on local issues helps explain several important traits of politics in this period. First, because political activity was a social activity as well as a civic responsibility, participation in political life was very widespread. Turnouts for elections were high and there was an exceptional degree of loyalty to one's club. The result was what historian Joel Silbey has termed an "almost cement-like electoral stability of voters in this period."[7] The challenge to antebellum politicians on the national scene was to direct this strong attachment to the local political club into an attachment to the political "party" at a national level – not always an easy task. A political party hoping for

6 The "first-party system" was that of the Federalists of Washington and later John Adams, who were opposed by Thomas Jefferson and the Republicans. The Federalist party had all but disappeared by the elections of 1824. An excellent analysis of the emergence of political parties in the 1820s and 1830s can be found in Richard P. McCormick, *The Second American Party System: Party Formation in the Jacksonian Era* (University of North Carolina, 1966).

7 Silbey, *The Partisan Imperative*, p. 57. Other works emphasizing the importance of local ties to the political organization include William E. Gienapp, *The Origins of the Republican Party, 1852–1856* (Oxford University Press, 1987); Michael Holt, *Forging a Majority: The Formation of the Republican Party in Pittsburgh, 1848–1860* (Yale University Press, 1969); idem, *The Political Crisis of the 1850's* (W. W. Norton, 1978); and Roland P. Formisano, *The Birth of Mass Political Parties: Michigan, 1827–1861* (Princeton University Press, 1971).

national appeal needed some common elements from which a consensus of voters could be forged. Two factors invariably played an important role in shaping that consensus: a leader charismatic enough to attract voters, or the exploitation of some issue with broad enough appeal to make an impact in communities throughout the country.

Through the late 1820s and mid-1830s, the Democrats had what seemed to be the perfect recipe. Their presidential candidate, Andrew Jackson, had a personal charisma that attracted a significant number of people to the party. But the solidity of the Democratic party did not rest simply on the popularity of the president. Equally important to Jackson's political success was the Democrats' ability to formulate positions on a number of key issues that appealed to specific interests in a changing economic and social environment.

As the expansion of the 1820s gradually grew into the economic boom of the 1830s, markets for American producers grew at an astounding pace. The marketplace, which had been of only secondary importance to colonial producers, suddenly became the driving force behind the decisions of farmers who found themselves drawn into commercial agriculture. Nowhere was the influence of the marketplace more evident than in the economy of the New England and the Middle Atlantic states, where manufacturing establishments appeared along the rivers and streams to make use of the waterpower that ran the machinery. With growing markets for their products, farmers and industrial entrepreneurs took an added interest in the role the state would play in shaping their economic environment. What in England had come to be identified as "political economy" came to the forefront of American political debates.[8] A variety of issues were in and out of the spotlight of debate, but none raised more heated argument than the role of the federal government in chartering a national bank. On this issue the split between Democrats and Whigs was so strong it touched off what became known as the "Bank War."

In 1791 Congress, with the urging of Secretary of the Treasury Alex-

---

8 For a review of the literature on the rise of "Jacksonian Democracy" and the changing society of the early nineteenth century, see Sean Wilentz, "On Class and Politics in Jacksonian America," *Reviews in American History* 10 (December 1982). Among the best general works dealing with the political economy of the Jackson era are Louis Hartz, *Economic Policy and Democratic Thought: Pennsylvania, 1776–1860* (Harvard University Press, 1948); and Edward Pessen, *Jacksonian America: Society, Personality and Politics* (Dorsey Press, 1969). For an excellent view of how the growing industrialization of the Middle Atlantic region affected Jacksonian politics, see Cynthia J. Shelton, *The Mills of Manayunk: Industrialization and Social Conflict in the Philadelphia Region, 1787–1837* (Johns Hopkins University Press, 1986).

ander Hamilton, had chartered the First Bank of the United States (BUS) as a quasi-public bank. In many respects, the BUS operated as any other private bank; it issued notes, made loans, and so forth. But because the BUS was the only bank with a federal charter, it enjoyed a distinct advantage over its competitors. The BUS was the fiscal agent of the federal government, which meant that all government receipts went to the bank. This arrangement, together with the fact that the bank had branches throughout the country, gave the bank considerable influence over the amount of specie and banknotes in circulation – and therefore over the level of credit in the economy. Although it was not what we would today call a "central bank," the BUS was able to exert a form of de facto control over the level of money credit in the economy.[9]

Initially, all this was of little importance because at the time of the bank's creation in 1790, very few people had need for banking services. But as the economy grew, the importance of credit increased to farmer and industrial entrepreneur alike, and the monopoly position of the BUS became more obvious. By 1811, when the charter of the BUS expired, the bank had become a target for those dissatisfied with the credit situation, and opponents of the bank successfully blocked renewal of the charter. The economic chaos surrounding the second war with Britain (1812–14) stymied efforts by supporters of the bank to get a new twenty-year charter approved by Congress, and it was not until 1816 that a rechartered BUS was able to resume business. As the postwar depression of 1816–19 gave way to a vigorously expanding economy in the 1820s and 1830s, the BUS once again found itself in the middle of a growing controversy over the demands for expanded credit. Those favoring the bank's efforts to limit the issuance of credit and bank notes by state-chartered and other "private" banks stressed the need for financial stability and the bank's role in guaranteeing that stability. Those opposed to the bank's policies insisted that the bank was the tool of a small cabal of directors who used the bank's preeminent position in the financial markets to further their own private interests, to stifle the legitimate operations of

9 The issuance of "bank notes" – a form of private debt issued by privately owned companies – as a form of money had become widespread by the end of the War of 1812. The importance of these notes lay in the ability of banks to make loans by issuing notes, thus providing credit and increasing the money supply. Because of its size, its exclusive control of government accounts, and its ability to establish branches throughout the economy, the BUS was in a position to exercise restraint on the issuance of bank notes by state banks. It did this through a policy of always promptly demanding specie for any notes of state banks that it received as payment. For an excellent analysis of how the bank operated, see Susan Previant Lee and Peter Passell, *A New Economic View of American History* (W. W. Norton, 1979), chap. 5.

state-chartered banks, and to constrain the continued expansion of agriculture to the West. Both sides employed colorful rhetoric in attacking
their adversaries.

Which brings us to Mr. Jackson and the "Bank War." Because he had
lost a considerable sum of money in a bank failure when he was young,
Jackson bitterly disliked *all* banks, and he quickly championed the cause
of those who opposed the largest bank of all.[10] Upon his election in
1828, he announced his opposition to renewal of the bank's charter,
which was due to expire in 1836. He proceeded over the next six years to
attack the bank relentlessly with every tool at his disposal. In 1832,
supporters of the bank succeeded in getting a bill to recharter the bank
through Congress. Jackson promptly vetoed the bill and turned the up-
coming presidential election into a referendum on the issue of rechartering the bank. The president was returned to office the following fall with
a substantial majority, which he took as a mandate to see that the charter
of the BUS was not renewed. The bank's fate was thus sealed. Its charter
expired in 1836 and the institution was forced to become an ordinary
private bank, chartered by the state of Pennsylvania. When the bank
failed in 1839, Jackson's victory was complete.[11]

Jackson's "war" against the BUS was the center of American political
debates for nearly a decade. Nor did the demise of the BUS end the
controversy. Indeed, there is a certain irony in Jackson's victory over the
bank. He greatly distrusted the power of the bank, and had little use for
the men who ran it. At the same time, the president regarded any bank as
something of a con game, and he was therefore an implacable foe of
banks that irresponsibly issued notes with little or no specie backing. By
destroying the Second Bank of the United States, Jackson opened the way
for an expansion of exactly the sort of banking practices that he personally abhorred. Consequently, the debate over "hard" and "easy" money
raged on.

The Whigs made several efforts to resurrect a federally chartered bank
in the early 1840s, but the efforts fell short and "free banking" ruled for
the remainder of the antebellum period. For all the ruckus it raised,

10 For an account of Jackson's early dealing with banks and credit, and how they affected
    his views on banking, see Robert V. Remini, *Andrew Jackson and the Bank War: A
    Study in the Growth of Presidential Power* (W. W. Norton, 1966), chap. 1.
11 The "Bank War" has received an enormous amount of attention from historians and
    economic historians. On the economic aspects of the dispute, see Peter Temin, *The
    Jacksonian Economy* (W. W. Norton, 1969); Hugh Rockoff, "Money, Prices, and
    Banks in the Jacksonian Era," in *The Reinterpretation of American Economic History*,
    eds. Robert Fogel and Stanley Engerman (Harper and Row, 1971); and Lee and
    Passell, *A New Economic View of American History*, chap. 5; for an account that
    stresses the political rivalry of Jackson and the president of the BUS, Nicholas Biddle,
    see Remini, *Andrew Jackson and the Bank War*.

economic historians have tended to downplay the significance of the bank war in terms of its impact on economic growth.[12] Political historians, however, point out that the disputes over chartering a central bank created the basis for a sharp and enduring political division into two political parties.[13] Democrats invariably characterized the bank a threat to democratic institutions in general and decried its tight-fisted monopoly of note issue and credit. Whigs saw the bank as the only thing standing between monetary stability and the chaos of irresponsible note issue. This deep division on the bank issue made other differences between the parties seem greater than they actually were.

There was one other aspect of the Bank War that bears notice at this point. The division on the question of rechartering the BUS was, in fact, quite close. In 1832 the Whigs succeeded in getting a bill renewing the charter through Congress, only to have the president veto it. The Whigs knew they did not have the votes to override the veto. Thus, despite the closeness of the division, there was no possibility of compromise so long as the president remained adamantly opposed to the recharter bill. "The Bank War," notes Robert Remini, "became the instrument by which the powers of the President were vastly expanded."[14] By first using the veto, and then making the rechartering of the bank the major issue in the 1834 campaign, Jackson clearly demonstrated the power of the presidency to shape legislation.

The bank was not the only issue at the center of Jacksonian political economy. Other issues included tariffs, internal improvements, and territorial expansion. Democrats generally opposed high tariffs and direct federal aid for internal improvements, and strongly supported territorial expansion, whereas their Whig opponents tended to favor protection for home manufacture, seek aid for transportation improvements, and take a more eclectic position on the benefits of territorial expansion.[15] However, unlike the question of whether there should be a Bank of the United States, these issues, by their nature, tend to be negotiable. The question of a tariff is basically over the degree to which domestic consumers should

12 Quantitative studies have tended to support the view that forces outside the U.S. economy played a more important role in promoting economic fluctuations than the institutional arrangements of the antebellum banking system. See in particular Temin, *The Jacksonian Economy*, and Rockoff, "Money, Prices and Banks."

13 See in particular Remini, *Andrew Jackson and the Bank War*, and Pessen, *Jacksonian America*.

14 Remini, *Andrew Jackson and the Bank War*, p. 177.

15 This characterization of party positions is a bit glib. As Edward Pessen has emphasized, apart from the Bank, there were few deep divisions between the parties. For a general overview, see Pessen, *Jacksonian America*, esp. chaps. 5, 6, and 12; for a more analytical view of Jacksonians and the role of the state, see Louis Hartz, *Economic Policy and Democratic Thought*.

be asked to pay a tax in order to protect domestic production. Most people were willing to concede some level of protection to domestic producers; the argument was over the *level* of protection. Nor did many people unequivocally oppose the construction of internal improvements to promote trade; the debate was over the extent of government assistance that was necessary, and whether the federal government should be involved in that decision. Territorial expansion was fine, if all that it implied was the voting of funds for the removal of "savage" Indian tribes.

In fact, notwithstanding the furor over the BUS, various scholars examining the political allegiances of this period have claimed that it is difficult to come up with any reasonable characterization of what made a "Whig" or a "Democrat." The distinction most often made is that upon which Jackson himself insisted: Democrats were led by common folk whereas Whigs were led by aristocrats. If so, it is hardly evident in the social and economic standing of the men who led each party. Edward Pessen summed up the situation by concluding that "it is very difficult to discern any difference in the social composition of Democratic and Whig party leaders."[16] Thus, for example, when he ran for president in 1828 on the Democratic ticket, Jackson was a very wealthy man with extensive holdings of lands and slaves in central Tennessee.

We are less concerned with the influences of class differences on politics during the Jacksonian era than with the influence of sectional differences that emerged in this period. Coalitions formed by the Whig and Democratic parties did involve sectional interests, but they were by no means uniform across all issues. Thus, for example, farmers in the West might stand together with southern farmers in opposing a tariff or a central bank while northern industrialists supported these measures. Yet Westerners interested in cheaper access to eastern or international markets would unite with northern interests in support of internal improvements. The second-party system functioned effectively precisely because both parties had considerable strength in all three of the major regions of the country. Only once did a sectional disruption on one of these issues threaten serious disruption of the political system. In 1828, Congress passed a new tariff law that particularly offended Southerners. John C. Calhoun, who had been elected vice-president with Jackson in 1828, launched a campaign in South Carolina to defy the federal government and "nullify" what he called the "Tariff of Abominations." In 1832 Calhoun and his allies received a boost when a new tariff bill – still

16   Pessen, *Jacksonian America*, p. 251. Not everyone is willing to accept the absence of class rivalries in the Jacksonian era. See Wilentz, "On Class and Politics in Jacksonian America."

resisted by southern interests – was passed by Congress. The nullifiers managed to gain sufficient power in the South Carolina legislature to organize a convention for the purpose of defying the federal statute. They met in November 1832 and passed an Ordinance of Nullification, which declared the tariff unconstitutional and prohibited the collection of duties. The state legislature thereupon took steps to implement the ordinance of nullification, and a confrontation with the federal government was inevitable.

President Jackson reacted swiftly to this crisis. Declaring that disunion was *treason*, he ordered federal military installations in Charleston Harbor reinforced and prepared to take military action. By early 1833 he had obtained from Congress a "Force Bill," which authorized collection of duties offshore and reaffirmed his right to call up the militia and use the military forces of the country to put down the challenge to federal power. Jackson's decisive action – together with a failure of the South Carolina nullifiers to gain support for their actions in other areas of the South – caused the nullification movement to collapse in disarray. To complete the rout of their opponents, Jackson forces passed a "compromise tariff" of 1833 with duties that were in many cases higher than those of the "Tariff of Abominations" that had started everything in 1832.

In fact, rhetoric about the tariff notwithstanding, most historians now argue that it was slavery, not economic issues, that was at the heart of the "Nullification Crisis." As Richard Latner observes, "The crisis laid bare southern anxieties about maintaining slavery and evidenced a determination to devise barriers against encroachments on southern rights."[17] Jackson's firm handling of the situation caused the nullifiers to back down, but Calhoun's philosophy of "states rights" remained on the southern political agenda from that time forward.

Jackson's handling of the nullification crisis is interesting in another respect as well. The tariff that sparked the controversy was a measure favored by the Whig, not the Democratic, legislators. Yet the president reacted to the challenge of governmental authority as if his own pet project had been threatened. His firm belief that "disunion" was, in fact, nothing short of treason, and his willingness to back up that belief with military action if necessary, produced the first major crisis over "states rights" with the southern states. Jackson's victory carried with it a mes-

17 Richard B. Latner, "The Nullification Crisis and Southern Subversion," *Journal of Southern History* 43 (1977). The definitive work on the nullification crisis is William Freehling, *Prelude to Civil War: The Nullification Crisis in South Carolina: 1816–1836* (Harper and Row, 1965); also see idem, "Nullification, Blackmail, and the Crisis of Majority Rule," in *A Nation Divided,* ed. George M. Fredrickson (Burgess, 1975).

sage that was not lost on Calhoun and his compatriots: The presidency is a powerful weapon in the hands of one who is willing to use the power of the office.

Apart from the incident over nullification in 1832, slavery was not an issue that was at the forefront of Jacksonian politics. Indeed, Jackson and his principal advisor, Martin Van Buren, went to considerable pains to see that slavery was kept out of the picture. Appointed secretary of state by President Jackson in 1828, and elected to the vice-presidency in 1832, Van Buren is generally regarded as having been the political mastermind behind Jackson's successful Democratic political machine in the late 1820s and 1830s.[18] Their political strategy was to form a political alliance between the Democratic "machine" that Van Buren had built in New York and the corresponding Democratic apparatus in Virginia. This North–South axis formed the core of Democratic politics for the next three decades.

Texas and Mexico: The Question of Slavery Revisited

In 1836 Martin Van Buren was elected president of the United States to succeed Jackson and carry on the Democratic tradition. The political position of Van Buren and the Democrats seemed secure. Unable to agree upon a single opponent, the Whigs had run four candidates in an effort to throw the election into the House of Representatives. The effort split only their own party, and Van Buren was elected with a comfortable margin. The country was experiencing unparalleled prosperity, and the opposition was in disarray. What more could an incoming president ask for?

There were, however, some distant storm clouds on the horizon. In the same year that Van Buren was elected president of the United States, a former member of the United States House of Representatives named Sam Houston was elected president of the newly proclaimed Republic of Texas. Like it or not – and Van Buren most certainly did not – the paths of the two republics were inextricably intertwined. It was apparent to even the most casual observer in the fall of 1836 that the Republic of Texas hoped someday to become a part of the United States. Should that happen, Texas would represent the addition of at least one, and possibly several, slave states to the Union – a prospect that threatened to undo the delicate balance fashioned by the Compromise of 1820. All the old

---

18 Several works on Van Buren have recently appeared emphasizing his role in shaping party politics in the 1820s and 1830s. See John Niven, *Martin Van Buren: The Romantic Age of American Politics* (Oxford University Press, 1983); and Major L. Wilson, *The Presidency of Martin Van Buren* (University Press of Kansas, 1984).

wounds would be reopened and the country would once again face a crisis over the extension of slavery.

The roots of the Texas problem date back to the early 1820s, when the Mexican government, anxious to populate its vacant northern territories, gave an American citizen, Stephen F. Austin, a grant of land and permission to distribute it to immigrant Americans. Austin succeeded in stirring great interest in the settlement of Texas, and by the mid-1830s the number of American colonists in Texas had grown to thirty thousand – four times the number of Mexicans in the region. Many American settlers brought their slaves with them into Texas. The Mexican government sought to curb this by prohibiting slavery, but its action did little to check the growth of slavery, because Americans circumvented the law by calling their black slaves "indentured servants." Alarmed by the presence and growing defiance of so many Americans, the Mexican government tried to regain control of its territory by a series of unfortunate acts, including legislation to abolish slavery in the territory, and an abortive attempt to disarm the Americans in 1835. The Mexicans' efforts succeeded only in sparking an armed uprising, which culminated in the Battle of San Jacinto on April 26, 1836, where the Mexican forces under Antonio Lopes de Santa Anna were decisively beaten by a Texan force under Sam Houston. Mexico agreed to Texan independence, but a bitter dispute over whether the southwestern boundary of the new republic was the Sabine River (as Mexico claimed) or the Rio Grande River (as Texas claimed) remained unsettled.

Despite the efforts of both Jackson and Van Buren to ignore the presence of the Texas republic, the United States was soon drawn into the intrigues surrounding the future of the new nation. Southern slaveholders had encouraged settlement of the area when it belonged to Mexico, and they now coveted the land along the coast and the Red River Valley for cotton production. No one seriously believed that Texas would remain truly independent; the question was whether it would ultimately be rejoined to Mexico, become attached to a European power (most likely Great Britain), or become a part of the United States. Southerners were particularly concerned over the possibility that England might gain control over Texas and abolish slavery there. Although such a possibility was remote at best, Texas President Houston cleverly played upon southern fears of an emancipation by offering to negotiate a treaty with England. To resolve this uncertainty, John Tyler, who became president of the United States in 1841, made the acquisition of Texas by the United States the top priority of his administration.

Tyler knew, of course, that the admission of Texas would represent a huge addition of slave territory, a move that opponents of the institution would vehemently oppose. Indeed, that opposition was so strong that Tyler's first efforts met with failure. A treaty of annexation that had been negotiated by Secretary of State John C. Calhoun was presented to the Senate in June 1844 and was soundly defeated. Undaunted, Tyler resorted to a more indirect approach. Although he was by this time a lame-duck president, Tyler succeeded in introducing a "Joint Resolution" to Congress approving the annexation of Texas in principle. The resolution was passed by the Senate on February 27, 1845, and by the House a day later. Tyler himself signed the resolution on March 1, 1845 – two days before he left office. The Texas legislature approved the resolution of annexation and Texas was formally admitted to the Union on December 29, 1845.

In his message to Congress accepting the admittance of Texas, Tyler's successor, James Polk, proudly announced that:

> This accession to our territory has been a bloodless achievement. No force of arms has been raised to produce the results. We have not sought to extend our territorial possessions by conquest, or our republican institutions over a reluctant people. . . . From this example European governments may learn how vain diplomatic arts and intrigues must ever prove on this continent against that system of self government which seems natural to our soil and which will ever resist foreign interferences.[19]

The president was being disingenuous to say the least. "American" blood *had* been shed, albeit in the guise of "Texans" fighting for their independence from the "tyranny" of Mexico.[20] Nor could Polk have been blind to the fact that the annexation of Texas was almost certain to trigger a war with Mexico that could hardly be "bloodless." To be sure, Polk would have preferred to avoid war with Mexico in the spring of 1846. The United States was hardly prepared to launch a military effort against the Mexicans, and his administration was already embroiled in an unsettled dispute with Britain over the boundary of the Oregon country in the Pacific Northwest. Nevertheless, the president was quite willing to fight if the Mexican government remained obstinate in frustrating his ambition to acquire California. In November 1845 Polk had sent James Slidell as a secret emissary to Mexico with an offer to purchase California from the Mexican Government for $25 million and an additional $5 million

19 Frederick Merk, *Slavery and the Annexation of Texas* (Alfred Knopf, 1972), p. 175.
20 Among the many anomalies about the Texan war for independence is the question of which "Texans" fought for their independence. Most of the men who fought in the Texan Army had been in Texas only a few weeks prior to joining the army. At the same time, most Americans who had settled in Texas did not fight for their own independence.

for the New Mexico Territory. The overture was rebuffed, and relations between the two governments continued to deteriorate.[21] Both sides sent troops to the disputed areas along the Texas border, and in early May 1846, U.S. troops commanded by General Zachary Taylor clashed with Mexican troops in the battles of Palo Alto and Resaca de la Palma. Congress formally declared war on May 13, 1846.

Although it is likely that a majority of Americans supported the Mexican War, a significant fraction of the electorate opposed it. Whigs, in particular, felt that "it is our president who began this war," and sixty-seven House members voted against the declaration of war. The president and his supporters were able to prosecute the war effectively, but there was a constant stream of criticism from those opposed to the conflict. By the time of the 1846 congressional elections, the unpopularity of the war had become sufficiently strong that the Whigs were able to regain control of the House of Representatives. A major issue in Congress involved the territorial settlement that should be demanded from Mexico as a price for peace. Mexico City had fallen to General Winfield Scott's army in September 1847, and Polk hoped to get a substantial portion of northern Mexico as well as California and New Mexico as a consequence of Scott's victory. However, the president no longer had a free hand in his negotiations with Mexico. In addition to congressional opposition, his own emissary in Mexico City, Nicholas Trist, had negotiated a treaty based on the president's instructions of ten months earlier, before the magnitude of Scott's victory had become apparent. The president reluctantly submitted the treaty to Congress, rather bitterly complaining that:

> If the treaty was now to be made, I would demand more territory, perhaps to make the Sierra Madre the line, yet it was doubtful whether this could ever be obtained by the consent of Mexico. I looked, too, to the consequences of its rejection. A majority of one branch of Congress is opposed to my administration; they have falsely charged that the war was brought on and is continued with a view to the conquest of Mexico; and if I were now to reject a Treaty made upon my own terms, as authorized in April last, with the unanimous approbation of the cabinet, the probability is that Congress would not grant either men or money to prosecute the war.[22]

21 There is some question how serious the offer really was. Slidell's trip was kept secret, and the president, in fact, had no authority to offer payment for the Mexican Territory. See Paul H. Bergeron, *The Presidency of James K. Polk* (University Press of Kansas, 1987), pp. 70–2. There was, of course, precedent for such an action; Jefferson had used a similar tactic to obtain Louisiana forty years earlier.

22 Quoted in David M. Potter, *The Impending Crisis: 1848–1861* (Harper Torchbooks, 1976), p. 4.

Anger and frustration over the Texas annexation and the Mexican War did not end with the signing of the Treaty of Guadalupe-Hidalgo in 1848. Northern opponents of slavery remained outraged over the tactics that the Tyler and Polk administrations had employed to pry Texas away from Mexico. Opponents saw the Texas affair as evidence of the lengths to which slave interests – what would soon come to be known as the slave power – would go to gain more territory and maintain continued dominance of national politics. The Texas annexation was identified as the product of political maneuvering by *southern* leaders. In June 1845, as the Senate debated the treaty of annexation with Mexico, Senator Thomas Hart Benton of Missouri rose to denounce the whole sordid affair to his colleagues. "I have often intimated it before, but now proclaim it," he said.

> Disunion is at the bottom of this long-concealed Texas machination. Intrigue and speculation cooperate; but disunion is at the bottom; and I denounce it to the American people. Under the pretext of getting Texas into the Union, the scheme is to get the South out of it. A separate confederacy, stretching from the Atlantic to California . . . is the cherished vision of disappointed ambition; and for this consummation every circumstance has been carefully and artfully controlled.[23]

Benton was not alone in his suspicions that more lay behind the machinations to admit Texas than met the eye. Tyler and Polk were both Southerners, and the leading figure in the Tyler administration negotiations for a treaty annexing Texas had been Secretary of State John C. Calhoun. Calhoun was still strongly identified as one who had promulgated the crisis of 1833 and his vociferous arguments that the annexation of Texas was essential for the continuation of slavery in the South were a factor in the Senate's rejection of the treaty of annexation in 1844.

When President Polk boasted that European powers should learn that the use of "diplomatic arts" and "intrigue" on this continent would be in vain, he failed to recognize who would "learn" from the Texas affair. The manner in which southern interests maneuvered Texas independence from Mexico and annexation into the United States was taken as evidence by many Americans that the South was an aggressive territorial power that would stop at nothing to protect its territorial interests. As we saw in Chapter 3, there was more than mere political rhetoric feeding such a suspicion; land to the west was important to southern slaveholders for economic as well as political reasons.

---

23 Thomas Hart Benton, June 15, 1844; cited in Merk, *Slavery and the Annexation of Texas*, p. 93.

The North Objects: The Wilmot Proviso

By the time peace negotiations were in the final stages with the Mexican government, there was a growing mistrust in the North over the motives as well as the tactics of southern leaders such as Calhoun and Tyler. This lack of trust surfaced in 1846 when President Polk requested funds to complete the peace negotiations. David Wilmot, a Democratic congressman from Pennsylvania, attached a proviso to the appropriations bill in the House stipulating that slavery would be excluded from any territory acquired from Mexico. Wilmot was acting as part of a group of antislavery northern Democrats who were becoming increasingly disenchanted with their party leadership in the White House.[24] He was well suited for the task because he was a Democrat who had, as he explained to his colleagues in the House of Representatives, "battled, time and again, against the Abolitionists of the North," and had "assailed them publicly, upon all occasions, when it was proper to do so."[25] He stood ready, he assured his audience, to "sustain the institutions of the South as they exist." "But sir," he continued, "the issue now presented is not whether slavery shall exist unmolested where it is now, but whether it shall be carried to new and distant regions, now free, where the footprint of a slave cannot be found."[26]

Wilmot had put his finger on what was to be the great issue of the next fifteen years: Was slavery to be allowed to extend to *new* regions as they became a part of the United States? There were many men in both parties of the North who were content to let slavery be where it already existed. But slavery had been introduced into Texas by Americans, and now, Wilmot claimed, they were doing the same in New Mexico. This was going too far. "Upon this question," the congressman contended,

> the North has yielded until there is no more to give up. We have gone on, making one acquisition after another, until we have acquired and brought into the Union every inch of slave territory that was to be

24 No one knows who actually wrote the language offered as the proviso to the appropriations bill. Jacob Brinkerhoff of Ohio claimed to be the author, saying that he asked Wilmot to introduce the proviso on the floor of the House because Brinkerhoff's antislavery views were so well-known that he would not be recognized by the speaker. Wilmot claimed authorship for himself, saying he discussed it with a number of antislavery Democrats before his action. What seems clear, as Eric Foner has pointed out, is that the proviso represents the sentiments of ten or more antislavery Democrats in the House; see "The Wilmot Proviso Revisited," *Journal of American History* 61 (September 1969).

25 Speech by David Wilmot in the House of Representatives, February 8, 1847; reprinted in Joel Silbey, ed., *The Transformation of American Politics, 1840–1860* (Prentice-Hall, 1967), p. 70.

26 Wilmot, in Silbey, *Transformation of American Politics*, p. 70.

found upon this Continent. Now, sir, we have passed beyond the boundaries of slavery and reached free soil.

Sir, as a friend of the Union, as a lover of my country, and in no spirit of hostility to the South, I offered my amendment. Viewing slavery as I do, I must resist its further extension and propagation on the North American Continent. It is an evil, the magnitude of which, no man can see.[27]

The Senate refused to go along with Wilmot's idea, and the final appropriations bill (which would have been vetoed by Polk had it included the proviso) was ultimately forwarded to the president's desk without the offending clause.

Wilmot's proviso did not simply fade from the scene, however. It became a symbol of resistance for antislavery forces seeking to check the further spread of slavery. "If any event in American history can be singled out as the beginning of a path which led almost inevitably to sectional conflict and civil war," claims historian Eric Foner, "it was the introduction of the Wilmot Proviso."[28] At the very least, the proviso heightened the rhetoric and made it increasingly difficult for politicians to find a middle ground in the slavery debates. This was particularly true for Democrats. In the mid 1840s northern Democrats were coming under increasing pressure to resist, and in some cases to repudiate entirely, what had become a very strong identification with southern slave interests. No less a person than Martin Van Buren, who was the architect of Democratic strategy in the 1820s and 1830s, pointed to the crux of the problem. Writing to a friend in the fall of 1842, he insisted that:

> The truth is that the Democrats of [New York] have suffered so often, and so severely in their advocacy of Southern men and Southern measures, as to make them more sensitive in respect to complaints of their conduct from that quarter, than I could wish. They say that . . . their party has suffered in every limb by the abolition question, and all this is undoubtedly true.[29]

The political maneuvering of Calhoun, Polk, and Tyler had further exacerbated those problems to the point where many northern Democrats felt they had to do something to head off criticism of being "proslave." Wilmot's proviso gave them that opportunity by going on record as opposing any further extension of slavery.

One of the great ironies of Wilmot's proviso is that it was a group of Democrats who introduced it in the House of Representatives. Whatever

27 Ibid., pp. 72–3.
28 Foner, "The Wilmot Proviso Revisited," p. 262.
29 Quoted in ibid., p. 266.

immediate relief the proviso may have offered to beleaguered antislave Democrats in the North, its eventual effect on the northern wing of the Democratic party was disastrous. Northern Whigs leaped at the chance to portray their opponents' opposition to the proviso as proof that they were "for" slavery. Democrats found themselves in an increasingly uncomfortable position trying to finesse the slave issue. Martin Van Buren is a case in point; he left the Democratic party in the late 1840s out of frustration over the party's waffling on the slave issue.

Nevertheless, party loyalty remained strong, and all this might have blown over had not a new and unexpected development occurred: Gold was discovered in California. Responding to the growing population from the "gold rush," President Zachary Taylor requested in his annual message to Congress on January 21, 1850, that Congress grant statehood for California. To lessen dissent from southern congressmen, he proposed at the same time the creation of a territory of New Mexico, which, he assumed, would lead to the formation of a new slave state to offset the newly admitted free state.

In calmer times such a proposal might have seemed reasonable. But in the winter of 1849–50, Taylor's message produced a crisis similar to that sparked by the proposal to admit Missouri in 1820. The South was outraged. Robert Toombs of Georgia indicated the extent of southern disaffection with the president's suggestion when he exclaimed on the floor of House that:

> If, by your legislation, you seek to drive us from the territories of California and New Mexico, purchased by the common blood and treasure of the whole people, and to abolish slavery in this District, thereby attempting to fix a national degradation upon half the states of this Confederacy, *I am for disunion*.[30]

Zachary Taylor was clearly caught off guard by the force of the southern response to his proposal. Old soldier that he was, Taylor's reaction was to stiffen his position and hold the line without any concessions to men like Toombs who threatened secession. The president's position had sufficient support in Congress to sustain a possible veto, and consequently the stalemate between a stubborn president and hard-line Southerners in Congress produced a major crisis in the government.

The political crisis of 1850 had been brewing ever since the appearance of the Texas problem in the late 1830s. To understand the dimensions of the problem, we need to back up a few years and see why neither of the

---

30 Toombs, in the House of Representatives, December 13, 1849, cited in Potter, *The Impending Crisis*, p. 94 (emphasis in original).

two major parties was able to deal with the problem of slavery when it reappeared in the late 1840s.

The Burden of the White House: Presidents and Slavery

We have seen that the driving force behind the creation of the Whig and Democratic parties was Andrew Jackson's forceful use of the presidency. From the last quarter of the twentieth century there is a tendency to view the power of the presidency as something that emerged out of the experience of the Great Depression and World War II.[31] In fact, the office of president has always been a position of considerable power in American politics. The person who wins the office automatically earns the right to be the titular head of his political party. At a more pragmatic level, the chief executive wields a considerable degree of power by virtue of having control over the bureaucratic apparatus of the government as well as the power of appointment and the dispensing of that bread and butter on which political parties live: political patronage. (It is surely not coincidental that the infamous "spoils system" appeared simultaneously with the organization of national political parties.)

Jackson's handling of the dispute over a central bank illustrated the extent to which the political clout of the president becomes greatly magnified in a situation where Congress is deadlocked over an important issue. The threat of a veto allows the president to dictate the limits of any acceptable compromise. The Compromise of 1820 could not have passed in the face of a president who opposed the measures: What were the chances of working something out in the face of an obstinate chief executive in 1850? Finally, as Andrew Jackson's handling of the nullification crisis in 1832 showed, a strong-willed president could use the executive power — including, if necessary, the military — to influence the level of enforcement of any actions taken by Congress.

So, for those with interests such as the protection of slavery, the competition for the White House involved high stakes. The game is complicated by the fact that electoral votes, not popular votes, are what it takes to win the election. Representatives to the electoral college are distributed according to each state's representation in Congress. The election of a president is, therefore, in reality a series of state elections in which the winner typically gets all the votes for a particular state. There is an inherent tendency in this system to reduce the competition to only

---

31   See, for example, the relative lack of importance attributed to the presidency prior to the Civil War by historians such as Arthur M. Schlesinger, Jr., *The Imperial Presidency* (Houghton-Mifflin, 1973); or Marcus Cunliffe, *American Presidents and the Presidency,* 2d ed. (McGraw-Hill, 1973).

two parties, each with a very broad geographical base of support. Parties that appeal to a narrow spectrum of the population will fall by the wayside because they will be unable to carry enough states to gain a majority in the electoral college. The winner-take-all aspect of each state election puts smaller parties at a disadvantage because voters perceive that they are "wasting" their vote on a candidate who has no chance to win.[32]

The emergence of the Democratic party and the subsequent formation of the Whig party in the 1820s and 1830s are examples of this tendency to weed out lesser parties. In 1824 Andrew Jackson lost the presidency even though he polled more votes in both the electoral college and in the total popular vote than did John Quincy Adams. With the help of Martin Van Buren he organized a strong national coalition – the "Democratic party" – which won in 1828. The success of Jackson's coalition eventually forced his opponents to adopt the same tactic and form the Whig party. In 1836, when Martin Van Buren ran for president, the Whigs fielded four candidates in the hope that the election would be thrown into the House as it was in 1824. The strategy failed, and Van Buren won handily. Four years later the Whigs put all their weight behind a single candidate – William Henry Harrison – and they won.

What all this means is that presidential politics have a special importance in the American political system quite apart from whatever goes on at the level of state or local party politics. This aspect of our political life was never more evident than in the three decades before the Civil War. What political historian Richard McCormick calls the "presidential game"

> exerted a singular appeal [on Americans] by the 1840s. It offered them identities as partisans in a contest with the entire nation as the arena. It enabled them to immerse themselves in an elaborate ritual with millions of their fellow citizens, to march in processions, chant slogans, sing songs, join clubs, exalt heroes, and confront the enemy.[33]

In the South, however, the presidential "game" was seen as much more than a ritual. The election of a chief executive, after all, involved the selection of someone who had the responsibility to protect the most important property right in the South: the ownership of slaves. To be

---

32 Numerous observers have commented on this tendency. For an excellent analysis of the evolution of presidential elections, and the two-party system, see Richard P. McCormick, *The Presidential Game: The Origins of American Presidential Politics* (Oxford University Press, 1982).

33 McCormick, *The Presidential Game*, p. 13.

sure, in the South as elsewhere, local issues played an important part in party politics. But when it came to the presidency, one "local" issue common to all southern communities was slavery. As one student of southern politics put it, "any political party that hoped to flourish in the South had to convince Southerners that it could protect slavery."[34] A presidential candidate's position on slavery became a litmus test that, if he failed, eliminated him from consideration. This situation worked fine so long as slavery remained basically a "southern problem." However, as the frictions between slave and antislave factions became more heated during the debates over territorial compromises and the annexation of new territory, any position that was perceived as "proslave" by voters in the North could pose a major obstacle to a candidate's appeal in that region. Consequently, slavery had became a very divisive issue at the national level by the early 1840s, which placed an enormous strain on party structures that were not well suited to deal with sectional strife. Between 1836 and 1852 the Democrats and Whigs met in five presidential elections. Table 4.1 presents the popular and electoral votes won by candidates of the two major parties by region in these elections. The first thing to note is that from 1836 to 1852 no incumbent president was reelected or even renominated by his own party, and no party in power stayed in the White House for more than one term.

This trend was in sharp contrast to the pattern of presidential elections prior to 1836. Each of the first eight presidents of the United States was nominated for reelection to a second term by his party, and five of them were reelected.[35] During the first half-century of the Republic, it seems, capturing the White House allowed a consolidation of power that persisted for at least a few more elections. The Federalist defeat of 1800 ushered in twenty-eight years of executive power exercised by Jefferson's "Democrat-Republicans," and Jackson's victory in 1828 produced twelve years of presidential power by the Jacksonian "Democrats."

To what can we attribute this change in the political fortunes of presidents? First, we can see that the popular vote in these elections was much closer than the electoral totals suggest. Here the importance of the winner-take-all aspect of the electoral college is evident. A small plurality in a few key states could result in a candidate capturing a huge block of electoral votes. But such victories were seldom secure; a few thousand votes either way often produced a different outcome next time. Two

34 William J. Cooper, Jr., *The South and the Politics of Slavery: 1828–1856* (Louisiana State University Press, 1978), pp. 370–1.
35 The five who were reelected were George Washington, Thomas Jefferson, James Madison, James Monroe, and Andrew Jackson. John Adams, John Quincy Adams, and Martin Van Buren ran for second terms but were defeated.

Table 4.1. *Presidential politics, 1836–52*

Candidate	Party	Popular votes Total	Popular votes %	Electoral votes Total	North	West	Border	South
1836		1,500,345	100.00	294	130	38	32	94
Martin Van Buren	Democrat	764,198	50.93	170	101	8	4	57
William H. Harrison	Whig	549,508	36.63	73	15	30	28	0
Hugh L. White	Whig	145,352	9.69	26	0	0	0	26
Daniel Webster	Whig	41,287	2.75	14	14	0	0	0
Person Magnum	Whig	—	—	11	0	0	0	11
1840		2,411,187	100.00	294	130	38	32	94
William H. Harrison	Whig	1,275,016	52.88	234	123	33	28	50
Martin Van Buren	Democrat	1,129,102	46.83	60	7	5	4	44
James Birney	Liberty	7,069	0.29	0	0	0	0	0
1841								
John Tyler[a]	Whig							
1844		2,698,605	100.00	275	112	49	30	84
James K. Polk	Democrat	1,337,243	49.55	170	77	26	7	60
Henry Clay	Whig	1,299,062	48.14	105	35	23	23	24
James Birney	Liberty	62,300	2.31	0	0	0	0	0
1848		2,871,906	100.00	290	112	57	30	91
Zachary Taylor	Whig	1,360,099	47.36	163	97	0	23	43
Lewis Cass	Democrat	1,220,544	42.50	127	15	57	7	48
Martin Van Buren	Free-Soil	291,263	10.14	0	0	0	0	0
1850								
Millard Fillmore[b]	Whig							
1852		3,157,326	99.59	296	110	66	32	88
Franklin Pierce	Democrat	1,601,274	50.72	254	92	66	20	76
Winfield Scott	Whig	1,386,580	43.92	42	18	0	12	12
John Hale	Free-Soil	156,667	4.96	0	0	0	0	0

Note: North: Connecticut, Maine, Massachusetts, New Hampshire, New York, New Jersey, Pennsylvania, Rhode Island, and Vermont; West: California, Illinois, Indiana, Iowa, Michigan, Minnesota, Ohio, Oregon, and Wisconsin; Border: Delaware, Kentucky, Maryland, and Missouri; South: Alabama, Arkansas, Florida, Georgia, Louisiana, Mississippi, North Carolina, South Carolina, Tennessee, Texas, and Virginia.

[a]Tyler became president upon Harrison's death, April 4, 1841.

[b]Fillmore became president upon Taylor's death, July 9, 1850.

occasions when there were enormous swings in electoral votes with relatively modest changes in the popular vote illustrate the point. In 1836 Democrat Van Buren got 170 electoral votes with 51 percent of the popular vote. Four years later, running against the same opponent, he received 47 percent of the popular vote, yet his electoral vote fell to only 60 (or 20 percent of the total). A similar turn-around occurred between the 1848 and 1852 elections, when the Whig party saw its electoral vote fall from 163 (for Zachary Taylor) to 42 (for Winfield Scott) despite a decline of less than 4 percentage points in the popular vote. Even though party loyalties were strong, population growth, together with occasional defections, produced a situation where neither party was able to establish any lasting regional loyalty over the entire period. The closeness of the elections would also tend to magnify the importance of an inflammatory issue such as slavery.

The region where this was most significant, of course, was the South. Both parties sought to nominate candidates who would tolerate the South's "peculiar institution" and at the same time urge national unity. But it was Democrats who most assiduously cultivated the Southern vote, and the significance of the South to the Democrats is immediately apparent in Table 4.1. In every election, the South delivered at least 44 electoral votes to the Democratic candidate, and only once – in 1840, when Van Buren narrowly lost the region to Harrison – did the Democrats fail to carry the South.

The political clout of the South in presidential elections was magnified by the infamous "three-fifths rule." Because its apportionment in Congress was weighted by a fraction of the nonvoting slave population, an electoral vote in the South represented less than half the number of eligible voters compared with the situation in the Northeast.[36] Consequently, the southern share of electoral votes remained at about 30 percent despite the fact that the free population of the North grew at a rate twice that of the South. By courting the South, Democrats were able, in effect, to gain political leverage in the national elections.

Events of history are not entirely the product of unseen "forces" that produce inevitable results. If, as we have argued, the office of the president is important, then it must have made some difference who held the office over this period. The presidents who presided between Andrew

---

36   An obvious measure of regional representation in the electoral college is the number of popular votes cast for each electoral vote. In 1836 there were 2,989 votes cast for each electoral vote in the South, which was less than half the 6,423 votes cast for each electoral vote in the free states of the North and the West. In 1860 the relative situation was about the same; 9,705 votes cast per electoral vote in the South compared with 18,639 in the West and North.

Jackson and Abraham Lincoln – Martin Van Buren, William Henry Harrison, John Tyler, James Polk, Zachary Taylor, Millard Fillmore, Franklin Pierce, and James Buchanan – are familiar names only because of an American penchant for naming our streets and public schools for presidents. Yet these men presided at a crucial period of our history. Each of them had to wrestle with the divisiveness created by the issue of slavery. Apart from the two who died in office, each of them found their political careers virtually destroyed by their tenure in the White House.

Martin Van Buren took over the leadership of the Democratic party upon the retirement of Andrew Jackson. Although economic events, not slavery, were the prime factor in Van Buren's inability to get reelected in 1840, the issue of Texas loomed on the horizon throughout his administration.[37] As president, Van Buren opposed annexation of Texas because of the sectional tensions that admission of a large slave territory was sure to create. After his retirement from the presidency in 1841, he remained active in politics and became increasingly outspoken on the question of slavery. He sought to find a middle ground that was no longer there. Always conciliatory toward the South, yet opposed to the expansion of slavery into the new territories, his efforts were viewed with suspicion and criticized in both the North and the South.

Van Buren's experience with the slave issue was a harbinger of things to come: Each of the men who followed him into the White House found that there was, in fact, no middle ground for the president on the slave issue. They were caught between competing interests and ideologies that saw any accommodation with the other side as nothing short of treason.

John Tyler of Virginia was not elected president; he assumed the office in April, 1841, when the newly elected president – William Henry Harrison – died after only thirty-one days in office. The Whigs had won the election of 1840 by drawing a substantial number of new voters to the polls to vote for a man who was viewed as a military hero. This tactic not only elected a Whig president, but wrested control of both the House and Senate from the Democrats as well.[38] The strategy backfired, however, when Harrison suddenly died and the Whigs found themselves with a

37 In 1837 there was a severe financial panic that was followed by a more general economic collapse in 1839. After twelve years of strident rhetoric on banks, tariffs, and economic policy, the Democrats were unable to escape blame for the economic catastrophe. For an account of the depression of 1839–43, see Douglass C. North, *The Economic Growth of the United States, 1790–1860* (Prentice-Hall, 1961); for an analysis of the impact of the depression on Van Buren's presidency, see Wilson, *The Presidency of Martin Van Buren,* chap. 3.

38 The Whigs controlled 133 seats in the House compared with 102 for the Democrats. In the Senate the Whigs had 28 while the Democrats had 22. The legislative majority was short-lived; Democrats regained control of the House in the off-year elections in 1842 and the Senate in 1844.

president who was far from the mainstream of the party on the two most important issues of the day: chartering a new federal bank, and the annexation of Texas. Over the objections of his cabinet and the Whig leaders in Congress, Tyler vetoed a bill in August 1841 that would have chartered a new federal bank. The veto created an irreparable split between Tyler and the rest of his party.[39] Having broken with his own party over the bank bill, Tyler revealed himself to be a narrow partisan championing his view of the southern cause. A slaveholder who deeply believed in westward expansion, Tyler proceeded to use every device available to him as president to pursue his goal of bringing Texas into the Union.

The Whigs had never intended to see John Tyler become president. In fact, Tyler was far closer to the Democrats on the issues of a federal bank and the annexation of Texas than he was to members of his own party. The unexpected turn of events that made him president had implications far beyond the 1844 presidential election. Historian William Cooper claims that "John Tyler had more influence on southern politics than any other southern politician between Andrew Jackson and the demise of the second party system. . . . By fundamentaliｙ altering the pattern of the 1844 campaign, Tyler guaranteed the continued supremacy of the politics of slavery in the South."[40]

The man who benefited the most from all this was James K. Polk, an obscure politician from Tennessee who capitalized upon the disarray in the Whig party to win the presidency in 1844. The last years of the 1840s were heady times for Americans, and Polk epitomized that exuberance and confidence that came to be known as "Manifest Destiny." Judged by his own goals, his administration was a stunning success. The annexation of Texas was completed; the dispute with Mexico resulted in a treaty whereby the United States gained California and New Mexico; and the dispute with England over Oregon was negotiated in a manner favorable to the United States without recourse to war. The policy succeeded because, despite critics who decried both his aims and his tactics, a majority of Americans – North and South – favored the acquisition of territories that would stretch the boundaries of the United States from the Atlantic to the Pacific.

39 Whig leaders put together a revised bank bill, which the president again vetoed. Five cabinet members, including the secretary of the Treasury, resigned in protest over the veto, and relations between the president and Whig leaders in Congress were never restored. The depth of the rift between the president and his own party is shown by the fact that over the next three years, eight cabinet nominations forwarded by Tyler were rejected by the Whig-controlled Senate, along with one Supreme Court nominee.

40 Cooper, *The South and the Politics of Slavery*, p. 176. Cooper's claim that Tyler has been ignored by historians is supported by the fact that there are no biographies that deal with his presidency in depth.

For all his success, Polk entered the final year of his presidency an embattled figure. Critics objected not only to the objectives of his administration, but to the way in which he used intrigue and secret diplomacy to attain his ends. Shortly after the end of hostilities with Mexico, Alexander Stephens, then a Whig in the House of Representatives, observed on the floor of Congress that "if a man were ambitious of acquiring a reputation for duplicity and equivocation, he could not select a better example in all history than to follow in the footsteps of our President."[41] Polk's greatest accomplishment – the acquisition of California from Mexico – ultimately produced a national crisis of monumental proportions. Polk died of ill health shortly after leaving office. It was left to Polk's successors to reap the whirlwind that his policy had sown.

The acquisition of Texas and then the Mexican Territory in quick succession propelled slavery to the forefront of the political scene as the elections of 1848 approached. The issue had been sharpened by the Wilmot Proviso, which made it more difficult for anyone seeking the presidency to avoid taking a stand on the issue of slavery in the West. The Democrats nominated Lewis Cass of Michigan, a man who strongly opposed the Wilmot Proviso and argued that people in the various territories should decide for themselves whether slavery would be allowed in their territories. In 1848 such an idea was novel, but it had little appeal outside of the West. The Whigs nominated Zachary Taylor, a hero of the recent war with Mexico. Publicizing his success in the Mexican War, Whig leaders convinced their candidate to say as little as possible about slavery. This allowed Whig supporters in the South to point to the fact that he was from Louisiana and had been a slaveholder, while in the North Whigs managed to get some antislave supporters to assure voters that the general did not favor the extension of slavery into the territories. The strategy worked; Taylor and his running mate, Millard Fillmore of New York, defeated Cass in an election that was extremely close. The only region that went solidly for Cass was his home area of the Midwest.

Although the Whigs could celebrate their victory, there were troubling signs that all was not well with their party in 1848. Martin Van Buren, running as the candidate of the Free-Soil party, which strongly opposed the expansion of slavery, polled over 10 percent of the total popular vote, with considerable strength in the Northeast and several western states.[42] Van Buren's strong showing did not bode well for either of the two major parties. Democrats, with their strength in the South, would be hard pressed to bring back a group of defectors who clearly opposed slave

---

41 Quoted in Merk, *Manifest Destiny*, p. 106.
42 Although he won no electoral votes, Van Buren got 16.3 percent of the total popular vote in the North. In four states – Massachusetts, New York, Vermont, and Wisconsin – he received at least 25 percent of the popular vote.

interests. Whigs faced an equally difficult challenge of capturing these votes without shattering the fragile coalition that had produced the narrow presidential victory of 1848. Illustrative of the Whigs' problem was the fact that they were unable to win control of either house of Congress in 1848, and the party lost still more ground in the off-year elections two years later.[43]

Almost as soon as Taylor took office the question of whether California should be admitted as a free state became a pressing problem. In a move characteristic of his military background, Taylor chose to confront the issue directly by favoring the admission of California, while at the same time proposing the formation of a new territory in the Southwest that might someday become a slave state. His proposal brought forth widespread criticism. Despite the furor his proposal caused, Taylor refused to back away from his unequivocal support for California statehood with no strings attached. Southerners were indignant, and at one point, the possibility that southern states might secede came up in a meeting with Taylor. The president reacted with great anger, stating that he would personally take the field against any such "insurrection."[44]

Taylor's intransigence on the question of any "compromise" on the issue of statehood for California threatened congressional efforts to find some solution without a presidential veto. The impasse was finally broken not by compromise, but by the sudden death of the president, who became seriously ill following an Independence Day celebration and died five days later. Millard Fillmore took the oath of office on July 10, 1850.

Zachary Taylor's death raises interesting questions. How would the impasse between the president and Congress have been resolved had Taylor survived? Commenting on Taylor's resolve not to give in to pressures for compromise, historian David Potter offers an interesting speculation:

---

43 Neither party won control of the House in 1848. The Democrats had 111 seats to 105 for the Whigs, with 13 seats going to Free-Soilers. In the Senate, Democrats held a more substantial 34 to 24 majority, with 2 seats held by Free-Soilers; see K. Jack Bauer, *Zachary Taylor: Soldier, Planter, Statesman of the Old Southwest* (Louisiana State University Press, 1985), p. 297. The elections of 1850 solidified the Democratic congressional power; they increased their majority in the Senate by 1 vote and their strength in the House rose to 140, compared with 88 for the Whigs.

44 Taylor's statement supposedly was made at a meeting at the White House involving the president and two of the leading Whig congressmen from the South: Robert Toombs and Alexander Stephens. Bauer places the date as February 23, 1849 (*Zachary Taylor*, pp. 302–4), but this date is disputed by Mark J. Stegmaier, "Zachary Taylor versus the Old South," *Civil War History* 33 (September 1987). There is no question, however, about the rift between Taylor and the southern Whigs. As Stegmaier notes, Taylor's "continued recalcitrance finally led Stephens and Toombs into an open opposition which threatened to diminish, if not destroy, whatever influence the president had over the southern wing of his own party" (p. 241).

One thing is clear, though frequently overlooked: Taylor had a definite and positive position. If he was correct in believing that the South would have yielded to a firm uncompromising attitude at this stage, before its separatist impulses had been hardened by a decade of contention, then the refusal of Congress to follow his policy cost the republic ten years of avoidable strife ending in a titanic Civil War. If he was wrong, his policy would have forced the North to face the supreme test of war for the Union before it had attained the preponderance of strength, or the technological sinews, or the conviction of national unity which enabled it to win the war that finally came in 1861.[45]

Whether the options were quite as threatening as Potter portrays them is open to question, but his point about the consequences of a firm stand by the president during this crisis is well taken. Taylor was prepared to force a showdown on the issue of slavery and secession. His unyielding stance in 1849 revealed once again the power of the presidency in such a crisis. Through the threat of a veto, which requires a two-thirds vote by Congress to overturn, a chief executive could effectively dictate the limits of any acceptable compromise sent forward by the Congress.

Crisis and Compromise: The Armistice of 1850

The situation facing the country in 1850 was not unlike that which had confronted Congress in 1820. The western territories acquired from Mexico required organization as free or slave territories, and the admission of the new state of California threatened to disrupt the delicate balance of free and slave states in Congress. Since the admission of Missouri and Maine in 1821, three free states (Michigan, Iowa, and Wisconsin) and two slave states (Arkansas and Texas) had been admitted to the Union. In addition two free territories (Oregon and Minnesota) had been organized. Now California wanted in as a free state. Southerners, concerned over the preponderance of free areas that would also be asking for statehood, sought some assurance that a portion of the large unorganized territory remaining from the Louisiana Purchase and the Mexican cession in 1848 would be open to slavery. An important part of this concern centered on the possibility that the western portions of Texas might be divided into one or two additional states, which presumably would enter the union as slave states. Opponents of slavery held to the Wilmot Proviso – that there be no slavery in the new areas.

Henry Clay, the man who was known as the "great pacifier" in recognition of his previous efforts at creating compromises on the slave issue, put together a package designed to gain enough support to carry both houses. Clay's Omnibus Bill was presented to the Senate on May 8, 1850.[46] The proposal addressed not only the question of statehood for California and territorial organization, but also the sensitive issues of fugitive slaves and slavery in the District of Columbia. Briefly stated, the Omnibus Bill would:

1. Admit California as a free state.
2. Establish boundaries for the state of Texas and have the United States government assume debts of Texas incurred during the Texan war against Mexico.[47]
3. Divide the area acquired from Mexico into a "Utah Territory" (roughly coinciding with the present-day states of Nevada, Utah, and part of Colorado) and a "New Mexico Territory" (roughly coinciding with the present-day states of Arizona and New Mexico).
4. Introduce a new and much more stringent Fugitive Slave Act, which would facilitate efforts of slave owners to reclaim slaves who had escaped to the free areas of the North.
5. Abolish the slave trade in the District of Columbia.

Clay had included something for everyone, yet he managed to please almost no one. On July 31, 1851, the Senate dismembered Clay's proposal piecemeal. The only part of the omnibus package that passed was a bill creating Utah as a territory. The old guard had failed; it was up to a new generation of leaders to fashion a compromise that would avoid bloodshed.

The man who would emerge as the clear "winner" from the congressional debates of 1850 was Stephen A. Douglas of Illinois. Douglas realized that, while all of the pieces necessary to form a compromise could not pass in a single bill, the five basic elements of Clay's Omnibus Bill might be successfully pushed through the two houses of Congress as individual bills. This tactic had worked thirty years earlier to produce the Compromise of 1820, and Douglas set out to repeat that accomplishment. That he succeeded in doing so is a testimony to his abilities as a politician and leader. Between July 31, when the Senate approved the bill creating the Utah Territory, and September 17, when the House approved the last of the five bills, Douglas and his allies put into law all of the provisions initially suggested by Clay. This accomplishment established Douglas as a leader who could offer the Democratic party an agenda for the 1850s that promised to resolve the squabble over slavery.

46   The discussion of this section draws heavily on the detailed discussion of Holman Hamilton, *Prologue to Conflict: The Crisis and Compromise of 1850* (Norton, 1964).
47   When Texas was admitted to the Union, it claimed the Rio Grande as its western boundary as far north as the Arkansas River. Most of this land was incorporated into the proposed territories of Utah and New Mexico.

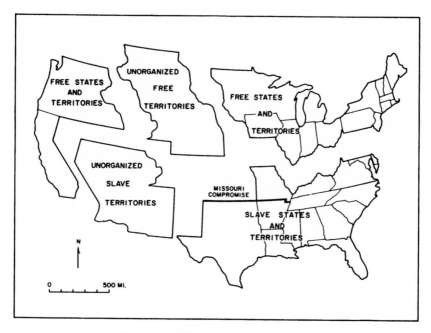

Map 4.1. The Compromise of 1850

In September 1850, the western territories of the United States had been reorganized as shown in the Map 4.1. One important feature of the compromise is that the status of the "unorganized" portion of the Louisiana Purchase, which had been excluded from slave settlement by the Compromise of 1820, was left unclear under the new law.

Unfortunately, although the operation was a great success, the patient died. The Compromise of 1820 had produced a lasting agreement on the question of slavery in the territory acquired through the Louisiana Purchase. The compromise fashioned by Douglas in 1850 failed to settle any of the major issues surrounding the territories acquired from Mexico, and actually reopened some issues settled by the agreement thirty years earlier. It was, as David Potter notes, not so much a "compromise" as an "armistice."[48]

The key votes in the package were the bill granting statehood to California, which was vital to the interests of the free states, and the passage of a new fugitive slave act, which was vital to the slave states. An exam-

48 Potter, *The Impending Crisis*, chap. 5.

Table 4.2. *Votes for California statehood and in favor of the Fugitive Slave Law in the Senate and the House of Representatives, 1850*

	California statehood			Fugitive Slave Law		
	For	Against	No vote	For	Against	No vote
Senate						
Total vote	34	18	8	27	12	21
By party						
Democratic	17	14	2	18	3	12
Whig	15	4	6	9	8	8
Other	2	0	0	0	1	1
By region						
Slave states	6	18	6	24	0	6
Free states	28	0	2	3	12	15
House of Representatives						
Total vote	150	56	17	109	76	38
By party						
Democratic	55	44	9	80	15	13
Whig	85	12	8	29	52	24
Other	10	0	0	0	9	1
By region						
Slave states	27	56	4	78	0	9
Free states	123	0	13	31	76	29

Source: Tabulated from data in Holman Hamilton, *Prologue to Conflict: The Crisis and Compromise of 1850* (Norton, 1966), appendix A.

ination of how the House of Representatives and the Senate voted reveals just how flawed the compromise really was. Table 4.2 presents the votes by party and by region on these two pivotal measures. The order in which the measures were taken up was crucial to the outcome, because the results of votes on one measure could have a decisive effect on the outcome of subsequent votes. All of the bills were acted on first in the Senate and then in the House. The vote on California in both houses preceded the vote on the Fugitive Slave Act.

Two overriding facts emerge from the table. First, both bills barely cleared their first hurdle – passage in the Senate. In fact, the Fugitive Slave Act failed to get an absolute majority in *either* the House or Senate. Second, most members voted according to regional interests, not party loyalty. Thus, no senator or congressman from free states voted against admission of California, and no senator or congressman from a slave state voted against the Fugitive Slave Act. Even after the California measure had cleared the Senate, the problem of convincing northern senators to vote for the Fugitive Slave Act remained. This was an extremely unpopular measure, and few Northerners – Democrat or Whig – were prepared to offer open support. To pass the act, Douglas and his allies prevailed upon northern senators to abstain on the Fugitive Slave Act vote. Fifteen free-state senators – including Stephen Douglas himself – abstained, and the law was enacted with only 27 favorable votes out of 60 possible votes. Once through the Senate, the major crisis was over, but a similar device had to be employed in the House, where 38 congressmen abstained on the Fugitive Slave Act vote. The act passed with only 109 favorable out of a 223 possible votes.

It is worth examining the pattern of votes in the House of Representatives in greater detail to search for clues to the nature of support or opposition for the compromise measure. Figures 4.1 and 4.2 present a breakdown according to four distinct "patterns" of votes by members on each of the five compromise measures. Table 4.3 presents the data in a tabular form.

The patterns are:

Strong Support includes members who did not vote against any of the compromise measures, although they might have abstained on either the Fugitive Slave Act or the measure abolishing slavery in the District of Columbia.

Strong Opposition includes those who basically rejected the compromise package, even though they voted for one or two measures. In the North this included those who voted *for* California statehood and the prohibition of slavery in the District of Columbia and *against* all the other measures; in the South this included those who voted *for* the Fugitive Slave Act and *against* all of the compromise measures.

Mixed or Weak Support: Any member not falling into one of the other two categories.

The results are revealing. Only twenty-eight congressmen, or 13 percent of all the House members, voted *in favor* of all five compromise

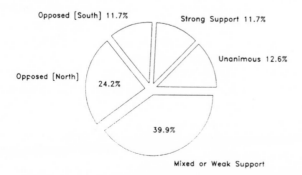

Figure 4.1. Support for the Compromise of 1850 in the House of Representatives

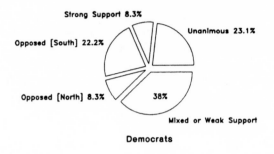

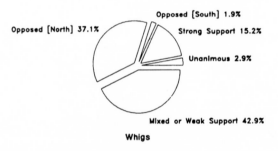

Figure 4.2. Support for the Compromise of 1850 in the House of Representatives
by political party

measures. If we add to those "unanimous supporters" the other members
who did not vote *against* any measure, then the total who "strongly
supported" the compromise package was fifty-four congressmen – just
over a quarter of the whole House. By contrast, eighty members, or more
than one-third of the House, strongly *opposed* the compromise package
from either a northern perspective or a southern perspective.

That party loyalty was *not* a determining factor in the overall voting
patterns is clear. A comparison of the support from each party presented
in Figure 4.2 with the aggregate voting pattern of Figure 4.1 shows that
each party provided roughly similar levels of support and opposition. If,
however, we look at both the *region* and *party affiliation* of each member, a very pronounced pattern quickly emerges. Opposition to the treaty
came from northern and western Whigs (thirty-nine strongly opposed
and only five strongly in favor) on the one hand, and southern Democrats
(twenty-four strongly opposed and only three strongly in favor) on the
other. Support for the compromise package came primarily from north-

Table 4.3. *Support for the Compromise of 1850 in the House of Representatives by region*

	North	West	Border	South	Total
All parties	89	47	22	65	223
Strong support	21	12	11	10	54
Unanimous	14	11	1	2	28
Except D.C.	0	0	10	8	18
Except Fugitive Slave	7	1	0	0	8
Weak or mixed support	32	17	11	29	89
Strong opposition	36	18	0	26	80
Democrat	21	30	12	45	108
Strong support	15	12	4	3	34
Unanimous	13	11	1	0	25
Except D.C.	0	0	3	3	6
Except Fugitive Slave	2	1	0	0	3
Weak or mixed support	3	12	8	18	41
Strong opposition	3	6	0	24	33
Whig	63	12	10	20	105
Strong support	5	0	7	7	19
Unanimous	1	0	0	2	3
Except D.C.	0	0	7	5	12
Except Fugitive Slave	4	0	0	0	4
Weak or mixed support	28	3	3	11	45
Strong opposition	30	9	0	2	41
Other parties	5	5	0	0	10
Strong support	1	0	0	0	1
Strong opposition	3	3	0	0	6
Weak or mixed support	1	2	0	0	3

Notes: North: Connecticut, Maine, Massachusetts, New Hampshire, New York, New Jersey, Pennsylvania, Rhode Island, and Vermont; West: California, Illinois, Indiana, Iowa, Michigan, Minnesota, Ohio, Oregon, and Wisconsin; Border: Delaware, Kentucky, Maryland, and Missouri; South: Alabama, Arkansas, Florida, Georgia, Louisiana, Mississippi, North Carolina, South Carolina, Tennessee, Texas, and Virginia.

Strong support: did not vote *against* any of the compromise measures; unanimous: voted in favor of all five compromise measures; except D.C.: voted for all compromise measures but *abstained* on the measure prohibiting slavery in the District of Columbia; except Fugitive Slave: voted for all compromise measures but *abstained* on the Fugitive Slave Act; strong opposition: in the North voting *for* California admission and the prohibition of slavery in the District of Columbia, but in the South voting *against* all of the compromise measures *except* for the Fugitive Slave Act; mixed or weak support: patterns of voting not falling into one of the other categories.

Source: Tabulated from data in Holman Hamilton, *Prologue to Conflict: The Crisis and Compromise of 1850* (Norton, 1966), appendix A.

ern and western Democrats (fifteen supporting and only three strongly opposed) and southern or border Whigs (fourteen supporting and only two strongly opposed).

The implication of this voting pattern on party structure is obvious.

The votes on the compromise measure split each party into distinct sectional factions that were at odds with each other. Southern Whigs sought a middle ground on slavery at the same time that their northern counterparts were strongly resisting compromise measures. Southern Democrats had no interest in compromise, which had become the cornerstone of the Democratic party in the North and the West. The large fraction of members falling into the "mixed or weak support" group attests to the fact that neither of the two extreme groups was strong enough to press for a showdown in 1850. Consequently, a compromise of sorts was possible. But it was seriously flawed because the package had no support from those who really mattered – the two factions with conflicting agendas regarding slavery. Southerners allowed another free state into the Union (although most of them voted against it), and Northerners agreed not to block passage of the proposed Fugitive Slave Act (although most of them opposed it). Consequently, the final result pleased no one. That, of course, is the nature of legislative compromises. But when the difference between the compromising groups is as deep-seated as that between slave and antislave forces was in 1850, the basis for serious dispute remains. The person caught in the middle of this situation was the president of the United States, who was charged with the task of enforcing the terms of the laws passed by Congress in the fall of 1850.

During the 1840s the presidency had been at the center of the disputes over territory and slavery. Although their policies were at times very controversial, John Tyler, James Polk, and Zachary Taylor each had exercised a firm leadership that shaped national policy. Millard Fillmore, who inherited the presidency upon Zachary Taylor's death, was in almost every respect the opposite of his predecessors in the White House. A seasoned politician who was inclined to accept compromise rather than force confrontation, he quickly let it be known that the new president was receptive to the possibility of compromise on the California issue. By the end of 1850 he had signed all five measures and in December of that year he sent Congress a message urging them to regard these measures as a "final settlement" of the slavery issue.

Did this produce a groundswell of support for the man who had averted a constitutional crisis? No, it did not. Unfortunately for Fillmore, the task of enforcing the various parts of the compromise package quickly made him unpopular.[49] Although he had been ambivalent about seeking a second term when he inherited the presidency in 1849, Fillmore had decided by the fall of 1852 to seek reelection. His bid was not successful,

---

49 Fillmore's problems with the compromise are spelled out in Benson Lee Grayson, *The Unknown President: The Administration of President Millard Fillmore* (University Press of America, 1981), pp. 64–70.

in large measure because of the enmity incurred as a result of his actions as a president committed to uphold laws that were very unpopular in various sections of the country.

In the presidential election of 1852 the Whigs sought to repeat their successes of 1840 and 1848 by turning to a military hero – General Winfield Scott. The Democrats responded by nominating a general of their own: Franklin D. Pierce of New Hampshire. In a campaign noted for its absence of any substantive discussion of issues, Pierce and the Democrats trounced the Whigs in every region of the country. Some viewed the Democratic victory of 1852 as evidence that the country was tired of controversy over slavery and consequently supported the more moderate position of the Democrats regarding the issue. The success of Pierce in winning all the electoral votes in the West, which in the 1840s had voted Whig on several occasions, seemed to confirm this notion. Lewis Cass had taken all 57 electoral votes in 1848, but he was a native son. Pierce, a New Englander with no perceptible identification on the slave issue, accomplished the same feat in 1852.

The Compromise of 1850 was the last gasp of the "second-party system" that had begun with the formation of the Whig party in the 1820s. Badly beaten in the 1852 election, the Whigs never again offered a candidate for the presidency. The political parties of the 1830s and 1840s, which had worked well in dealing with quarrels over banks, internal improvements, and tariffs, were not able to deal with the divisive sectional split created by slavery. A country weary of crisis gave Pierce and the Democrats an overwhelming vote of confidence in the election of 1852. Neither Scott nor Pierce had any appreciable following among his own party; each was a compromise chosen over stronger leaders who would have alienated one wing or another of the two parties.

The voting patterns behind the compromise measures provide a better guide to the political future than the apparent consensus election of Pierce. By the fall of 1850 it was clear that the alignment of political parties in the United States was undergoing drastic changes. The ideological splits over slavery in each of the two parties meant that no single group controlled a powerful enough block of votes to ensure passage of its agenda. A coalition of at least two groups was required to enact any significant changes. In 1850, such a coalition, composed of moderates from both parties, had prevailed to enact the compromise. The challenge facing moderate leaders was how to keep the more radical elements of their party sufficiently placated to avoid defections in the future. To appreciate the magnitude of that challenge, we need only look at Figure 4.3, which presents a breakdown of members of Congress by party and regional affiliation elected to the Thirty-first Congress in the fall of 1850.

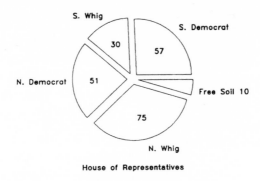

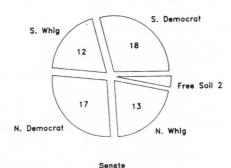

Figure 4.3. Party affiliation of members of Congress elected in 1850 by region

Perhaps the most obvious portent of the changing times was the election of twelve members of the Free-Soil party.

Democrats would seem to have the easier task, inasmuch as a middle-of-the-road policy toward slavery had been the cornerstone of Democratic politics since the time of Jackson and Van Buren. Successful though this policy had been, it was becoming increasingly difficult to sustain. Whigs from the South, not southern Democrats, provided the needed support to pass the compromise measures in the summer of 1850. Outspoken in their denunciations of the compromise package, the more radical southern Democrats were already looking toward secession as a means to "solve" the slave issue. Despite the rhetoric, events of 1849–50 had clearly shown that the southern wing of the Democratic party was not yet strong enough to break away from their northern comrades.

So long as the Democrats controlled the White House, the two wings of the party would find it in their interest to maintain a coalition at the national level. The best hope for this, of course, was to keep the slavery issue as far in the background as possible. The Democratic leaders clearly understood this point. The platform adopted by the party at its convention in the fall of 1852 stated that the party "will abide by and adhere to a faithful execution of the acts known as the compromise measures settled by the last Congress." In addition, the platform urged Democrats to "resist all attempts at renewing, in Congress or out of it, the agitation of the slavery question."[50] In 1852 that strategy worked well. The furor over the compromise had, indeed, calmed down, and an electorate weary of disputes over slavery was ready to accept the advice of those who asked that the compromise measures be given a chance to work. Franklin Pierce, the Democratic nominee, was elected president by an overwhelming margin and the Democrats regained substantial majorities in both the House and the Senate. The party seemed to have put its house back in order. There was, to be sure, some disquieting evidence that party unity was more fragile than the electoral support might suggest. Pierce, who was a political nonentity, had obtained the nomination only after two more prominent leaders – Stephen Douglas and James Buchanan – had created a deadlock that was finally broken on the ninth ballot. The rivalry of these two men would pose problems for the Democrats for the remainder of the decade.

Whigs faced a far more formidable task in maintaining their national unity. A majority of northern Whigs voted against the Compromise of 1850 and were becoming increasingly inflexible on the slavery issue. To them, both the strident position of the southern Democrats and the compromise measures of the northern wing of that party were now unacceptable. This put the southern wing of the Whig party in an untenable position. The primacy of the slave issue in southern politics meant that no politician from that region could openly join forces with antislave advocates from the North and remain politically alive. Their own party offered no real alternative, and the "compromise" position on slavery had already been preempted by the moderate wing of the Democratic party. The result was that the Whig party ceased to be an effective political force in the South. Unable to maintain an effective coalition at the national level, the party had disappeared from the American political scene by 1856.

The implication of this ideological split within each party was that each party was compelled to nominate a moderate candidate if it hoped

50 Reproduced in Silbey, *The Transformation of American Politics, 1840–1860*, p. 75.

to win the White House. But once in office, the "moderate" president was compelled to deal with the radical leaders who frequently dominated the debates in Congress. The situation was inherently instable, and the party structure that had governed presidential politics in the United States since the late 1820s was rapidly collapsing. This brought up an alarming possibility: What if one of the more extreme wings gained control of the White House?

The answer would not be long in coming.

Appendix Table

Table A.4.1. *Party affiliation in Congress by region, 1850*

Party	South	North	Total
House of Representatives			
Democrat	57	51	108
Whig	30	75	105
Free-Soil	0	10	10
Total	87	136	223
Senate			
Democrat	18	17	35
Whig	12	13	25
Free-Soil	0	2	2
Total	30	32	62

Source: Tabulated from data in Holman Hamilton, *Prologue to Conflict: The Crisis and Compromise of 1850* (Norton, 1966), appendix A.

5

The Politics of Compromise

A gigantic fraud has been committed in the name of slavery, which has aroused a keen sense of wrong, and filled the dullest understandings with apprehensions for our future liberties. The Kansas–Nebraska bill – which repealed the Missouri Compromise, sprung like a trap, as it was, upon a Congress not chosen in reference to it; hurried through the forms of legislation, under whip and spur, by a temporary majority; alleging a falsehood in its very terms, and having the seizure of a vast province, secured to freedom by thirty years of plighted faith, as its motive – was the fatal signal which, after astounding the nation by its audacity, rallied it to battle.

Parke Godwin, 1856[1]

The demise of the Whig party following the presidential election of 1852 created an enormous vacuum in the American political scene. For two decades, Whigs and Democrats had vied for the presidency, each with some degree of success. Now there was only one truly national party: the Democrats. But even that solidarity was illusory. No party could maintain any consistent degree of unity in the face of the slave issue. In the early 1850s no politician could avoid taking *some* stand on the question of slavery and the territories. The situation created by the Compromise of 1850 allowed three broad stances that politicians could offer the voters when asked about slavery and the West.[2]

According to *The Free-Soil Doctrine,* it was the duty of Congress to prevent any further expansion of slavery in the West. The most outspoken proponent of this doctrine was Salmon Chase of Ohio, a former Democrat who represented the Free-Soil party in the Senate from 1848 to 1854. Although a relatively small group in the late 1840s, Free-Soilers posed a serious threat to both major parties. Their enthusiastic support of the Wilmot Proviso in 1846 proved to be a decisive factor in the Democratic defeat of 1848, when Martin Van Buren bolted the Democratic party and garnered 10 percent of the presidential vote as the Free-Soil candidate. Free-Soilers also exacerbated the split in the Whig party

1 Parke Godwin, *Political Essays* (Dix Edwards, 1856), pp. 254–5.
2 An excellent discussion of these "doctrines" can be found in Robert R. Russel, "Constitutional Doctrines with Regard to Slavery in the Territories," *Journal of Southern History* 32 (November 1966).

over slavery. Men such as William Seward of New York insisted that no further concessions should be made that might allow slavery in the territories. By the mid-1850s the Free-Soil doctrine had become the rallying cry of dissident northern Democrats and Whigs who were adamantly opposed to slavery. Southern Whigs, of course, were extremely discomfited by a policy that obviously undermined the position of men such as Alexander Stephens and Robert Toombs of Georgia, who sought a middle ground on the slavery issue. Eventually, the Free-Soil position would become a part of the Republican platform of 1856 and 1860.

Supporters of *The States' Rights Doctrine*, the Southern counterpart to the Free-Soilers, insisted that the federal government had no authority whatever to rule on the question of slavery in the territories. The most outspoken advocate of this position was John C. Calhoun of South Carolina, who opposed both the Compromises of 1820 and 1850 on these grounds. Although support for the states' rights position was concentrated in the plantation regions of the deep South, Calhoun played a very prominent and visible role in the Democratic administration of James Polk, and his states' rights supporters were also able to secure posts in the Pierce administration. With Calhoun's death in 1849, leadership of this group fell to Calhoun's fellow South Carolinian Robert Barnwell Rhett together with William Yancey of Alabama and John Quitman of Mississippi.

The Doctrine of Popular Sovereignty was first articulated by Lewis Cass in the presidential election campaign of 1848. Its basic tenet was that the question of slavery should be decided by those living in the territories. By conveniently finessing the issue of whether there was some inherent right to allow or prohibit slavery, the notion of popular or "squatter's" sovereignty had a simplistic appeal to the many voters in both the North and the South who viewed either of the first two doctrines as too extreme. The champion of popular sovereignty was Stephen A. Douglas of Illinois, who made the concept the cornerstone of his compromise measures in 1850. There was, however, one serious political liability associated with the concept of popular sovereignty when applied to the unsettled areas of the Louisiana Territory: It negated the agreement established by the Missouri Compromise of 1820. A rather large area of the Louisiana Purchase remained unsettled in 1850. Thirty years earlier Thomas Jefferson had warned of the danger of fixing a line that coincided with a "moral and political principle." Now what he had feared had come to pass. To those opposed to slavery, changing that line would be an egregious breach of faith on the part of those seeking to overturn the earlier agreement. If the Compromise of 1820 had no lasting force, what importance should one attach to the proposals being debated in Congress in 1850?

The Kansas–Nebraska Act: Overturning the Missouri Compromise

Stephen Douglas and his allies understood the dangers in overturning the Missouri Compromise. They had carefully avoided the issue in 1850 by remaining silent on the question of slavery in unorganized portions of the Louisiana Purchase. But that was clearly only a temporary solution; the territory had to be organized soon, and slave interests made it clear that they considered the Nebraska Territory to be a test case for the newly established policy of popular sovereignty. By 1853 the issue could no longer be avoided and debate on the organization of a Kansas–Nebraska Territory began. A second problem with popular sovereignty immediately became apparent. Far from defusing the slavery issue by making it a "local" decision, the debate over slavery in the unorganized area of the Louisiana Purchase once again catapulted the slave issue to the forefront of national politics. The consequences would be disastrous for both of the major political parties.

Douglas would have gladly let the issue of slavery and the organization of new territories sit quietly on the sidelines were it not for the pressures of a relatively new force in American politics: the competition for railroad lines to the West. The late 1840s and 1850s had been a period of frenetic construction of railroads. By 1853 at least four roads were on the verge of completing "trunk lines" from the east coast to the tier of states just west of the Mississippi River. The next step was a giant one: to leap across the "great American Desert" and the Rocky Mountains to California and the Pacific Coast. Everyone knew that a transcontinental railroad could not be built without some form of financial support from Congress. To get that support, two great issues had to be resolved. The first involved the dispersal of government lands to railroads and settlers as an inducement to construction of the roads and the settlement of the regions west of the Mississippi. The second was to determine the route to be followed by the first transcontinental line. Both issues brought forward regional rivalries that made any political settlement difficult at best. But before that issue could be tackled, Congress had to organize the Nebraska Territory.[3]

3 On the construction of railroads in this period, see George Rogers Taylor, *The Trans-portation Revolution, 1815–1860* (Holt, Rinehart and Winston, 1951); Carter Good-rich, *Government Promotion of American Canals and Railroads* (Columbia University

There was a large area of land between the Mississippi and the western coast that remained unorganized by any of the previous acts of Congress. Map 4.1 shows the situation as it existed in the early 1850s. The northern half of this area – what today comprises the states of Montana, Wyoming, and the Dakotas – was either too arid or mountainous to be valued for settlement in 1850. The southern third of the territory, which lay due west of Missouri, was coveted by both slave and free settlers. It was also directly astride the major rail routes to the West. This region attracted the attention of Douglas and his railroad friends in early 1854.

Seldom has the old adage "haste makes waste" proved so true as in the consideration of a bill to organize the territory of Kansas–Nebraska in the winter of 1854. Stephen Douglas had for many years publicly favored organizing the area as a free territory in accordance with the principles of the Missouri Compromise. As we noted earlier, he had carefully avoided raising the issue of slavery in the unorganized Kansas–Nebraska Territory while shaping the Compromise of 1850. Suddenly, on January 4, 1854, he abandoned this position and introduced an act to organize the territory of Kansas–Nebraska applying the same language with regard to slavery as that employed earlier in the Utah and New Mexico acts. After some further consultation with southern senators, he modified his bill to reflect the principle of popular sovereignty.[4] He then devoted his considerable energy toward getting his bill passed through Congress as quickly as possible.

Why the haste? Douglas, like many of his colleagues in Congress, had a personal as well as a political interest in seeing that the construction of a railroad to the western coast be undertaken as expeditiously as possible, preferably from a point that would favor Illinois interests. In 1850 he had been one of several politicians behind the passage of a bill pioneering subsequent government aid to railroads by granting large blocks of land to the Illinois Central Railroad.[5] Now he had even grander ambitions

Press, 1960); and Frederick L. Paxson, "The Railroads of the Old Northwest before the Civil War," *Wisconsin Academy of Science, Arts, and Letters* 15, pt. 1 (1914). On railroads and the politics of the Nebraska Act, see Allan Nevins, *Ordeal of the Union* (Charles Scribners and Sons, 1947), 2: chap. 6; and David M. Potter, *The Impending Crisis: 1848–1861* (Harper Torchbooks, 1976), chap. 7.

4   The language proposed in the initial bill stated that the new territory would be admitted to the union "with or without slavery, as their constitution may prescribe at the time of their admission." Several days later the bill was amended to read "that all questions pertaining to slavery . . . are to be left to the people residing therein, through their appropriate representatives" (Nevins, *Ordeal of the Union*, 2: 94–5.

5   The Illinois Central was the first railroad to receive substantial assistance from the federal government in the form of land grants along the route of the road. In this case, the route paralleled the Mississippi River from Cairo, Illinois, south to New Orleans. See Taylor, *The Transportation Revolution*, and Goodrich, *Government Promotion of American Canals and Railroads*.

that required that the new territory be organized. But territorial organization was a thorny issue. Douglas was aware that a bill to organize the Kansas–Nebraska Territory had been defeated in the previous session, largely because of southern opposition. Now southern Democrats in the Senate, led by David Atcheson of Missouri, insisted that the question of slavery in the new territory be reopened. Convinced that southern support for his bill was essential, Douglas wrote his bill to allow slavery in the new territory.

It may be that Douglas was not so cynical; perhaps he simply believed that he could finesse the slavery problem by proposing "popular sovereignty." In itself, this was a serious political miscalculation, which Douglas then compounded by agreeing to accept an amendment to his original bill that explicitly repealed the Missouri Compromise. Archibald Dixon, a Whig senator from Kentucky, convinced him that this would allow southern Whigs to support Douglas's bill enthusiastically. Dixon's amendment was, in fact, the brainchild of William Seward, who had no intention of supporting Douglas's bill. Seward reasoned, correctly as it turned out, that outright *repeal* of the Missouri Compromise would be doubly offensive to the moderate Northerners opposing slavery.[6] With southern support assured, the Kansas–Nebraska bill passed the Senate on March 4, 1854, by a vote of 37 to 14. The House was more recalcitrant, but eventually passed the bill on May 22, 1854, by a vote of 113 to 100. Thanks to the Dixon amendment, Southern Whigs supported the measure. Indeed, only nine congressmen from the South voted against the bill. Northern Whigs and Free-Soilers opposed the bill, as did almost one-half the northern Democrats.[7] Douglas had his victory, but at what cost? In retrospect the price seems very high indeed.

That the Kansas–Nebraska bill was a political miscalculation of massive proportions is beyond dispute. Alan Nevins labeled the entire episode a "disaster"; David Potter termed the act "the apex of futility"; Michael Holt thought it a "serious miscalculation"; and William Gienapp regarded it as "one of the most fateful measures ever approved by Congress."[8] As these writers point out, the act had a result that was completely opposite from what was intended. Far from strengthening the two parties, the act inflicted irreparable damage on both. Nor did it take

6 Nevins provides a full account of the arguments used to persuade Douglas to accept the Dixon amendment (*Ordeal of the Union*, 2: 92). Seward's role is also highlighted in the account by William E. Gienapp, *The Origins of the Republican Party, 1852–1856* (Oxford University Press, 1987), p. 70.
7 The votes are reported by Gienapp, *Origins of the Republican Party*, p. 78.
8 Nevins, *Ordeal of the Union*, 2: chap. 3; Potter, *The Impending Crisis*, p. 173; Michael Holt, *The Political Crisis of the 1850's* (W. W. Norton, 1978), p. 148; and Gienapp, *Origins of the Republican Party*, p. 83.

long for the effects of the acts to be apparent. Reaction in the North over the repeal of the Missouri Compromise was explosive. Speeches and editorials following the passage of the act attacked Douglas's motives as well as his political leadership. Perhaps the most ironic outcome was the plight of the southern Whigs. They had hoped to generate some political capital through their support of the repeal of the Missouri Compromise. But the vituperative outbursts of northern Whigs so offended most people of the South that the label "Whig" became a political liability almost anywhere south of the Mason–Dixon Line.

Yet, for all its faults, and there were many, the Kansas–Nebraska Act represented an attempt to compromise on the question of extending slavery to the West. Popular sovereignty was the closest thing to a middle ground on which any agreement might be reached by the contesting groups. Earlier compromises in 1787 and 1820 had been fashioned by offering both sides enough territory in which to pursue their separate development. But by 1854 the United States no longer had vast areas of unorganized land that could be divided among competing groups to maintain territorial balance.[9] Popular sovereignty offered a possible way to resolve the problem of which group got the land, and Douglas's attempt to apply this to the Kansas–Nebraska Territory was, in a sense, an experiment that would determine whether the concept could work. He was confident that the furor his bill stirred up would be short-lived. "The storm will soon spend its fury," Douglas wrote to a colleague shortly after passage of the bill, "and the people of the North will sustain the measure as they come to understand it."[10] Nor was this optimism wholly without foundation. Particularly in the western states, where interest in a compromise solution on the western land issue remained strong, Douglas expected growing support as time went on.[11] Popular sovereignty, he insisted, would work.

With the benefit of hindsight we know that it did not work, and the reasons for its failure are apparent enough. The basic premise behind

---

9 As noted in Chapter 3, much has been made of the fact that there were huge areas of land that were not "settled" in 1860. In this *economic* sense land was still quite abundant. At issue here was the question of who will control territory for *future* settlement by slave or free farmers.

10 Letter from Douglas to Howell Cobb of Georgia, April 2, 1854; cited in Gienapp, *Origins of the Republican Party*, p. 79.

11 William Gienapp, who is generally critical of Douglas's handling of the Nebraska question, concedes that Douglas's optimism was "not without foundation," and notes the possibility of support for the measure from western congressmen (*Origins of the Republican Party*, pp. 78–81). David Potter credits Douglas with being opposed to slavery; his criticism of the Nebraska bill is that it "contaminated" popular sovereignty by attaching it to a bill that opened up a previously closed area for a new vote on slavery (*The Impending Crisis*, p. 173).

popular sovereignty requires that the competing groups be willing to coexist under whatever arrangement is agreed upon. It also requires that people outside the region are willing to accept the outcome of the local determination. Neither of these premises was valid for the determination of slavery in the Kansas–Nebraska Territory. For a variety of reasons, some of which we explored in Chapter 3, slave and free settlers were unable to live peaceably with each other. Nor were people in neighboring states willing to remain disinterested spectators to the drama. Slave and nonslave groups in the South and North felt they had strong vested interest in the outcome of the popular sovereignty of western territories. This proved ultimately to be the fatal flaw in the idea of popular sovereignty. No matter which side – slave or free – triumphed in a territorial vote on slavery, one major region of the country would be unwilling to accept the outcome.

Ethnic Politics: Immigrants, Nativism, and "Know-Nothings"

Land and slavery were not the only issues on people's minds in the 1850s. While the southern states continued to expand their agricultural system of cotton and slaves in much the way as their forefathers had, economic growth in the northern states was producing a series of profound social and economic changes. Perhaps the most far-reaching of these changes was the development of an industrial system that required the creation of a wage labor force and the development of an economic system geared to an urban rather than a rural environment.

By the end of the 1840s, increasing numbers of Americans were leaving their farms and moving to the city, where they took up jobs in a wide array of industrial and related occupations. Just how rapidly urbanization progressed can be seen in Figure 5.1 and Table 5.1. In 1820 just over 7 percent of Americans lived in a "city"; forty years later 20 percent of the population was urban.[12] In the Northeast, where roughly two-thirds of the urban population resided, the fraction living in cities reached one-quarter by 1850 and exceeded one-third in 1860.

Moving to a city involved profound changes in a family's life-style. They were going from a world in which the farm family was fairly isolated from neighbors and largely self-reliant for its needs, to a world where contact with neighbors on a daily basis was unavoidable, and

---

12 We must be careful not to exaggerate the meaning of "urban" in this period. The censuses defined urban as any person living in a town of twenty-five hundred or more inhabitants.

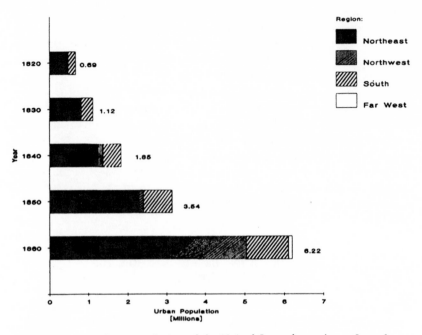

Figure 5.1. Urban population of the United States by region, 1820–60

where one depended on others for a wide range of basic needs. The economic and social interdependence that came with urban life carried over into the political arena. To the city dwellers of mid-nineteenth-century America, political parties served a very important social role by offering a vehicle for people to deal collectively with an environment that was constantly changing and at times seemed very threatening. Joel Silbey describes what he terms "an intricate web of interactive institutions" working within the community and functioning "in a most partisan fashion." Parties, he notes, had a variety of means to keep in touch with their constituencies, including newspapers and pamphlets, with no commitment to objectivity, and social organizations such as volunteer fire companies that tended to be highly partisan.[13]

Factories offered jobs, and jobs attracted people to the city thereby creating more jobs, and so on, in a pattern that is all too familiar to twentieth-century Americans. But the cities not only attracted farm fami-

13 Joel H. Silbey, ed., *The Partisan Imperative: The Dynamics of American Politics before the Civil War* (Oxford University Press, 1985), p. 100.

Table 5.1. *Urban population of the United States by region, 1820–60 (thousands)*

Year	Population			Region as % of U.S. urban	% change in urban population
	Total	Urban	% urban		
United States					
1820	9,638	694	7.20	—	—
1830	12,860	1,128	8.77	—	62.54
1840	17,064	1,845	10.81	—	63.56
1850	23,193	3,543	15.28	—	92.03
1860	31,443	6,216	19.77	—	75.44
Northeast					
1820	4,360	480	11.01	69.16	—
1830	5,542	785	14.16	69.59	63.54
1840	6,761	1,253	18.53	67.91	59.62
1850	8,627	2,289	26.53	64.61	82.68
1860	10,594	3,787	35.75	60.92	65.44
West					
1820	859	10	1.6	1.44	—
1830	1,610	42	2.61	3.72	320.00
1840	3,352	129	3.85	6.99	207.14
1850	5,404	499	9.23	14.08	286.82
1860	9,097	1,263	13.88	20.32	153.11
South					
1820	4,419	204	4.62	29.39	—
1830	5,708	301	5.27	26.68	47.55
1840	6,951	463	6.66	25.09	53.82
1850	8,983	744	8.28	21.00	60.69
1860	11,133	1,067	9.58	17.17	43.41
Far West					
1850	179	11	6.15	0.31	—
1860	619	99	15.99	1.59	800.00

Notes: Northeast: Connecticut, Maine, Massachusetts, New Hampshire, New Jersey, New York, Pennsylvania, Rhode Island, and Vermont; West: Illinois, Iowa, Indiana, Kansas, Michigan, Minnesota, Missouri, Nebraska, Ohio, and Wisconsin; South: Alabama, Arkansas, Delaware, District of Columbia, Florida, Georgia, Kentucky, Louisiana, Maryland, Mississippi, North Carolina, South Carolina, Tennessee, Texas, and Virginia; Far West: California, Colorado, New Mexico, Nevada, North Dakota Territory, Oregon, Washington, and Utah.
Source: U.S. Census Office, *Historical Statistics of the United States, Colonial Times to 1870*, part 1, (U.S. Government Printing Office, 1975), series A178–9, p. 22.

lies from New England or upstate New York; between 1820 and 1860 over five million people came to the United States from other countries, primarily from northern Europe. Figure 5.2 and Table 5.2 document the annual influx of immigrants from abroad. These data reveal an enormous wave of immigrants during the decade 1845 to 1854, when just under three million people entered the United States, and show that two out of every three immigrants came from just two countries, Ireland and Germany.

In 1850, the first year for which census data on birthplace was tabulated and published, one out of every ten Americans was foreign born. By 1860 this fraction had increased to 14 percent. Another way of looking at this is to say that in 1850 there was one immigrant for every eight native-born Americans; and by the end of the decade that ratio had fallen to less than one in five for every region except the South. Figure 5.3 and Table 5.3 present the distribution of the foreign-born population of the United States by region for 1850 and 1860. These figures reveal not only that there were large numbers of immigrants, but also that their numbers relative to the native population was expanding very rapidly at a time

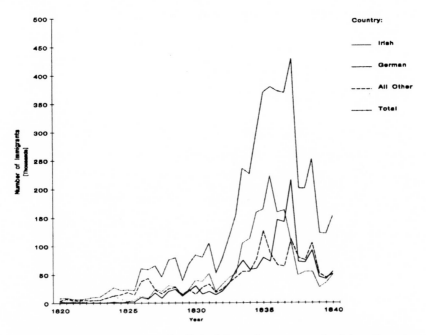

Figure 5.2. Immigration into the United States by country of origin, 1820–60

Table 5.2. *Immigration into the United States by five-year intervals, 1820–59 (thousands)*

Years	Total	Irish	German	Other
1820–4	74.8	11.7	1.9	25.1
1825–9	130.3	40.0	3.8	46.0
1830–4	326.5	54.1	39.3	137.1
1835–9	389.8	116.6	85.5	105.8
1840–4	481.2	181.7	100.5	117.8
1845–9	948.8	474.4	284.9	268.0
1850–4	1,808.8	809.1	654.3	453.2
1855–9	831.3	220.4	321.8	354.8
1820–59	4,024.7	1,907.9	1,492.0	1,507.9

Source: Table 5.A.2.

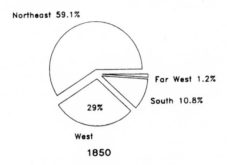

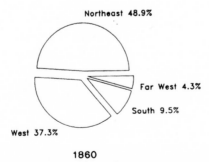

Figure 5.3. Foreign-born population of the United States by region, 1850 and 1860

Table 5.3. *Free native and foreign-born populations of the United States by region, 1850 and 1860 (thousands)*

	Total	Free native	Foreign born	Foreign born as % of total	Ratio of native to foreign born
1850					
Northeast	8,627	7,289	1,326	15.37	5.50
West	5,404	4,747	650	12.03	7.30
South	8,983	5,617	242	2.69	23.21
Far West	179	151	27	15.08	5.59
Total	23,193	17,804	2,245	9.68	7.93
1860					
Northeast	10,594	8,570	2,019	19.06	4.24
West	9,097	7,439	1,543	16.96	4.82
South	11,133	6,902	392	3.52	17.61
Far West	619	440	179	28.92	2.46
Total	31,443	23,094	4,390	13.96	5.26

Note: For regional definitions, see Table 5.1.
Source: U.S. Census Office, *Historical Statistics of the United States, Colonial Times to 1970*, part 1 (U.S. Government Printing Office, 1975).

when pressures for realignment in political parties were reaching a peak. Moreover, this increase in the foreign-born population was spread very unevenly over the United States. In 1850, 59 percent of the total foreign-born population of the United States lived in the Northeast, and another 29 percent lived in the West. By contrast, only 11 percent of the foreign population lived in the South, and that fraction fell to less than 10 percent by 1860.[14]

Statistics on the foreign-born population understate the overall impact of immigration, because the data include only those who were actually born abroad. A better measure of ethnic influence would be what the U.S. Census Offices called "people of foreign stock," a concept that grouped people who were born abroad together with those whose parents were born abroad. These data are not available for 1850 or 1860, but based on data for 1890, one can surmise that the total number of people of "foreign stock" comprised at least 20 to 25 percent of the total

14 The data in Figure 5.3 are tabulated by census division, and the "South" therefore includes the border states of Delaware, the District of Columbia, Kentucky, Maryland, and Missouri. Apart from areas immediately adjacent to the Mississippi River and a few cities such as New Orleans, the foreign-born population of the cotton-growing regions of the South was negligible.

population of the United States in the 1850s.[15] In the North the fraction was much higher, and in urban areas it often exceeded one-half.

Immigration was hardly something new to the United States in the 1840s, and the Irish and Germans had always composed the largest group of arrivals from abroad. Still, there had never been a wave of foreigners comparable with that of the 1840s and 1850s, and the result was a far-reaching reaction from "native" Americans. The source of the irritation is easy to identify. Large numbers of immigrants settled in northern urban areas, and the closeness of urban life magnified ethnic differences and provided ample ammunition for those who were upset by the intrusion posed by outsiders entering their community. The Irish were overwhelmingly Catholic, giving rise to strong anti-Catholic sentiment in areas where they settled. The Germans were more likely to be Protestant, but they did not speak English. Not surprisingly, members of both groups looked to each other for support, and this togetherness was easily channeled into partisan politics. The Democratic party sought to capitalize on the solidarity of immigrant voters in the city, a situation that its political opponents lamented with increasing frequency and a growing resentment. The *New York Times* editorialized in 1854 that "our adopted citizens" had a "duty" to "imbue themselves with American feelings. They should not herd themselves together for the preservation of their customs, habits, and languages of the countries from which they came."[16]

The increase in foreign population was also blamed for what seemed to be an alarming increase in social disorder. Having estimated that 1 out of every 154 immigrants was a criminal, the author of a tract titled *Immigration: Its Evils and Consequences* concluded that "pauperism and crime are the inevitable results of foreign immigration."[17] It is easy to see why such casual empiricism carried great weight. The immigrants who

15 In 1890 the fraction of the population that was foreign born was 14.69 percent, almost exactly equal to the fraction for 1860. Adding those with at least one foreign parent brings the fraction of persons with "foreign stock" to 33 percent of the population. The estimate of the text takes this rule of thumb and applies it to the fraction of the foreign-born population in 1850 and 1860. The data are from U.S. Bureau of the Census, *Historical Statistics of the United States, Colonial Times to 1970* (U.S. Government Printing Office, 1975), vol. 1, series A172; A191–4.

16 *New York Times*, June 23, 1854; cited in Eric Foner, *Free Soil, Free Men and Free Labor: The Ideology of the Republican Party before the Civil War* (Oxford University Press, 1970), p. 229.

17 Samuel C. Busey, *Immigration, Its Evils and Consequences* (Dewitt and Davenport Publishers, 1856; reprint, Arno Press and the New York Times, 1969), p. 126. Busey's estimate for criminals among the native population was 1 in 1,619. The statistic was computed by dividing the foreign population reported in the 1850 census by "the whole number of persons convicted of crime in the United States, during the year ending June 30, 1850" (p. 117).

remained in the cities tended to be relatively poor, and the crowded living quarters typical of immigrant neighborhoods in New York, Boston, and the other cities along the Atlantic seaboard did little to "imbue American feelings" in the foreign-born residents.

The friction between "nativist" and immigrant groups spilled over into a variety of specific issues that confounded the political leaders of the early 1850s. In New England, most notably in Maine, nativists launched a temperance campaign based on the allegation that immigrants drank too much. Religion and language became a burning issue because of the immigrant, and particularly Irish Catholic, resistance to sending their children to public schools in America. Where the newcomers sought work in factories, economic competition between immigrant and native workers became a source of friction between the two groups. Although politicians recognized these forces, mobilizing nativist support was a difficult task. The most serious problem was the difficulty of framing a coherent "pronativist" program on a national or even regional level. What might appeal to nativists or immigrants in one area could be anathema to the group in some other area. An even more serious obstacle to political organization was the secretive nature of nativist societies that sprang up throughout the Northeast and Midwest. The most famous of these was the Know-Nothings, a secret group that took its name from the answer that members gave in reply to questions about their political beliefs: "I know nothing."

The Know-Nothing societies burst upon the political scene as a potent force in the elections of 1854. Whigs such as William Seward hoped to capitalize on the discontent among antislave groups over Democratic support of the Kansas–Nebraska Act and at the same time appeal to the nativist groups by stressing the extent to which Democratic machine politics in the cities rested on support from immigrant voters. Things did not work out the way Seward had planned. The Democrats did take a beating in the congressional elections, losing forty-one seats in the House. But only twelve of those seats went to the Whigs; the rest went to Free-Soil and Know-Nothing candidates. In the Senate the Whigs fared even more poorly; the Democrats gained two seats, and the Whigs lost seven seats. Again, it was the splinter parties who gained the most. Far from reestablishing order, the election of 1854 was a disaster for both national parties, which signaled the onset of six years of political chaos.

By the end of 1855, a major realignment of political parties was taking place. The Whig organization had disintegrated to the point where the party was no longer in a position to field a slate of candidates for national office. The Democrats, who had swept to a huge victory in 1852, lost heavily only two years later. Why? The simple explanation was to blame their support of the Kansas–Nebraska Act. But if antislavery sentiment was the major reason for the Democratic defeat, why did the Whigs fail to pick up substantial gains? The answer, according to Douglas, was that Kansas–Nebraska was not the only important factor in the election. The Democratic defeat, he argued, stemmed from "a crucible into which [was] poured Abolitionism, Maine Liquor lawism, and what there was left of northern Whiggism, and then the Protestant feeling against the Catholic and the native feeling against the foreigner."[18] That the Democratic troubles stemmed from a combination of antislavery sentiment and the emergence of nativism seems plausible enough. And it may well have been the case that the nativist issue was the more important of the two. In the mid-1850s the highly secretive societies, built around strong resentment against Catholics and immigrants, probably represented the most rapidly growing political groups in the United States.

The Know-Nothing movement was something endemic to American politics: a protest movement by people disaffected with a political system that did not seem to be responding to their particular needs. "*Americans must rule America*," proclaimed article 3 of the party's platform in 1856, "and to this end, *native*-born citizens should be selected for all state, federal, or municipal offices of government employment, in preference to naturalized citizens."[19] The platform proceeded to enumerate a series of grievances against the intrusion of foreign influences; and it proclaimed that in the future, naturalized citizenship should be given only to those who had resided in the United States for at least twenty-one years, were not "paupers," and had been convicted of no crimes since coming to the United States.[20] This was a program that blatantly appealed to religious and racial bigotry, and that played on the fears and frustrations of many Americans stemming from their inability to check the flow of immigrants into the cities. The sentiments expressed by the Know-Nothings were by no means novel, but they took on new force in the context of a period of rapid social and economic change, and they were especially difficult to deal with because of the secret nature of the societies. Until they began to support candidates openly in 1856, no one really knew how much importance to attach to the Know-Nothing sentiments.

Because the political system creates strong incentives to form broadly based political parties that can win national elections, established political parties in the United States have always had trouble dealing with protest movements of this sort. The anti-Catholicism and nativist protest proved

18 Cited in Foner, *Free Soil, Free Men and Free Labor*, p. 238.
19 Cited in Joel Silbey, ed., *Transformation of American Politics, 1840–1860* (Prentice-Hall, 1967), p. 62; emphasis in original.
20 Ibid., pp. 62–3.

as much a thorn in the side of the Whigs as the slavery issue was to the Democrats. Whig leaders hoped to navigate a narrow middle ground, but they soon found that it was difficult to find a path that would not offend as many as it would attract. Unlike slavery, the nativist issue offered no single overriding question upon which one could call for a division. As we already noted, taking strong stands on specific issues, such as temperance or schools, was fraught with danger when carried to a national scale. The strongest single unifying force in the Know-Nothing movement was anti-Catholicism. However, for many years the Whig leadership had preached moderation with regard to the anti-Catholic issue. The result, as Michael Holt points out, was that although the Whigs often made nativist appeals, the party rarely acted against Catholics.[21] Regional differences further complicated the issue; anti-Catholicism had far less appeal in western states such as Illinois and Wisconsin, where immigrants were more likely to be German Protestants than Irish Catholics, than it did in the cities along the eastern seaboard that were populated with the Irish.

Nativism, in short, did not generate political pressures that might support the creation of a *national* party; at best, it created a group of state parties whose only common ties were anti-Catholicism and fears of a foreign influence. As a basis for protest, they represented a powerful political voice. But the protesters were far more successful in bringing about the demise of the Whig party than they were in constructing the basis for a new political party. By the middle of the decade, the effect of having so many political groups protesting this or that aspect of slavery, immigration, urbanization, or religion was to create political confusion on a grand scale. As Parke Godwin put it in 1856: "What with whigs, democratic whigs, democrats, true democrats, barnburners, hunkers, silver grays, woolly heads, national reformers, fire-eaters, and fillibusteros, it is easy to imagine how the exotic intellect should get perplexed!"[22] Although some of the parties mentioned by Godwin were variants on some major party, and hence remained in the fold for most elections, it was clear that a major realignment of parties had occurred.

Figures 5.4 and 5.5 show the number of representatives and senators by major party affiliation from 1848 through 1858. Three points are immediately evident from the figures. First, the Democrats, who had been the dominant party in Congress since the time of Jackson, began losing ground rapidly after 1854. They had only a plurality in the House in 1856, and in 1858 they had become the minority party. Second, the

---

21 Michael Holt, "The Politics of Impatience: The Origins of Know-Nothingism," *Journal of American History* 60 (1973): 314.
22 Godwin, *Political Essays*, p. 1.

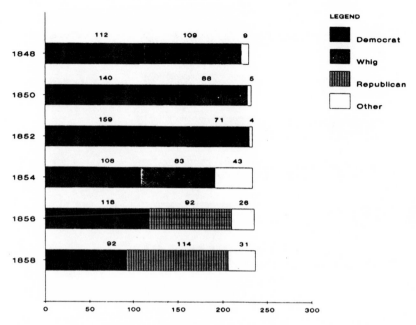

Figure 5.4. Party affiliation of members elected to the House of Representatives, 1848–58

growing importance of third parties, primarily the Free-Soilers and nativists, gave these groups the balance of power in the House of Representatives by 1856. Finally, and most significant, we see the disappearance of the Whig party and the rise of the Republican party after 1854.

The phenomenal speed with which that party emerged belies the difficulties facing its founders. George W. Julian, one of the men who was instrumental in establishing the Republican party, reflected about what it had taken to form a new party:

> Such were the elements which mingled and commingled in the political ferment of 1854, and out of which an anti-slavery party was to be evolved capable of trying conclusions with the perfectly disciplined power of slavery. The problem was exceedingly difficult, and could not be solved in a day. The necessary conditions of progress could not be slighted, and the element of time must necessarily be a large one in the grand movement which was to come. The dispersion of

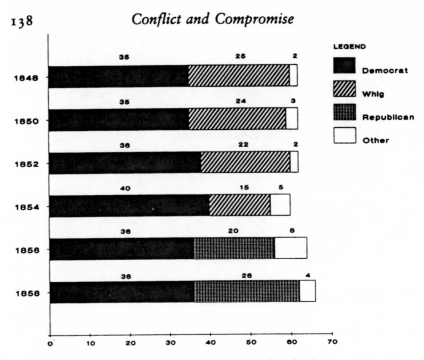

Figure 5.5. Party affiliation of members elected to the Senate, 1848–58

the old parties was one thing, but the organization of their fragments into a new one on a just base was quite a different thing.[23]

We are left, then, with the question of how the Republican party was able to emerge from this political chaos as the dominant party in the northern states? Clearly neither slavery nor ethnic differences by themselves were enough. What was missing was a unifying cause or idea around which the dissident Whigs or Democrats could rally.

The Power of Ideas: Free Labor, Free Soil, and the "Slave Power"

Political historians have recently stressed that ethnic politics of the 1850s created a chaotic political environment that made the task of forming a new political party to challenge the Democrats very difficult.[24] But the

23 George W. Julian, *Political Recollections, 1840 to 1872* (Jansen, McClung, 1884), p. 143.
24 Most notable among those emphasizing this point are Michael Holt, *Forging a Majority: The Formation of the Republican Party in Pittsburgh, 1848–1860* (Yale Univer-

political divisiveness produced by the nativist–immigrant clashes must be kept in perspective. For all their problems with each other, the nativists and immigrant groups in the North shared a deep-seated antipathy toward the South, and this antipathy was the foundation upon which a new political coalition – the Republican party – could be formed in the North.

As the data presented in Figure 5.3 clearly show, immigrants did not settle in the South. Fewer than one in ten of all Americans born abroad lived in the South in 1860; the foreign-born population of that region in 1860 represented only 3.5 percent of the population. This was no accident; immigrants made a conscious judgment that the South was a distinctly less desirable region in which to settle than either the North or West. Although the specific reasons for that judgment obviously varied widely, the presence of black slaves was surely a factor. Immigrants, many of whom were fleeing from economic or political repression in their mother country, saw the South's system of chattel labor as a singularly unappealing institution that was completely at odds with their view of the "new world."

Slavery also discouraged settlement by fostering a plantation system that was totally unfamiliar to northern Europeans, most of whom had no experience with an agricultural environment that used slave labor and specialized in growing cotton, sugar, or tobacco. Northern agriculture was a far more attractive opportunity, but farming of any sort required both land and capital to get started. The southern emphasis on staples and slaves not only increased these costs; slavery and cotton also stifled urban development. Without cities, southern states offered few jobs outside of agriculture. Even those immigrants who were indifferent to slavery were more likely to find economic opportunities more to their liking outside the South. Would-be farmers took jobs as wage laborers in the cities of the North until they could earn a "stake" to start farming in the West.

The reluctance of immigrants to settle in the South meant that the issues of concern to ethnic groups produced political alliances that followed geographical boundaries that just happened to coincide with the division between slave and nonslave areas. This fact was not lost on antislavery leaders such as Seward of New York or Chase of Ohio. The

sity Press, 1969), and idem, *Political Crisis of the 1850's*; Roland P. Formisano, *The Birth of Mass Political Parties: Michigan, 1827–1861*) Princeton University Press, 1971); Silbey, *The Partisan Imperative*; and Gienapp, *Origins of the Republican Party*. As Gienapp notes, "emphasis on the Kansas–Nebraska Act has obscured the importance of other factors in the antebellum realignment, and consequently historians have underestimated the extent to which the Republican party's organization was a lengthy and difficult process" (p. 103).

difference between North and South, they argued, was that a system of *free labor* was the cornerstone of the northern society, whereas a system of *slave labor* was the cornerstone of southern society. "Political anti-slavery," writes Eric Foner,

> was not merely a negative doctrine, an attack on southern slavery and the society built upon it; it was a reaffirmation of the superiority of the social system of the North – a dynamic, expanding, capitalist society, whose achievements and destiny were almost wholly the result of the dignity and opportunities it offered the average laboring man.[25]

By stressing the "dignity" of free labor, opponents of slavery were able to appeal to all of the laboring classes of the North. As Foner notes, the virtues of a world in which there was "free labor" carried considerable weight among both native and immigrant workers.

Despite the growing importance of the industrial sector in the Northeast, the availability of land retained a special importance to those who came from a world where the right to land offered the only true means of economic security. Linked with the idea of "free" labor was the importance of "free" land. The fact that far more immigrants found employment as urban workers than as farmers tends to obscure the fact that most of them came from agricultural backgrounds, and many had arrived in their new land with hopes of starting anew as farmers just as soon as they could raise the capital. For these people, the promise of farmland in the West remained an important part of their ideology, even though those expectations might never be realized. This, of course, was a dream they shared with many native-born Americans who had come to expect the availability of western land as an option for those seeking economic opportunities beyond the confines of their present family or community.

In fact, the settlement of the western lands had been a preeminent part of American life since before the Revolution. From Jefferson's administration on, government land policies had encouraged Americans – from both the North and South – to move west. From the time of the compromise of 1787, which barred slavery from the Old Northwest, territories had been designated as being "slave" or "free." As we saw in Chapter 3, the presence of slavery produced a very different pattern of farming than that in the free territories. This difference was reflected in the geographical origins of the people who settled there. Table 5.4 gives the percentage

---

25 Foner, *Free Soil, Free Men and Free Labor*, p. 11. Foner's book is an excellent analysis of the role of ideology in fostering a cohesive political force that became the Republican party; also see his essay "Politics, Ideology and the Origins of the American Civil War," in *A Nation Divided,* ed. George Fredrickson (Burgess Publishing, 1975).

Table 5.4. *Percentage distribution of the
native white population by census region of
residence and birth, 1850 and 1860*

Census division of residence	Born in same region	Born in other region in	
		North	South
1850			
New England	97.72	2.03	0.25
Middle Atlantic	93.49	5.21	1.30
South Atlantic	96.68	2.54	0.78
East North Central	65.13	22.92	11.94
East South Central	77.23	2.29	20.48
West North Central	48.14	20.89	30.97
West South Central	53.67	8.83	37.51
1860			
New England	97.04	2.65	0.30
Middle Atlantic	94.64	4.14	1.22
South Atlantic	96.36	2.74	0.90
East North Central	70.76	20.98	8.27
East South Central	80.69	2.74	16.57
West North Central	44.41	35.34	20.25
West South Central	52.68	7.03	40.29

Notes: New England: Connecticut, Maine, Massachusetts, New Hampshire, Rhode Island, and Vermont; Middle Atlantic: New Jersey, New York, and Pennsylvania; East North Central: Illinois, Indiana, Michigan, Ohio, and Wisconsin; West North Central: Iowa, Kansas, Minnesota, Missouri, Nebraska; South Atlantic: Delaware, District of Columbia, Florida, Georgia, Maryland, North Carolina, South Carolina, and Virginia; East South Central: Kentucky, Tennessee, Alabama, and Mississippi; West South Central: Arkansas, Louisiana, and Texas.
Source: Table A.5.3.

of the native-born population born within the same census region, together with the percentages born outside the region for the North and South respectively. As one would expect, along the Atlantic Coast, most natives were living in the region where they were born.[26] In the two East Central regions, by contrast, between 20 and 35 percent of the native-

26 The data on white native-born populations of Table 5.4 make the slave and free regions seem much more similar than they really were. As Table 5.3 shows, there are two enormous differences not shown: the large number of black slaves in the South, and the foreign-born immigrants in the North.

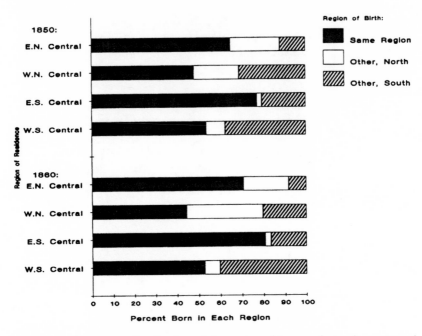

Figure 5.6. Percentage distribution of the native white population by region of birth and residence, 1850 and 1860

born population was born in another census region. In the two West Central regions, half the native population had migrated from another region.

The sources of internal migration to the western regions were quite different. Figure 5.6 compares data for the four western regions. Fewer than 3 percent of the people living in the East South Central area in 1860 were born outside the South, and only 7 percent in the West South Central region were from outside the South. By contrast, the nonslave areas of the West were settled by people from every part of the country, including a significant fraction from the South. What stands out from an examination of these data is that people living in the free regions of the western United States came from a far more varied background than those living in the slave states of the Southwest.

This asymmetry in birthplaces reveals a striking fact about internal migration in the United States during the antebellum period. A significant number of Southerners migrated from the South to free areas of the West.

Peter McClelland and Richard Zeckhauser estimate that at least two hundred thousand people left the South between 1840 and 1860. "The implication is a significant exodus from the South as the nation became progressively divided."[27] Northerners, by contrast, did not tend to move to the western slave areas. The result was a far more heterogeneous population in the Northwest than in the Southwest. Aggregate data of this sort cannot reveal the motives behind migration from one region to another. Nevertheless, these demographic characteristics and estimates of internal migration suggest several important influences on the political ideology of the 1850s.

First is the northern view of slavery. When it came to a choice of where to live, neither native nor foreign-born Northerners wanted to live in a region dominated by the plantation-slave agriculture. Martin Van Buren stated the case as well as anyone when he wrote:

> Free workers are unwilling to work side by side with negro slaves; they are unwilling to share the evils of a condition so degraded and the deprivation of the society of their own class; and they emigrate with great reluctance and in very small numbers to communities in which labor is mainly performed by slaves.[28]

We have commented on this antipathy of free settlers toward slavery before. An additional factor that Van Buren did not mention was the racial antagonism that free settlers felt toward black slaves.

Equally important is the fact that a sizable number of Southerners elected to move away from slavery. While hardly conclusive, the data in Table 5.4 are certainly consistent with an argument that nonslaveholders in the South who faced serious obstacles in the form of high costs of establishing a slave farm exercised their option of going north where the costs of establishing a family farm with free labor were much lower. Finally, the large number of people who must have left slave states for the West underscores once again the point that the ownership of slaves in the United States was by choice. Those who disagreed with either the morality or the economics of slavery could escape the system by simply leaving. Over time, this self-selection reinforced the proslave ideology of those who remained behind. Unlike the free regions of the West, which were

27 Peter D. McClelland and Richard J. Zeckhauser, *Demographic Dimensions of the New Republic: American Interregional Migration, Vital Statistics, and Manumissions, 1800–1860* (Cambridge University Press, 1982), p. 52. The estimate of two hundred thousand is, in fact, an understatement of the actual emigration out of the South, because McClelland and Zeckhauser include the movement to California as a part of the region considered for the calculation.

28 Quoted in John Niven, *Martin Van Buren: The Romantic Age of American Politics* (Oxford University Press, 1983), p. 569.

populated by a very heterogeneous group of people, the "new" South was settled by the sons and daughters of the "old" South.[29]

Every major crisis over land in the West brought these differences into sharp focus, and such crises occurred whenever it came time to organize a new territory into states. Both Northerners and Southerners wanted more land, and each wanted it exclusively for their system of agriculture. We have already examined the expansionist pressures that operated in the slave society of the South. In the North, "Free Soil" – the rallying cry of the Free-Soil party in the 1840s – became a political slogan that had powerful appeal in the 1850s to those who feared that these expansionist tendencies might interfere with their own hopes to stake out a claim in the West. Even if they did not expect to settle land themselves, free laborers and farmers in the North came increasingly to view any intrusion of slavery into free territories as a threat. This attitude made the Kansas–Nebraska Act abhorrent to everyone in the North, because it reversed a long-standing ruling on slavery in the territory north of the compromise line of 1820 and opened up the *possibility* that Kansas would be another Missouri – a slave state in the "North." Southern resistance to the Homestead Act provided added irritation to those who interpreted it as further evidence that the slave interests would consistently oppose the establishment of family farms in "free" territories to the West.[30]

Arguments that a system using "free labor" was superior to one using slave labor fell on sympathetic ears in the West, as did the contention that western territories should be free from the presence of slave agriculture. But Democrats such as Stephen Douglas could accept these points and still insist that his policy offered a viable way to stem the westward push of slavery. He was convinced that popular sovereignty would eventually lead to the exclusion of slavery from the West precisely because free labor *was* superior to slave labor. The final element in the effort to make the

---

29 The argument that Southerners settling in the free West were "escaping" the influence of slavery is admittedly only suggestive. Many of these transplanted Southerners came from the Upper South, not the cotton regions, where the problems associated with the plantation-slave agriculture would be greatest. Nor do we have any idea how many of these people actually owned slaves before moving to free territory. Some simply were doing what their northern counterparts were doing: seeking more fertile land. Whatever their reasons for moving, the striking fact remains that significant numbers of people left the South for free western territories, whereas the reverse was not true: neither Northerners nor immigrants settled in the South.

30 In fact, the economic implications of free land in the West created some schisms in the South that may not have been apparent to those looking at the southern opposition to homesteading in the Senate. See Susan Previant Lee, *The Westward Movement of the Cotton Economy, 1840–1860: Perceived Interests and Economic Interests* (Ph.D. diss., Columbia University, 1975; reprint, Arno Press, 1977).

antislavery crusade a far-reaching political coalition was an argument that would convince immigrants and nativists alike that the mere presence of slavery posed a *threat* to "free labor" and "free soil."

The idea that a *slave power* – a sinister and largely invisible group with slave interests – controlled the national government had been implicit in some of the rhetoric surrounding the Missouri Compromise, and it surfaced even more clearly in the arguments over Texas fifteen years later.[31] Use of the term slave power by antislave activists started with Senator Thomas Morris, a Jacksonian Democrat from Ohio, but the man who is generally credited with turning the expression into a potent political slogan of the 1850s was Salmon Chase of Ohio.[32] To Chase, the repeated attempts by Southerners to extend slavery into new territories was a complete subversion of the original intent of the Constitution. Writing in 1850 to Charles Sumner he claimed:

> 1. That the original policy of the Constitution was that of slavery restriction. 2. That under the Constitution Congress cannot establish or maintain slavery in the territories. 3. That the original policy of the Government has been subverted and the Constitution violated for the extension of slavery, and the establishment of the supremacy of the Slave Power.[33]

Chase was one of the first prominent politicians to clearly state that the only effective way to fight slavery was through the formation of a new political party committed to stopping the expansion of slavery. To this end he left the Democratic party in the 1830s and joined the fledgling Liberty party. When that movement failed to take hold, Chase became a stalwart of the Free-Soil party, for which he served in the Senate during the debates of 1849 to 1854. In 1855 he joined the Republican party, and his election as governor of Ohio in 1855 was a major breakthrough for the nascent Republican party.[34] Chase provided an eloquent intellectual argument that the slave power was a sinister threat to the country. The idea that a group of proslave politicians manipulated national politics to their own advantage was hardly new; many Northerners had believed

31 Recall that a major source behind Thomas Hart Benton's anger over the machinations of the Polk administration was that such actions were aimed at breaking the South away from the Union.

32 In 1849 Morris had attacked "the power of these two great interests – the slave power of the South, and banking power of the North," and subsequently lost his seat in the Senate. As Foner points out, he was one of the earliest political "martyrs" of the antislavery cause. See Foner, *Free Soil, Free Labor and Free Men*, p. 91.

33 Quoted in ibid., p. 87.

34 William Gienapp provides an analysis of the importance of Chase's gubernatorial victory in 1855 (*Origins of the Republican Party*, pp. 192–203).

that for many years. What gave real force to these arguments were the events of 1856 and 1857.

By the middle of 1856 the attempt to form a national party by "fusing" anti-Democratic groups was making only modest progress. The Republican party had progressed to the point where it was able to field a candidate for president – John C. Fremont of California – and a large slate of candidates for Congress. Although they lost the 1856 presidential campaign to James Buchanan, the combined votes of Fremont and the Know-Nothing candidate, ex-president Millard Fillmore, totaled 55 percent of the popular vote, and the Republicans captured 92 House seats and 20 Senate seats.[35] Notwithstanding these successes, the position of the Republican party remained tenuous. It was still only a loose coalition of antislave, anti-Democrat groups, and the future of the coalition was far from assured, because the Democrats held a sizable plurality in the House and were in firm control of the Senate.

James Buchanan, the newly elected Democratic president, faced two major crises almost as soon as he took office in March 1857. One was a pending decision by the U.S. Supreme Court dealing with the petition of a slave named Dred Scott claiming that, because he had lived in a free state since 1834, he was entitled to his freedom. The other was statehood for Kansas, the first great test of popular sovereignty.

The Failure of Compromise: Dred Scott and Kansas

Dred Scott was a slave who had been sold to an army surgeon named John Emerson. In 1834 Emerson, who had been posted in Fort Armstrong, Missouri, moved to Illinois and thence, in 1936, to Fort Snelling, which is near the present site of St. Paul, Minnesota. The surgeon took his slave with him to his new assignment, which meant that Dred Scott was now in territory that, under the terms of the Missouri Compromise, forbade any slavery. Subsequently, Emerson and his slave moved to a number of posts in the South, and returned for one more tour of duty at Fort Snelling. Upon Emerson's death in 1843, Dred Scott became the property of Emerson's wife who was living in Missouri. On April 6, 1846, Dred Scott sued for his freedom from Mrs. Emerson on the grounds that he had "lived" in a free state, albeit as a slave. His claim to freedom was upheld by a lower court, but reversed by the Missouri Supreme Court.[36]

35 See Table 4.1 for the presidential vote; Figures 5.4 and 5.5 give the breakdown of congressional seats. Note that twenty-six House seats and eight Senate seats also went to opponents of the Democratic party.

36 Little is known about the early years of Dred Scott's life. The best account of the events leading to the court case in 1846 is Donald E. Fehrenbacher, *Slavery, Law, and Politics: The Dred Scott Case in Historical Perspective* (Oxford University Press, 1981), chap. 5.

By the time the U.S. Supreme Court was ready to announce its decision on Scott's appeal, the case was regarded as a test of the legality of the Missouri Compromise. In his inaugural address, President James Buchanan alluded to the importance of the decision by saying that the issue of who should decide on slavery in a territory "is a judicial question, which legitimately belongs to the Supreme Court of the United States where it is now pending, and will, it is understood, be speedily and finally settled. To their decision, in common with all good citizens, I shall cheerfully submit."[37] Buchanan's confidence that the issue of slavery in the territory would be resolved was badly misplaced. When Chief Justice Roger Taney read the decision on March 3, 1857, he announced that the Court had ruled on three matters in the Dred Scott decision.[38]

First, Dred Scott was not a free man. This was the only point on which all nine justices gave an opinion. Seven justices concluded that Dred Scott had not gained his freedom simply by virtue of living as a slave with his master for a prolonged period in a place where slavery was prohibited. Although antislave groups were unhappy with this ruling, it was hardly a surprise.

Second, Congress did not have authority to legislate on the legality of slavery in the territories. With five justices assenting on this point, the Court, in effect, pronounced the Missouri Compromise unconstitutional. This decision touched off an angry reaction in the North. Men such as abolitionist William Cullen Bryant challenged the legitimacy of the Court itself:

> Hereafter, if this decision shall stand for law, slavery, instead of being what the people of the slave states have hitherto called it, their peculiar institution, is a Federal institution, the common patrimony and shame of all the states. . . . Are we to accept, without question, these new readings of the Constitution – to sit down contentedly under this disgrace – to admit that the Constitution was never before rightly understood, even by those who framed it – to consent that hereafter it shall be the slaveholders' instead of the freemen's Constitution? Never! Never![39]

This ruling was a blow not only to the ardent opponents of slavery, but to the moderate Democrats as well. Popular sovereignty, which was the cornerstone of the Kansas–Nebraska Act, was threatened by the ruling that slavery was a constitutional right that could not be abrogated by Congress or any state.

Third, free blacks could not be citizens of the United States. The chief

37 Quoted in Nevins, *Ordeal of the Union*, 3: 88.
38 For an excellent summary of the Court's ruling, see Fehrenbacher, *Slavery, Law, and Politics*, pp. 174–5 and chap. 7.
39 Quoted in Nevins, *Ordeal of the Union*, 3: 96.

justice and two of his colleagues ruled that blacks could never have rights equal to those of whites in the United States. In reaching this ruling, they were following accepted practice in the free states of the union, where free blacks were routinely denied full citizenship. Nevertheless, the opinion of citizenship for free blacks carried with it an ominous implication, for it meant, as Bernard Schwartz notes, that "without constitutional amendment, the Negro was consigned to a permanent second-class status which could not be changed even if all the slaves were ultimately free."[40]

By itself, the Dred Scott case would hardly have been controversial enough to touch off sectional conflict. With the possible exception of the ruling on the ability of Congress to legislate slavery, the Court was basically following legal precedents that had evolved over the past half century. Even the ruling that the Missouri Compromise was unconstitutional had only a limited impact. Congress, after all, had all but overturned that arrangement with the Kansas–Nebraska Act. In 1857, however, the Dred Scott case was not viewed as an isolated ruling on the freedom of a slave. The Court's decision had a very polarizing effect. To opponents of slavery in the North it was seen as a ruling that clearly supported slave interests, rendered by a court that was blatantly pro-South. It gave men like Salmon Chase and William Seward an issue with which to attack the credibility of the Supreme Court and raise the specter that the sinister *slave power* controlled not only the executive, but the judiciary branch of the national government as well. The fact that Chief Justice Roger Taney was a slaveholder from Maryland who consistently defended the rights of slaveholders added fuel to the fire. Several politicians, most notably Seward, went so far as to claim that this was all a conspiracy between the Court and the Buchanan administration. Benjamin Curtis, one of the northern justices on the Court resigned in protest, claiming that Taney had changed the decision between agreement and publication.[41]

Applause from Southerners and President Buchanan was just as loud as were the protests from the North. The Court's decision encouraged the southern advocates of slavery, who cried for even stricter enforcement of

40 Bernard Schwartz, *From Confederation to Nation: The American Constitution, 1835–1877* (Johns Hopkins Press, 1973), p. 129. Schwartz notes that Taney's interpretation supported numerous laws in the North and South that denied rights of citizenship to free blacks and had been upheld by the courts in the North. He cautions, however, against looking at "the problem presented to the Taney Court through the distorting lenses of the Fourteenth Amendment. Before the Civil War the question of Negro Citizenship was by no means clearly settled. What authority there was tended to support Taney . . . on the matter" (p. 127).

41 Schwartz notes correspondence between justices of the Court and President-elect Buchanan, which formed the basis of the charges of collusion (*From Confederation to Nation*, pp. 117–20). Also see Nevins, *Ordeal of the Union*, 3: 115–18.

the controversial Fugitive Slave Act of 1850. It also increased the determination of proslave forces to bring Kansas into the Union as a slave state.

It was a foregone conclusion at this point that Kansas would soon apply for statehood. The terms under which statehood would be granted had become an important issue for all three of the major political groups in the United States. For northern and moderate Democrats from the South, it would be the first major test of the popular sovereignty issue that they had written into the Kansas–Nebraska Act three years earlier. Proslave Southerners regarded Kansas as the only realistic possibility of having a sixteenth slave state admitted into the Union, and accordingly placed enormous importance on it being admitted with slavery. Northern opponents of slavery saw in the issue of Kansas statehood an opportunity to test their strength against the slave power.

The history of territorial government in Kansas provided little basis for optimism that the slavery issue might be resolved. From the outset, elections in the Kansas Territory had sparked violence and threats of intimidation from both sides. In both the North and the South, groups of immigrants were organized to go out to Kansas and secure it for their cause. An election for the territorial legislature in March 1855 produced a massive proslave majority; but opponents charged that the vote totals were inflated by fraud and that a massive influx of proslave Missourians on election day seriously distorted the results. Antislave groups were further outraged by the expulsion of all the free-state representatives once the legislature met in session. With no opposition, the proslave legislature proceeded to enact a legal code patterned after that of Missouri. Among the more offensive measures was one that made it a felony to maintain that slavery was not legal in the territory and imposed a death penalty for anyone assisting a runaway slave.[42]

Claiming that "we owe no allegiance or obedience to the tyrannical enactments of this spurious legislature," the free-state supporters held their own elections in early 1856 and elected a governor and legislature, which took up residence in Topeka.[43] Thus, there were two territorial governments "governing" Kansas by mid-1856. In fact, civil order had deteriorated to the point that in May of that year a group of proslavery ruffians "sacked" the city of Lawrence, which was a center of the free-state supporters. Several days later ardent free-staters led by abolitionist John Brown killed a number of prominent proslave supporters in an

---

42 See Gienapp, *Origins of the Republican Party*, p. 171.
43 The slogan is attributed by David Potter to Andrew Reeder, a former territorial governor who became a leading free-state supporter (*The Impending Crisis*, p. 205).

incident known as the "Pottawatomie Massacre." Events such as these were widely publicized by the press in both the North and the South, and gave rise to the expression "Bleeding Kansas."[44]

So it was that, in the spring of 1857, Kansas prepared to apply for statehood. Some semblance of order had been restored to the territory through the efforts of territorial governor John Geary, but the truce was fragile, and Geary resigned at the end of 1857. President Buchanan then chose Robert J. Walker, who had lived in both Pennsylvania and Mississippi, to be governor of the territory. Walker was a proslavery Democrat who insisted he would abide by the rules of popular sovereignty. To the surprise of everyone, he tried to do exactly that.

When Walker arrived on the scene in the spring of 1857, there were about 22,000 adults living in the territory, 9,250 of whom had registered to vote. The contesting parties were locked in a dispute over the election of representatives for a state constitutional convention that would meet in the little town of Lecompton. Convinced that their opponents had once again rigged the electoral process to produce a proslavery victory, the antislavery forces boycotted the election. Although their fears of manipulation were well founded, the decision to boycott proved to be an unfortunate one. With only 2,200 votes cast, a strongly proslavery slate of delegates was elected in June 1857 to draw up a state constitution. Not surprisingly, the convention drafted a document that recommended that slavery be permitted in Kansas, and provided no provision that would submit the entire document to a vote of the electorate. To placate objections to such a blatant approval of slavery, the document stipulated that there be a referendum to select one of two proposed clauses dealing with slavery. The "strong" version would place no limits at all on the right to own or bring more slaves into the territory; the "weak" clause would allow ownership of slaves, but restrict the importing of more slaves into the state.

Slave interests had clearly won the first round. The "Lecompton Constitution" was a document to which the free settlers of Kansas, who by this time were clearly in the majority, strongly objected. Yet, according to the procedures for statehood, this proposed constitution had to be offered to Congress for approval. The situation was further complicated by the results of another election for seats in the territorial legislature and a representative to Congress that was held in October 1857. This time the

44 The battle over statehood for Kansas has been told many times. The fullest account is that of James A. Rawley, *Race and Politics: "Bleeding" Kansas and the Coming of Civil War* (J. B. Lippincott Company, 1969). Also see Nevins, *Ordeal of the Union,* 3: chap. 6, and 9–11; and Potter, *Impending Crisis,* chaps. 9 and 12. Unless otherwise noted, events and election totals reported in the text are taken from these sources.

free settlers participated in the election. The result was another proslavery victory, but the fraud was so obvious that Governor Walker invali-
dated the fraudulent returns and called for a new election.[45] This time
the free-state party prevailed, and the territorial legislature was now
firmly in the hands of those who opposed slavery in Kansas.

In December 1857 the two constitutional clauses on slavery were put
to a popular vote. Once again the free-state forces abstained from voting,
because a vote for either clause would provide a legal basis for slavery in
Kansas. The predictable outcome was that the "strong" slavery clause
passed by an overwhelming margin, 6,226 to 569, and the Lecompton
Constitution was forwarded to Congress for approval. Governor Walker, who strongly opposed the Lecompton Constitution, went to Washington to lobby against approval by Congress. In his absence, acting
Governor Frederick Stanton, an antislavery advocate, maneuvered a bill
through the newly elected territorial legislature calling for a nonbinding
referendum on the Constitution. The referendum was held on January 4,
1858, and this time the proslavery voters abstained. The result was a
smashing victory for opponents of the proposed constitution: 10,226
voted against approval of the constitution; 138 favored the "strong"
slave clause, and 24 favored the "weak" slavery clause.

The results of the referendum revealed just how far the process of
implementing "popular sovereignty" in Kansas had gone awry. If one
takes the results of various elections as an indication of the relative
strength of the two groups, it appears that the ratio of antislavery voters
to those favoring slavery was about 1.5 to 1.[46] Yet the proposed constitution contained a clause that favored unrestricted ownership of slaves
in the new state. Further attempts to resolve this contradiction at the
territorial level were not likely to prove fruitful, because both sides stead-
fastly refused to recognize the legitimacy of the other. Antislave forces
disputed the election of delegates to the constitutional convention, and
therefore denied the legitimacy of the document itself. Proslave forces
insisted that the constitution had been drafted and approved according to
the prescribed procedures, but refused to recognize the legitimacy of the
territorial legislature because of Governor Walker's actions in throwing
out the results of the October 1857 election. Neither side would partici-
pate in an election in which it appeared the other side might win. The
result was a stalemate that had to be resolved by Congress.

45 The most glaring examples of fraud were two districts where a total of 2,828 proslavery votes were returned even though less than 30 votes were cast in one district and no
election was held in the other.
46 In the election approving the constitution, 6,226 voted in favor, while in the January
referendum, 10,226 voters opposed the constitution.

Once again, the power of the presidency was brought to bear on the sectional division over slavery. President Buchanan decided to throw his support in favor of the Lecompton Constitution. "Seldom in the history of the nation," notes Allan Nevins, "has a President made so disastrous a blunder."[47] Buchanan and Stephen Douglas had struggled for leadership of the Democratic party for many years. Outraged by Buchanan's support of a document that he felt made a mockery out of the process of "popular sovereignty," Douglas announced his vehement opposition to the Lecompton document. Nevertheless, Buchanan and the Democrats carried the day in the Senate; on March 3, 1858, a bill accepting the Lecompton Constitution for Kansas passed by a vote of 33 to 25. In the House, however, the administration forces were stymied when opponents introduced a substitute motion stipulating that Kansas be admitted only if the entire Lecompton Constitution was put to a popular vote in Kansas. Backed by a coalition of ninety-two Republicans, twenty-two northern Democrats, and six Know-Nothings, the amended bill passed the House 120 to 112.

To break the deadlock between House and Senate, representative William English of Indiana suggested that the Lecompton Constitution be put to another vote in Kansas, but with some curious stipulations. If the Lecompton Constitution passed, Kansas would be admitted as a slave state. If the voters rejected the Lecompton Constitution, Kansas would have to wait until it had a population of 90,000 before it could become a state. Although Douglas objected to these stipulations, the compromise measure passed the Senate by a vote of 31 to 22, and the House by a vote of 112 to 103. The Lecompton Constitution was once again put to a vote in Kansas on August 2, 1858, and it was overwhelmingly rejected.

In the midst of this maneuvering in Kansas, an incident occurred in the United States Senate that further excited the emotions of disputing parties. On May 19 Charles Sumner, one of the most outspoken critics of slavery, rose to deliver a speech entitled "The Crime against Kansas." Even by the standards of the day, Sumner's speech was particularly vituperative, and he included a very personal attack on his fellow senator from South Carolina, Andrew P. Butler.[48] Sumner's comments about

---

47 Nevins, *Ordeal of the Union*, 3: 259.
48 Sumner referred to "murderous robbers from Missouri" and the "rape of a virgin territory, compelling it to the hateful embrace of slavery." He portrayed Butler as a "Don Quixote" who "has chosen a mistress to whom he has made his vows, and who, though ugly to others is always lovely to him; though polluted in the sight of the world, is chaste in his sight . . . the harlot slavery." See Rawley, *Race and Politics,* pp. 126–9; and James M. McPherson, *Battle Cry of Freedom: The Civil War Era* (Oxford University Press, 1988), pp. 149–52. Excerpts from Sumner's speech are reprinted in Silbey, *The Transformation of American Politics.*

Senator Butler particularly infuriated Butler's cousin, Representative Preston Brooks. Two days after Sumner's speech, Brooks entered the Senate and approached Sumner, who was seated at his desk. "Mr. Sumner," he announced, "I have read your speech with care . . . and I feel it my duty to tell you that you have libeled my State and slandered a relative."[49] Brooks then proceeded to beat Sumner senseless with the head of his cane before striding out of the Senate chambers.

Moderates from all regions were appalled both by the language of Sumner's speech in the Senate, and by the brutality of Brooks's attack on a senator of the United States. Extremists hastened to make the most of the incident for their own purposes. Coming shortly after the infamous "sack" of Kansas, the "caning of Sumner" became a symbol of the "barbaric" nature of the slave society and all who associated with the slave power. Southern zealots, for their part, praised Brooks as standing for the honor of the South. In the weeks following the incident, Brooks, who went unpunished save for a fine of three hundred dollars, received numerous canes to replace the one he had broken while "punishing" Sumner. "Never was the country in such a crazy state," wrote New Yorker George Templeton Strong in his diary, "North and South [are] farther alienated than ever before. . . . The Carolinas are decaying into barbarism."[50]

For the Democrats, the debates on Kansas statehood and the Sumner affair were nothing short of disastrous. The battle between administration supporters and the Douglas-led opponents in Congress irrevocably split the Democratic party. Because he had led the effort to defeat the proslave Lecompton Constitution, Douglas was henceforth regarded as an opponent of slavery by people in the South. In the North his policy of popular sovereignty was discredited by the fiasco of the Kansas elections. "Popular Sovereignty," exclaimed Charles Sumner, "which, when truly understood, is a fountain of just power, has ended in Popular Slavery."[51] Administration Democrats fared no better: They had alienated many northern moderates by their avowed support of slavery and, because they lost the battle to get Kansas into the Union as a slave state, picked up no additional support in the South.

For Republicans, the Kansas issue and the appearance of a martyr in the form of Charles Sumner were political godsends. Needing an issue

49 This statement comes from an account of the incident written by Brooks to his brother, cited in Rawley, *Race and Politics*, p. 126. Sumner's injuries were so severe that he did not return to the Senate until December 1857.
50 Cited in Rawley, *Race and Politics*, p. 127.
51 Speech by Charles Sumner, May 19 and 20, 1856; reproduced in Silbey, *Transformation of American Politics*.

that might unite the disparate groups in the North, leaders of the Republican party were given just that. The attack on Sumner and the machinations of proslave groups in Kansas revealed once more the pattern of aggressive expansion that had been so evident in the furor over Texas and the Mexican territories a decade earlier. Moreover, President Buchanan's ill-advised support of the Lecompton Constitution gave added fuel to those arguing that the Democratic party was dominated by the slave power. Finally, the Kansas affair proved to be the undoing of the Know-Nothings, who could not come up with an effective response to the crisis. Hoping to maintain support in the border states, the Know-Nothings equivocated on the slave issue and lost support among both the border Whigs and the northern nativists.[52] By stressing Kansas at every opportunity, the Republicans succeeded in finally gaining control of the House of Representatives in the 1858 elections.

For the South, the Lecompton affair was a bitter defeat. Kansas did not come in as a slave state, and it seemed unlikely that there would be another territory that could be organized as a slave state in the near future. The antislave forces had finally managed to forge a strong enough coalition to obviate the need for compromise. Honest Quitman of Mississippi reflected both the dejection and the anger of Southerners when he insisted that:

> Should the [Lecompton] constitution be rejected, the South must regard the plighted faith of the Northern Democracy [as] violated. It will assure us that no more reliance can be placed on them to aid us in protecting our rights; that National Democracy is worthless. We must also see in the act, a fixed and inexorable determination on the part of the majority never to admit another slave state, to stop forever the extension of slavery, and thus to bind the South to a triumphant car [sic] of an antagonistic majority.[53]

The lesson was clear. Even a friendly president had been unable to provide the necessary support to carry the day for the South's cause. Quitman was articulating a fear that an increasing number of Southerners would express many times over the next two years: An "antagonistic majority" from the North was now in a position to dictate national policy and (at least in the eyes of Southerners) threaten the viability of slavery.

52 For more on the problem of Kansas and the Know-Nothing party, see Holt, "The Politics of Impatience," and Gienapp, *Origins of the Republican Party*, pp. 229–37. On the significance of the Sumner affair on support for Kansas, see William E. Gienapp, "The Crime against Sumner: The Caning of Charles Sumner and the Rise of the Republican Party," *Civil War History* 25 (1979).
53 Quoted in Nevins, *Ordeal of the Union*, 3: 284–5.

We have examined the Kansas affair in such detail because a simple chronicle of events by itself reveals the deep divisions over slavery and just how irreconcilable these differences had become by 1858. Popular sovereignty had failed, and with it went the most promising hope for a compromise on the question of slavery. It failed because neither side could afford to lose to the "popular" will, and because the division over slavery went far beyond the borders of Kansas. Consequently, the national government was unable to act as an arbiter to resolve the issue. Finally, popular sovereignty failed because the act of voting on slavery in Kansas rekindled all the old passions and once again made slavery front-page news throughout the nation. Indeed, feelings about the outcome of the various territorial elections were probably more deeply held in many other parts of the country than they were in Lawrence or Topeka or Lecompton.[54] The option of whether Kansas was to be free or slave, therefore, could not be left to Kansans. When the decision eventually fell to the national government, the same old antagonisms surfaced. Only this time there was no more territory to divide between the contending factions. Someone had to lose. It was the South that lost, and they knew it.

A House Dividing: Republican Triumph and Southern Secession

The person caught in the middle of all this was the president of the United States, who found himself continuously torn between the pro- and antislave factions in his own party as well as those in the country as a whole. This tension is reflected in the pattern of voting in Presidential elections in the 1850s. Table 5.5 presents information on the three presidential elections between 1852 and 1860. In 1852, as we have seen, the Democrat Franklin Pierce swept into office with an overwhelming margin. The regional breakdown of support by party presented in Figure 5.7 shows that Pierce did very well in every region of the country. He was clearly a consensus choice of the people.

Franklin Pierce lived up to the expectations of those who wanted cooperation with Congress, not bold or independent leadership from the White House. He was content to support the efforts of the northern Democrats in the Senate, most notably Douglas of Illinois, in their efforts to implement the terms of the compromise so carefully worked out in

---

54 David Potter, for example, insists that many Kansans were initially far more concerned over establishing their title to land than whether or not slavery would be in the territory (*Impending Crisis*).

Table 5.5. *Presidential politics, 1852–60*

Candidate	Party	Popular votes		Electoral votes				
		Total	%	Total	North	West	Border	South
1852		3,157,326	100.00	296	110	66	32	88
Franklin Pierce	Democrat	1,601,274	50.72	254	92	66	20	76
Winfield Scott	Whig	1,386,580	43.92	42	18	0	12	12
John Hale	Free-Soil	156,667	4.96	0	0	0	0	0
1856		4,053,967	100.00	296	110	66	32	88
James Buchanan	Democrat	1,838,169	45.34	174	34	28	24	88
John C. Fremont	Republican	1,341,264	33.09	114	76	38	0	0
Millard Fillmore	Know-Nothing and Whig	874,534	21.57	8	0	0	8	0
1860		4,682,069	100.00	303	110	73	32	88
Abraham Lincoln	Republican	1,866,452	39.86	180	107	73	0	0
Stephen Douglas	Northern Democrat	1,376,957	29.41	12	3	0	9	0
John Bell	Conservative Union	849,781	18.15	39	0	0	12	27
John Breckinridge	Southern Democrat	588,879	12.58	72	0	0	11	61

Notes: North: Connecticut, Maine, Massachusetts, New Hampshire, New York, New Jersey, Pennsylvania, Rhode Island, and Vermont; West: California, Illinois, Indiana, Iowa, Michigan, Minnesota, Ohio, Oregon, and Wisconsin; Border: Delaware, Kentucky, Maryland, and Missouri; South: Alabama, Arkansas, Florida, Georgia, Louisiana, Mississippi, North Carolina, South Carolina, Tennessee, Texas, and Virginia.

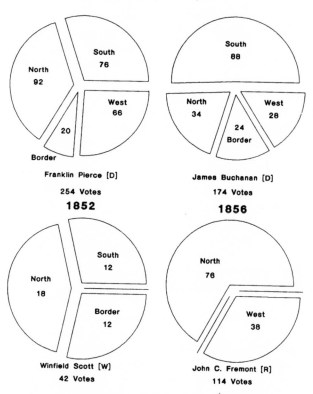

Figure 5.7. Electoral votes by region, 1852 and 1856

1850. Unfortunately, Pierce, who in the words of Allan Nevins, "was one of the quickest, most gracefully attractive, and withal weakest, of the men who have held his high office," proved to be unequal to the task of steering a course through the storms gathering in Congress.[55] By 1856 the question facing the Democrats was: Who should replace Pierce? The party's most outspoken leader, Stephen Douglas, had been seriously hurt by the furor over Nebraska, and nominating a Southerner was out of the

55 Nevins, *Ordeal of the Union*, 2: 40. Nevins notes that Pierce's wife and friends viewed the announcement of his candidacy "with alarm." This assessment is generally shared by other historians of the period, although Roy Nichols offers a slightly more sympathetic view, noting that "it was Pierce's misfortune to be elected chief-magistrate at a moment when probably no one was prepared for it or when no one could have occupied it successfully." See Roy F. Nichols, *Franklin Pierce: Young Hickory of the Granite Hills*, 2d ed. (University of Pennsylvania Press, 1958), p. 544.

question. Yet it was essential that the party's candidate be a "friend" of the South. After some bitter arguments, the delegates finally turned to an old party regular: James Buchanan. "Buchanan," notes one biographer, "had always shown a talent for shifting positions under political stress, and the balancing of issues had been a major part of his success."[56] That, of course, is precisely why the Democrats supported him for president. He was a diplomat who had served ably as secretary of state under Polk, and as emissary to Great Britain under Pierce. If anyone could quell the rising tide of violence and disunion, Buchanan appeared to be the man for the job.

He was opposed in the general election by two candidates. Former president Millard Fillmore accepted the nomination of the newly formed American party in February 1856.[57] In June the Republicans nominated John C. Fremont as their choice for president. Buchanan won the election handily enough, with 45 percent of the vote compared with Fremont's 33 percent. But, in addition to the large defection represented by the vote for Fillmore, Democrats had to be concerned with the pattern of regional support for the three candidates. More than half of Buchanan's electoral support (88 out of a total of 174 votes) came from the South, and an additional 24 votes came from the slave-holding border states. In the West, which had been swept by the two previous Democratic candidates, Buchanan got only 28 of the region's 66 votes. The Republican strategy was clear enough; concentrate on the free states of the North. It worked fairly well; they captured 76 electoral votes in the North and 38 in the West. This was a portent of things to come. The North and the West had enough electoral votes (176 out of 296) to elect a president even if the candidate received no support from other regions of the country.

As we have already seen, Buchanan proved unable to meet the challenge he faced over the next four years. Whether events had already proceeded beyond the point where any man could effect a compromise, or whether this failure reflected shortcomings of the new president can be debated.[58] But Buchanan's inability to deal with the situation in Kansas is a good example of the problems confronted by someone attempting to

56 Elbert B. Smith, *The Presidency of James Buchanan* (University Press of Kansas, 1975), p. 31.
57 The American party was a coalition formed from the Know-Nothing party of the North and what remained of the Whig party in the Upper South.
58 Buchanan has not fared well at the hands of historians. For a recent treatment of Buchanan's life that paints a favorable picture of his efforts to wrestle with the problems of his presidency, see Smith, *The Presidency of James Buchanan*. Potter is somewhat more equivocal (*The Impending Crisis*, pp. 517–24); Nevins is highly critical of Buchanan, particularly on his handling of the Lecompton affair (*Ordeal of the Union*, 3: 239).

straddle the slave issue. More and more people were considering turning to a candidate who would take the bull by the horns and confront the slavery issue. Something had to be done to end the paralysis that had griped the executive office since the death of Zachary Taylor.

In fact, the defeat of the bill for Kansas statehood had marked the end of serious attempts at compromise on slavery. Southern radicals bent their energies toward building up their political base and making sure that there would not be a repeat of the 1832 or 1849 fiascoes, when efforts to lead the South out of the union fell upon deaf ears within their own region. In the North, Republican leaders consolidated their gains and built a solid political base from which to make opposition to further extension of slavery an issue in 1858 and 1860. A key race was the 1858 senatorial contest in Illinois, which pitted Abraham Lincoln against Stephen Douglas. Accepting his party's nomination on June 16, 1858, Lincoln attacked Douglas's stand on slavery. In so doing, he eloquently stated what was to become the theme of the Republican party for the next two years:

> We are far now into the fifth year since a policy was initiated with the avowed object and confident promise of putting an end to slavery agitation. Under the operation of that policy, that agitation not only has not ceased, but has constantly augmented. In my opinion, it will not cease until a crisis has been reached and passed. "A house divided against itself cannot stand." I believe that this government cannot endure permanently half slave and half free. . . . Either the opponents of slavery will arrest the further spread of it, and place it where the public mind shall rest in the belief that it is in the course of ultimate extinction; or its advocates will push it forward until it shall become alike lawful in all the states, old as well as new, North as well as South.[59]

The senatorial race in Illinois in 1858 produced one of the most remarkable series of debates in American political history. Lincoln and Douglas met a total of seven times throughout the state. Thousands of people came to hear the two speakers, and the meetings drew national coverage from the news media. Douglas was by now the leader of the northern wing of the Democratic party, having narrowly lost the presidential nomination to Buchanan in 1856. He was a leading contender for his party's presidential nomination in 1860. Lincoln was a prominent politician in Illinois who had yet to make his mark on the national scene. In 1856 he had challenged the Democrats for the other senatorial seat in Illinois, held by James Shields. Although he lost that bid, he was instru-

---

59 Quoted in Nevins, *Ordeal of the Union*, 3: 361.

mental in getting Lyman Trumbull chosen over Shields, who had been Douglas's choice.[60] Now he was once again making a serious bid for the Senate, and an upset victory over Douglas would catapult him into national prominence as a leader of the young Republican party.

Lincoln sought to tie Douglas as closely as possible to the policy of "popular sovereignty" – allowing the voters in a territory to choose if they wanted slavery – that had produced such a furor in Kansas. At the debate in Freeport he asked Douglas: "Can the People of a United States territory, in any lawful way, . . . exclude slavery from its limits prior to the formation of a state constitution?"[61] This, of course, was the essence of popular sovereignty, and the Dred Scott decision had clearly stated that the Constitution guaranteed the right to own slaves. Douglas did not back away from supporting the policy that was embodied in the Kansas–Nebraska Act. He replied:

> As Mr. Lincoln has heard me answer a hundred times, the people of any territory can, by lawful means, exclude slavery from their limits. . . . It matters not what way the Supreme Court may hereafter decide as to the abstract question whether slavery may or may not go into a territory under the Constitution, the people have the lawful means to introduce it or exclude it as they please, for the reason that slavery can not exist a day or an hour unless it is supported by local police regulations.[62]

What became known as the "Freeport Doctrine" remained the cornerstone of Douglas's policy on the slave issue, and he defended it with great vigor. "I will never violate or abandon that doctrine," he proclaimed, "if I have to stand alone." His words were to prove prophetic as the 1860 election neared.

For his part, Douglas sought to portray Lincoln as the "friend of the Negro" and champion of emancipation. His attack threw Lincoln on the defensive. In response to one of Douglas's barbs Lincoln angrily retorted:

> I am not, nor ever have been, in favor of bringing about in any way the social and political equality of the black and white races . . . and I will say in addition to this that there is a physical difference between the black and white races which I believe will forever forbid the two races living together on terms of social and political equality.[63]

60 Lincoln's support for Trumbull paid large dividends when Trumbull bolted the Democratic party and joined Lincoln as a Republican. See Gienapp, *Origins of the Republican Party*, pp. 172–76.
61 Quoted in Fehrenbacher, *Slavery, Law, and Politics*, p. 262.
62 Ibid., pp. 262–3.
63 Cited in Nevins, *Ordeal of the Union*, 3: 386.

As to emancipation, Lincoln tried to make it clear that he had "no purpose, either directly or indirectly, to interfere with the institution of slavery where it exists." Yet he left little doubt that he believed in the right of blacks eventually to be free. "In the right to eat the bread, without the leave of anyone else, which his own hand earns," Lincoln went on, the black man "is my equal, and the equal of Judge Douglas, and the equal of every living man."[64] In the seventh and last debate, Lincoln eloquently stated the question facing the country:

> [Slavery] is the issue which will continue in this country when these poor tongues of Judge Douglas and myself shall be silent. It is the eternal struggle between these two principles – right and wrong – throughout the world. . . . And whenever we can get rid of the fog that obscures the real question – when we can get Judge Douglas and his friends to avow a policy looking to its perpetuation – we can get out from among them that class of men and bring them to the side of those who treat it as a wrong. Then there will be an end of it, and that end will be its "ultimate extinction."[65]

Two observations emerge from our brief look at the Lincoln–Douglas debates. First is the extent to which slavery dominated a series of debates by two men who were clearly aspiring to higher office. From the time of Martin Van Buren through James Buchanan, men seeking the presidency had carefully avoided taking strong stands on the slave issue. Lincoln and Douglas talked of little else. Obviously they realized that the next president would have to tackle the slave issue head on *before* he took office. The second observation is that the debates clearly reveal the deep-seated ambivalence of many Americans who wanted to eradicate slavery on the one hand, yet deny blacks social and economic equality on the other. The tensions produced by talk of immediate emancipation of four million black slaves were particularly high in the Midwest. Only the Ohio River separated Illinois from the slave South. However abhorrent slavery might be, racial fears of free blacks coming north across the river deterred many from supporting any form of emancipation. Neither candidate emerged as a champion of black rights.

Lincoln lost the battle for the Senate to Douglas in the fall of 1858, yet the victory proved to be a hollow one for Douglas. Two years later, it was Lincoln's Republican party that emerged victorious in the presidential election of 1860, and the debates of 1858 clearly aided Lincoln in this goal. His articulate statement of a policy of containment of slavery had stamped him as someone who could hold the strong antislavery vote without driving away the more moderate voters in the North.

64 Cited in ibid., p. 379.
65 Cited in ibid., p. 391.

Lincoln had claimed that a "house divided" could not stand. Others in the Republican party took an even more aggressive position on the possibility of conflict between slave and free societies. In December 1858, William Seward, after noting the differences between North and South, bluntly asked:

> Shall I tell you what this collision means? Those who think that it is accidental, unnecessary, the work of interested or fanatical agitators, and therefore ephemeral, mistake the case altogether. It is an irrepressible conflict between opposing and enduring forces, and it means that the United States must and will sooner or later, become entirely a slaveholding nation or entirely a free-labor nation.[66]

Such rhetoric did not go unanswered. Replying to Seward's speech, Senator James Hammond of South Carolina in effect agreed with Seward's conclusion:

> But the true issue is now made. The South is to be Africanized and the elections of 1860 are to decide the question. In other words it is emancipation or disunion after 1860, unless Seward is repudiated. If he is not we shall make jelly of him and his party in 1860, if we promptly accept and fight the battle right through on the issue tendered; or, failing in that, we are consolidated, organized, and trained for a Southern Republic.[67]

The emphasis on the 1860 elections is significant. For more than a decade, the strategy of nominating a candidate who represented a compromise on the slave issue had proved successful. In 1860, however, a major political party had emerged based on a strategy of confronting the slave issue. Even before the election, Southerners such as Senator Hammond were serving notice that a Republican victory would prompt a move to secede by southern extremists. In the past such threats had carried little weight. This time would be different.

Moderate Democrats hoped to avoid a sectional confrontation over slavery by once again presenting a united front against the Republican threat. However, the events of the past four years made such hopes illusory. When the Democrats convened in Charleston, South Carolina, toward the end of April, Stephen Douglas thought he had the nomination in his grasp. But Southerners refused to forgive Douglas for his opposition to the Lecompton Constitution. After fifty-seven ballots, he remained just a few votes short of nomination, and the convention adjourned without a nominee.

The scene now shifted to Chicago, where the Republicans were gather-

---

66 Quoted in Foner, *Free Soil, Free Labor and Free Men*, pp. 69–70. As Foner notes, Seward's theme was not new; he had been saying much the same thing for many years.
67 Quoted in Nevins, *Ordeal of the Union*, 3: 412.

ing. This also produced a surprise. Abraham Lincoln, the articulate Midwesterner from Illinois, was at best a "dark horse" candidate for his party's nomination when he arrived at the Republican convention. Although he had acquired a modest level of fame with his celebrated debates over slavery with Stephen Douglas two years earlier, he was still outside the inner ring of Republican leaders in the East, and few expected him to emerge as the party's standard bearer in the presidential election. William Seward of New York seemed a more likely choice. But, just as Douglas had fallen short in the Democratic convention, Seward did not have the votes to carry the day in Chicago. The difference was that the Republicans had someone to turn to. On May 19, in a burst of enthusiasm that literally brought down the canvas roof over the delegates, Abraham Lincoln was nominated.[68] His selection proved to be a masterful choice that marked a major turning point in the evolution of the Republican party. Republicans had always been a party with limited appeal outside the North, and there was no point in selecting a candidate who might appease the South. At the same time, it was important that the Republican candidate be viewed in the North as sufficiently moderate to attract dissident northern Democrats. Lincoln fit the bill.

The ball was now in the Democrats' court as that party reassembled on June 19 in Baltimore. This time the Douglas people prevailed, but it was a Pyrrhic victory. Dissatisfied Southerners refused to accept this outcome. Even before the party had selected Douglas, the Southerners bolted and convened their own convention a few blocks away. There they proceeded to nominate John Breckinridge of Kentucky as the nominee of the *southern* Democratic party. The rupture of the Democratic party was complete. While Republicans in Chicago had hailed Lincoln's nomination with unbridled enthusiasm, the Democrats departed Baltimore shouting recriminations at each other.

In May a group of those dissatisfied with the policies of both the major parties met in Baltimore in an effort to find a candidate who would represent an alternative to either the Republicans or the two factions of the Democrats. Representing what was left of the Know-Nothing or American party, old-line Whigs and a few Democrats from the border states, they chose John Bell of Tennessee as their candidate for president.

On November 6, 1860, Abraham Lincoln was elected president of the United States. As the distribution of electoral votes presented in Figure 5.8 shows, it was a purely sectional victory. Lincoln got barely 40 percent of the popular vote, and the Republicans did not even appear on the ballot in ten of the southern states. The fate of Stephen Douglas reveals how important the coalition between northern and southern Democrats

---

68 There are numerous accounts of this convention; none is better than that supplied by Nevins, *Ordeal of the Union*, 4: 229–60.

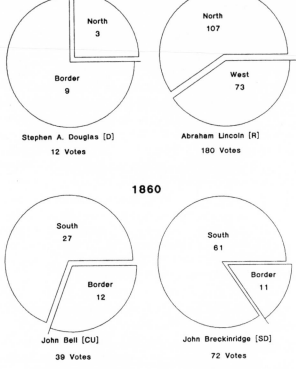

Figure 5.8. Electoral votes by region, 1860

had been. Douglas garnered 30 percent of the popular vote, but managed only 3 electoral votes from the free states. Breckinridge, by contrast, gained 72 electoral votes (all from the southern or border states) with only 12.5 percent of the popular vote. Even Bell, who got only 18 percent of the popular vote, did better than Douglas in the electoral college, receiving 39 votes. One fact jumps out from these numbers. Unless they could have cracked the Republican solidarity in the North and the West, the old coalition of Democrats would not have carried the day. Although he got only 40 percent of the vote, Lincoln received a substantial majority of the electoral votes.

Viewed in the context of presidential politics over the previous two decades, we can see why the South took such alarm over Lincoln's election. The cornerstone of southern political strategy since the founding of the Republic had been based on controlling the Senate and the presidency. Now they had lost both. The executive power, which had in the past tipped the balance of power to the South, would now swing the other way. The South's dominant position in the Republic had been over-turned.

Southern radicals promptly launched their campaign for secession. The South Carolina legislature, after learning the outcome of the election, passed a bill calling for a state convention to meet on January 15, 1861.[69] Within weeks, four other states – Georgia, Alabama, Florida, and Mississippi – had followed suit by calling for state conventions in January. Louisiana joined the movement by calling for a special session of the legislature to meet on the question of secession.[70] When the South Carolina convention met on December 20, 1860, the delegates unanimously voted to secede from the Union. By February 1861, seven states, all in the lower South, had left the Union.

Meanwhile, back in Washington, Congress made a last-ditch effort at compromise. In mid-December, at a time when only the South Carolina congressional delegations had gone home, a "Committee of Thirteen" was appointed in the Senate by Vice-President Breckinridge to seek a solution to the crisis. The committee was carefully chosen to balance both parties and regions, and it was agreed that a majority of both parties was needed for any action to be reported to the full Senate.[71] Brecken-ridge put forward a proposal that attempted to defuse the situation by reinstating the terms of the Missouri Compromise. Moderates were prepared to support such an idea, but Republican members, following the lead of their president-elect, demurred. The Breckenridge proposal, a desperate effort that really offered no new ideas, died in committee. In the House, efforts at compromise were even less successful. A committee of one representative from each state was appointed to investigate the crisis. The committee failed to report any viable solutions. Secession was a fact to which the federal government had to respond.

President Buchanan thought that secession was unconstitutional, but he also believed that he was not empowered to act against the authority of a sovereign state government. So he did nothing beyond an authorization to resupply the forts off the southern coast. By the time of Lincoln's inauguration on March 3, 1861, everyone was waiting for the new presi-

---

69 That date was moved forward to December 17 when the South Carolinians heard a rumor that Robert Toombs of Georgia had resigned his seat in the Senate and that the governor of Georgia had called for a state convention on the question of secession. The rumor proved to be false, but the Carolinians proceeded with their plans for an early convention.

70 In Texas, Governor Sam Houston, the man who had done so much to bring his state into the union, temporarily blocked the rush to secede by refusing to call the legislature into session.

71 The committee included, in addition to the vice president, Robert Toombs of Georgia and Jefferson Davis of Mississippi from the deep South; John Crittenden of Kentucky; Douglas of Illinois; and William Seward of New York and Benjamin Wade of Ohio from the Republicans.

dent's reaction to the crisis. The most pressing issue was the threat by South Carolina troops against the forts in Charleston Harbor. On April 6, 1861, Lincoln gave the order to reinforce Fort Sumter. His action gave the South Carolinians the excuse they needed to start a shooting war. On April 10 the bombardment began, and the rebellion had exploded into armed conflict.

Within a few weeks the remaining slave states acted on their decision to secede. The pivotal state was Virginia. Although it wavered momentarily, the institution of slavery proved too strong a tie to break. The Old Dominion went with the lower South on April 17, 1861. Three others followed in short order: Arkansas (May 5), Tennessee (May 7), and North Carolina (May 20). There were now two nations where there had been only one: the Confederate States of America and the United States of America.

Irrepressible Conflict and Bumbling Politicians: A Final View

Let us return for a moment to the question we posed at the outset of our investigation: Was war inevitable in the spring of 1861? Or was it a case of political leaders seeing it in their own narrow interests to keep the issue of slavery in the public's eye and then losing control of the situation?

When all is said and done, the question of "inevitability" comes down to an analysis of the tactical shortcomings of the politicians in the 1850s. The political decision that did more than anything else to keep slavery at the center of political debate during the 1850s was the Kansas–Nebraska Act. It is easy enough to indict Douglas and his colleagues in 1854 as cynical politicians who failed to appreciate the full consequences of what they were doing. Yet we should pause in this indictment long enough to note that, although the political maneuvering that went into the Kansas–Nebraska Act may have left much to be desired, it is unclear exactly what alternatives were open to Congress in 1854. The main criticism leveled at Douglas is that he should have stayed with his earlier position that Kansas was a free territory under the Compromise of 1820. This would have placated the North. But what of the South? If popular sovereignty was to mean anything to proponents of slavery, it meant there would be a "choice" for slavery in Kansas. Any attempt to organize the Kansas–Nebraska Territory was going to reopen the debate on slavery. Even with the benefit of a century or more of hindsight, critics have been unable to offer alternatives that would accomplish anything more than a few years of uneasy peace under the "truce" of 1850. The events that followed as voters in Kansas wrestled with popular sovereignty drove home the point that there no longer was any middle ground on which to shape a compromise between slave and free states.

Simply put, the situation in the 1850s was such that, if either side was prepared to press the issue of limiting or expanding slavery, armed conflict would surely result. In the crisis of 1850, neither side was prepared to take that step. What had changed by 1860, was that both sides were prepared to fight. Southerners had determined that leaving the Union was the only sure protection for their slave society. Northerners had become convinced that such an action was detrimental to their interests and should be prevented. Therein lies the final piece to our puzzle. Why were Northerners prepared to fight rather than simply let the South secede?

Americans had been "at each other's throat," so to speak, for almost two decades. And, as Lincoln had noted in his famous speech, a "house divided against itself can not stand." The irritation, frustration, and tension of almost continual political crises made it relatively easy to stir up strong feelings on either side of the Mason–Dixon line. In the North, a deep-seated belief in the sanctity of the American Union and the evils of slavery made the actions of the "rebels" seem even more reprehensible. But the North's determination to stand up to the southern challenge and keep the Union together rested on more than either patriotic ideology or a moral conviction that slavery was evil. There were very practical reasons for insisting that the South not be allowed to secede. Events of the past seventy years had shown that the two societies, slave South and free North, could not live side by side within the union. Why then, would one expect them to coexist peacefully as separate states outside the Union? If the slave South were allowed to leave the Union, what then would check the expansion of the slave power? We have seen that the South of the mid-nineteenth century was an expansionist system that coveted land to the west and to the south. That expansionism had surfaced time and again: in Missouri, in Texas, in Mexico, and most recently in Kansas.

One clear outcome of the elections following the Kansas dispute was that the North finally had contained the slave power within the political framework of the United States. Secession threatened to make that a hollow victory. If they gained status as an independent nation, slave-owners would be free to pursue a "foreign policy" just as inimical to the North's interests as that pursued by the "slave power" when it had control of the federal government within the union. To let the slave states secede would, in effect, be returning everything to ground zero. Lincoln, among others, understood this point quite clearly. In a letter to Lyman Trumbull of Illinois, he stated why he opposed further compromise with the South: "Let there be no compromise on the question of extending slavery. If there be, all our labor is lost, and ere long, must be done again. . . . The tug has to come, and better now than at any time here-after."[72] In short, Northerners went to war to preserve their security in a political union of states in North America. Their forefathers had equivo-cated on the slave issue in 1776 and again in 1790 in order to form a union in the first place. Now the time of reckoning had finally come and the North was prepared to fight rather than back away. Lincoln never wavered in his determination neither to compromise with the southern states at the last moment on the crucial issue of slavery, nor to allow them to leave the union. He hoped that a "show of force" might bring the rebellion to a speedy halt. His greatest gamble in this regard was the hope that Virginia would throw its lot with the Union. He lost that gamble when Virginia seceded, but it was a gamble he had to take.

Finally, it is worth remembering that wars are notoriously easy to start but, once fighting starts, very difficult to bring to an end. No one was likely to put out the fire touched off by the bombardment of Fort Sumter. This war would not end until 625,000 men had lost their lives. And it would not end until slavery had finally been abolished.

72 Quoted in Nevins, *Ordeal of the Union,* 4: 294.

Appendix Tables

Table A.5.1. *Immigration into the United States, 1820–60*

Year	All countries	Ireland	Germany	Other countries
1820	17,197	3,614	968	12,615
1821	15,688	1,518	383	12,787
1822	15,723	2,267	148	13,308
1823	13,017	1,908	183	10,926
1824	13,203	2,345	230	10,628
1825	14,980	4,888	450	9,642
1826	19,732	5,408	511	13,813
1827	30,330	9,766	432	20,132
1828	33,236	12,488	1,851	18,897
1829	32,018	7,415	597	24,006
1830	40,142	2,721	1,976	35,445
1831	58,269	5,772	2,413	50,084
1832	77,422	12,436	10,194	54,792
1833	69,346	8,648	6,988	53,710
1834	81,311	24,474	17,686	39,151
1835	51,075	20,927	8,311	21,837
1836	89,826	30,578	20,707	38,541
1837	89,307	28,508	23,740	37,059
1838	89,817	12,645	11,683	65,489
1839	69,810	23,963	21,028	24,819
1840	89,113	39,430	29,704	19,979
1841	83,256	37,772	15,291	30,193
1842	10,145	51,342	20,370	38,433

Table A.5.1. (cont.)

Year	All countries	Ireland	Germany	Other countries
1843	74,199	19,670	14,441	40,088
1844	88,554	33,490	20,731	34,333
1845	25,068	44,821	34,355	45,892
1846	74,936	51,752	57,561	65,623
1847	239,897	105,536	74,281	60,080
1848	240,671	112,934	58,465	69,272
1849	293,243	159,398	60,235	73,610
1850	290,783	164,004	78,896	47,883
1851	373,324	221,253	72,482	79,598
1852	363,842	159,548	145,918	58,376
1853	360,505	162,649	141,946	55,910
1854	420,292	101,606	215,009	103,677
1855	196,671	49,627	71,918	75,126
1856	196,458	54,349	71,029	71,080
1857	247,031	54,361	91,781	100,889
1858	120,507	26,873	45,310	48,324
1859	118,011	35,216	41,784	41,011
1860	149,321	48,637	54,491	46,193

Sources: For all countries: Peter D. McClelland and Richard Zeckhauser, *Demographic Dimensions of the New Republic: American Interregional Migration, Vital Statistics and Manumissions, 1800–1860* (Cambridge University Press, 1982), p. 113; for Ireland and Germany: U.S. Bureau of the Census, *Historical Statistics of the United States, Colonial Times to 1970*, part 1, (U.S. Government Printing Office, 1975), series C89, C92, C95, p. 106.

Table A.5.2. *Party affiliation of members of Congress for the elections of 1848–58*

Year	Democrat	Whig	Republican	Other
House of Representatives				
1848	112	109	0	9
1850	140	88	0	5
1852	159	71	0	4
1854	108	83	0	43
1856	118	0	92	26
1858	92 -	0	114	31
Senate				
1848	35	25	0	2
1850	35	24	0	3
1852	38	22	0	2
1854	40	15	0	5
1856	36	0	20	8
1858	36	0	26	4

Source: U.S. Bureau of the Census, *Historical Statistics of the United States, Colonial Times to 1970*, part 2 (U.S. Government Printing Office, 1975), series Y204–10, p. 1083.

Conflict and Compromise

Table A.5.3. *Native white population of the United States by census region of residence and birth, 1850 and 1860 (thousands)*

Census division of residence	Total native population	Census division of birth			
		New England	Middle Atlantic	East North Central	West North Central
1850					
New England	2,821.8	2,367.9	237.4	171.2	9.4
Middle Atlantic	5,484.0	46.6	4,566.5	725.1	39.1
East North Central	2,757.4	2.4	16.3	2,582.6	96.7
West North Central	373.5	0.2	0.6	12.8	334.7
South Atlantic	3,764.8	5.1	60.7	286.2	80.8
East South Central	2,179.5	0.5	1.8	184.6	131.1
West South Central	286.0	0.4	0.9	2.8	3.4
Mountain	59.8	0.0	0.0	0.0	0.0
Pacific	9.9	0.0	0.0	0.0	0.0
Total	17,736.7	2,423.2	4,884.3	3,965.3	695.2
1860					
New England	3,144.6	2,584.3	212.2	224.2	57.3
Middle Atlantic	6,944.0	64.5	5,582.9	946.1	185.0
East North Central	4,562.9	5.1	29.7	4,044.3	358.7
West North Central	848.7	0.7	2.0	27.5	756.0
South Atlantic	4,264.7	6.8	67.0	265.6	126.0
East South Central	2,781.4	0.8	3.1	202.8	211.0
West South Central	550.0	0.5	1.6	4.3	7.8
Mountain	100.7	0.0	0.0	0.0	0.0
Pacific	101.5	0.5	0.6	1.1	0.5
Total	23,298.8	2,663.1	5,899.0	5,716.0	1,702.2

Notes: New England: Connecticut, Maine, Massachusetts, New Hampshire, Rhode Island, and Vermont; Middle Atlantic: New Jersey, New York, and Pennsylvania; East North Central: Illinois, Indiana, Michigan, Ohio, and Wisconsin; West North Central: Iowa, Kansas, Minnesota, Missouri, and Nebraska; South Atlantic: Delaware, District of Columbia, Florida, Georgia, Maryland, North Carolina, South Carolina, and Virginia; East South

Table A.5.3. (*cont.*)

South Atlantic	East South Central	West South Central	Mountain	Pacific
11.1	5.9	5.5	1.1	12.3
55.2	19.8	12.7	2.3	16.7
7.0	21.8	14.6	2.5	13.3
0.5	3.0	11.6	1.3	8.9
2,811.3	446.4	65.5	0.5	8.3
22.0	1,705.0	123.3	0.8	10.4
0.9	5.8	270.1	0.1	1.6
0.0	0.0	0.0	59.8	0.0
0.0	0.0	0.0	0.0	9.8
2,907.9	2,207.7	503.3	68.5	81.3
12.2	7.3	5.9	6.0	35.1
68.5	24.0	15.7	10.3	47.1
10.4	32.2	24.0	17.1	41.4
0.9	5.8	23.5	7.2	25.2
3,236.2	411.9	133.7	3.0	14.6
28.9	2,048.7	263.1	4.3	18.8
1.2	8.9	518.8	0.9	5.9
0.0	0.0	0.0	100.7	0.0
0.1	0.1	0.2	0.5	98.0
3,358.5	2,538.9	984.9	150.1	286.2

Central: Kentucky, Tennessee, Alabama, and Mississippi; West South Central: Arkansas, Louisiana, and Texas; Mountain: Colorado, New Mexico, Nevada, North Dakota Territory, and Utah; Pacific: California, Oregon, and Washington.

Source: U.S. Bureau of the Census, *Historical Statistics of the United States from Colonial Times to 1970*, part 1 (U.S. Government Printing Office, 1975), series C15–24, pp. 89–91.

6

Slavery and the War

> If there be those who would not save the Union unless they could at the same time *save* slavery, I do not agree with them. If there be those who would not save the union unless they could, at the same time, *destroy* slavery, I do not agree with them. My paramount object in this struggle is to save the union and it is not either to save or destroy slavery. If I could save the Union without freeing *any* slave I would do it, and if I could save the Union by freeing some and leaving others alone, I would also do that. What I do about slavery and the colored race I do because I believe it helps the union; and what I forbear I forbear because I do not believe it would help save the union.
>
> Abraham Lincoln, August 1862[1]

Abraham Lincoln's claim that preservation of the Union, not the ultimate fate of slavery, was the paramount objective in the Civil War reveals a long-standing American dilemma that was brought to the fore by the outbreak of war. On the one hand, men such as Lincoln clearly felt that it was the presence of slavery, and the political arrogance of the slave power, that had brought about the conflict between the states. Slavery, in their eyes, was an abhorrent institution that had to be brought under control – controlled, but not necessarily eliminated. For if slavery were eliminated, what would become of the four million freed blacks? Only a small fraction of Americans regarded immediate emancipation for black Americans as a desirable social objective; most regarded such a drastic step with considerable fear. "Control of the slave power" was a political slogan that had gained ready support through the 1850s; "freedom and equality for black Americans" would attract far less enthusiasm from the northern electorate in the 1860s.[2]

At the root of this tension was the racial prejudice that characterized

---

1 Letter to the New York *Tribune* dated August 22, 1862. Quoted in Allan Nevins, *Ordeal of the Union* (Charles Scribners and Sons, 1960), 6: 232.
2 An excellent study of the problem of racism and opposition to emancipation in the midwestern states is V. Jacque Voegeli, *Free But Not Equal: The Midwest and the Negro during the Civil War* (University of Chicago Press, 1967). For a more general analysis of the role of racism and the question of black rights, see Barbara J. Fields, "Ideology and Race in American History," in *Region, Race and Reconstruction: Essays in Honor of C. Vann Woodward*, eds. J. Morgan Kousser and James M. McPherson (Oxford University Press, 1982).

northern as well as southern society on the eve of the Civil War. However repugnant the South's peculiar institution may have been, it served as a very effective policy of race control working to the advantage of those in the North as well as in the South. So long as blacks were locked in bondage in the South, Northerners need not worry about the race question in their own part of American society. As the treatment of free blacks in the years prior to the war rather clearly demonstrates, Americans in the free states were not at all eager to see large numbers of free blacks in their midst.[3] Even most "radical" Northerners had no intention of allowing blacks to become citizens on an equal plane with white Americans.

Equality for black Americans, of course, had never been the mainspring of antislavery sentiment in the North. The political debates of the 1850s, as we have seen, stressed the need to *contain the spread of slavery*, not to eliminate it through emancipation. So long as containment remained the focus of the debate, the racism of Northerners did not pose an obstacle to the support for antislavery proposals. Indeed, racist views tended to support the movement to limit the expansion of black slavery. An important element of the Free-Soilers' objection to slavery in the territories was an objection to allowing blacks – slave or free – to settle in the western lands. Emancipation of slaves on anything approaching a grand scale was never seriously considered for discussion in the antebellum period because the property rights of slaveholders were protected by the Constitution. The costs attached to any feasible scheme to convince slaveowners to relinquish that right were simply prohibitively high.[4]

The outbreak of open rebellion in 1861 changed all that. Southern slaveholders clearly forfeited the constitutional protection of their human property by attempting to dissolve the Union. Yet the question of

3   For a view of northern racism toward free blacks before 1860, see Eugene Berwanger, *The Frontier against Slavery: Western Anti-Negro Prejudice and the Slavery Extension Controversy* (University of Illinois Press, 1967); and Leon F. Litwack, *North of Slavery: The Negro in the Free States, 1790–1860* (University of Chicago Press, 1971). Bernard Schwartz makes a particular point of the enactment of northern prejudice into law in his interpretation of the Dred Scott case in *From Confederation to Nation: The American Constitution, 1835–1877* (Johns Hopkins Press, 1973), pp. 127–9.

4   Emancipation did occur in the northern states; however, because most slaveowners had ample time either to leave the state or to sell their slaves before any emancipation act took effect, the number of slaves affected by this emancipation was quite small. On northern emancipation, see Arthur Silversmit, *The First Emancipation: The Abolition of Slavery in the North* (University of Chicago Press, 1967); and Claudia Dale Goldin, "The Economics of Emancipation," *Journal of Economic History* 33 (March 1973). As we noted in Chapter 3, the only feasible option would be purchase of slaves by the government, and the costs of such a scheme – even if spread over many years – would be enormous.

whether blacks would be emancipated even if the Union prevailed in the forthcoming struggle was far from settled. Lincoln detested slavery. But, whatever his personal feelings toward full emancipation of blacks may have been, the president was acutely aware that many of his countrymen were ambivalent in their support of emancipation. As the quotation from his letter to the *Tribune* suggests, Lincoln's first priority with regard to emancipation was whether any action might have an effect on the outcome of the war. Neither the president nor his advisors were prepared to rule out the possibility that the "rebellion" might end with slavery still in place throughout the southern states.

So, in the spring of 1861, as the two armies prepared for combat, the struggle to emancipate slaves still had a long way to go, even if the Union won the war. An immediate problem, however, was posed by the growing presence of blacks who, by the summer of 1861, were already fleeing to the Union lines seeking their freedom. Were they to be denied that freedom? Were they to remain slaves irrespective of the outcome of the war? Although the Union government hoped to equivocate for as long as possible on the issue of a general emancipation of all slaves, the growing number of blacks who had left their masters and sought freedom in the North made that equivocation increasingly difficult. By taking matters into their own hands, the slaves forced Congress and the president to deal with the question of freeing slaves from the outset of the war.

Southerners were also called upon to reassess their "peculiar institution." We have seen how slavery fostered a class society in the South with a relatively small number of rich slaveholders at the top of the wealth pyramid, and a much larger number of poor nonslaveholders at the bottom. Most of these nonslaveholders, the "yeoman" farmers of the South, had little use for slavery. They regarded it as necessary to control the black labor required to run the plantation economy, but they resented the presence of black slave labor. Still, the slave system required very little from yeoman farmers in the way of explicit "costs," and the prosperity of the plantation economy offered very real benefits in the form of readily accessible markets for the small surpluses of staple crops produced on the nonslave farms. There had always been tensions between slaveholders and those without slaves in the South, but before the war these tensions were masked behind a common interest of opposing northern interference with their system of chattel labor.[5]

The question of secession and war presented nonslaveowning South-

5 On the tensions between slave and nonslave farms, see Emory M. Thomas, *The Confederate Nation: 1861–1865* (Harper Torchbooks, 1979), chap. 1; and Steven Hahn, *The Roots of Southern Populism: Yeoman Farmers and the Transformation of the Georgia Upcountry, 1850–1860* (Oxford University Press, 1983), chap. 3.

erners with a Hobson's choice: Support the slave oligarchy of the South, or support the "Black Republicans" of the North. Of the two, support for slavery seemed the lesser evil. A surge of southern "nationalism," fueled by the outbreak of hostilities in April 1861, tipped the decision in favor of supporting the slave masters. But as the war went on, it became increasingly apparent that the real burden of defending slavery was falling most heavily on those who stood to gain the least from victory – white farmers who owned no slaves. The tensions that had been suppressed during the political struggles to defend slavery against the outside agitation of Northerners during the antebellum period were brought to the surface and magnified by the strains of the war on the South.

In the end, those strains had a profound effect on the South's war effort. The slave system that had been so instrumental in bringing on the war, proved to be equally instrumental in determining the outcome of the fight.

Defending Slavery: Military Strategy in the North and the South

Despite the saber rattling and rhetoric of the previous decade, neither side was prepared for war when it came. At the time of Lincoln's election, the United States Army had a total of only 15,259 enlisted men and 1,105 commissioned officers scattered, for the most part, along the western frontier and in a few coastal forts. Both Lincoln and Jefferson Davis called for volunteers to carry the fight to a quick conclusion, and both received an enthusiastic response. With Richmond and Washington less than one hundred miles apart, each side hoped to strike a knockout blow by capturing the opponent's capital. Both sides assembled sizable armies in front of their own capitals.

Urged on by his commander in chief, the Union general Irwin McDowell broke his camp outside Washington on July 21, 1861, and advanced south to engage the Confederate Army commanded by P. T. Beauregard, the man who had orchestrated the bombardment of Fort Sumter three months earlier. McDowell's maneuver instigated the first major engagement of armies in the Civil War: the Battle of Bull Run. McDowell's plan of attack was sound enough, but the raw troops he commanded were not equal to the challenge of carrying it out. The Union forces pressed their attack and came close to carrying the day. However, the timely arrival of Confederate troops from the Shenandoah Valley late in the afternoon allowed the rebels to launch a decisive counterattack against the weary federal troops. What began as an orderly Union retreat toward Washington soon turned into a full-scale rout. The organization of units simply disintegrated, and disorganized and demoralized troops continued to wander back into Washington for the next three days. The first major battle of the war was an unmitigated disaster for the Union.[6]

Bull Run was one of the most decisive victories gained by either side during the entire war. The Union army had been routed and the road to Washington seemed open. But the Confederates were themselves badly disorganized, and hardly in a position to capitalize on their enormous success.[7] An obvious lesson to be learned from Bull Run was that this war would require more than a few months of hasty preparation. The high commands on both sides sat down to consider what sort of strategies would be required.

The Confederates had one enormous advantage over their opponent: Theirs was basically a defensive situation. So long as the South's armies could repel any Union invasion, the Confederacy could survive. Being on the defensive not only greatly enhanced the Confederates' strategic options, it also provided them with a huge tactical advantage because of the introduction of the rifled musket in the 1850s. Prior to the introduction of rifled barrels, a muzzle-loading musket could fire accurately perhaps eighty to one hundred yards, and anything beyond three hundred yards was effectively out of range. A rifled musket had an effective range of about one thousand yards, and a decent marksman could hit a target at about five hundred yards. This meant that the distance over which an attacker had to move while under accurate fire was increased by a factor of five, an enormous advantage to the defender. The rifled musket also meant that effective fire power no longer depended so heavily on close-order drill and discipline. A few men with rifles behind a fence or ridge

6 Surprisingly, there are relatively few detailed studies of this first major battle of the Civil War. For a good account of the efforts to mobilize raw troops and to fight a battle for which neither side was really prepared, see William C. Davis, *Battle of Bull Run: A History of the First Major Campaign of the Civil War* (Louisiana State University Press, 1977).

7 The failure of the Confederates to follow up their victory was the subject of considerable debate in the months and years that followed. With the advantage of hindsight, most observers seem to agree that a Confederate advance toward Washington immediately after the battle would not have produced a decisive outcome to the war, or even the capture of Washington. They point out that the Confederate Army was itself quite disorganized, and no preparations had been made for such an advance. Rain, which began immediately after the battle, would have posed insurmountable difficulties in keeping the advancing army supplied. Finally, although many of the federal units that had been engaged in the battle were disorganized, McDowell still had a force of at least 11,000 reserves at his immediate disposal, and a force of 18,000 troops was only a few miles away at Harpers Ferry under the command of General Robert Patterson. It seems very unlikely that the Confederates could have pressed their advantage to the point of capturing Washington. The problem, in the eyes of contemporary critics, is that they did nothing at all, thus allowing the disorganized Union troops to regroup in front of Washington.

could lay down a very effective fire against advancing troops. This made it much easier for units to fall back in the face of an attack and establish a new line of defense further to the rear.[8] Consequently, even when one side won a stunning tactical victory, as the Confederates achieved at Bull Run, the advantage was difficult to exploit. Battles seldom produced a strategic advantage sufficient to produce a major change in the larger picture of the war. Typically, the victors of a battle licked their wounds and the losers regrouped to fight another day. All of this worked to the South's advantage; it would be difficult for the Northerners to gain a clear decision on the battlefield.

The advantage of being on the defensive was partially offset by two problems facing the Confederates. The first was that, so long as they were willing to press the attack, time was on the Union's side. With each month that passed, the larger population and greater economic power of the union would become more evident on the battlefield. At some point, therefore, the Southerners had to carry the war to the North if they wished to avoid a prolonged test of strength that would eventually work very much to their disadvantage. Unfortunately, attempts to execute this policy proved to be costly. Twice in the course of the war, Robert E. Lee, the brilliant Confederate commander, led his Army of Northern Virginia onto northern soil, and both times he was sharply rebuffed. This inability of the South to launch an effective counterstroke left the initiative of carrying on the war in northern hands, and placed a relentless pressure on Confederate defenses.

The second problem confronting the South's military commanders was the need to defend *territory*. To take maximum advantage of being on the defensive, a commander would prefer to choose both the time and place where any battle would be fought. If southern commanders had been free to move anywhere and choose whether to fight, then the enormous area of the South would have made it extremely difficult for northern commanders ever to gain a decisive edge in battle. One had only to look back to the campaigns of George Washington in the American Revolution to see a classic example of how such a strategy could wear down a militarily

---

8 While many writers have stressed the advantage of the rifled musket to the defenders, it should be noted that the longer range of the rifle could produce a distinct advantage to the *offense* when an attacking force had a significant numerical superiority. This is because the greater range of the rifle enabled a larger number of men to engage the enemy at any point in time. Thanks to the accuracy of the rifle, the concentration of firepower from the larger force could inflict a proportionately greater number of casualties on the defenders than on the attackers. For an argument that this is why casualty rates between the two armies of the Civil War were often quite similar regardless of who was attacking or defending, see Richard E. Beringer, Herman Hattaway, Archer Jones, and William N. Still, Jr., *Why the South Lost the War* (University of Georgia Press, 1986), pp. 468–76.

superior enemy. Over the course of the Revolutionary War, British troops occupied every major city in the colonies, typically without even being challenged by Washington's troops. But these were meaningless victories, for as Washington commented, "it is our arms, not defenseless towns they have to subdue."[9] The British knew Washington was right; unless they could defeat his army, they could not destroy the colonists' ability to carry on the fight. Simply by keeping his army in the field, Washington was eventually able to gain the decisive victory he needed at Yorktown in 1781 – after nearly six years of fighting on the defensive.

Why was the South unable to follow a similar strategy in the Civil War? Because they could not afford to let the Union army occupy large areas of Southern territory. To do so would undermine the very foundation of the southern cause: the defense of slavery. Southern commanders had to protect territory from invasion because of the need to protect slave property. The stability of Confederate society required that the South's armies be able to keep territory secure from invasion. Confederate armies also needed to control territory in order to feed their troops. Unfortunately for the South, the structure of the slave economy did not serve them well in this regard. The plantations of the South produced food for themselves, but did not generate large surpluses of food to feed others. The most productive food-producing areas of the Confederacy were the Shenandoah Valley in Virginia and the areas of eastern Tennessee and northern Georgia and Alabama. These areas were vulnerable to Union attack, because they were along the borders of the Confederacy.

The South, in short, had to defend southern soil from northern invaders. This negated some of the advantages inherent in being on the defensive. In particular, it made the vast size of the South something of a liability rather than an asset because of the need to defend long frontiers. Nevertheless, as long as they were patient enough to wait and see where the Union forces planned to strike, the Confederate high command could use their "interior lines" of communication and supply to concentrate their forces to meet the threat.[10]

For the Union, of course, the problem was exactly the reverse of that facing the Confederacy. After Bull Run, it was apparent to Lincoln and

---

9 Quoted in Alan R. Millett and Peter Maslowski, *For the Common Defense: A Military History of the United States of America* (Free Press, 1984), p. 66.

10 Having "interior lines" of communication refers to a situation where one side has established a position such that the supply lines connecting different army groups are shorter for them than for the enemy. The Confederates enjoyed interior lines along most of their frontiers, particularly in the east. An excellent introduction to these and other concepts of tactical and strategic maneuvers is in Herman Hattaway and Archer Jones, *How the North Won: A Military History of the Civil War* (University of Illinois Press, 1983), appendix A.

his generals that they must devise a strategy that would, in effect, conquer the South. This was no mean feat. The Confederacy encompassed a huge area, much of which was only sparsely settled. Supplying an invading army over long distances in hostile country would be difficult even with a good transportation network, and the South was not known for having good roads. To be sure, the Upper South, where the bulk of the fighting took place, did have excellent rivers to serve as transportation. But to an invading army a system of rivers was a two-edged sword. Although they offered an effective means of transportation, rivers and streams also provided highly effective lines of natural defense for the defenders. Nowhere was this more evident than in northern Virginia, where, after crossing the Potomac, an invader is confronted with the Rappahannock, York, and James rivers along with all of their lesser tributaries, "creeks," and "runs" that honeycombed the areas north of Richmond. In the hands of a tactician such as Lee, these waterways provided formidable obstacles to Union advances into Virginia. In the West, the Ohio, Tennessee, Cumberland, and Mississippi rivers offered Confederate defenders natural lines of fortification against invasion.

The ranking officer in the Union army in the spring of 1861 was Winfield Scott, a man who had fought in the War of 1812 and led the victorious American army into Mexico City in 1848. Scott recognized a need for an overall strategic plan for the Union war effort. The plan that he eventually devised had four key elements, which are illustrated in Map 6.1.

First priority was for the Union to gain control of the Mississippi River (point 1). This would not only cut the Confederacy in half, but would also give Union commanders an invaluable basis for supplying all of their subsequent operations in the West. Second was to establish a naval blockade of the Southern coast (point 2). Scott recognized that the South's slave economy had always depended on external sources for the supply of manufactured articles. He was convinced that an effective naval blockade would eventually have a telling effect on the Confederate war effort. Finally, although he gave it considerably less importance than his commander in chief, Scott proposed that the Union army should try to capture the Confederate capital at Richmond and knock Virginia out of the war (point 3). Lincoln quickly endorsed these objectives and added a fourth: to hold Kentucky and attack the heart of the Confederacy through Tennessee (point 4).

The plan was both ambitious in its scope and cautious in its method. It called for a massive build up of forces, and counseled a "divide and conquer" approach rather than an attempt to occupy large areas of the South. Critics dubbed it *Anaconda* after the South American snake that

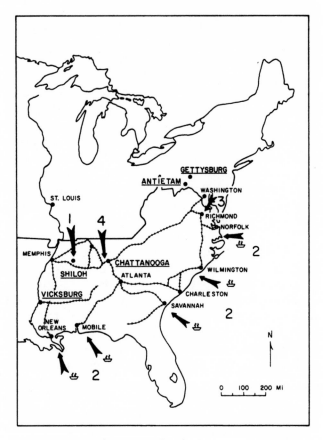

Map 6.1. The Union plan for victory, 1861

slowly strangles its victims, and complained that blockades and control
of rivers would never bring the South to its knees. The only element of
the plan that was met with enthusiasm was the frontal assault on Richmond, an operation that Scott felt was not as important as the blockade
or operations in the West. Although this initial proposal underwent
many minor modifications as the war went on, the four major objectives
it outlined provided the strategic overview that guided military decisions
by the Union high command, and particularly Lincoln, throughout the
war.

The Fortunes of War: From Shiloh to Chattanooga

In the fullness of time, Scott's Anaconda plan provided a blueprint for Union victory. But the best-laid plans of mice and men can easily go awry. To win the war, the Union had to defeat the Confederate armies in the field and ultimately occupy the South. This proved to be no mean feat. Confederate victories such as those at Bull Run (twice), Fredericksburg, and Chancellorsville testify to the success of the outnumbered rebels in holding off their stronger opponent for nearly four years. Yet these and other battles that the South either won or fought to a draw tend to obscure the fact that, apart from Bull Run in April 1861, the South *lost* the five crucial battles of the war: Shiloh, Antietam, Gettysburg, Vicksburg, and Chattanooga. The collective effect of these Confederate defeats was to eliminate any threat of further offensive action by the Southern armies, and to open the Confederacy to invasion by the Union armies in the spring of 1864.

Moreover, the significance of these battles goes beyond the impact they had on armies and military strategy. Morale, both at the front and at home, rose and fell with news of success or failure on the battlefield. Unlike past wars, when it took weeks, or even months, for news of battles to reach people back home, the advent of the telegraph meant that news of victories or defeats could be broadcast within a day of the outcome. Each of these battles was followed by a serious erosion of morale in the South, much of which could not be recovered. Equally important was the boost of morale that the victories at Antietam, Vicksburg, and Gettysburg gave to people in the North. Unlike the leaders of the South, who could counter discouraging news by rallying people to defend their homes against the invading Yankees, the North's leaders depended on military success to maintain morale to carry on the fight. Finally, military success proved to be vitally important in sustaining the campaign for emancipation. It is therefore worth taking a brief look at these battles.

A key to Confederate defenses in the West was their control of the Mississippi, Tennessee, and Cumberland rivers. In February 1862 the Union general Ulysses S. Grant captured two key Confederate positions: Fort Henry on the Tennessee River, and Fort Donelson on the Cumberland River.[11] Grant then proceeded south down the Tennessee River, and by the first week in April his army had reached a place on the

---

11 For an excellent analysis of the significance of Grant's victories at Fort Donelson and Fort Henry, see Benjamin Franklin Cooling, *Forts Henry and Donelson: The Key to the Confederate Heartland* (University of Tennessee Press, 1987).

Tennessee River near the Shiloh courthouse (see map 6.1). There he
paused until he could be joined by the troops of Don Carlos Buell, who
was marching south through Nashville.

Grant's successful piercing of the Confederate line of defense along the
rivers posed a serious threat to the South's military situation in the West.
The Confederate commanders responded by concentrating all their available forces at Corinth, and then quickly moving to attack Grant before
he could be joined by Buell's army. The plan nearly worked. Early on the
morning of April 6, 1862, the Confederates launched an attack that took
Grant's army by surprise and drove his troops back toward the Tennessee River. Though badly mauled, the northern troops were able to
rally from the shock of the initial attack and subsequently held their line
in the face of repeated Confederate assaults. Unfortunately for the Confederate army, its commander, Albert Sydney Johnston, had been mor-
tally wounded in the day's action. Amid the ensuing confusion, the new
commander, P. T. Beauregard, elected to let his troops rest rather than
pressing the attack further late in the afternoon. This decision proved to
be a fatal mistake; Buell's troops arrived late in the day and crossed the
river to reinforce Grant's beleaguered troops. The following morning
Grant ordered a counterattack that drove the rebels from the field. Beauregard managed an orderly retreat to Corinth, but he was forced to
abandon that city at the end of May.[12]

Grant's victory at Shiloh, together with the Union capture of New
Orleans later the same month, proved to be a pivotal turning point in the
war. Grant was now free to concentrate his attention on Vicksburg and
closing the Mississippi. Although another fifteen months would pass
before Vicksburg finally fell, the die was cast by the outcome at Shiloh.
The Confederates would never again regain the initiative in the West.[13]

---

12 For a detailed account of the fighting around Shiloh Courthouse, see James Lee
   McDonough, *Shiloh – In Hell before Night* (University of Tennessee Press, 1977). The
   subtitle of the book is a reference to the ferocity of the fighting at Shiloh. In this battle,
   the first major engagement after Bull Run, the North suffered over 13,000 casualties
   out of a total force of 55,000 (including Buell's troops); the South suffered 10,700
   casualties from an army of about 40,000.

13 In retrospect, Shiloh was important not only for strategic reasons, but in terms of its
   effect on the generals involved as well. Grant, who had been absent from his army at
   the time of the attack, would surely have been discredited had the Confederates
   succeeded. Sherman, who commanded the Union right wing, showed incredible laxity
   in failing to have his troops dig in when confronted by a large enemy force only a few
   miles away, and would similarly have been blamed. Even with the victory, the high
   number of casualties produced pressure to remove Grant. Lincoln demurred, claiming
   that "I need this man; he fights." The Confederates suffered the death of one of their
   more able commanders, Albert Sydney Johnston. Although Beauregard took temporary command, the Confederates were unable to find anyone of Johnston's stature to
   replace him, and the command structure in the West remained in disarray for some
   time.

Once the Mississippi River was under Union control, their armies in the West could focus their full attention on the final element of the Union plan: an invasion of the heartland of the Confederacy. What had been a crack in the Confederate defenses at Forts Donelson and Henry had grown to a gaping hole. Nor did it take a military mind to assess the importance of the situation. "Those western men have not held their towns as we held and hold Charleston or as the Virginians hold Richmond," observed Mary Boykin Chesnut in the fall of 1864.[14] She was right; the Confederacy's inability to defend its western territory proved eventually to be its downfall.

Still, as summer turned to autumn in 1862, the downfall of the Confederacy was hardly obvious. The great Union offensive of the previous spring had been far less successful in the East. Robert E. Lee had assumed command of the Army of Northern Virginia, and had successfully turned back the Union threat to Richmond in a series of bloody battles.[15] Lee followed this success with a second victory not far from where the first battle of the war took place. In the West, things were also going poorly for the Union cause. After occupying Corinth at the end of May, Grant had found his lines of supply badly extended. By the end of the year, Confederate raids on his rear had forced him to pull back into Tennessee.

The Union invasion had been checked; now it was time for the Confederates to assume the offensive. Another victory over the federal army would push the dispirited Union morale even lower. "When the Second Bull Run campaign closed," claimed General James Longstreet after the war, "we had the most brilliant prospects the Confederates ever had."[16] Lee was also optimistic; writing to President Davis on September 3, 1862, he explained that "the present seems to be the most propitious time since the commencement of the war for the Confederate Army to

14 Mary Chesnut, dated August 6, 1864, in C. Vann Woodward, ed., *Mary Chesnut's Civil War* (Yale University Press, 1981), p. 634. Mrs. Chesnut was wife of James Chesnut of South Carolina, who had served in the United States Senate and was a prominent leader during the war. Her diary offers a very candid and valuable view into the reactions of people back home to the changing military fortunes of the Confederacy.

15 A Union army led by General George B. McClellan had advanced up the Yorktown Peninsula toward Richmond. Despite the fact that he enjoyed a sizable numerical superiority, McClellan was excessively cautious and allowed Lee to outmaneuver him and eventually force abandonment of his attack on Richmond. Although he failed to capture Richmond, McClellan's "Peninsular Campaign" was the most successful Union effort against the Confederate capital until the very end of the war. One of the more notable outcomes of the fighting was the appointment of Lee as commander of the Army of Northern Virginia, a post he held for the rest of the war.

16 James Longstreet, "The Invasion of Maryland," in *Battles and Leaders of the Civil War*, eds. Robert U. Johnson and Clarence C. Buel (The Century Company, 1884), 2: 663. Longstreet was at that time one of Lee's division commanders; he would eventually rise to become the second in command of the Army of Northern Virginia and one of Lee's most trusted commanders.

enter Maryland."[17] Davis heartily agreed. More than a tactical advantage might be gained from an invasion; a victory of southern arms on northern territory might tempt the European powers to intervene in the American conflict. Certainly the British were toying with the idea; on September 4, Viscount Palmerston, the British prime minister, wrote to his foreign minister, Lord John Russell, that:

> The detailed account given in the *Observer* to-day of the Battles of August 29 and 30 between the Confederates and the Federals show that the latter got a very complete smashing; and it seems not altogether unlikely that still greater disasters await them, and that even Washington or Baltimore may fall into the hands of the Confederates. If this should happen, would it not be time for us to consider whether in such a state of things England and France might not address the contending parties and recommend an arrangement upon the basis of separation?[18]

A week later, Palmerston wrote his foreign minister again, noting that "it is evident that a great conflict" was taking place between the two armies, and adding that:

> If the Federals sustain a great defeat, they may at once be ready for mediation, and the iron should be struck while it is hot. If, on the other hand, they should have the best of it, we may wait a while and see what may follow.[19]

Palmerston's suggestion that Britain and France intervene to mediate a peace was a possibility that held out the best hope for Confederate victory. Demoralized by past military failure, impressed with the seeming invincibility of Lee's veterans, and faced with pressure from France and Britain, the North might be forced to accept the reality of southern independence.

So, as the Army of Northern Virginia headed into Maryland, much hung in the balance. In a bold gamble, Lee split his army and sent "Stonewall" Jackson on a circuitous route to capture Harpers Ferry while the remaining part of his forces were dispersed over a twenty-mile front foraging for supplies, and perhaps gaining a few recruits to the Confederate cause, in eastern Maryland. Lee knew that he was exposing

---

17 Lee to Jefferson Davis, September 3, 1862; letter reproduced in James V. Murfin, *The Gleam of Bayonets: The Battle of Antietam and the Maryland Campaign in 1862* (1965; paperback ed., Louisiana State University Press, 1982), p. 378.

18 Palmerston to Russell, September 14, 1862, reproduced in ibid., p. 394. The Union defeat Palmerston refers to was Pope's defeat at the Second Battle of Bull Run on August 29–30, 1862.

19 Palmerston to Russell, September 23, 1862; reproduced in ibid., pp. 397–8.

his army to extreme risk should the Union commander, George Mc-Clellan, move his army to engage the Confederates, but he was confident that McClellan would act with his usual caution. Alas, fortune, which had smiled on him often in the past, suddenly turned against the Confederate commander. A copy of the field orders to Lee's corps commander, detailing his army's scattered movements, fell into the hands of a Union soldier. McClellan was elated. "Here is a paper," he exclaimed to a fellow officer, "with which, if I cannot whip Bobbie Lee, I will be willing to go home."[20] With uncharacteristic promptness, he issued orders for the Army of the Potomac to set out after the Confederate invaders. Lee scrambled to reassemble his army, and the two forces met along Antietam Creek, which flows just east of Sharpsburg, Maryland (Map 6.1).

The battle of Antietam (or, as the Confederates preferred to call it, the Battle of Sharpsburg) was one of the decisive battles of the war. With only three-quarters of their army hastily reassembled, the Confederates were outnumbered two to one. Lee's troops were hungry and weary from the series of long marches, and his army was backed up against the Potomac River. That he was able to extract his army from this predicament is testimony to both Lee's extraordinary skill as a military commander and the mettle of the Confederate troops. In this instance they were helped by the inability of McClellan and his generals to coordinate their attacks in a manner that would make use of their overwhelming numerical superiority, and by the timely arrival of A. P. Hill's corps, which had left Harpers Ferry early on the morning of the battle. Hill arrived just in time to save the right wing of the Confederate army from collapse. Had that last Union attack been successful, Lee's army would surely have been crushed, and the Confederate position in Virginia would have been precarious indeed. As it was, the Confederate army escaped back across the Potomac after surviving the bloodiest day of the war.[21]

President Lincoln, furious that Lee had escaped, urged pursuit of the battered Confederate army. When McClellan hesitated and finally lost the opportunity altogether, Lincoln relieved him of command.[22] The

20 Quoted in ibid., p. 133.
21 The two armies suffered a total of twenty-four thousand casualties at Antietam, with losses about equal to both sides. For the Confederates, that implied a casualty rate of almost 25 percent; see Grady McWhiney and Perry D. Jamieson, *Attack and Die: Civil War Military Tactics and the Southern Heritage* (University of Alabama Press, 1982), p. 8. An excellent account of the battle of Antietam is by Stephen W. Sears, *Landscape Turned Red: The Battle of Antietam* (Ticknor and Fields, 1983).
22 Ironically, McClellan's only victory over Lee ended his career; he was never given another command. The president's frustration with "little Mac" is revealed by an exchange that occurred during his visit to Antietam shortly after the battle. "Do you know what this is?" he asked a friend as they viewed the army at camp. "It is the Army

president's exasperation was well founded; the Union had lost a golden opportunity to destroy Lee at Antietam. Nevertheless, the battle was clearly a costly setback to the Confederates. The British lost their enthusiasm for active intervention. "The best thing," observed Palmerston on October 1, "would be that the two parties should settle details by direct negotiation with each other." As for the possibility of Britain or France's role in mediating the dispute, the prime minister felt that "the whole matter is full of difficulty, and can only be cleared up by some decided events between contending armies."[23] With the loss at Antietam went the best chance for recognition of the Confederacy by the European powers. Richmond papers proudly proclaimed another victory by Lee, but Jefferson Davis summed up the reality of the situation when he remarked after the battle, "Our maximum strength has been mobilized, while the enemy is just beginning to put forth his might."[24]

Davis's words were prophetic. Never again would the South have an opportunity to gain such an advantage on the battlefield. Looking back, it can be argued that Antietam was the high-water mark of the Confederacy. For, in addition to turning back Lee's invasion, the Union victory at Antietam prompted Abraham Lincoln to make the preliminary announcement of his intent to free all the slaves in the rebellious states. Lincoln's Emancipation Proclamation set in motion forces that were to have a profound impact on the course of the war.

The Confederate cause had received a serious jolt by Lee's defeat at Antietam, but there was still a great deal of fight in the South as the armies resumed their campaigns in the spring of 1863. In fact, the war went well for the South in the first half of that year. Once again, the Union advances in the East met with bloody reverses, and Grant, who had seemed on the verge of cutting the Confederacy in half a year ago, was still struggling to take Vicksburg in late May. And so, in an effort to relieve the pressures of supplying his army from Virginia, and in order to carry the burden of the war to the North, Lee once again determined to invade Pennsylvania. Prospects for success seemed good. "We were all hopeful, and the army was in good condition," General Longstreet recalled.[25] But as the Army of Northern Virginia once again headed north, the men knew that the South could not afford another Antietam. As

---

of the Potomac," answered his companion. "So it is called," Lincoln said, "but that is a mistake; it is only McClellan's bodyguard" (quoted in Murfin, *Gleam of Bayonets*, p. 315).

23 Palmerston to Russell, October 1, 1862; reproduced in ibid., p. 401.
24 Quoted in Nevins, *Ordeal of the Union*, 6: 231. On the reaction of southern newspapers, see Murfin, *Gleam of Bayonets*, pp. 306–7.
25 James Longstreet, "Lee's Invasion of Pennsylvania," in Johnson and Buel, *Battles and Leaders*, 3: 247.

Longstreet noted: "The war had advanced far enough for us to see that mere victory without decided fruits was a luxury we could not afford. Our numbers were less than the Federal forces, and our resources were limited while theirs were not."[26] In Washington, Lincoln reacted to Lee's invasion of Pennsylvania by appointing General George Meade commander of the Army of the Potomac and urging him to give chase and destroy the Confederate Army at the earliest opportunity. Without a clear idea of where their opponent was, the two armies moved northward along parallel paths into Pennsylvania. They met, largely by accident, just north of the little town of Gettysburg (see Map 6.1).[27]

Gettysburg was the quintessential Civil War battle. It pitted two evenly matched armies fighting in the major theater of the war.[28] It was a battle characterized by incredibly intense fighting between opposing infantry concentrated in a relatively small area – the Union position at Gettysburg was only about two and a half miles in length. Fittingly enough, the outcome of the battle ultimately came down to the success or failure of a charge by fifteen thousand infantry commanded by General George Pickett across a mile and a quarter of open field into the center of the Union line, which was expecting the attack.[29] Over seven thousand of Pickett's men were left on the field that fateful afternoon – an awesome testimony to the power of rifled muskets and cannon to defend a fixed position. As was so often the case in the Civil War, both armies were so exhausted by the effort of the battle that neither had the strength to carry on the fight. Meade, with casualties totaling over 20 percent of his forces, was content to let the Confederates retreat back across the Potomac to the sanctuary of Virginia. Lee had lost 30 percent of his strength, yet his army survived its defeat to fight for almost two more years.

Gettysburg was a crushing defeat for the South. What was worse, on

---

26 Ibid., p. 247.
27 Long after the fact, there remains considerable uncertainty exactly what Lee had in mind as his principal objective in this invasion; it appears to have been to capture the city of Harrisburg, Pennsylvania. One of the most complete accounts of Lee's Pennsylvania campaign, and the events that led to the climactic battle at Gettysburg, is Edward B. Coddington, *The Gettysburg Campaign: A Study in Command* (Scribners, 1984).
28 Lee had about seventy-five thousand troops at Gettysburg; Mead just over eighty thousand. Initially, the Confederates had an advantage because their troops were more concentrated and arrived on the scene before the entire Union Army could take up positions.
29 General John Gibbon, whose unit was in the center of the Union line, gave the following account of a conversation with Meade the evening before the fateful charge: "Meade said to me, 'If Lee attacks to-morrow, it will be in your front.' I asked why he thought so, and he replied, 'Because he has made attacks on both our flanks and failed, and if he concludes to try it again it will be on our center.'" John Gibbon, "The Council of War on the Second Day," in Johnson and Buel, *Battles and Leaders*, 3: 313.

the same day that Pickett's futile charge ended Confederate hopes in Pennsylvania, Vicksburg fell to Grant's besieging army. Following his setbacks the previous summer, Grant had hit upon a bold plan to capture the Confederate bastion by crossing the river and attacking the city from the east. On the night of April 16, 1863, the Union fleet under Admiral David Porter succeeded in sailing past the Confederate batteries at Vicksburg and establishing a post south of the city. Two weeks later Grant was able to land forty-one thousand troops south of Vicksburg at Port Gibson. Having abandoned his supply lines to the north, Grant proceeded to march east toward Jackson, the capital of Mississippi, which he captured on May 14. He then turned west and in a series of sharp engagements, forced General John C. Pemberton's force of thirty-two thousand Confederate troops back into the city of Vicksburg. Finding the city's defenses too strong for direct attack, Grant sat back and waited for hunger to take its toll. The Confederate garrison held out for forty-eight days before Pemberton asked Grant for terms. On July 4, 1863, while Lee's weary veterans trudged south from their defeat at Gettysburg, Pemberton's troops marched out of Vicksburg and surrendered the last major Confederate outpost on the Mississippi River to Grant's army. The Confederacy was split in two.

The Confederates launched one last major offensive in October 1863 by attacking the Union army under General William Rosecrans in eastern Tennessee. After a stunning success at the battle of Chickamauga, the Confederates under Braxton Bragg had the Union army trapped in the city of Chattanooga. The success was short-lived, however. Lincoln placed Grant in command of the entire western theater, and provided reinforcements for the relief of the beleaguered Union army at Chattanooga. Arriving in mid-November, Grant directed a counterattack that drove Bragg's army out of Tennessee and effectively ended Confederate offensive operations in the West.[30]

At the end of 1863 the military outlook for the Confederacy looked bleak indeed. After two years of hard fighting its armies had failed to check the Union advances in the West, and they had been unable to carry the war effectively to the North. Grant's success at Shiloh and Vicksburg had given the Union control of the western rivers, and his victory at Chattanooga cleared the last obstacle to a Union invasion of Georgia. As spring approached, William Tecumseh Sherman prepared to march on Atlanta. On his only two attempts at invasion of the North, Lee had been sharply rebuffed, and there seemed little chance of his launching a third

30 For an account of this campaign, see James Lee McDonough, *Chattanooga: A Death Grip on the Confederacy* (University of Tennessee Press, 1984).

try in 1864. Finally, although the effectiveness of the Union blockade is a subject of some debate, by the beginning of 1864 the Union Navy was intercepting a high enough fraction of the southern blockade runners to reduce significantly the flow of supplies from abroad. Moreover, blockade runners found that luxuries, not war supplies, brought the best prices in the South, which meant that those supplies that did slip through did little to help the Confederate war effort.[31] As the fourth year of fighting began, the South was reduced to hoping that the defense of Richmond and Atlanta would take a sufficiently high toll of northern casualties to discourage further prosecution of the war.

It proved to be a forlorn hope. To see why, we must retrace our steps and look at what was happening on the home fronts in both the North and the South.

Mobilizing for War: Men, Slaves, and Money

As early as the spring of 1862, it was evident that warfare had changed since the days when Napoleon and Wellington had squared off at Waterloo. Military historians use adjectives such as "total," "organized," or "modern" to describe the form of warfare that was emerging. They point to changes in weaponry (such as the rifled musket and repeating rifle); a difference in the soldiers of both armies (from professionals and volunteers to conscripts); and the treatment of noncombatants (such as Sherman's destruction of civilian property in Georgia) as proof that the nature of warfare had changed over the course of three years of fighting. War had also changed on the home front. The effort needed to sustain the military effort of this war required the involvement of the civilian population in the war effort. Society had to be mobilized for the war effort. The success or failure of that mobilization effort had much to do with the outcome of the war.

Tactics and strategy in the middle of the nineteenth century were primarily a matter of deploying men in a way to achieve numerical advan-

---

31 Some historians argue that the blockade failed because it was so "leaky" that large amounts of cotton were exported, and huge quantities of arms were imported. See, for example, Frank L. Owsley, *King Cotton Diplomacy: Foreign Relations of the Confederate States of America*, 2d ed., rev. Harriet C. Owsley (University of Chicago Press, 1959); and Frank E. Vandiver, "Editor's Introduction," in *Confederate Blockade Running through Bermuda, 1861–1865*, ed. Frank E. Vandiver (University of Texas Press, 1947). For a convincing case that despite the "leaks" the Union blockade was quite effective, see Beringer et al., *Why the South Lost*, chap. 3. Nevins provides evidence from the diary of a Charleston resident that graphically illustrates the shortages produced by the blockade (*Ordeal of the Union*, 6: 289), and McPherson provides a similar example from the diary of Mary Chesnut (*Battle Cry of Freedom: The Civil War Era* [Oxford University Press, 1988], p. 381).

tage at the point of attack. Improvements in weaponry had, to be sure, greatly increased the damage that a single soldier could inflict on his foe, but the outcome of battles in the Civil War rested in the final analysis on the infantrymen who charged or defended a particular position. Although the quality and morale of soldiers counted for a great deal in battle, the strategies on both sides of the war stressed, above all, having large numbers of men. This war would not be won with a few thousand volunteers; it would eventually involve roughly one out of every three men of fighting age in the population being pressed into military service.

The Union had a significant advantage in manpower. Table 6.1 presents a breakdown of human resources available to each side; Figure 6.1 presents a more detailed breakdown of human resources for the Confederacy and the free states of the Union by percentage. Out of a total population of 31 million in the United States at the outbreak of the war, 19 million lived in the free states of the Union, 9 million lived in the Confederacy, and 3 million lived in the four "border" states of Delaware, Kentucky, Maryland, and Missouri (Table 6.1). Thirty percent of the population in each of these regions were children under ten years of age, and another 8 to 10 percent were adults over the age of fifty (Figure 6.1). In terms of men available for military service, then, the free states could draw upon a pool of some 6.1 million men ten to forty-nine years of age; the Confederates on a pool of 3.9 million.[32]

From the outset, however, the military effort of the South was crippled by the fact that a sizable segment of its manpower – the 1.1 million military-aged male slaves – could not be used as fighting men at the front. The South, therefore, could count on a pool of only 1.7 million fighting men living in the Confederate states. The extent of this handicap can be seen in Figure 6.1. Whereas the northern pool of military manpower represented 32 percent of the population in that region, the South had only 19 percent of its population available for military service. Figure 6.2 presents the same data in terms of the total male population aged ten to fifty in the United States in 1860: Of all military-aged males, 61 percent lived in the free states of the Union, whereas only 17 percent lived in the Confederacy. The South's inability to enlist male slaves, who represented 12 percent of the eligible population, meant that the North had an

---

32 It is common to regard men in the age group fifteen to forty-five as the appropriate pool of military manpower. I have chosen ten years as the lower limit to reflect the fact that, as the war went on, youths in the age group ten to fifteen became eligible for duty. Although the Union did not draw heavily on this youngest cadre of would-be soldiers, the Confederates did enlist substantial numbers of fourteen- and fifteen-year-old boys toward the end of the war. At the outbreak of the war, the most common age of those enlisting was eighteen years.

Table 6.1. *Human resources in the free and slave states, 1860*

	Total population	Adult population over 10 years	Male population 10 to 49 years
All races			
Confederate states	9,101,450	6,299,697	2,837,819
Border states	3,211,897	2,235,217	1,019,340
Free Union states	19,086,250	13,846,835	6,128,138
Total	31,399,597	22,381,749	9,985,297
Whites			
Confederate states	5,447,220	3,779,721	1,712,064
Border states	2,650,243	1,849,012	850,552
Free Union states	18,860,008	13,675,972	6,057,644
Total	26,957,471	19,304,705	8,620,259
Slaves			
Confederate states	3,521,470	2,425,751	1,088,464
Border states	432,586	291,043	131,708
Total	3,954,056	2,716,794	1,220,172
Free blacks			
Confederate states	132,760	94,225	37,291
Border states	129,068	95,162	37,080
Free Union states	226,242	170,863	70,494
Total	488,070	360,250	144,866

Note: Border states are Delaware, Kentucky, Maryland, and Missouri.
Source: Table A.6.1.

initial manpower edge of better than 3 : 1. This advantage would become even greater when the Union eventually began to enlist blacks, including freed slaves, to fight against the South.[33]

A final element in the balance of manpower between the two sides were the 850,000 potential soldiers who lived in the border states (Figure 6.1). Both sides eagerly sought to tap this valuable manpower resource. Although we can only guess where these men served, it is likely that no more than 30 percent went to the South while 70 percent went to the North. This would add about 250,000 men to the southern pool and

33 By the end of the war, almost 200,000 blacks were serving in the armed services of the United States. Of that total, about half were southern blacks (Hattaway and Jones, *How the North Won*, p. 17). A further resource was available to the North and not the South during the course of the war: immigrants who came to the North during the years 1861 through 1864.

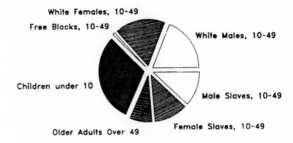

Confederate States

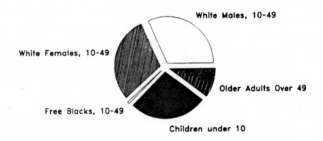

Free States of the Union

Figure 6.1. Human resources available in 1860 (thousands)

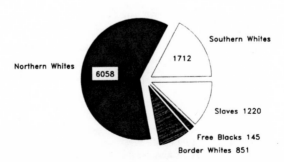

Figure 6.2. Males ten to forty-nine years of age in 1860 (thousands)

530,000 to the northern pool.[34] All told, then, the North could draw on a pool of 6.7 million eligible males; the South had about 2.1 million white males together with an additional 1.1 million male slaves.

How effectively did the two sides exploit this available manpower? Most observers agree that the Union was able to mobilize about 2.1 million men in the course of the war, or just about one-third of our estimated manpower pool. The South, with a far smaller pool, was able to get about 900,000 soldiers in its armies, implying a mobilization rate of over 40 percent.[35] The success of the South in enlisting a higher fraction of eligible males as soldiers reduced the North's overall manpower advantage to 2.3 to 1. At first glance this advantage seems overwhelming, but we must remember that the South was on the defensive, and conventional wisdom of the day dictated a ratio of at least 2 : 1 for the attacker to succeed. Moreover, the weight of northern numbers would not become a major factor until the final year and a half of campaigning, when the North was finally able to mobilize the full range of resources at hand.

Unfortunately, manpower was not the only area where the Southerners were at a distinct disadvantage. Armies in the middle of the nineteenth century consumed huge quantities of supplies. The North had an enormous edge in industrial capacity. Perhaps the best measure of relative productive capacity is the value added by manufacture, which in the North totaled $1.6 billion, compared with $193 million in the South.[36]

34　James McPherson claims that "nearly three-quarters of the white men in Missouri and two-thirds of those in Maryland who fought in the Civil War did so on the side of the Union"; he places the fraction at 40 percent for Kentucky (*Battle Cry of Freedom*, p. 293). Hattaway and Jones add a total of 600,000 "southern sympathizers" from all of the northern and border states to their estimates of the southern manpower pool (*How the North Won*, p. 17). My estimate that 30 percent of the white males were available to the South may slightly overstate the contribution to the Confederacy, but it should be remembered that there were also over 430,000 slaves in these states, many of whose masters presumably favored the South and may have contributed their slaves' efforts to the Confederate cause.

35　The number of troops for the Union is based on War Department records and reported by several sources. See McPherson, *Battle Cry of Freedom*, p. 306, and Millett and Maslowski, *For the Common Defense*, p. 154. The number of Confederate troops is more difficult to ascertain. Thomas Livermore calculated a total of just over 1 million, but as McPherson notes, Livermore was a former Union officer prone to exaggerate the strengths of the enemy he fought; see Thomas L. Livermore, *Numbers and Losses in the Civil War in America 1861–1865* (Houghton-Mifflin, 1901). McPherson used records of surviving veterans in 1890 to reach a total of 882,000 for the Confederate armies (*Battle Cry of Freedom*, p. 306).

36　Fred Bateman and Thomas Weiss, *A Deplorable Scarcity: The Failure of Industrialization in the Slave Economy* (University of North Carolina Press, 1981), p. 17. Value added represents the net increase in value (i.e., the total value of output minus the cost of materials) that is attributable to each producer. Almost half of the small southern total was in one state, Virginia.

Even this ratio understates the North's dominance in key areas; the South lagged particularly far behind in industries such as machinery and metals, and produced only about 2 percent of the munitions in the United States. One must view these statistics of industrial production with considerable care as a guide to military effectiveness in the early years of the war, however. Neither side had any significant productive capacity in the production of armaments when the war broke out, and both armies depended initially on imported arms. Until the federal blockade shut off the supply of weapons from abroad, the South's lack of industry was therefore not a crippling deficiency. More than six hundred thousand rifles were imported into the South during the course of the war, and its armies usually had adequate supplies of ammunition.

The same could not be said for food. The aspect of supply that proved most vexing to the South throughout the wear was feeding and clothing its troops. A major consideration behind Lee's invasions of the North in 1862 and 1863 was the need to supply his army. These problems appeared early in the war. Prior to this first invasion of the North in September 1862, Lee noted that his army was "feeble in transportation, the animals being much reduced, and the men are poorly provided with clothes, and in thousands of instances are destitute of shoes."[37] In the summer of 1863, when he launched his next invasion of the North, Lee again was motivated by a need for supplies. As one of his veterans wrote home from Pennsylvania: "[Our] army likes this country very well, and – O! what a relief it will be to our country to be rid of our army for some time. I hope we may keep away for some time and so relieve the calls for supplies that have been so long made upon our people."[38] In fact, Confederate troops from Jubal Early's division were foraging for shoes and clothing when they encountered Federal cavalry outside Gettysburg. It is a fitting comment on the South's war effort to note that the site of the climactic battle of the war was determined not by careful tactical or strategic considerations, but by the location of shoes.

Shortages of southern industrial production might account for the shortages of clothing and shoes, but it was logistical difficulties that left the Confederate armies continually short of food. As Sherman's march through Georgia in the summer of 1864 clearly demonstrated, there were ample supplies of food in the Confederacy even in the last year of the war. The problem was that the transportation network of the Confederacy was not up to the task of moving large quantities of supplies to the

37 Lee to Jefferson Davis, September 3, 1862; quoted in Sears, *Landscape Turned Red*, p. 65.
38 Jedediah Hotchkiss to his wife, June 25, 1863; cited in Edwin Coddington, *The Gettysburg Campaign: A Study in Command* (Scribners, 1984), p. 159.

armies of Virginia. The southern railway network, which was far below the standards of the North, is often blamed for this problem. But, despite their problems with a shortage of locomotives and rails, southern railways performed reasonably well during most of the war. Eventually, the wear and tear of heavy use without adequate repairs took its toll. Because of the concentration on production of armaments, no new locomotives were built in the South during the war, and there was almost no production of rails. Another handicap of the railway system of the South was that the "trunk lines" usually ran from the interior to a coastal city. Consequently, connections between two interior cities often required very roundabout shipments.[39]

More crippling to the Confederate supply effort than the problem of railroads was a shortage of draft animals and deficiencies of organization. The backbone of military supply on both sides were the horse and the mule. Here the North enjoyed a substantial advantage because the antebellum South depended on the border states of Kentucky, Tennessee, and Missouri to supply mules for its plantation agriculture. As the ravages of war took its toll of animals as well as men, the shortages of horses and mules in the Confederacy became more and more acute.

Neither side was prepared to wage a long war, and the full mobilization of men and resources took time. If the South could mobilize faster than the North at the outset of the fight, it might gain a military decision before the full effect of the North's superiority in men and equipment could be brought into play. The structure of a slave society did seem to work in the South's favor in terms of mobilizing quickly in 1861. Although the one million male slaves were excluded from military service, they continued to work behind the front. The release of white manpower was made easier, in the eyes of some observers, by the presence of a slave labor force that would remain to keep the slave farms going. The class structure of the South may also have accelerated mobilization. Slaveowners were an aristocracy of sorts. They were fond of assuming military airs, calling each other "colonel," sending their sons to military academies, and adhering to a code of "honor" patterned after an officer class. In the spring of 1861, the planter elite eagerly accepted the challenge of war. They organized and equipped regiments, often at their own expense, which they then led off to "whup" the hated Yankees. The troops in these volunteer units had grown up together in a world where elements of coercion and control were a dominant factor in everyday life. The presence of a large slave population, and an obsessive fear of insurrection by

39 An example of this problem could be seen in the effort to concentrate troops around Shiloh in the spring of 1862. Troops from central Georgia and Alabama had to be routed through Mobile and, in some instances, New Orleans.

blacks, had produced a level of military preparedness far greater than found in the North. Most Southerners were familiar with firearms as a matter of course, and in the plantation districts, many had served in the armed "patrols" that were organized to enforce restriction of movements by black slaves. This martial atmosphere, in a society organized around the principle that a large fraction of its population must remain forcibly enslaved, facilitated the creation of an effective fighting force.[40]

In the afterglow of the victory at Bull Run there was reason enough for optimism among the leaders of the Confederacy, but there were also signs of what was to come. Amid all the self-congratulatory editorials and proclamations of victory, Mary Boykin Chesnut, privy to the inner circles of influence and information at Richmond, was frustrated at the failure to follow up the victory. "Yes, here we will dillydally and Congress orate and generals parade," she observed, not long after the battle. "until they get up an army three times as large as McDowell's that we have just defeated. . . . This victory will be our ruin. It lulls us into a fool's paradise of conceit at our superior valor."[41]

Mrs. Chesnut's fears were well founded; by the following spring the North had mobilized over half a million men and its armies were pressing Confederate defenses on two fronts. Southern efforts to match their foe's increased manpower soon revealed that reliance on volunteers alone would not be sufficient. On March 29, 1862, the Confederate Congress enacted a conscription law that extended the terms of those already serving in the army to the end of the war, and made every white male aged eighteen to thirty-five liable for military service. Conscription was, in effect, an admission that it would take more than just the "superior valor" of those who volunteered in 1861 to win the war; every able-bodied man would be needed in the war effort. Within a year the Union was forced to adopt the same expedient. Lincoln signed a draft bill in July 1863.

From the outset of this race to mobilize resources, the presence of slavery created enormous problems for the Confederates. The most obvious, which we have already noted, was that the one million able-bodied male slaves of military age were not pressed into military service. This disadvantage could have been at least partially offset if the slaves had

---

40 Not all of the martial traits of the slave society worked in the South's favor. Some historians have argued that the southern culture engendered a commitment on the part of its military leaders to attack the enemy recklessly, a tactic that produced horrendous casualties from the early days of the war to the end. The most outspoken proponents of this view are Grady McWhinney and Perry Jamieson, who claim that thanks to the "attack and die" attitude of its generals, the Confederacy quite literally bled to death (*Attack and Die*). Others remain skeptical; see Beringer et al., *Why the South Lost*.

41 *Mary Chesnut's Civil War*, p. 111; dated July 24, 1861.

been made available for noncombat military labor. Ironically, one of the major principles for which the South was fighting, the right of a slave-owner to control his slave property, proved to be a major obstacle to the effective use of slave labor in support of the military effort of the South. Slaves were the private property of owners, and the government had no direct control over how they were used. Military authorities could, to be sure, impress slaves for army work if they deemed it necessary. In fact, slave labor contributed substantially to the construction of defenses throughout the Confederacy, and slaves were used in a variety of industrial enterprises, most notably railroads, armaments, and ironworks.[42] But slaves were seldom kept in the proximity of the fighting. In part this reflected owners' reluctance to have their valuable property placed at risk on hazardous jobs. The absence of slaves in the war zone was also simply a matter of geography. Most slaves remained on their owner's plantation, and the largest concentration of slaves was in the cotton growing regions of the South. Except for some areas in Mississippi and Tennessee, these regions remained outside the area of major military activities until the very end of the war. (Even Sherman's march through Georgia missed the heart of the southern cotton belt.) Finally, the reluctance to use slaves near the front lines reflected planters' fears that slaves placed in the proximity of Union troops would attempt to reach the Union lines. Slaves and masters alike knew that the "enemy" offered a prospect of freedom. Historian Barbara Fields provides an insightful analysis of this situation:

> The [slaveholders] knew from the outset what their fellows would soon learn: that the arrival of the federal army would inevitably incite the slaves to disobedience and escape. Slaves and secessionist masters developed remarkably similar analyses of the situation. There was no coincidence in this, for they had learned from each other. Slaves knew that the election of a Republican president portended the abolition of slavery – long before the Republican president himself knew it – because slaveholders had been saying so for years.[43]

42 Clarence L. Mohr claims that over ten thousand slaves were employed in the construction of defenses in Georgia, and he provides evidence that slaves made a substantial contribution to the South's industrial sector; see *On the Threshold of Freedom: Masters and Slaves in Civil War Georgia* (University of Georgia Press, 1986), chap. 5. Although Mohr's point is well taken, it should be noted that the number of slaves in industrial employment represented a very small fraction of the total slave labor force.

43 Barbara J. Fields, *Slavery and Freedom on the Middle Ground: Maryland during the Nineteenth Century* (Yale University Press, 1985), p. 93. For another excellent account of the reaction of slaveholders to the prospect of emancipation by federal troops, see James L. Roark, *Masters without Slaves: Southern Planters in the Civil War and Reconstruction* (W. W. Norton, 1977), chap. 3.

Southerners might still have made good use of their labor on the home front. But, for the most part, they did not. Planters who had always produced staple crops with slave labor were reluctant to change their ways just because of the war. The high price of cotton at the outbreak of the war encouraged planting of more cotton than ever in the spring of 1861. Placing their confidence in the power of "King Cotton" to force European intervention, planters throughout the South placed an informal embargo on cotton shipments to Europe in 1861. The government did not endorse the move, but the embargo was a success, leading to the stockpiling of cotton in the South. Unfortunately, the ploy failed to have the desired effect on England, and when the planters finally decided to sell the cotton in an effort to obtain supplies from abroad, the Union blockade was becoming effective. Nevertheless, planters continued to plant cotton through the 1862–3 season, and many continued into the 1863–4 season, despite efforts by both the state and Richmond governments to discourage production of cotton. Too late, Southerners realized their error. They had accumulated vast stockpiles of raw cotton that were virtually worthless to the war effort at home. The South had squandered the better part of three years' labor of slaves on production of a useless commodity.[44]

The class structure of the slave South affected the mobilization effort of the South in more subtle ways. From the outset of the war, there were those who charged that this was a "rich man's war, poor man's fight." The view was expressed by a Georgian, writing to the editor of a local paper in 1861:

> Is it right that the poor man should be taxed for the support of the war, when the war was brought about on the slave question, and the slave at home accumulating for the benefit of his master, and the poor man's farm left uncultivated and a chance for his wife to be a widow, and his children orphans?[45]

44 On the effectiveness of the cotton embargo, see Nevins, *Ordeal of the Union*, 6: 100; and McPherson, *Battle Cry of Freedom*, pp. 383–9. On the reluctance of Southerners to cease growing cotton, see Roark, *Masters without Slaves*, pp. 39–42; Paul D. Escott, *After Secession: Jefferson Davis and the Failure of Confederate Nationalism* (Louisiana State University Press, 1978), chap. 4; and Thomas, *Confederate Nation*. David M. Potter estimates that about 1 million bales of cotton were exported from the South after 1861, and about 2.5 million bales were destroyed by the Confederates themselves toward the end of the war ("Jefferson Davis and the Political Factors in Confederate Defeat," in *Why the North Won the Civil War*, ed. David Donald (Collier Books, 1962).

45 Letter to the Rome, Georgia, *Weekly Courier*, January 25, 1861; quoted in Escott, *After Secession*, p. 95. Escott provides an excellent discussion of the disaffection of the "common people" toward the mobilization measures of the Confederate government in chapter 4 of that book.

The draft law intensified the perception that the poor were carrying the brunt of a war favoring the rich. Conscription, of course, applied only to white males, which raised a touchy problem. If all the eligible males on a plantation were drafted, who would remain behind to oversee the plantation and control the slave work force? The Confederate Congress, which had already allowed the purchase of a substitute as exemption from the draft, enacted in October 1862 an exemption for anyone owning twenty or more slaves. Only a small number of people were actually exempted from the draft by the "twenty nigger law." But the exemption so clearly favored wealthy slaveowners that resistance to conscription, which had been vigorous from the outset, became more fierce than ever.[46] Farm families, from which the principal source of male labor had been taken by the army, were infuriated by the sight of planters with their slave labor force intact being exempted from the draft. In an angry letter to the Confederate secretary of war, James Sedden, a Virginian warned that "the people will not *always* submit to this *unequal, unjust* and partial distribution of favor and wholesale conscription of the *poor* while the able-bodied & healthy men of property are all occupying *soft places*."[47]

The poor, of course, invariably bear the major burden of war. There was substantial resentment in the North against inequities of the Union draft and the burden of the war. In July 1863, while the Union was still celebrating the victory at Gettysburg, rioting broke out in New York City over Irish discontent that the burden of the draft was falling differentially on them. Mobs rampaged through the city for four days until troops were finally called in to restore order.[48] Yet, although the mobilization effort on both sides exacerbated class tensions, the problem of inequality was far greater in the South than in the North.

The antebellum South was a curious blend of a cash-crop agriculture that produced for an international market for staples on the one hand, and "walk-away" farming that eschewed the gains of market specialization in favor of a self-sufficient independence on the other. The slaveholding plantations dominated production of the cash crops; self-sufficient farming was more common among the nonslave farms. Many small farms throughout the South had only marginal contact with the cash

46 On the impact of the law, see ibid., p. 120, and McPherson, *Battle Cry of Freedom*, pp. 610–11.
47 R. M. Radford to James Seddon, October 17, 1864, quoted in Escott, *After Secession*, p. 119 (emphasis in original).
48 By the time peace was restored, there had been at least 105 deaths, and about twenty thousand regular troops had been assigned to keep order in the city. See McPherson, *Battle Cry of Freedom*, pp. 609–11; a full account of the riots is in Adrian Cook, *The Armies of the Streets: The New York City Draft Riots of 1863* (University of Kentucky Press, 1974).

economy. Nevertheless, the small amount of income they earned through market sales was an important element in determining their well-being, because they depended on outside suppliers for various implements, some clothing, and necessities such as salt.[49] Merchandising arrangements for these people were relatively simple. Farmers either handled sales through neighboring plantations, traveled to the nearest town, or, most likely, relied on traveling peddlers. The marketing arrangements for staple crops such as cotton were far more sophisticated, involving cotton factors, banks, commission merchants, shipping interests, and the like. But these institutional arrangements were largely external to the Southern economy, with agents from the major cotton centers of the North or Europe located in a few key places such as Charleston, New Orleans, Mobile, or Memphis.[50]

These features of the Southern economy made it difficult to rely on market arrangements to mobilize resources for the war effort. The problem was not just getting guns and munitions. In fact, the absence of domestic manufacturing markets posed little problem for the supply of munitions. A fact that is often overlooked in assessing the South's lack of industrial capacity at the outset of the war is that the Confederacy was actually rather successful in creating a military–industrial complex that was able to provide reasonably ample supplies of munitions to its armies throughout the war. This was accomplished through direct government production of munitions. Existing factories such as the Treadegar Ironworks in Virginia were simply taken over, and new facilities such as the gunpowder works at Augusta, Georgia, or Selma, Alabama, were constructed by the government.[51] Centralized control of government pro-

49 This is not to argue that smaller farms produced no cotton, or that they ignored the influences of the marketplace. The data discussed in Chapter 3 suggest that large farms accounted for a disproportionate share of the total amount of cotton and tobacco produced. Many small farms produced cotton as a surplus above and beyond their basic food needs. On the nature of agriculture in the "upcountry," see Hahn, *Roots of Southern Populism*, pp. 29–49. Gavin Wright presents an economic model of such behavior that he terms "safety-first" farming; see *The Political Economy of the Cotton South: Households, Markets, and Wealth in the Nineteenth Century* (W. W. Norton, 1978), chap. 6.

50 On the southern merchandising system before the war, see Harold D. Woodman, *King Cotton and His Retainers: Financing and Marketing the Cotton Crop of the South, 1800–1925* (University of Kentucky Press, 1968); for an excellent view of the country store and peddlers in the antebellum period, see Lewis E. Atherton, *The Southern Country Store, 1800–1860* (Louisiana State University Press, 1949).

51 Raimondo Luraghi has argued that the efforts to supply the South's war needs created a miniindustrial revolution in the South, in "The American Civil War and the Modernization of American Society: Social Structure and Industrial Revolution in the Old South before and during the War," *Civil War History* 18 (September 1972). I think his argument exaggerates the extent of social change, but he documents the prodigious efforts of Southerners to become self-sufficient in the production of military goods. An

duction was not, however, a feasible way of supplying animals and foodstuffs for the army. Here the army's quartermaster corps needed a way of encouraging the necessary production from the thousands of farms throughout the South, and then getting the supplies to the armies. The rudimentary state of the cash economy in the rural South made this a difficult task.

In the North, domestic financial markets were well developed and cash transactions in the agricultural sector were more common. This allowed the Union government to purchase supplies at market prices from a wide range of producers. The government could pay for these cash purchases with revenues generated through taxes or the sale of government bonds. In fact, these two sources of revenue accounted for over 85 percent of the Union's wartime government financing.[52] The Confederate government, by contrast, faced severe limitations in its effort to raise revenues through either taxation or bond sales. Taxation was a particularly vexing problem. The shortage of cash throughout much of the rural South meant that a substantial fraction of the tax revenues had to be collected in kind – that is, paid for with commodities rather than money. This had two disadvantages. First, it was extremely inefficient in the sense that the government got agricultural commodities, principally foodstuffs or feed for animals, at the point of collection, rather than cash which could be taken anywhere and converted into specific supplies needed by the army at the front. Second, taxation in kind meant that a tax collector quite literally carried away a farm family's food as payment for the war effort, a practice that infuriated upcountry southern farmers.[53] Attempts to raise cash through the sale of bonds also encountered problems. The South had always relied on northern or British capital markets. Northern

excellent account of that effort can be found in the biography by one of the men who directed the production of guns and munitions in the South – Josiah Gorgas; see Frank E. Vandiver, *Ploughshares into Swords: Josiah Gorgas and Confederate Ordnance* (University of Texas Press, 1952).

52 Efforts to compute an exact total of war expenditures and revenues for the war are imprecise at best. In terms of current dollars, expenditures of the federal government of the United States on defense between 1860 through 1865 totaled $3.2 billion. Total revenues over the same period were: taxes, $860 million; interest-bearing bonds, $2.16 billion; and the issue of currency, $458 million. This suggests that something on the order of one-quarter of the war costs was financed through taxes and another two-thirds through bond issues. The figures are computed from United States Bureau of the Census, *Historical Statistics of the United States, Colonial Times to 1970* (U.S. Government Printing Office, 1975), part 2, series Y457–63, pp. 1114–15.

53 The taxation was all the more onerous because most of these farms had already lost a major portion of their manpower to the army. For a detailed discussion of the taxes and reaction to them, see Eugene M. Lerner, "Money, Prices and Wages in the Confederacy, 1861–65," *Journal of Political Economy* 62 (October 1955); and Escott, *After Secession*, pp. 67–8.

capital was obviously no longer available, and as the war progressed poorly for the South, it became increasingly difficult to raise funds through the London capital market. Consequently, the Confederate government was able to raise only about one-third of its war costs through taxes or bond financing.[54]

The manner in which the government raises revenues has a significant impact on economic activity. A rapid and large increase in government spending that is not offset by revenues from taxes or borrowing will create substantial inflationary pressures in any economy. Deficit spending in the North, which accounted for 15 percent of total government outlays, pushed the general price level to about double the 1861 level by the end of the war. In the South, where over 60 percent of the expenditures were backed by neither taxes nor borrowing, wartime strains on production and the success of the Union blockade created a curtailment of aggregate supply concurrent with a vast increase in the amount of money in circulation. The result was an inflation that caused prices to rise to the point where, by early 1865, the Confederate currency was practically worthless.[55] Inflation is a form of taxation. The government uses its power to print enough money to "outbid," as it were, other buyers for scarce resources. A doubling of prices, such as that experienced in the North, is irritating, but in a reasonably well-developed market situation, consumers and producers can make the necessary adjustments to the changes in prices and cope with the problem.[56] However, even a mild rate of inflation can be extremely unsettling in a situation where farmers rely on the market for only a few essential items, and where prices have been fixed for long periods of time. With fewer options in a more limited market setting, the effect of a price increase is far more damaging. When the rate of increase in prices reaches the proportions experienced in the Confederacy by mid-1864, the decline in the value of the currency brings about a collapse of the market system itself. Mary Chesnut's story of the purchase of eggs from a woman at a local market

54 Because the Confederates collected a sizable share of their taxes "in kind," tax revenues are difficult to estimate. The best estimates of Confederate finances are those of Eugene Lerner, who argues that less than 5 percent of revenues came from taxes, and about 30 percent came from bonds; see Lerner, "Money, Prices and Wages."

55 Between January 1861 and January 1864, the level of commodity prices in the Confederacy increased by a factor of twenty-eight. By 1865 prices had risen to a level ninety-two times that in 1861 (Lerner, "Money, Prices and Wages," pp. 24–8).

56 An important element in the impact of inflation is the extent to which wages keep up with the price level. They did not keep pace with the rise in prices in the North, but they did rise substantially over the period. The classic analysis of this problem is Rueben A. Kessel and Armen A. Alchian, "Real Wages in the North during the Civil War: Mitchell's Data Reinterpreted," in *The Economic Impact of the American Civil War*, ed. Ralph Andreano (Schenkman Publishing Company, 1967).

reveals the attitude most Southerners held about the value of Confederate money by the spring of 1864:

> She asked me 20 dollars for five dozen eggs and then she said she would take it in "Confederick." Then I would have given her 100 dollars as easily. But if she had taken my offer of yarn! I haggle in yarn for the millionth part of a thread! . . . When they ask Confederate money, I never stop to chafer. I give them 20 or 50 dollars cheerfully for anything.[57]

Mrs. Chesnut's comment about the value of yarn in bartering for goods is particularly revealing. In the heart of Charleston, one of the South's major commercial centers, the use of currency had given way to bartering yarn for food. By the middle of 1863, when Confederate paymasters "paid" for supplies with government money or vouchers, it was tantamount to confiscating the goods. In many areas the government or army officials did not bother with the formality of payment of any kind. In 1863 the Confederate Congress authorized army quartermasters to "impress" foodstuffs to supply troops in the field. Although this was termed a "tax," it fell directly on those unfortunate enough to be located in the areas where troops were stationed. City folk were not spared the trials of confiscation, however. Noting that "prices are inconveniently high for poor folks," an editorial by the *Richmond Whig* in October 1864 offered an opinion that this situation

> must be expected so long as the necessities of life are impressed on their way to market by the government agents, who are too lazy to go through the country in search of supplies. Half the troubles of the army and nearly all the troubles of the people are due to the existence of the pestiferous commissaries.[58]

As the war continued, it became increasingly clear that the slave economy was not equipped to handle the problem of total mobilization. In the North, government use of the marketplace produced abuses of profiteering and gains that detracted from the war effort. But the production decisions involving the North's military effort were effectively *decentralized* through the market process. Market decentralization was able, in spite of its shortcomings, to provide coordination for production of a vast array of goods needed by the military machine as well as enough consumption items to satisfy the home front. Because markets in the South were far less developed, the mobilization effort was forced to rely on *centralized* decisions made by the government in Richmond. Had the

---

57 *Mary Chesnut's Civil War*, p. 749; dated March 7, 1864.
58 Lerner, "Money, Prices, and Wages," p. 39.

Confederate government bureaucracy been up to the task, this approach might have worked, as it did in the case of munitions. But because the government apparatus was not equal to the task before it, the South wound up with a decision-making apparatus that became overcentralized and was ultimately unable to meet either military or civilian needs. Eugene Lerner points out that the South may have actually overmobilized its military effort.[59] That is, the government's war effort stripped away so much from civilian production that production for the home front collapsed. Shortages of food and the necessities of life created the inflation that ultimately caused the Confederate economy to collapse in the spring of 1865.

To Free or Not to Free: The Question of Emancipation

As both sides wrestled with the problem of mobilizing resources for the war, Lincoln and his administration struggled with another problem: What to do about the question of freeing slaves? When he took office in the spring of 1861, the president had assured the South that he had no intention of expropriating slave property. Shortly before the first major battle of the war at Bull Run, Congress backed up these executive assurances by passing resolutions coauthored by John Crittenden of Kentucky in the Senate and Andrew Johnson of Tennessee in the House declaring that the federal government had no intention of "overthrowing or interfering with the rights or established institutions" of the rebellious states. The government sought merely to "defend and maintain the *supremacy* of the Constitution, and to preserve the Union with all the dignity, equality, and rights of the several states unimpaired."[60] In late August 1861, General John C. Fremont, union commander in Missouri, issued a proclamation freeing the slaves of any Confederate activist in the state. Lincoln promptly demanded that Fremont rescind his order. In December of the same year, Secretary of War Cameron issued a report endorsing not only the confiscation of slaves, but arming them against the rebels. Again Lincoln intervened to force the secretary to recall and amend the report, deleting the offending paragraph.[61]

These actions demonstrate the caution with which both Congress and

---

59 Eugene M. Lerner, "The Monetary and Fiscal Programs of the Confederate Government, 1861–65," *Journal of Political Economy* 62 (December 1954), and idem, "Money, Prices, and Wages."

60 David H. Donald and James G. Randall, *The Civil War and Reconstruction*, 2d ed. (D. C. Heath, 1961), p. 280; also see Nevins, *Ordeal of the Union*, 5: 190; and McPherson, *Battle Cry of Freedom*, p. 312.

61 See Donald and Randall, *Civil War and Reconstruction*, pp. 371–2; and McPherson, *Battle Cry of Freedom*, pp. 352–8.

the president approached the emancipation issue. Congress did act, in August 1861, to pass a "confiscation act," which threatened any property used "for insurrectionary purposes . . . in aid of the rebellion" with confiscation. But the interpretation of this act was such that, apart from those slaves who came to the Union lines of their own accord, confiscation of slaves was rare.[62] Radicals were unhappy with this reluctance to act against slaveholders, but could do little about it in the early months of the war. A complex set of forces acted to restrain any precipitous action by either Lincoln or Congress with regard to emancipation. Foremost among these were considerations of the impact that any action might have on the course of the rebellion. Would freeing slaves demoralize the South, or would such an action spur the rebel states to even stiffer resistance? What of slaves in the border states that had remained in the Union? Lincoln was willing to put off any definitive action on emancipation of slaves in order to keep open the option of negotiating a settlement with the rebel states.

Such pragmatism was reinforced by the strong prejudice in the North against any scheme that might produce a flow of free blacks to the North. As we saw in our discussion of the territorial disputes over slavery before the war, racial antagonism toward blacks had been a strong factor in drawing the support of Free-Soilers to the antislave cause. This support for containing slavery did not extend to the point of favoring general emancipation of blacks. In fact, there was a persistent resistance, particularly in the Midwest, to any emancipation scheme. "The truth is," wrote an editor of Springfield's *Illinois State Journal*, "the nigger is an unpopular institution in the free States."[63] This was a political reality that plagued the Republicans' seeking emancipation throughout the war.

Finally, there was a lingering fear that a confiscatory emancipation of slaves would set a dangerous precedent for the future. Whether or not such arguments were entirely sincere, the constitutional issues associated with the confiscation of property provided a useful means for those opposing emancipation to slow down or even halt the efforts to free the slaves. Another set of forces, however, placed increasing pressure on the federal government to take some decisive action with regard to emancipation. The most pressing of these was the problem of refugee slaves who came to the camps of the Union armies occupying slave areas of the South. In May 1861, General Benjamin Butler, whose troops had occupied Fort Monroe, Virginia, declared all slaves who came to his camp to be "contraband of war" and confiscated them. Butler's actions were

---

62 Donald and Randall, *Civil War and Reconstruction*, p. 283. The act did stipulate that slaves reaching Union lines were not to be returned to their rebel masters.
63 Quoted in Voegeli, *Free But Not Equal*, p. 28.

subsequently supported by the president and by the terms of the confiscation act of July 1861. Refugee slaves were henceforth termed "contraband" and deemed subject to confiscation. In July 1862, Congress made the first definitive move toward emancipation by enacting a much more sweeping Confiscation Act that allowed seizure of all "enemies' property" and stipulated that slaves in such cases should be set free. This act for the first time put teeth into the confiscation of slaves by the army, but it met with considerable resistance. Indeed, Lincoln thought it far too sweeping in its notion of who would be subject to confiscation, and threatened to veto the legislation.[64] He eventually relented, but again we see that it was caution, not boldness, that governed the president's handling of the emancipation issue.

The pressure continued to grow, not only at home but also abroad. Lincoln was becoming concerned that the image of the United States abroad was tarnished by the government's failure to act on the slave issue. By mid-1862 the president was convinced that some bolder step must be taken on the question. But he needed a propitious moment to act. Finally he saw his chance. Meeting with his cabinet on September 21, four days after the Union army had turned back Lee at the Battle of Antietam, Lincoln told them that the time had come to do something dramatic on the emancipation question. He read a statement that he had prepared:

> That on the first day of January in the year of our Lord, one thousand eight hundred and sixty-three, all persons held as slaves within any state, or designated part of a state, the people whereof shall be in rebellion against the United States, shall be then, henceforward, and forever free, and the executive government of the United States, including the military and naval authority thereof, will recognize and maintain the freedom of such persons, and will do no act or acts to repress such persons, any of them, in any efforts they might make for their actual freedom.[65]

He was not, Lincoln informed the cabinet, interested in their advice "about the main matter — for that I have determined for myself." He asked only for opinion as to the wisdom of releasing the statement. The cabinet, after expressing some mild reservations, unanimously agreed

---

64　Opponents of the law were concerned because the term "enemy" was taken to include anyone, including foreigners, residing in the rebellious states. See the discussion in Donald and Randall, *Civil War and Reconstruction*, pp. 284–5.

65　Nevins, *Ordeal of the Union*, 6: 234. The account of the meeting comes from the recollections of Secretary of the Treasury Salmon Chase.

with the draft. The Emancipation Proclamation appeared in newspapers throughout the United States the following day.

It was a remarkable document. In one sense it maintained the cautious policy pursued up to that time by doing very little of substance. It would have no effect on the status of slaves in the Confederacy until Union troops occupied the enemy's territory, and very little Confederate territory was in Union hands in September 1862. Nor would it have any effect on slaves in the United States, since Lincoln's statement had deftly side-stepped the delicate question of whether slaves in his own country would eventually be emancipated. As the London *Spectator* wryly noted, the principle behind the proclamation seemed to be "not that a human being can not justly own another, but that he cannot own him unless he is loyal to the United States."[66] The Proclamation was also a bold step that moved the North further along the path of full emancipation. By issuing the Emancipation Proclamation, Lincoln had, in the words of Allan Nevins, "irrevocably committed the United States, before the gaze of the whole world, to the early eradication of slavery from those wide regions where it was most deeply rooted."[67] With the stroke of a pen, the president had turned the war into a revolution.

Still, the *Spectator* was right; Lincoln's proclamation had not freed a single slave. As we have seen, his reluctance to deal with the issue of slavery in the United States was designed not to offend slaveholders within the Union. Emancipation by the federal government of the more than four hundred thousand slaves in the border states would have a demoralizing effect on the loyal population of those states. Emancipation for slaves in rebel territories, by contrast, could be defended on the grounds that it would demoralize and weaken the enemy. But Lincoln was not simply playing a cynical game of politics. He knew the limits of executive power. Issuing a proclamation freeing slaves in areas controlled by people in open rebellion against the United States government was a legal exercise of the war powers of the president. Freeing slaves in areas loyal to the United States would almost certainly be seen as an aggrandizement of presidential power subject to challenge by Congress. His proclamation, he knew, amounted to little more than getting a foot in the door on the question of emancipation. But once he got his foot in the door, Lincoln was confident that the door could be opened all the way.

If it had little immediate impact on the situation of slaves, the proclamation promised to bring about profound change once the Union armies advanced into Confederate territory. Up to this point, the question of

66 Quoted in McPherson, *Battle Cry of Freedom*, p. 298.
67 Nevins, *Ordeal of the Union*, 6: 236–7.

how black slaves who came through the Union lines would be treated at the end of the war was unclear. Lincoln's proclamation unequivocally answered that question: "Contraband slaves" were henceforth declared to be free. Many blacks did not wait for the army to come to them. By mid-1863, large numbers of ex-slaves had managed to make their way to the Union lines. Camps of "contraband" collected around each of the major federal armies located in the South. In 1864, as Sherman's army marched through Georgia, the flow of refugees reached mammoth proportions. "Every day as we marched on," wrote one of Sherman's generals,

> we could see, on each side of our line of march, crowds of these people coming to us through roads and across fields, bringing with them all their earthly goods, and many goods that were not theirs. . . . They were allowed to follow in the rear of our column, and at times they were almost equal in numbers to the army they were following.[68]

And with each group of escaped slaves arriving at the Federal army's lines the Union's commitment to total emancipation became stronger.

As late as 1864, however, the only formal evidence of that commitment was the Emancipation Proclamation, an executive order that would have questionable force once the war ended. Although few doubted that slaves freed by the armies would retain their freedom, there was considerable concern over those not freed by the proclamation. What if the South were willing to negotiate for peace in return for not freeing slaves still in the Confederacy? What about blacks still enslaved in the Union? Republicans were determined to extend the basis of emancipation by passing a constitutional amendment prohibiting slavery. In the Senate they had little trouble getting their amendment through, but Democrats opposed to the measure defeated it in the House. Frustrated in their attempt at constitutional reform, the radicals attached a provision to a bill dealing with the establishment of a Unionist government in Louisiana insisting that before any state could be readmitted to the Union slavery must be abolished. Lincoln vetoed the bill, insisting that constitutional amendment, not legislative action, was the only legal way to accomplish emancipation.[69] He would settle for nothing less.

---

68 Henry W. Slocum, "Sherman's March from Savannah to Bentonville," in Buel and Johnson, *Battles and Leaders*, 4: 688–9.

69 Lincoln maintained that secession was illegal, therefore the states in rebellion *had never left the Union*. Setting terms for "readmission," even on something as crucial as emancipation, would be tantamount to an admission that secession *was* legal. Lin-

The difficulty in getting a consensus to support the amendment abolishing slavery points again to the ambivalence of many Northerners toward freedom and equality for blacks. The Republican convention in June 1864 approved a platform strongly endorsing a constitutional amendment to end slavery in the United States, but Democrats continued to oppose strongly such a move. Not until the surprisingly large Republican victory in the November elections of 1864 was passage of the amendment finally assured, and even then only after the new Congress took office in March 1865. Hoping for at least the appearance of bipartisan support, Lincoln applied pressure to several lame-duck Democrats in the House, and on January 31, 1865, the House of Representatives approved the Thirteenth Amendment for ratification by the states. The last major legal hurdle to the permanent eradication of slavery in the United States had finally been cleared.

Enactment of emancipation was a singular achievement that had a profound effect on the nature of the conflict. In the end, Lincoln decided to steer a course that was clearly headed toward a goal of total emancipation for all slaves. He knew that with each step he took in that direction, he was raising the stakes of the war. The South could no longer look for a settlement that included anything short of complete emancipation. If it were going to protect its peculiar institution, the South must fight to the bitter end.

A Fight to the End: Total War and Unconditional Surrender

By the fall of 1864, the South's only hope for victory hinged on the fact that Lincoln faced an election in November. The people of the North were getting weary of the incredible toll exacted by the effort to win this war. Despite the military reversals of the past six months, the South still retained most of its territory. The Federal armies would now be forced to carry the war deep into enemy territory, something neither side had effectively done up to this point. If the southern armies could hold on for just one more season of fighting and impose enormous losses on the Union, that might influence the fall elections. Lincoln and his Republicans would be voted out of office by an electorate weary of a costly and seemingly endless war.

Unfortunately for the South's hopes, Lincoln had finally found a gener-

coln's veto of the Wade-Davis bill was part of a larger dispute between the president and Congress over how the policy of "reconstruction" after the war should proceed.

al who understood what was required to win the war. In December 1863, he appointed Ulysses S. Grant commander in chief of all the Union armies. Grant, in turn, gave command of the West to William T. Sherman. Grant and Sherman had fought together since Shiloh. They had a trust and confidence in each other that made truly coordinated operations in the East and West a reality for the first time in the war. Moreover, both of these generals were prepared to wage a war of attrition to bring the South to its knees. Grant's plan was simple enough. He would assault Lee's position in Virginia, while Sherman attacked through Georgia. Grant knew that even if Lee succeeded in holding off the Union advance in Virginia, the effort would put so great a strain on the Confederacy's limited resources that there would be nothing left to check Sherman's advance into Georgia.

Grant was right. Despite heavy casualties, he relentlessly continued the attack on Lee's position through the summer of 1864, vowing to fight on "if it takes all summer." Meanwhile, Sherman advanced into Georgia and captured Atlanta on September 1, 1864. He then pondered his next move. The problem that had plagued previous attempts to invade the Confederacy had been the vulnerability of the invader's supply lines. Sherman proposed to solve this problem by simply abandoning his supply lines and living off the land. On November 15 he left Atlanta with 62,500 men and launched the grandest "raid" of the war; his army marched through Georgia, living off the land and leaving a path of destruction in its wake. "I will make Georgia howl," Sherman claimed as his army left Atlanta, and he proceeded to make good his boast. On December 20, 1864, he wired the president that he wished to present "as a Christmas gift, the city of Savannah."[70]

Sherman's capture of Atlanta broke the apparent stalemate that had persisted since the late spring. Northern morale received a huge boost, and Lincoln was easily reelected to a second term on November 8, 1864, over the disgruntled general, George McClellan.[71] With Lincoln's election, the last slim hope for a negotiated peace had vanished. With hindsight, it is tempting to argue that the decision by Davis and his generals to keep fighting in early 1864 was a tragic error of judgment

---

70 An excellent account of Sherman's march is the book by Joseph T. Glatthaar, *The March to the Sea and Beyond: Sherman's Troops in the Savannah and Carolinas Campaigns* (New York University Press, 1985).

71 Lincoln received 212 electoral votes to 21 for his opponent. McClellan carried only three states: New Jersey, Kentucky, and Delaware. An interesting facet to the election results was that among the soldiers, Lincoln received 116,887 votes to 33,748 for the former army commander; see Tim Taylor, *The Book of Presidents* (Arno Press, 1972), p. 188.

that cost the lives of thousands of soldiers on both sides. No one seriously doubted the eventual outcome of a protracted military struggle. The offensive capabilities of Lee's army had been so reduced after Gettysburg that he could, at best, only temporarily stymie Grant's advance. By June 1864, Lee's army was only half the size of Grant's and had resorted to tactics of digging an intricate web of trenches around the outskirts of Petersburg, Virginia. The war in the East had evolved into a contest between two armies crouched in a massive network of trenches.[72]

Why not simply admit that the cost of such a war would not produce any measurable gains to either side and agree to negotiate a peace? The answer, of course, is that ever since the Emancipation Proclamation, there was no room for negotiation. Lincoln's commitment to emancipation was, in effect, a commitment to unconditional surrender on the part of the Confederacy.[73] Southern leaders, who had gone to war to defend slavery, were left two choices: Abandon the military effort and accept the end of slavery; or gamble that by carrying on the fight, the North would be forced to reassess its priorities in the fall of 1864. Long shot though it was, continued fighting seemed the better choice in early 1864.

The Union victories at the end of the summer of 1864 tend to obscure the fact that the odds facing the Confederates in the early summer were not insurmountable. In the opinion of some observers, morale in the North dipped lower that summer than at any time since Bull Run. Grant's war of attrition was exacting a huge toll of casualties as he hammered away at Lee's defenses, and the results were disappointing. Indeed, Lincoln was so depressed by the military stalemate in mid-August that he became convinced he would lose the fall election. But if Northerners could find little to cheer about in the summer of 1864, Southerners were becoming equally desperate. In relative terms, Lee was losing men just as fast as Grant, and there were no more men to replace those he lost. The Southerners had thrown everything they had into the fight.

Or had they? In January 1864, General Patrick Cleburne and thirteen officers in his division had proposed to his superiors that the Confeder-

---

72 Edward Hagerman argues that Lee's understanding of the advantages of trench warfare dates from the day when he commanded the defense of Richmond against McClellan's peninsula campaign in the spring of 1862. He proved to be a master of defensive tactics in the battle of Richmond two years later; see "The Tactical Thought of R. E. Lee and the Origins of Trench Warfare in the American Civil War, 1861–1862," *The Historian* 38 (November 1975).

73 For an excellent discussion of the evolution of Lincoln's policy of unconditional surrender, see James M. McPherson, *Lincoln and the strategy of Unconditional Surrender,* Twenty-Third Annual Report Fortenbaugh Memorial Lecture (Gettysburg College, 1984).

acy "commence training a large reserve of the most courageous of our slaves, and further, that we guarantee freedom within a reasonable time to every slave in the South who shall remain true to the Confederacy in this war."[74] Jefferson Davis quickly suppressed Cleburne's report. The South, he felt, was not yet ready for a suggestion that blacks be armed to fight for southern independence. After a lifetime of living with the fear of an insurrection of black slaves, it was too much to expect Southerners to accept slaves as their possible saviors.

But the issue of arming blacks was not likely to go away. The willingness of the North to enlist blacks, including freed slaves, in the Union Army gave Southerners additional food for thought on the subject.[75] The Confiscation Act of July 1862 had given the president power to arm "contraband" ex-slaves and use them as a military force. Lincoln was not prepared to go so far as to arm blacks, although he was willing to see them used as military labor. An effort by General David Hunter to organize a regiment of black volunteers in the Sea Islands off the coast of South Carolina and Georgia was overruled by the president in the spring of 1862. But the inevitable could not be long delayed. On August 25, 1862, Secretary of War Edwin Stanton authorized the creation of a regiment of five thousand black soldiers to be recruited in the Union-occupied areas of Louisiana. This time Lincoln did not object, and the first regiment of free blacks was mustered into service on September 27, 1862 – less than a week after Lincoln announced the Emancipation Proclamation. With emancipation now an official policy, resistance to enlisting black soldiers began to abate, although it hardly disappeared. At first, black troops were assigned to guard and other duties behind the fighting. Finally, in 1863, black regiments appeared at the front lines and performed well in battle for the duration of the war.

The use of blacks as soldiers in the Union army infuriated southern whites. The appearance of black soldiers may have strengthened the hand of those in the South who argued that the Confederacy should also use its black manpower to fight the war. By the fall of 1864, Jefferson Davis was quietly suggesting that slaves might be armed and promised their freedom if they would fight for the South. The response was not enthusiastic. Here again, there was an interesting psychology at work. Three and a

---

74 Quoted in Beringer et al., *Why the South Lost*, p. 370.
75 The best account of the movement to use black troops in the North is Dudley Taylor Cornish, *The Sable Arm: Black Troops in the Union Army, 1861–1865* (1956; reprint, University Press of Kansas, 1987), with a foreword by Herman Hattaway. My account draws heavily on Cornish's pioneering study.

half years of fighting had made independence from the hated "yankees" more important to the South than the continued enslavement of blacks. The loss of so many young men in the war convinced many who would have rejected any proposal to arm slaves at the outset of the war to consider it now. "If I were convinced that we would be subjugated," a Georgia member of the Confederate Congress declared in October 1864, "unless the negroes be placed in the army, I would not hesitate to enrol our slaves and put them to fighting."[76] Yet, even with defeat staring them in the face, the Confederate Congress continued to equivocate on the issue. Finally, the one man who might sway public opinion in favor of arming slaves gave his support to the idea. "I think that we must decide," wrote Robert E. Lee in January 1865, "whether slavery shall be extinguished by our enemies and the slaves used against us, or use them ourselves at the risk of the effects which may be produced upon our social institutions. My own opinion is that we should use them without delay."[77] Lee's support carried the day, and the Confederate Congress finally passed a law providing for the arming and freeing of slaves.[78]

It was a case of far too little far too late. The belated attempt to get slaves in the Confederate military effort had no direct effect on the outcome of the war. Yet it reveals just how far the strains of wartime mobilization had changed the South by the end of the fight. Surely one of the greatest ironies of this conflict is that the South had endorsed emancipation by the end of the war. Had it done so sooner, it might even have won the war. As it turned out, the South's inability to use its slave resources and the divisiveness created by slavery were major reasons why it lost the war.

When all was said and done, the South was not simply outgunned and outmanned by superior resources and manpower. The Confederacy had ample manpower and resources at its disposal to wage an effective defensive war and hold the North at bay. The South lost because the slave society upon which the Confederacy was built was unable to muster the will to outlast a determined foe. The presence of slavery, which hampered mobilization and crippled morale on the home front, led to the collapse of morale at the end of the war.

76 Akin to Nathan Land, October 31, 1864; quoted in Beringer et al., *Why the South Lost*, p. 372.
77 Lee to Andrew Hunter, January 11, 1865; quoted in Beringer et al., *Why the South Lost*, p. 373. Lee went on to endorse a plan of gradual emancipation for slaves who fought to defend the South.
78 For a more complete account of the fight to arm black slaves in the Confederacy, see Escott, *After Secession*, chap. 8, and Beringer et al., *Why the South Lost*, chap. 16.

Conflict and Compromise

Appendix Table

Table A.6.1. *Population of the free and slave states by age and race, 1860 (thousands)*

	Children aged 1 to 9			Adults aged 10 to 49		
	Male	Female	Total	Male	Female	Total
All races						
Confederacy	1,415	1,387	2,802	2,838	2,734	5,571
Border states	495	481	977	1,019	958	1,978
Free union	2,652	2,588	5,239	6,128	5,770	11,898
Total	4,562	4,456	9,018	9,985	9,462	19,447
Whites						
Confederacy	852	815	1,667	1,712	1,671	3,329
Border states	408	394	801	851	787	1,637
Free union	2,624	2,560	5,184	6,058	5,695	11,752
Total	3,884	3,769	7,653	8,620	8,098	16,719
Free blacks						
Confederacy	19	19	39	37	43	80
Border states	17	17	34	37	42	79
Free union	27	28	55	70	75	146
Total	64	64	128	145	160	305
Slaves						
Confederacy	543	553	1,096	1,088	1,074	2,162
Border states	71	71	142	132	129	261
Total	614	623	1,237	1,220	1,203	2,423

Note: Border states are Delaware, Kentucky, Maryland, and Missouri. The totals for ages unknown reported in the census were allocated to the various age groups in proportion to each group.

Table A.6.1. (*cont.*)

Adults 50 and older			All ages		
Male	Female	Total	Male	Female	Total
376	352	728	4,629	4,472	9,101
133	124	257	1,648	1,564	3,212
1,005	943	1,949	9,785	9,301	19,086
1,515	1,420	2,934	16,062	15,338	31,400
236	215	451	2,800	2,647	5,447
111	100	212	1,370	1,281	2,650
993	930	1,924	9,675	9,185	18,860
1,340	1,246	2,586	13,845	13,113	26,957
6	8	14	63	70	133
7	9	16	61	68	129
12	13	25	110	116	226
26	29	55	234	254	488
135	129	264	1,766	1,755	3,521
14	15	30	217	216	433
149	144	293	1,983	1,971	3,954

Source: U.S. Census Office, Eighth Census, *Population of the United States in 1860* (U.S. Government Printing Office, 1864).

7

The Impact of Emancipation

Section 1: Neither slavery nor involuntary servitude, except as a punishment for crime whereof the party shall have been duly convicted, shall exist within the United States, or any place subject to their jurisdiction. *Section 2:* Congress shall have power to enforce this article by appropriate legislation.

Constitution of the United States of America, Amendments, Article 13, Ratified December 18, 1865

The words were terse and to the point, echoing those of Thomas Jefferson as he had struggled to ban slavery from the Northwest Territory. In 1865 the ban was applied not just to a few states or territories, but to all of the United States. The Thirteenth Amendment demonstrated that at least one great question had been resolved by four years of war: Slavery was abolished, and four million black slaves were freed.

What was next? In the summer of 1862, the editor of a Boston newspaper had commented that the "great phenomenon of the year is the terrible intensity" with which the support for emancipation had swept through New England. "A year ago," he continued, "men might have faltered of proceeding to this extremity, [but now] they are in great measure prepared for it."[1] The editor's observation was overly sanguine. Even if he was correct that northern men might have prepared themselves to accept the idea of emancipation (and we have seen that this was by no means obvious elsewhere in the United States at this time), three years later they were still not prepared to deal with the reality of its consequences. For most, it was a distant problem that was supposed to work itself out. The victory of northern armies had given blacks their freedom, and with the "slave power" finally put to rest, free labor – black and white – in the South could now develop in combination with capital and land just as it did in the North. A "New South" would rise from the ashes of the "Old."

There were those in the South who shared such a dream. James De-Bow, a constant critic of the South's dependence on cotton before the war, welcomed the possibility that with the demise of slavery "King

---

1 *Boston Advertiser*, August 20, 1862; quoted in James M. McPherson, *Battle Cry of Freedom: The Civil War Era* (Oxford University Press, 1988), p. 496.

Cotton" might finally be displaced. "The soils and climate of this vast region," he proudly proclaimed, "are favorable to every product upon which industry and capital are expended in any country." Developing these natural resources, DeBow asserted, "will open up results for [the South], which nothing in the history of the times have equalled, dazzling and magnificent as have been its past achievements."[2] Initially, prospects did seem bright. Marveling at the speed with which his countrymen had already recovered from the devastating impact of the war, the comptroller general of Georgia wrote in October 1866 that "we have every reason to hope that this is but the beginning, the ground swell of a great and glorious future, if fortune will continue to favor us."[3] Such predictions proved to be premature. Fortune did not continue to favor either Georgia or its sister states of the defunct Confederacy, and the future proved to be anything but "glorious." Although a full account of the reasons for the failure of that future to materialize lies beyond the scope of this book, we can see the genesis of the problem in the reactions of people to the events that followed on the heels of the North's victory and the emancipation of slaves.[4]

Institutional change is never easy, even in the best of times, and the years immediately following 1865 were hardly the best of times in the South. Americans were attempting to "reconstruct" a defeated society following a bitter and devastating war. On April 16 they learned to their horror that Abraham Lincoln, the man who had led the North through the war and whom many counted on to bind the nation back together again, had been murdered as he watched a play in Washington, D.C. Lincoln's death removed from the political scene an extraordinary politician who possessed both the stature and leadership skills to formulate and implement a policy for "Reconstruction" acceptable to a broad spectrum of people in the North. If nothing else, Lincoln's continued leadership might have avoided the bitter clash that developed between Andrew Johnson and the radical Republican leaders in Congress. Johnson was a former governor and senator from Tennessee who was not even a member of the Republican Party when he was nominated as vice-

---

2 James D. B. Debow, "The Future of the South," *Debow's Review* 1 (January 1866): 8–9.

3 John T. Burns, *Annual Report of the Comptroller General of the State of Georgia . . . October 16, 1866* (J. W. Burke and Company, 1866), p. 28.

4 The arguments presented in this chapter draw heavily on the extensive body of research that Richard Sutch and I have conducted on the postbellum South. For a much fuller analysis of the economic consequences of emancipation, see Roger L. Ransom and Richard Sutch, *One Kind of Freedom: The Economic Consequences of Emancipation* (Cambridge University Press, 1977); and the essays in Gary M. Walton and James F. Shepherd, eds., *Market Institutions and Economic Progress in the New South, 1865–1900: Essays Stimulated by One Kind of Freedom* (Academic Press, 1981).

president in 1864; he was a southern Unionist whose candidacy was intended to draw support from the border states at a time when Lincoln's reelection was by no means assured. Unfortunately, the new president lacked Lincoln's skill as a politician. In attempting to assert the power of the presidency in directing Reconstruction, he produced a rift between the White House and congressional leaders that crippled the formulation of Reconstruction policy. Congress had the power of the purse and the authority to legislate change. But enforcement of any policy rested with the military authorities in the South, and they were responsible to the president, who was the constitutional commander in chief of the armed forces. At a time when cooperation between the legislative and executive branches was crucial, relations had deteriorated to the point where, shortly before the end of his term, congressional leaders tried to remove the president from office through impeachment.

Even had he lived, Lincoln would have faced formidable problems, many of which were not well understood at the time. Most observers' attention was focused on problems associated with the *physical* destruction and dislocation from the war. Yet this proved to be the least of the South's worries. Damage from the fighting was greatly exaggerated at the time, partly because of the publicity given Sherman's march through Georgia and the Carolinas, together with the destruction of cities such as Columbia, South Carolina, and Richmond, Virginia, in the closing months of the war. In fact, the greatest disruption to the southern economy was not destruction from fighting; it was the neglect of farms and machinery that occurred because of labor being away at the front. Most of the effects of wartime damage and neglect could be repaired within a few years.[5] A more significant problem was that the social and economic institutions in the South had been completely destroyed by the war and abolition. The system of labor that had been practiced in the South for two and a half centuries had been abolished. The financial institutions that had provided the agricultural credit for the antebellum plantation system were gone, ruined by the financial collapse of the Confederate government. All of this was evident enough in the spring of 1865, yet neither the victorious Northerners nor the defeated Confederates had any clear picture of how to go about reestablishing these institutional arrangements. No one seems to have really understood just how far-reaching the impact of freeing four million black slaves would be. The misunderstandings that arose in the years immediately after the war

---

5 For more on this point, see Roger L. Ransom and Richard Sutch, "The Impact of the Civil War and of Emancipation on Southern Agriculture," *Explorations in Economic History* 12 (January 1975).

seriously interfered with the establishment of a set of institutional arrangements that might allow a "New South" to arise from the ashes of the war.

Free at Last: Blacks' Reaction to Freedom

One group of people who did understand the initial impact of emancipation were the freed blacks. "What my people wants first," exclaimed an ex-slave to journalist Sidney Andrews in the fall of 1865, "what dey fust wants is de right to be free."[6] They were free at last. But what did freedom mean? Although many – perhaps most – slaves had heard that they would be set free when the victorious Yankees came, they were often unprepared for the event when it finally arrived. A former slave from Virginia recalled how he and his fellow freedmen had been overwhelmed by the realization that they were now free: "It came so sudden on 'em they wasn't prepared for it. Just think of whole droves of people, that had always been kept so close, and hardly left the plantation before, turned loose all at once, with nothing in the world, but what they had on their backs, and often little enough of that."[7]

The first problem was convincing blacks – and in more than a few cases, their former masters – that the ex-slaves were really free. Given conditions in the rural South in the spring of 1865, this was no easy task. The most common source of information was from the Yankee troops that came through the area. But the troops seldom stayed in one place for long, and once they departed, the freedmen and their families were left with little or no means of support, and they were forced to deal with the authority of their former masters.[8] Not surprisingly under these circumstances, it did not take blacks long to want to "test" their newly won freedom. Several manifestations of this desire to see if they were really "free" are evident in the actions of free blacks soon after the end of the war.

Restrictions on slaves' movement had been one of the most onerous elements of slavery. As Carl Schurz observed, "Large numbers of colored people left the plantations; many flocked to our military posts and camps to obtain the certainty of their freedom, and others walked away merely for the purpose of leaving the places on which they had been held in

6 Sidney Andrews, *The South since the War as Shown by Fourteen Weeks of Travel in Georgia and the Carolinas* (1866; reprint, Houghton-Mifflin Company, 1970), p. 188.
7 Parke Johnston, cited in Leon F. Litwack, *Been in the Storm So Long: The Aftermath of Slavery* (Vintage Books, 1979), p. 215.
8 On the initial reaction to freedom on the part of the ex-slaves, see Litwack, *Been in the Storm so Long*, chaps. 4 and 5; and Peter Kolchin, *First Freedom: The Response of Alabama's Blacks to Emancipation and Reconstruction* (Greenwood Press, 1972).

slavery, and because they could now go with impunity."[9] Although they often went only a short distance, and many returned to their antebellum homes in the fullness of time, the ex-slaves were anxious to prove that their former master could not compel them to stay on the plantation. To assist freedmen, as well as white Southerners who had lost their means of support in the confusion of the immediate postwar period, Congress established the Bureau of Refugees, Freedmen, and Abandoned Lands. Because it was operated by the U.S. Army, the bureau was the most visible evidence of a northern military presence in the South. Although it had other responsibilities, the bureau soon found that its major task would be to act as an intermediary between whites and freedmen. By the end of 1865 it was known simply as the "Freedman's Bureau," and for four years it acted as the principal agent of Reconstruction policy in the South.

The Bureau quickly established centers in most of the major towns of the South to distribute rations for refugees displaced by the war. One effect of these centers, as Carl Schurz noted, was to attract freedmen to the towns. In fact, the centers attracted whites as well as blacks. However, whereas the blacks often tended to stay in the vicinity of the center, whites tended to collect their rations and return to their farms.[10] Consequently, towns throughout the South experienced a large influx of blacks, a phenomenon that was not greeted with great enthusiasm by white inhabitants. A Baton Rouge newspaper noted that "before the war there were but six hundred Negroes in this place; now there are as many thousand. . . . We have to support them, nurse them, and bury them."[11] He need not have worried; the influx of blacks to urban areas was only a temporary phenomenon. Whether or not they eventually returned to their antebellum plantations, almost all blacks remained in agriculture after the war.[12] The hostility of whites in the cities encouraged them to return to their farms, as did the pressure applied by the agents of the

9 Carl Schurz, "Report of Carl Schurz on the States of South Carolina, Georgia, Alabama, Mississippi, and Louisiana," in *Message of the President of the United States, Communicating . . . Information in Relation to the States . . . Lately in Rebellion (December 19, 1865)*, Senate Executive Document no. 2, 39th Congress, 1st Session (U.S. Government Printing Office, 1865), p. 15.

10 According to the reports of the bureau, more rations were given to white refugees than to "colored people." John W. DeForest's account of his activities as a bureau officer in Georgia provides an excellent overview of the bureau's handling of rations for refugees of both races; see *A Union Officer in the Reconstruction* (1867; reprint, Yale University Press, 1948).

11 *Baton Rouge Advocate*, February 21, 1866; reported by John Richard Dennett, *The South As It Is: 1865–66* (1867; reprint, Viking Press, 1967), pp. 343–4.

12 For an analysis of the impact of black migration on the cities of the South, see Kolchin, *First Freedom*; and Ransom and Sutch, *One Kind of Freedom*, pp. 61–4.

Freedmen's Bureau to find jobs. Now that they were free, slaves had to provide for themselves and their families. Jobs in the South were on farms, not in the cities. The reality of this situation soon became apparent to the freedmen. Ex-slaves, recalled one black, "had an abundance of dat somethin' called freedom." But, she continued,

> they soon found out dat freedom ain't nothin', 'less you is got some-thin' to live on and a place called home. Dis livin on liberty is lak young folks livin' on love after they gits married. It just don't work. No, sir, it las' so long and not a bit longer. Don't tell me! It sho don't hold good when you has to work, or when you gits hongry.[13]

There was ample work available. After four seasons of war, cotton prices were high in the spring of 1865, and planters were anxious to plant their fields. All that was needed for production to resume was for landlords and laborers to agree on terms of work.

That seemed simple enough, but the efforts to reach agreement on labor contracts between planters and freedmen brought forth a second manifestation of freedom on the part of the former slaves. Blacks, it turned out, were more than willing to work, but they wanted employment as free labor, not as slave labor. Under the slave regime, masters had been able to extract far more labor from the slave labor force than might be expected from free workers. Not unnaturally, free black families wished to enjoy some of the free time they were denied as slaves. Freedmen demanded the right to work fewer hours; to have at least one day off; and, if they were married, to have more free time with their wives and children. The result was a dramatic fall in the amount of labor that free blacks were willing to offer as free laborers.[14] This decline in labor effort produced what contemporaries claimed was a "shortage" of farm labor, a phenomenon that whites attributed to an unreasonable refusal on the part of blacks to work for wages. In fact, what had oc-curred was a perfectly reasonable response to freedom on the part of blacks. What really bothered whites was the disappearance of a major source of exploitation under black slavery – the extraction of labor through a system of coercion. This was the first unexpected shock of emancipation: There would be less labor available now that the slaves were free workers.

13 Slave narrative from South Carolina, cited in Litwack, *Been in the Storm So Long*, p. 328.
14 We can get a pretty firm idea of the order of magnitude of this decline in labor by noting that the free black population in the 1870s offered between 28 and 37 percent fewer men-hours of labor per capita than had been obtained from slavery. The decline is calculated as the net effect from three factors: fewer hours worked per day; fewer days worked per year; and a lower rate of participation in the labor force by free blacks. For details, see Ransom and Sutch, *One Kind of Freedom*, pp. 44–7.

Blacks not only wanted to have more time to spend as they pleased; they wanted to have more to say about the conditions under which they would be working. Throughout the South, freedmen stubbornly resisted attempts by planters to reinstitute the old work gangs so reminiscent of slavery. Planters who insisted on having their black workers work in gangs and live in the old slave quarters found it difficult to get labor. Necessity might force blacks to seek work, but a pressing need for labor produced enough competition among employers to enable the ex-slaves to gain some concessions from their former masters before agreeing to once again supply their labor. Blacks' reluctance to work under the old terms forced planters to acquiesce in offering more reasonable working conditions.

Another aspect of the slave regime that had been especially offensive to blacks was the prohibition against teaching slaves to read or write. Based on evidence after the war, it seems clear that over 90 percent of the adult slave population could not read or write.[15] Free from slavery, blacks were, in the words of journalist Whitelaw Reid, "far more eager than any other to secure the advantage of education for themselves, and especially for their children."[16] Considering the obstacles, efforts made to meet this demand for education were nothing short of heroic. Schools for blacks were established throughout the South, supported by contributions from the North, by the Freedman's Bureau, and, to a limited extent, by public funds. Prior to the war, no southern state had a statewide system for supporting education; by 1880 all of them had superintendents of education and tax support for schools. In the face of strong and often violent opposition by whites, the freedmen pressed forward on a program of education. The legislation establishing public school systems was a direct result of the determination on the part of blacks to provide education for their children. Although they were to fall into disrepair later in the century, schools for black children established in the 1870s represented one of the most significant accomplishments of reconstruction governments.

Blacks in the years after emancipation displayed a keen appreciation of their freedom. Their desire to move about, their demands to have some control over their working conditions, and their eagerness for education were all reactions of a people who had been denied these rights for all their lives. Occasionally, the spirit behind this sense of freedom reached extraordinary heights. In August 1865, Jourdan Anderson, who had mi-

15 The 1870 census reported about 90.4 percent of blacks aged twenty or more were illiterate, compared with 19.8 percent of whites (Ransom and Sutch, *One Kind of Freedom*, table 2.4, p. 30).
16 Whitelaw Reid, *After the War: A Tour of the Southern States, 1865–1866* (1866; reprint Harper and Row, 1965), pp. 302–3.

grated to Ohio, received a letter from his ex-master in Tennessee offering him a "good chance" if he and his wife Mandy would return to the old homestead. In response, Jourdan offered the following proposal:

> Mandy says she would be afraid to go back without some proof that you are sincerely disposed to treat us justly and kindly – and we have concluded to test your sincerity by asking you to send us our wages for the time we served you. This will make us forget and forgive old scores, and rely on your justice and friendship in the future. I served you faithfully for thirty-two years and Mandy twenty years. At $25 a month for me and $2 a week for Mandy, our earnings would amount to $11,680. Add to this the interest for the time our wages have been kept back and deduct what you paid for our clothing and three doctor's visits to me, and pulling a tooth for Mandy, and the balance will show what we are in justice entitled to. Please send the money by Adams Express, in care of V. Winters, esq, Dayton Ohio. If you fail to pay us for faithful labors in the past, we can have little faith in your promises for the future. . . .
>
> You will also please state if there has been any schools opened for the colored children in your neighborhood, the great desire of my life now is to give my children an education and have them form virtuous habits.
>
> P.S. – Say howdy to George Carter, and thank him for taking the pistol from you when you were shooting at me.[17]

Most blacks wanted to do more than simply "test" their freedom. Like Jourdan Anderson, they wanted to establish themselves as independent families with an economic livelihood to support themselves. In the agricultural South, the ex-slaves soon discovered that to do this they needed access to land. One hope was that the land confiscated from their former masters might be given to the freedmen by the government in Washington, D.C. In 1865 and early 1866, this was not pure fantasy. Acting under an order issued by General William Sherman in January 1865, General Rufus Saxton supervised the distribution of confiscated land on the coast of Georgia and South Carolina to about 40,000 freedmen.[18]

17 Cited in Litwack, *Been in the Storm So Long*, p. 335. Dated August 22, 1865, the letter was published in the *Cincinnati Commercial* and reprinted in the *New York Times* as a "letter dictated by a servant." As Litwack notes, "few individuals – white or black – have ever articulated the meaning of freedom more clearly or more precisely than Jourdan Anderson" (p. 335).

18 Sherman's *Field Order Number 15*, which was issued without consulting officials in Washington, created considerable consternation when it became known that land had actually been distributed to the freedmen. Sherman's order was contested after the war by planters who petitioned President Johnson to get their land back. The correspondence between Freedman's Bureau Commissioner O. O. Howard and Secretary of War Stanton provides good insights into the problems of land distribution after the war. See the letters reproduced in Lawanda Cox and John H. Cox, *Reconstruction, the Negro,*

General O. O. Howard, the first commissioner of the Freedman's Bureau, clearly thought that a major task of his bureau would be to oversee the distribution of confiscated land to blacks. In his initial report to President Johnson, Howard stated that "with respect to abandoned lands, it was the evident intention of [Congress] to give the bureau control, solely for the purpose of assigning, leasing, or selling them to refugees or freedmen."[19] General Howard, together with several other military commanders such as General Saxton and General Wager Swayne, conveyed this impression to freedmen in the South. Congressional rhetoric gave added encouragement to freedmen who hoped for land from the government. Thaddeus Stevens proposed giving some 394 million acres of land owned by about 70,000 former Confederates to blacks. To those who objected to distributing land to the freedmen, Stevens responded that it would be "far easier and beneficial to exile 70,000 proud, bloated, and defiant rebels than to expatriate 4,000,000 laborers, native to the soil and loyal to the government."[20] The Stevens bill never came to a vote. One result of all this speculation was that blacks held off making labor contracts in the spring of 1865 and again in 1866 in the hope that they would be given land of their own to work.[21] The notion that the government owed freedmen "forty acres and a mule" was still very much in evidence as late as the presidential election of 1868.

Blacks wanted to own land because land ownership offered the only sure means of security. Without government help, they clearly lacked the means to purchase it, and following the elections of 1866 it became increasingly apparent that ownership of land by blacks would not come quickly, if it came at all. If they could not own the land they worked, they could at least insist on getting away from the odious supervision and control of the plantation-gang system. A rented farm did not offer the security of ownership, but it offered some degree of independence for the farm family. At the very least, the tenant family could make its own choices with regard to when they would work.

and the New South (University of South Carolina Press, 1973), pp. 315–26; also see Kenneth Stampp, *The Era of Reconstruction, 1865–1877* (Vintage Press, 1965), p. 125.

19 O. O. Howard, "Report of the Commissioner of the Bureau of Refugees, Freedmen, and Abandoned Lands," December 1865; reprinted in Cox and Cox, *Reconstruction, the Negro, and the New South*, p. 317.
20 Thaddeus Stevens, cited in Stampp, *Era of Reconstruction*, p. 127.
21 The classic studies of land for the freedmen are Oscar Zeichner, "Transition from Slave to Free Agricultural Labor in the Southern States," *Agricultural History* 13 (January 1939); Martin Abbott, "Free Land, Free Labor, and the Freedman's Bureau," *Agricultural History* 30 (October 1956); and Lawanda Cox, "Promise of Land for the Freedmen," *Mississippi Valley Historical Review* 45 (December 1958).

The Prostrate South: Whites' Reaction to Emancipation

Contemporary accounts of the slaves' reaction to their liberty stressed the emotional response of a people suddenly released from two and a half centuries of bondage. That is not surprising, but such accounts provide a somewhat misleading guide to the deeper feelings that lay behind the actions of blacks once they established that they were, indeed, free. Those deeper feelings – which prompted the blacks' insistence on being allowed to move around and their insistence on the right to choose working conditions as free workers, as well as their intense desire for education and a parcel of land to call their own – were misunderstood by most whites at the time. And those misunderstandings produced serious problems as both races sought to work out a new set of economic and social arrangements in the turbulent times of Reconstruction.

To most southern whites, emancipation was seen as an unmitigated disaster. Those who had owned slaves suffered enormous financial losses and experienced a profound threat to their social and economic status. Those who had not owned slaves found themselves confronted with a situation where slavery no longer acted as a buffer that protected them from having to deal with blacks. The issue of black equality affected all Southerners, whatever their feeling about slavery might have been. Moreover, emancipation had been forced upon the South as a consequence of losing a costly and bitter war. The sight of their former slaves being free produced a resentment in the minds of most Southerners every bit as strong as that felt toward the Yankee invaders. One of the most obvious manifestations of this resentment over emancipation was a marked increase in the level of racial antagonism on the part of whites toward blacks in the South.

The freedmen's reaction to freedom exacerbated this antagonism. Seen from a distance, the ex-slaves' behavior can be understood as a natural response to obtaining their freedom – they no longer wished to live or work like slaves. But to white observers such attitudes were "proof" that blacks could never be expected to deal with the responsibilities of freedom. Thus, for example, the freedmen's migration to cities was taken as evidence of an inherent laziness on the part of the Negro race. A Northern army surgeon in Natchez, Mississippi, commenting on the condition of blacks who had come to the city observed that:

> Large numbers of *idle* negroes . . . now throng the streets, lanes and alleys, and overcrowd every hovel. *Lazy* and *profligate,* unused to caring for themselves, thriftless for the present and recklessly improvident of the future, the most of them loaf idly about the streets

and alleys, prowling in secret places, and lounge lazily in crowded hovels.[22]

Black resistance to returning to the conditions of the plantation reinforced the racist predilections of planters who were convinced that blacks would not provide labor simply in return for wages. "I tell you," an Alabamian told Whitelaw Reid in 1865,

> the nigger *never* works except when he is compelled to. It isn't in his nature, and you can't put it in. He'll work a day for you for good wages, and then will go off and spend it; and you'll not get another lick out of him til he's hungry, and has got nothing to eat.[23]

This view of the black response to freedom obviously influenced the bargaining over wages and employment in the first seasons after the war. Convinced of the unreliability of black labor, white landlords offered terms of employment that blacks found offensive. Not surprisingly, the result was a high level of dissatisfaction on the part of both parties. "The number of complaints made at this office is very large," reported an officer of the Freedman's Bureau to Commissioner O. O. Howard in November 1867:

> The white man complains generally that the freedman is lazy, impudent and unreliable, and that he will not fulfil his contract any further than it suits his convenience, that he claims the right to lose as much time as he pleases and when he pleases but wants full rations all the time. . . . The freedman, on the other hand, generally complains that the white man has made him sign a contract, which he does not understand to mean what the white man says it does mean, and that the white man wants him to do work which he did not contract to do.[24]

As if these problems were not enough, the weather provided still more obstacles to those trying to work out the new arrangements. John De-Forest, an agent of the Freedman's Bureau stationed in Greenville, South Carolina, described conditions that existed in most parts of the cotton South in 1866: "The crop of 1866, both of cereals and other productions, had been a short one for various reasons. Capital, working stock, and even seed had been scarce; a new system of labor had operated, of course bunglingly; finally, there had been a severe drought."[25]

22　Cited in Litwack, *Been in the Storm So Long*, p. 320 (emphasis in original).
23　Reid, *After the War*, p. 363 (emphasis in original).
24　Report of Charles Rauschenberg to O. O. Howard, November 14, 1867; reprinted in Cox and Cox, *Reconstruction, the Negro, and the New South*, pp. 340–1.
25　DeForest, *A Union Officer in Reconstruction*, p. 73. For more on the crop problems of 1866–7, see Ransom and Sutch, *One Kind of Freedom*, pp. 64–5.

Responsibility for sorting all of this out and making the system of free labor "work" fell ultimately on the officers of the Freedman's Bureau, who adjudicated all disputes between freedmen and planters. Although they were more likely to give the freedmen their due than were the local planters, northern officers still fell prey to racial and ideological stereotypes that affected their judgment in these matters. Reports coming to the bureau after the spring of 1866 increasingly expressed concerns over the blacks' reluctance to sign contracts and get to work. Agents of the bureau, who came from a world where wage labor was common in agriculture as well as industry, became impatient with black resistance to terms offered by landlords. In many areas the agents exerted strong pressure on freedmen to sign contracts and get to work on whatever terms the planters offered.

Emancipation not only necessitated the reorganization of the labor system, it also had profound consequences on the financial structure of the South. Table 7.1 presents data on the wealth of farmers in 1860 and 1870. Planters who owned slaves and operated a "plantation" in 1860 reported an average total wealth of $81,382 in 1860, more than half of it in "personal estate."[26] The average wealth reported by all farm operators in 1860 was $22,819. In 1870, the average total wealth reported by white farm operators was $3,168; the personal estate was $849. This enormous fall in the wealth of farm operators reflected more than simply the disappearance of slaves. In the confusion of the postwar adjustments, real estate values plummeted as well. The average value per improved acre in 1860 had been almost $30; in 1870 it had fallen to less than $15. The price of unimproved land fell even more in relative terms.[27] Small wonder that the southern planter felt "wiped out" by the war.

Such a dramatic decline in the level of wealth held by whites had a significant effect on the level of income flowing to whites each year. Although there are no reliable estimates of income over the Civil War

26 A *farm operator* was defined as the person living on the farm, based on an examination of the Population and Agricultural Schedules of the manuscript censuses. Slaves were counted as personal estate in 1860. The definition of a "plantation" was a farm with at least one hundred improved acres operated by someone who was listed by the census as owning at least twenty slaves. See the appendix to Chapter 3 for details about the samples of farms used in this analysis.

27 The value of land per acre is estimated using the same procedures employed in the estimates of value per acre presented in Chapter 3. The calculations are reported more fully in Roger L. Ransom and Richard Sutch, "Capitalists without Capital: The Burden of Slavery and the Impact of Emancipation," *Agricultural History* (Fall, 1988), table 3, p. 148. A contributing factor to the decline in land values was the withdrawal of slave labor, which made land a redundant factor of production immediately after the war. See the discussion of Ransom and Sutch, "Impact of the Civil War," and idem, *One Kind of Freedom*, chap. 3.

Table 7.1. *Average value of reported wealth by class of farm and
real and personal estates in eight counties in the South,
1860 and 1870 (dollars)*

| Year | Number of farms sampled | Average value reported per farm | | |
		Real estate	Personal estate	Total wealth
1860				
All farms	643	9,542	13,276	22,819
Plantations	126	35,324	45,057	81,382
Small slave	291	4,445	8,904	13,348
Nonslave	226	1,174	1,188	2,362
1870				
All farms	947	1,683	658	2,340
White	685	2,318	849	3,168
Black	262	20	158	178

Source: Computed from the sample of farms in eight counties in the South; see the appendix
to Chapter 3 for details of the samples.

decade, we can gain some appreciation of the relative change by comparing the value of agricultural output per capita in 1857 and 1879. Our
estimates of crop output suggest that black incomes rose by about 40
percent (from about $30 to just over $40), while white incomes fell by
about 35 percent (from $125 to just over $80).[28] In fact, the income of
whites who owned slaves was almost surely more than this aggregate
estimate of per capita output suggests.[29] The reason for the decline in
white incomes is evident enough: Slaveholders no longer received the
fruits of exploitation from their chattel labor. Southerners at the time
saw this a little differently; they placed the blame for their financial losses
on the war and emancipation. Having to pay their former bondsmen to

28 The estimates of crop output per capita are discussed more fully in Roger L. Ransom
and Richard Sutch, "Growth and Welfare in the American South in the Nineteenth
Century," *Explorations in Economic History* 16 (April 1979): 224–6. Obviously,
these figures offer only a very rough index of the change in real welfare of blacks
because they measure only the change in output per capita, and make no allowance for
the value of being "free." The "income" of blacks in 1857 was the estimated value of
their rations.

29 The estimates of per capita crop output are for all white farmers in the Ransom–Sutch
sample of farms for 1880; see Ransom and Sutch, *One Kind of Freedom*, appendix F.
The loss of income for slaveholders, particularly large slaveholders, may have been
considerably more than this because, as we point out, the loss of income from slave
capital alone could have produced a decline of as much as 42 percent of income (Idem,
"Growth and Welfare in the American South," pp. 225–6).

perform labor further increased their resentment over these losses and fed the fires of racial antagonism.

Slavery was gone and there was nothing that the ex-slaveowners could do to regain their lost slave property. They could, however, do something about the pressures by blacks for economic and social equality. Despite the popular notion of a class that had been "prostrated" by the war, the wealthy families who had controlled the political structure of the South before the war retained enormous economic and political power in the postwar era. The key to this power was that they still controlled the land, and land remained the cornerstone of economic power in the postbellum South.[30] Playing on the virulent racism of whites, landowners were able to deny blacks ownership of farms through a combination of strong social pressure or, when necessary, outright coercion. Whitelaw Reid observed that:

> In portions of the Mississippi Valley the feeling against any owner-ship of the soil by negroes is so strong, that the man who should sell small tracts to them would be in actual danger. Every effort will be made to prevent negroes from acquiring lands; even the renting of small tracts to them is held to be unpatriotic and unworthy of a good citizen.[31]

The denial of land ownership to freedmen constrained both the eco-nomic and the social status of blacks. Violence directed against education had the same effect. Schools – particularly schools for blacks that were affiliated with the Freedman's Bureau or supported by private northern interests – were a constant target of white anger. Schoolhouses were burned, teachers were intimidated, and both students and parents of black students were subjected to threats of white reprisals against those who were involved with education for the freedmen.[32] The success of

---

30 On the persistence of large landholdings, see Roger W. Shugg, "The Survival of the Plantation System in Louisiana," *Journal of Southern History* 3 (August 1937); idem, *Origins of Class Struggle in Louisiana: A Social History of White Farmers and La-borers during Slavery and After, 1840–1875* (Louisiana State University Press, 1939); Jonathan M. Wiener, "Planter Persistence and Social Change in Alabama, 1850–1871," *Journal of Interdisciplinary History* 7 (Autumn 1976); Ransom and Sutch, *One Kind of Freedom*, chap. 5; and Gavin Wright, *Old South, New South: Revolu-tions in the Southern Economy since the Civil War* (Basic Books, 1986), pp. 47–50.

31 Reid, *After the War*, pp. 564–5.

32 One need only glance through the reports of the various assistant commissioners of the Freedman's Bureau of the testimony before the Joint Select Committee of Congress investigating the Ku-Klux conspiracy to find abundant evidence of white antagonism toward black education. Excellent accounts of the efforts to educate blacks in the face of this resistance can be found in Henry A. Bullock, *A History of Negro Education in the South from 1619 to the Present* (Harvard University Press, 1967); and Litwack, *Been in the Storm So Long*.

white resistance to land ownership and education for blacks ensured that white Southerners would retain control over the economic structure of southern society.

Gaining political power was a bit more difficult, given Republican support for black equality and the presence of Yankee troops throughout the South. But the very presence of the Northerners worked to the advantage of those who stubbornly refused to accept the outcome of the war. This group, in the opinion of many observers, constituted a large fraction of the southern white population. A report submitted to a northern newspaper in June 1865 noted that:

> With the exception of the younger class of hot-headed rebels, the external conduct of all is proper, and shows an outward respect for authority. But underneath this calm, society is seething and boiling, as if a volcano were struggling beneath it. All here is chaos, and designing politicians are busy with schemes to save all that can be saved of the old order of things. Everything looks as if the South had only laid down the sword and rifle as weapons, and changed the fighting ground to the political arena.[33]

This determination to reinstate the "old order of things" was to play a crucial role in the politics of Reconstruction.

The unreconstructed "rebels" got help from an unexpected source in the spring of 1865. President Andrew Johnson, claiming to be following the plan laid down by Lincoln, recognized the validity of the first postwar "reconstruction Government" in Virginia on May 9, 1865 – barely a month after Appomattox. At the end of May, the president issued two proclamations that, in effect, offered a full pardon to anyone willing to take an oath of allegiance to the United States. The pardon restored full civil rights to the person, including the right to run for office, and restored all confiscated property.

Under the president's plan, the "rebel" states had never left the Union. Thus, as soon as a state could form a new government, it could resume its representation in Washington, D.C. The terms for establishing a new government required that at least 10 percent of the electorate had taken the loyalty oath to the Union. "Loyal" ex-Confederates greeted the news of Johnson's pardon and the formation of state governments with great enthusiasm. Northern radicals were far less enthusiastic, claiming that the president's actions had undermined any effective basis for Reconstruction.[34] Their fears proved well founded. During the summer and fall

---

33 Quoted in Michael Perman, *Reunion without Compromise: The South and Reconstruction, 1865–1868* (Cambridge University Press, 1973), p. 22.

34 Lincoln had formulated the 10 percent rule at a time when he was trying to set up a wartime government loyal to the Union in Louisiana. Radicals in Congress had strongly objected at the time, insisting on at least 50 percent loyalty, a figure they knew

of 1865 southern states elected state officers and legislatures. The impact of the presidential policy was immediately apparent: Throughout the South former Confederates were elected to office. Once elected, these state legislatures lost little time in showing their intent to restore the "old order." They passed laws, commonly termed "black codes," that placed severe restrictions on the political and economic rights of blacks. The codes encouraged collusion among employers, placed heavy penalties on freedmen who "broke" their contracts, and prescribed harsh penalties against "vagrancy." The actual effect of the codes was probably not as great as the publicity surrounding their passage suggests. The scarcity of labor undermined agreements not to compete for labor. Nevertheless, the psychological effect of such a blatant denial of rights to freedmen brought forth a storm of protest from the North. What made the codes particularly threatening to blacks was the arbitrariness with which the provisions on vagrancy could be enforced.

Johnson insisted that his actions in establishing state governments were following the plans that Lincoln had sketched out for Reconstruction after the war. A key part of this plan was the assertion that postwar governments could be established by executive action as soon as a sufficient fraction of loyal citizens were registered to vote. Who should frame the guidelines for these elections was a point that had first been raised by Lincoln in 1863–4. This issue soon became the basis for a fundamental disagreement between Congress and the chief executive. The failure of congressional leaders and the president to agree on the underlying principles of a Reconstruction policy meant that, for a period of almost four years, the two branches of the government were essentially working at cross-purposes with each other.

An important element in this struggle was that the traditional balance of power was initially tilted very much in the president's favor by the absence of any civil government in the rebel states. The only recognized authority of the United States government in the South immediately after the war was the Union Army, and the military commanders were responsible to their commander in chief. Consequently, the president could control policy in the South by executive order – as Johnson did with his amnesty proclamation. Congressional attempts to impose its will could be partially offset by the manner in which the executive enforced the laws. Ultimately, an enormous amount of effort was expended by the president and his foes in Congress attempting to offset the actions of the other. By late 1867, a time when the initial efforts at reorganizing the South's economic and political institutions were just beginning to be

would be impossible. Johnson's application of Lincoln's policy after the war completely alienated the radical wing of the Republican party from the new president.

tested, Johnson and congressional leaders were preoccupied with efforts to remove the president from office. By the time of the celebrated impeachment trial and acquittal of the president by the Senate in May 1868, the damage had been done.[35]

Johnson had utilized the power of the executive to implement his policy of Reconstruction in 1865–6. Following the elections of 1866, Republicans in Congress were determined to take Reconstruction into their own hands. They passed a series of "Reconstruction Acts" that called for the formation of new governments throughout the South based on the participation of black voters. A "Civil Rights Act" was passed in 1867 in an effort to ensure the enfranchisement of blacks. Convinced that congressional action was not enough, radicals initiated two amendments to the Constitution. In June of 1866 an amendment had been submitted to the states guaranteeing that "no state shall make or enforce any law which shall abridge the privileges or immunities of citizens of the United States; nor shall any state deprive any person of life, liberty, or property, without due process of law." The Fourteenth Amendment was ratified on July 28, 1868. This still did not explicitly mention the right to vote, so in February 1869, Congress approved still another constitutional amendment that simply stated "the right of citizens . . . to vote shall not be abridged." The Fifteenth Amendment was declared ratified by the states on March 30, 1870.

Congress could initiate constitutional amendments and pass legislation calling for the protection of black civil rights and participation in elections. But without a policy of enforcement backed by the presence of federal troops in the South, such guarantees were empty gestures. Southern whites, in the words of one officer of the Freedman's Bureau, "are yet unable to conceive of the negro as possessing any rights at all." He went on:

> The people boast that when they get freedmen affairs in their own hands, to use their own classic expression, "the niggers will catch hell."
> . . . The reason for all this is simple and manifest. The whites esteem the blacks their property by natural right, and however much they may admit that individual relations of masters and slaves have been destroyed by the war and the president's emancipation, they still have an ingrained feeling that blacks at large belong to whites at

---

35 It is interesting to note that the incident that precipitated the impeachment of Johnson was his attempt to remove Edwin Stanton as secretary of war. Stanton had consistently opposed the president's policies and used his position to undermine Johnson's authority over the military.

large, and whenever the opportunity serves they treat the colored
people just as their profit, caprice or passion may dictate.[36]

Feelings such as these posed an insurmountable obstacle to the restoration of open elections in the South. Congress could prevent conservative whites from dominating the political apparatus of the southern state governments through the presence of troops to guarantee black rights. But a Congress dominated by northern Republicans could never convince southern whites, nearly all of whom were adamantly opposed to any black participation in elections, to support the governments thus established. Therein lay the Achilles' heel of radical Reconstruction policy. Conservative opponents to Reconstruction responded to congressional action by simply refusing to recognize the legitimacy of governments that had, in their eyes, been established by force of arms.

This placed the northern radicals in an awkward position. Congressional support for "black Republicans" in the South was certain to alienate a large block of white southern voters. Yet, to gain a widespread support from these white voters, southern Republicans would have to abandon their black supporters and allow "unreconstructed rebels" to gain control of the political apparatus of state governments. The radicals' situation was made still more awkward by charges from northern Democrats that black enfranchisement in the South was nothing more than a political ploy by northern Republicans to increase their power at the national level. Emancipation, in short, had presented northern Republicans with a dilemma for which they had no answer. They had hoped that the destruction of slavery in the South would create a situation where poorer whites would join hands with the freedmen to form an effective Republican coalition that could govern the South.

Whites' reaction to emancipation shattered that hope. Although the Republican tickets in the South attracted some support immediately after the war, poor whites did not stay with the Republican banner for long. Racial prejudice proved stronger than class animosities. Poor whites chose to support southern conservatives who promised to exclude blacks from economic or political power. Thus, the option of allowing "home rule" (as Johnson's policy had done) would give away the most significant gain won in the war: the freedom of black Americans. The alternative – imposing a policy of Reconstruction based on black political power – could work only if there were strong support for equality of black rights in the northern states, or if blacks were able to establish a firm economic and political base. As we have already seen, black equality was never very high on the list of political priorities for most Norther-

36 Colonel Samuel Thomas to Carl Schurz; quoted by Schurz, "Report," p. 81.

ners. The constitutional amendments abolishing slavery and guaranteeing the civil liberties of blacks were in place. From there, things should have taken care of themselves.

One reason things did not take care of themselves is that the economic situation of blacks was as tenuous as was their political situation. As noted earlier, blacks understood the importance of having their own farm. Widespread ownership of land for blacks was largely out of the question because of the strident opposition of whites, together with the inability of black farmers to obtain capital for the purchase of land. President Johnson's amnesty, which was upheld by the courts, returned the confiscated lands to their original owners, thus vitiating any chance of land redistribution on the part of the federal government. After the 1868 election it was apparent that blacks would be farming the land owned by their former masters. That is not to say they would be working on the old plantation. This they refused to do, and their resistance proved effective in forcing a major reorganization of southern agriculture.

Agricultural Reconstruction: Breaking Up the Plantation

By the spring of 1868, a growing number of planters had abandoned efforts to farm large parcels of land, and turned instead to a system of renting small parcels of land to their former slaves. This change in strategy on the part of landowners produced one of the most dramatic changes associated with emancipation: the breakup of the antebellum plantations. In 1860, one-third of the total land in farms was organized in holdings of five hundred or more acres of land. Figures 7.1 and 7.2 graphically illustrate what happened over the next ten years. While the number of large farms in the five cotton states of the South fell by one-half, the number of farms reporting fewer than 50 acres more than doubled over the Civil War decade. By 1870, these smaller units held almost 30 percent of the total acreage in farms. Because the number of holdings with between fifty and one hundred acres also increased markedly, farms with less than one hundred acres, which had accounted for less than 20 percent of the land in farms before the war, represented almost 60 percent of the total acreage in 1870. What made the impact of this transformation of landholdings even more dramatic was the fact that it was completed in the space of barely five years.

Although many large farms were subdivided into small holdings, land ownership in the South remained in the hands of those who had owned land and slaves before the war.[37] What had changed was the manner in

---

37 For data on land ownership, see Ransom and Sutch, *One Kind of Freedom*, pp. 78–80. Data on persistence are presented by Wiener, "Planter Persistence," and idem, *Social*

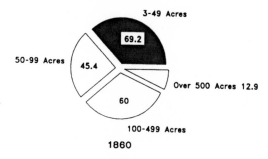

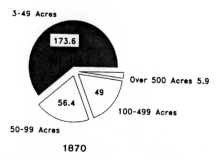

Figure 7.1. Number of farms in five cotton states by size of farm
in 1860 and 1870 (thousands of farms)

which landowners attracted labor to farm their land. The renting of small
landholdings, a practice that was relatively uncommon before the war,
became very common after 1868. Table 7.2 presents data on the
ownership of real estate and the size of farms in 1860 and 1870.[38] The
most striking difference between the two census years is the much higher
fraction of farms operated by tenants in 1870. Before the war, nine out of

Origins of the New South: Alabama, 1865–1885 (Louisiana State University Press,
1978), chap. 1.
38 The censuses of 1860 and 1870 did not collect data on tenure. The marshals did,
however, record any "real estate" owned by the farm operator. The analysis of the text
assumes that a farm operator who reported real estate was a farm "owner," while
those reporting no real estate are regarded as "nonowners" and therefore tenant
farmers. Because this procedure says nothing at all about the tenure of farms whose
operators reported no real estate, it cannot distinguish from a variety of possible
tenure arrangements for these farms. It does, however, provide a reasonable approx-
imation to the extent of farm ownership. The measure probably *overstates* the extent
of tenancy among whites, because the largest single bias is likely to be owners who fail
to report ownership of land.

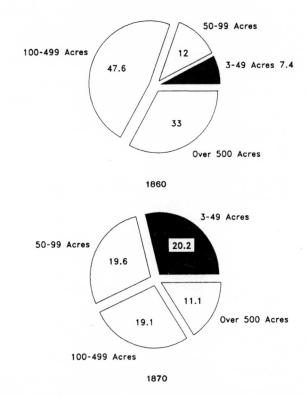

Figure 7.2. Percentage of land in farms in five cotton states
by size of farm, 1860 and 1870

ten farms were operated by people reporting real estate. In 1870, less
than half of the farm operators reported any real estate. The appearance
of black farm operators, who represented over one-fourth of all farm
operators in 1870, was an important element in this change. Roughly
three out of five tenant farms were managed by blacks. Considering that
blacks made up a group that had no claim to land whatsoever five years
earlier, the number of black farm operators in 1870 represents a very
significant achievement. Blacks had forced the white landowners to recognize their demand for some degree of autonomy in the management of
land.

Although many blacks had succeeded in becoming tenant managers,
the reluctance of whites to give blacks land is evident in the statistics on
farm size and value of output per acre. Virtually no blacks owned their

Table 7.2. *Number of improved acres and value of crop output in 1860 prices in eight counties in the South by ownership of real estate, 1860 and 1870*

Year	% of farm operators reported as		Average number of improved acres		Average value of crop output in 1860 prices	
	Owner	Nonowner	Owner	Nonowner	Owner	Nonowner
1860						
All farms	88.6	11.4	216.5	199.1	10.85	10.84
Nonslave	82.3	17.7	58.2	63.0	8.91	8.34
1870						
All farms	56.3	43.7	123.9	74.9	8.06	15.61
White	55.4	16.9	124.2	119.1	7.96	9.96
Black	0.8	26.8	102.1	47.1	14.21	19.18

Source: Computed from the sample of farms in eight counties in the South; see the appendix to Chapter 3 for details of the samples. Prices and definition of crop output are from Table A.3.1.

own land, and black tenant farms were noticeably smaller than those of whites who either owned or rented. Moreover, data on the value of output per acre in Table 7.1 indicate that black tenants produced twice the crop output per acre than the levels on white farms either before or after the war.[39] One interpretation of these high levels of real output per acre on black-operated farms in 1870 is that black farmers worked their land more intensively than did whites in a comparable position. The high levels of output per acre also strongly suggest that – contrary to the claims of whites immediately after the war – freedmen who were able to obtain land of their own were both willing and able to work their own land when they were able to operate a farm.[40]

How did these blacks become farm operators? The arrangements that

39 The prices of agricultural commodities rose substantially between 1860 and 1870. To reflect changes in the real level of production on farms, Table 7.1 presents the value of farm output in 1870 using the 1860 prices. See Table A.7.1 for details on the commodities and prices used in this calculation.

40 A full analysis of the productivity of these tenant farms would require more detailed information on labor inputs, particularly hired labor, than is available in the census data for either 1860 or 1870. A rough calculation of crop output per worker on farms reporting less than fifty improved acres suggests that output per worker on black-operated tenant farms was slightly higher than on comparably sized farms rented by whites.

emerged were the product of trial and error at a time when neither the laborers nor the landowners were sure of what was best. Blacks resisted a return to the work-gang system of the plantation; whites resisted giving freedmen their own land. An added complication in the seasons immediately after the war was the extreme shortage of cash. Out of this emerged an arrangement that seemed well suited to both parties at the time: sharecropping. In the typical sharecropping agreement, the landlord provided land and some working capital; the tenant provided labor. At the end of the season the tenant and landlord split all crops grown on the farm down the middle.[41] Sharecropping contracts appealed to both tenants and landlords because they were very simple arrangements that required a minimum of cash. Moreover, at a time when prices were uncertain and the idea of contracting for labor was still rather new, sharing the crop meant that both sides shared the risk of success or failure equally. For blacks, sharecropping offered an additional advantage; it gave the family some degree of independence. Although it did not provide the security of owning a farm, having a claim to half the harvest meant that the return to farming would be based on performance rather than the racist white perceptions of black productivity. For their part, landowners found that the better laborers were attracted by this incentive effect. Finally, sharecropping appealed to whites because the contract called for the landlord to retain considerable degree of control over the operation of the farm.[42]

At first glance, it seemed to some contemporaries that the agricultural reorganization following emancipation offered Southerners a chance to break away from the staple-crop dependency that had characterized the antebellum slave plantation system. With the influence of slave labor gone, farms in the South could adopt a pattern of crop production more akin to that of the "yeomen farms" that eschewed slavery in the antebellum period. Yet it gradually became apparent that, if anything, the replacement of the plantation with small farms had produced a shift

---

41 The use of payment of shares of a crop began with *share wages*, where workers were paid as little as one-sixteenth of the crop. This arrangement was not at all popular with black laborers, and the idea quickly disappeared as the idea of renting for shares gained favor. Although examples of many varieties of contracts can be found in surviving contract records, the fifty–fifty split of crop output was by far the most common sharecropping arrangement in the cotton belt. See Ransom and Sutch, *One Kind of Freedom*, chap. 5.

42 This is not entirely a matter of racial prejudice. By its nature, sharecropping requires considerable supervision on the part of the landowner. This is one reason why sharecropping invariably produces small farms that are worked very intensively. See the discussion in Ransom and Sutch, *One Kind of Freedom*, chap 5; and also idem, "Sharecropping: Market Response or Mechanism of Race Control?" in *What Was Freedom's Price?*, ed. David S. Sansing (University Press of Mississippi, 1978).

toward greater specialization in cotton and other staples rather than a move toward a more diversified crop mix. This was evident throughout the South, but it was most pronounced in the heart of the cotton belt. Table 7.3 presents data on crop output for four cotton-belt counties in 1860 and 1870. The increased emphasis on cotton is immediately apparent. A greater fraction of farms were "cash farms" (i.e., they grew some cotton), and on these farms the cash crop represented a far greater share of total output on postbellum farms than had been true in 1860. This change is particularly noticeable when we compare the antebellum farms that had no slave labor with white farms after the war. In 1860, 20 percent of the nonslave farms grew no cotton, and on those that did, the cotton crop represented less than half the value of crop output. After the war, virtually every farm grew cotton, which now represented over 70 percent of the average value of crop output. Compared with the output of free farms before the war, the output of cotton per improved acre doubled.

Was this move to greater emphasis on cotton simply a result of a doubling in price? Surely such an increase in the price of cotton encouraged farmers to plant more of the fiber. What is interesting about the data of Table 7.3, however, is that the degree of specialization in cotton differed markedly among the different tenure groups. For white owners,

Table 7.3. *Acreage and value of crop output in the cotton-growing regions of the South, all farms and free farms in 1860, all farms by race and tenure in 1870*

	% of farms growing cotton	Improved acres per farm	Value of crop output per acre	Farms growing cotton	
				Bales of cotton per acre	% of crop output in cotton
1860					
All farms	84.8	217.1	12.7	0.205	53.4
Free farms	81.7	62.3	9.6	0.120	43.8
1870					
All farms	97.0	96.1	28.1	0.237	71.2
White owners	96.6	130.3	15.4	0.104	59.1
White tenants	94.8	123.2	25.4	0.208	70.1
Black farmers	98.3	45.7	43.6	0.398	85.1

Source: Sample of southern farms in four cotton counties: Attala, Mississippi; Dallas, Alabama; Madison, Louisiana; and Coweta, Georgia. For a fuller description of the sample, see the appendix to Chapter 3. For prices and definition of crop output, see Table A.7.1.

the increased importance of cotton appears not to have involved fundamental changes in the nature of farming. Compared with the output of
antebellum nonslave farms, the number of bales of cotton produced per
acre actually fell, and as we saw in Table 7.2, the total value of crop
output per acre valued in 1860 prices remained virtually unchanged from
1860 to 1870. Tenants are another story. White tenants produced twice
as much cotton per acre as white owners in 1870, and black tenants
produced almost four times the cotton per acre of white owner-operated
farms. Cotton on these black-operated farms represented 85 percent of
the total value of output on the farm – almost twice the ratio exhibited
by nonslave farms before the war.

Cotton had emerged as a more dominating force in southern agriculture than ever, and this was not merely a response to the situation
produced by the wartime famine of cotton. As cotton prices declined
through the 1870s southern farms continued to produce more and more
cotton and less and less food crops. In 1850 and 1860 production of food
crops in the South exceeded thirty-five bushels per person. After the war,
food production fell to less than twenty bushels per capita.[43] Those who
hoped that emancipation would free southern agriculture from the grips
of cotton were concerned over this change. "The farmers who prosper at
the South," claimed Henry Grady, "are the 'corn raisers,' i.e., the men
who raise their own supplies, and make cotton their surplus crop."[44]
Southern farmers in the 1870s were obviously not making cotton their
"surplus crop"; it was the mainstay of their farm income. Still, farmers in
the Cotton South had always put most of their effort into the production
of cotton and corn. Why so much concern over a continuation of that
trend after the war?

Two aspects of the extreme specialization in cotton emerged as major
problems in southern agriculture. The first was what might be termed a
"macro" concern over the poor performance of the southern agriculture
in the decades following the war; the second was a "micro" concern over
poverty and the seeming inability of cotton farms to adjust to changing
market conditions.

Long Live the King: Cotton, Corn, and Credit

The antebellum slave economy had exploited a natural economic advantage in the production of cotton to sustain a rapid rate of economic

---

43 Production of food crops was converted to corn-equivalent bushels for these computa-
tions. See Ransom and Sutch, *One Kind of Freedom*, table 8.1. p. 152.
44 Henry W. Grady, "Cotton and Its Kingdom," *Harper's New Monthly Magazine* 63
(October 1881): 723–4. Grady was editor of the *Atlanta Constitution* and a leading
spokesman for those who advocated that the farmers of the South should grow their
own supplies. See the discussion in Ransom and Sutch, *One Kind of Freedom*, chap. 8.

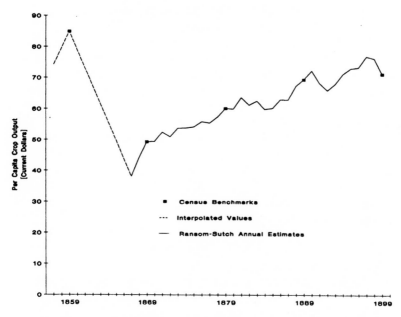

Figure 7.3. Growth of per capita crop output in five cotton states,
1857–99

expansion. Indeed, as we saw in Chapter 3, per capita income in the southern states on the eve of the Civil War was about equal to the level for the United States as a whole. After the war, the southern economy lagged so far behind the economic performance of the United States as a whole that southern income per capita by 1880 was barely one-half that of the nation as a whole, and this relative position did not change for the rest of the century.[45] Agricultural stagnation was at the heart of this problem. Figure 7.3 presents estimates of crop output per capita for five cotton states between 1857 and 1899. The enormous impact of the war and emancipation is immediately apparent; in 1867 per capita output was only half the 1857 level.[46] There was a postwar recovery but it was

45 Estimates of per capita income by region for 1880 and 1900 are in Stanley L. Engerman, "Some Economic Factors in Southern Backwardness in the Nineteenth Century," in *Essays in Regional Economics*, eds. John F. Kain and John R. Meyer (Harvard University Press, 1971), table 1, p. 282. In 1880 and 1900 per capita income in the South as a whole was 51 percent of the national average respectively.
46 Note that the crop of 1859 was about 13 percent above the 1857 level. This increase reflected an unusually good crop that year, together with high prices buoyed by the expectations of war and an interruption of supply. Consequently, the 1857 figure provides a better benchmark for measuring trends. See Ransom and Sutch, "Growth and Welfare."

soon aborted. By the time of the 1870 census, the recovery had ended and the South settled into a pattern of agricultural stagnation to the end of the century.[47]

This poor performance of an agricultural system that before the war had been so productive could hardly go unnoticed. For the first decade it was easy to blame the slow growth on the effects of the war. But by the mid-1870s it was becoming evident that more than wartime disruption was involved. Focus shifted to the decline of the world cotton market. The growth in the demand for cotton, which had been so spectacular in the two decades before 1860, was not sustained after the war. By the mid-1870s, the volume of cotton production in the South had regained its prewar level. If demand did not keep pace, continued expansion of cotton production was bound to put downward pressure on the world prices of the staple. The decline in world cotton prices provided a ready scapegoat for those seeking an explanation for the South's economic ills. In 1895 a special committee of the U.S. Senate issued a report, "The Present Condition of Cotton-Growers of the United States Compared with Previous Years," that placed a major share of the blame for the depressed condition of cotton farmers on a falling price in the world market.[48]

The decline in international cotton prices undoubtedly had something to do with the plight of southern farmers. But if cotton prices were being depressed, why did southern farmers keep specializing so heavily in cotton? The real economic failure of the postwar South was the unwillingness or inability of farmers to adjust to changing agricultural markets. This was a *micro* problem. Producing enough food for the farm family had been a primary concern of farmers without slaves before 1860. Why did farmers of the 1870s and 1880s disregard Henry Grady's advice to make cotton the surplus crop?

Our discussion to this point has focused on the relationships that evolved to deal with the physical factors of production – most notably land and labor – following the demise of slavery. A third element also enters into the production of agricultural commodities grown to be sold in the marketplace: credit. Farmers plant their crop in the spring, nurture

47   The annual growth in crop output per capita of the cotton South averaged 1.17 percent from 1869 to 1899, and 0.85 percent per year from 1879 to 1889. By way of comparison, growth in per capita gross national product in the United States over the period 1869 to 1899 averaged 2.74 percent per year. For a more complete discussion of these trends, see Ransom and Sutch, "Growth and Welfare."

48   United States Congress, Senate Committee on Agriculture and Forestry, "Present Conditions of Cotton-Growers of the United States Compared with Previous Years," in *Senate Report Number 986*, 53rd Congress, 3d session, 2 vols. (U.S. Government Printing Office, 1895).

it along through the growing season, and collect the harvest in late summer or early fall. Only after the harvest does the farmer reap the benefits of his labor, whether in the form of cash from crops sold in the market or the consumption of products grown on the farm. Consequently, the farmer must acquire some means of support to get through the growing season. In a simple world of complete self-sufficiency, the farmer can borrow from himself, so to speak. By putting aside a portion of production each season, the farmer can provide for consumption demands during the subsequent growing seasons. So long as all such needs can be met on the farm, obtaining "credit" from an outside party is not necessary. At the other extreme, if all the crops grown on the farm are sold for cash, the farmer must obtain enough credit to finance the entire consumption needs of the family for a whole year. In the South of the mid-nineteenth century, most farms fell somewhere between these extremes. Few were so specialized that they produced none of their supplies; most required at least some credit for needs that could not be produced on the farm. The terms on which credit is offered represent one of the most important constraints on the cash-crop farmer's options.

Unlike crops, agricultural credit does not simply "grow" on the farm; it must be provided by lenders who worry about the return on their capital. In the antebellum plantation economy, the demand for credit to finance the cotton came almost exclusively from the slaveholders who produced 95 percent of the crop. These men, as the data in Table 7.1 convincingly demonstrate, owned substantial assets in real and personal estate that could be offered as security to offset the risk of crop failure. The breakup of the plantation and the decline in land values after the war drastically changed the nature of the demand for agricultural credit. In 1870 tenant farmers, who had no real estate to offer as security for a loan, produced about half the cotton crop.[49] How could lenders secure their short-term loans to these producers?

The solution was to offer a *crop lien* whereby the farmer pledged the forthcoming crop as collateral to secure the loan. This arrangement seemed to offer a reasonable way of allowing farmers with no security other than the produce of their labor to secure credit for the growing season. In theory, the sale of the crop provided the means to liquidate the debt and leave the farmer with a balance as income earned for his effort. In practice, it was seldom that simple. Storekeepers offering credit and supplies to the operators of small farms soon realized that the crop lien represented a powerful means of controlling the options of the farmer. As

49 Among farms in the cotton-producing counties of our 1860 and 1870 sample, tenant farmers accounted for 48.2 percent of all cotton produced. Nonslave farms had contributed only 5.1 percent of the cotton crop in the 1860 sample.

early as 1871 Robert Somers noted the problem. "A new class of houses are springing up," he noted, "whose conditions of advance are almost necessarily marked by a degree of rigor that was unknown in former times."[50]

The "degree of rigor" to which Somers referred consisted not only of charging extremely high rates of interest; lenders also insisted that the crop pledged as collateral against the loan be cotton, not corn or other food crops. The high interest rates by themselves would have imposed a serious burden on tenant farmers.[51] But the insistence on growing cotton to the exclusion of other crops proved to be the most pernicious feature of the system of credit in the South. The merchants' insistence that the farmers grow cotton was defended on the grounds that they were simply asking for the collateral that could be easily liquidated should the need arise. But a second interest soon became apparent: If the merchant insisted that the bulk of the farm's resources be devoted to cotton production, the farm would be unable to produce enough food. This would increase the demand for supplies purchased from the store at "credit prices."[52] So effective was the merchant's power that by the beginning of the 1880s, seven out of ten family farms in the South were not producing enough food to meet the food needs of the farm family.[53] These farm families had to purchase food from the merchant. In the event that the value of the crop was insufficient to cover the cost of supplies advanced at the outset of the year, the family would be obligated to contract again with the same merchant to plant cotton for the coming season. What emerged was a cycle of debt that bound the farmer to the same merchant year after year. Critics of the system termed it "debt peonage."

The crop-lien system not only lined the pockets of merchants with monopoly profits; it also crippled the ability of the southern agricultural system to adjust to changes in prices. Left to their own devices, farm

50 Robert Somers, *The Southern States since the War: 1870–1* (Macmillan, 1871), p. 198.
51 Interest rates of between 60 and 100 percent per annum were commonly charged by storekeepers in the postbellum South. For a detailed analysis of the level of rates and the basis for such charges, see Ransom and Sutch, *One Kind of Freedom,* chap. 7 and appendix D.
52 The manner in which interest was charged by storekeepers was to maintain two sets of prices: those for goods paid for in cash, and those bought on "time" and paid for at the end of the season.
53 Over 60 percent of all farms in the cotton South had food deficits in 1879. A "food deficit" is defined as a situation where the production of food crops on the farm remaining after all animals have been fed is less than fifteen bushels of corn per capita. See Ransom and Sutch, *One Kind of Freedom,* pp. 156–62; and idem, "Debt Peonage in the Cotton South after the Civil War," *Journal of Economic History* 32 (September 1972).

operators caught in the crop-lien system would be better off producing less cotton and more corn. Yet merchants insisted that they not do so. The result was that many farmers who expanded their production of cotton to take advantage of the high prices of the late 1860s were unable to respond to the decline in the price of cotton relative to other crops in the 1870s and 1880s. They found themselves "locked in" to cotton as the crop demanded as collateral for their credit needs.

The use of crop liens met the need for some form of debt instrument that would allow farm operators who owned few if any assets to obtain credit for the coming season. This sort of arrangement had worked well enough in the antebellum period, when planters had used the proceeds from selling the crop to cover debt incurred over the past year. But the changes that accompanied emancipation drastically altered the nature of the lender–client relationship. Antebellum planters had ample collateral to cover any shortfall that might arise from year to year, whereas tenant farmers after the war could offer no such financial buffer. Nor was the operator of a small farm in the central cotton belt likely to establish the same sort of long-term personal relationship that had been an essential aspect of the prewar credit system of factors and planters. The provision of credit became a very local arrangement between a merchant or land-lord and a relatively small number of client farmers. This, indeed, was the basis of the lender's power; he had a territorial monopoly.[54]

The problems posed by the use of the crop-lien system and the rise of tenancy affected everyone in southern agriculture; however, blacks were particularly vulnerable to the exploitive aspects of the system. In part this vulnerability was because they were given nothing more than their freedom when they were set free in 1865. Left to fend for themselves, freedmen found it difficult to make much progress in a system that inherently favored those with economic power. Their problems were compounded by the attitudes of whites toward black abilities – attitudes that had been shaped over years of slavery and the more recent experience of emancipation. Perhaps the most significant measure of success in an agricultural society such as the South was the ability to operate a farm of one's own.

54 The role of both tenure and credit in the postwar South has drawn a great deal of attention from economic historians, not all of whom agree with the analysis sketched out here. For a fuller treatment of the concept of a territorial monopoly, see Ransom and Sutch, *One Kind of Freedom*. Other works on the postwar southern economy include Harold D. Woodman, *King Cotton and His Retainers: Financing and Marketing the Cotton Crop of the South, 1800–1925* (University of Kentucky Press, 1968); Gavin Wright, *The Political Economy of the Cotton South: Households, Markets, and Wealth in the Nineteenth Century* (W. W. Norton, 1978); idem, *Old South, New South;* and Robert Higgs, *Competition and Coercion: Blacks in the American Economy, 1865–1914* (Cambridge University Press, 1977).

To become a farm operator one had to have some capital, and for blacks that meant borrowed capital.

Who would lend to blacks? In addition to their hostility toward any sign of black independence, most whites had a very low opinion of blacks' abilities. Lending to blacks was seen by whites as involving high risks. Consequently, even those blacks who became farm operators seldom had the level of capital equipment, fertilizer, or animal power that white farmers enjoyed. In 1870 black farm operators worked fewer tilled acres than white tenants, and the disparity in amount of unimproved land available was even greater. Blacks, in short, faced discrimination in the credit market that further reduced their options.[55] We have already seen that the choice of tenure was similarly constrained by racial prejudices of whites. The composite effect of discrimination in the availability of both credit and land meant that for many blacks operating a farm was only a dream, and for those who got a farm, the dream all too often turned into a nightmare.

One of the great ironies of this situation was that both the crop lien and the new tenure arrangements were responses to emancipation that were initially favored by freedmen because they seemed to enhance their situation. Because they lacked any other physical assets, borrowing against the coming crop was the only hope most freedmen had of obtaining capital for farming. Sharecropping was far from perfect, but it did offer them an opportunity to live on their own farm – however small a parcel that might be. Yet within 15 years these arrangements had become exploitive devices that held blacks in a form of peonage that effectively blocked any hopes of economic advancement by the ex-slaves. Moreover, the exploitive arrangements caught large numbers of whites in a similar debt trap and produced an institutional rigidity that crippled southern agriculture for three quarters of a century.

An Unfinished Revolution: The Failure of Radical Reconstruction

The success of northern arms in the Civil War eliminated the scourge of slavery in the United States. Now the challenge to the northern radicals was to move beyond the act of emancipation and "reconstruct" southern society in the image of free labor in the North. As we have seen, the image that emerged was not what they had hoped to see. Why not? What

---

55   For evidence on the nature and extent of discrimination against blacks in the cotton regions, see Roger L. Ransom and Richard Sutch, "The Ex-Slave in the Postbellum South: A Study of the Economic Impact of Racism in a Market Environment," *Journal of Economic History* 33 (March 1973).

turned the triumph of civil war into the tragedy of Reconstruction? Our analysis of slavery and the war suggests that there were fundamental flaws in the Northerners' perception of the problems facing them in rebuilding the economy of the South. In addition to these flawed perceptions, radical Reconstruction faced an uphill struggle because the rank and file of Northerners did not share their leaders' commitment to the cause of black equality. An unwillingness to establish firmly black civil rights crippled attempts to erect a system of free labor in the South after the war.

No one seems to have anticipated just how great the economic shock created by a sudden emancipation of four million slaves would be. Whites misinterpreted the reaction of blacks to freedom as evidence that the transition to free labor could not work without strong elements of coercion or control of the freedman. This perception, which was shared by many northern observers, continually undercut efforts to establish a reasonable basis for contracts between landowners and the freedmen. In light of such prejudice, it is surprising not how poorly labor markets functioned in 1865 and 1866 but that they functioned at all. Equally important was a failure to appreciate the impact that uncompensated emancipation had on the credit markets of the South. Northern radicals might gloat with Thaddeus Stevens over the setbacks suffered by the "bloated and defiant rebels" who had lost their slaves. But the failure of the federal government to replace those losses with some other forms of financial assets seriously disrupted the equilibrium of capital markets in the South. Slaves represented financial assets that had been an integral part of the credit arrangements that supported antebellum agricultural production. Their disappearance, coupled with a plummeting value of land, wiped out the basis for agricultural credit, which now had to be secured by the only means available – a lien against the coming crop. This arrangement worked well enough in the initial years, but over the long term it proved exploitive and a barrier to flexibility in responding to changes in agricultural markets.

Expecting Northerners to reward the rebel slaveowners by restoring the value of their expropriated property would hardly be reasonable. There was, however, another possibility: Give the freedmen land and perhaps some capital. The failure to redistribute land is commonly cited as the one great opportunity for change that was "lost" by those shaping Reconstruction policy. Certainly such a subsidy was feasible. But would it have made a difference? Let us suppose Congress had instituted a substantial redistribution of land to freedmen. Although the eventual impact of such a policy is highly conjectural, there were areas of the South – most notably the Sea Islands off the coast of Georgia and South

Carolina – where blacks did get land after the war, and the experience there provides some clue as to the impact of a more general distribution of land.[56]

One claim seems fairly certain: Distribution of land to freedmen could only have improved their situation in 1865–6. The prospects for the longer term are less clear. At best, the opportunity for blacks to begin farming with some land of their own could have created a class of owner-operators that mirrored the ideal of farming in the Old Northwest. At worst, blacks would have lost their title to land and wound up with a situation not very different from what actually occurred. The most likely scenario is somewhere in between. Giving blacks title to farms in 1865 would surely have resulted in a significantly higher fraction of blacks owning the farms they operated in the years that followed. Even those who lost their title to a farm would, in many cases, have managed to remain as tenant farmers rather than become laborers. Because of the success with which whites prevented blacks from ever gaining ownership of land in most places of the South, it is natural to conclude that blacks would have been unable to retain their right to land distributed by the government. But this is not necessarily so. The tenacity with which blacks fought to keep their claim to farms in the Sea Islands and coastal Georgia suggests that many of the ex-slaves might have kept land had it been given to them. Describing the efforts of planters and authorities to displace blacks in South Carolina, Eric Foner notes that "It was one thing for the state to suppress labor organization, but quite another to intervene directly to dispossess black renters and owners."[57] A key point here is that, if there had been widespread distribution of land, the black owner would not have been an isolated exception who could be easily intimidated. When they were allowed actually to own or to settle on land in reasonable numbers, freedmen did rather well in keeping their claims to land.

Was this a Pyrrhic victory? Eric Foner points out that the black landowners who retained their land in the South Carolina rice districts were hardly more than peasants whose physical standard of living may well

---

56 The Sea Islands were occupied by Union troops early in the war and became an experiment that showcased the success of freedmen as farmers. An excellent description of these efforts is Willie Lee Rose, *Rehearsal for Reconstruction: The Port Royal Experiment* (Alfred A. Knopf, 1964). For an analysis of the situation of blacks in these areas, see Eric Foner, *Nothing But Freedom: Emancipation and Its Legacy* (Louisiana State University Press, 1983). One must be cautious in generalizing from such experiences, however. They occurred in areas that produced rice and long-staple cotton before the war and were hardly typical of the cotton belt where the bulk of the black population lived after the war.

57 Foner, *Nothing But Freedom*, p. 107.

have been below those who toiled as laborers in the cotton fields. One of the more obvious lessons from the experience of the American South after 1865 is that land distribution alone would not have been sufficient to allow black farmers to escape the trap of debt peonage that had engulfed the South by 1880.[58] Emancipation instantly created a huge class of propertyless people in a rural, agrarian society. The tenure and the credit institutions of the South were totally unprepared to deal with this situation, and the arrangements that evolved were seriously flawed. What is important to realize is that by the time these "flaws" had become apparent, the arrangements could not be easily adjusted. Once in place, tenure and credit arrangements tended to reinforce the monopoly position of the merchant and the landowner. Despite the repeated advice that farmers should stop borrowing to finance production of cotton, "King Cotton" remained firmly in place through the rest of the nineteenth century.

The reorganization of the southern economy presented formidable problems, and the misperception of those problems added to the difficulties of adjustment to emancipation. It would be naive, however, to insist that the failure of radical Reconstruction was solely the result of economic forces that doomed the South to agricultural stagnation. Behind the economic failures lay the real reason for the inability to construct a free society in the South: the racial prejudice of whites in both the North and the South. Among white Southerners this prejudice manifested itself in a racial antagonism and hostility toward any attempt to form a government predicated on equality for blacks. In the North, racial prejudice produced an antipathy toward the situation of the freedmen that first weakened and finally destroyed the resolve of Northerners to see the rights of blacks firmly established in the South.

Ultimately, northern radicals "lost" the peace for the same reason that slaveholders in the South had earlier lost the war. They were unable to sustain sufficient resolve to carry the fight in the face of a determined foe. Radical Republicans succeeded in passing an imposing set of constitutional amendments and legislation "guaranteeing" the civil rights of all Americans. Southern whites simply refused to recognize these actions and openly dared Congress to force compliance. When Congress responded with a policy that supported black equality through the presence

---

58 Ibid., pp. 109–10. "The peasantry survived," notes Foner, "but its growth was stunted. Its economic opportunities were limited, its standard of living increasingly impoverished. Command over credit, capital, and other scarce resources remained in white hands" (p. 109). The same point emerges from a study comparing the southern experience with land reform in Mexico by Roger L. Ransom and Kerry Ann Odell, "Land and Credit: Some Historical Parallels between Mexico and the American South," *Agricultural History* 60 (Winter 1986).

of federal troops, southern opponents were able to portray the radicals as a group of mean-spirited men imposing "black rule" on a white majority in the defeated South. Over time, this "myth" of a defeated South proved to be an extremely effective appeal. In the fall of 1867, one of the most visible radical leaders, Thaddeus Stevens, failed in a bid for a seat in the United States Senate. Stevens's defeat was an early indication that the support for black equality and radical Reconstruction was beginning to wane. On August 11, 1868, the great "commoner" died. Stevens's death, claimed the *New York Herald*, "sounds the death knell of the extravagant hopes of the radicals."[59] The *Herald* was somewhat premature in announcing that radical hopes would expire with Stevens's death. But the suggestion that radical hopes were "extravagant" struck home to a growing number of northern voters. As Southerners remained as intractable as ever on the race question, political slogans of both parties in the North began to emphasize *reunion* with the southern states rather than *reconstruction* of their social system.

The presidential election of 1876 was one of the most hotly contested elections in the history of that office. When the electoral votes were counted, Democrat Samuel Tilden had 184 votes, 1 less than a majority, while the Republican candidate, Rutherford B. Hayes, had 165 votes. Twenty votes from four states – Florida, Louisiana, Oregon, and South Carolina – were claimed by both candidates. The situation was further muddied by the fact that partisan control of Congress was split; Republicans controlled the Senate, whereas Democrats controlled the House. To resolve the issue, a bipartisan commission was created in January 1877. The commission consisted of five members each from the House and the Senate, plus four judges (two from each party) of the U.S. Supreme Court who would choose the fifteenth and final member of the commission from the Court. Not surprisingly, the Senate selected three Republicans and two Democrats; the House chose three Democrats and two Republicans. Because there were only two Democrats serving on the Supreme Court, the final balance of power on the commission favored the Republicans by a margin of eight to seven.

Tilden needed only 1 of the disputed electoral votes to win the election. Beginning with the Florida results, the commission ruled, eight to seven in every case, to give all 20 electoral votes to Hayes. That made the outcome 185 for Hayes and 184 for Tilden. Hayes was inaugurated on

---

59 *New York Herald*, August 13, 1868; cited in Hans L. Trefousse, *The Radical Republicans: Lincoln's Vanguard for Racial Justice* (Louisiana State University Press, 1968), p. 436.

March 4, 1877, but there was more to this than met the eye. Democrats initially expressed outrage at having the election "stolen" from their man on a strictly partisan vote that accepted very questionable election returns. There were widespread fears that dissidents would dispute the outcome and disrupt Hayes's inauguration. Yet, by the time Hayes took office, the furor had largely died down and he was sworn in without incident. Why had the Democrats backed away? Because Hayes and his supporters offered to strike a bargain. At this time the three southern states with contested electoral votes still had "carpetbag" Republican governments that were supported by the presence of federal troops. If the Democrats agreed not to challenge the ruling of the electoral commission, Hayes would agree to remove the last troops from the South as expeditiously as possible. The bargain was struck and two months after his inauguration the last remaining troops left the South.

Today, the political bargain that gave Hayes the presidency is regarded as one of the most infamous political deals in American history. In effect, the Republican candidate sold the future of his own party in the South – which included most of the black leaders in the region – down the river in return for the presidency. Within a year the reconstruction governments had been replaced by "redeemer" governments controlled by conservative southern Democrats. Yet, as William Gillette observes, "the drama and timing of the disputed election have led many historians to exaggerate the importance of its effect on reconstruction."[60] By the time Hayes and his colleagues struck the deal that removed troops from the South, any semblance of northern political presence had already disappeared from eight of the former Confederate states, and keeping troops in the other three had become an unpopular issue with Republicans in the North. "We must get rid of the Southern Question," wrote the editor of the Springfield *Republican,* echoing the sentiments of many of his fellow Republicans.[61] By returning control of the South to the conservatives, the deal that Hayes made "got rid" of the problem. The radical flame that had burned so brightly during and immediately after the war to abolish slavery in the United States had been all but extinguished. The one great outcome of that war was to give four million blacks their freedom from slavery. But as Americans celebrated the centennial of the Declaration of Independence, black equality remained a distant dream.

---

60 William Gillette, *Retreat from Reconstruction, 1869–1879* (Louisiana State University Press, 1979), p. 333.
61 St. Louis *Republican,* October 16, 1876; cited in Gillette, *Retreat from Reconstruction,* p. 301.

Appendix Table

Table A.7.1. *Prices of agricultural products, 1860 and 1870*

Crop	Units	1860 price	1870 price
Cash crops			
Cotton	Bale	40.00	96.69
Rice	Pound	0.02	0.04
Tobacco	Pound	0.078	0.10
Other crops			
Barley	Bushel	0.40	—
Corn	Bushel	0.33	1.18
Molasses	Gallon	0.40	1.05
Oats	Bushel	0.40	—
Peas	Bushel	0.73	1.37
Potatoes, Irish	Bushel	0.50	0.88
Potatoes, sweet	Bushel	0.50	1.33
Rye	Bushel	0.84	1.54
Wheat	Bushel	1.30	1.73

Source: Roger L. Ransom and Richard Sutch, "Capitalists without Capital: The Burden of Slavery and the Impact of Emancipation," *Agricultural History* (Fall, 1988), table 2.

8

After the War

The Republican Conservatives wanted to end the war as quickly as possible without deranging the essential *political* and *social* patterns of the nation. They were neither Abolitionists nor egalitarians: the unequal status of the Negroes and poor southern whites were of no interest to them. But, as spokesmen for industrial capitalism, the war furnished them with the opportunity to round out the *economic* program of the class which they represented. Industrial capitalism was now in control of the state.

Louis M. Hacker, 1940[1]

In the aftermath of the war, most people in the North genuinely wanted to put the conflict behind them. They hoped to bind up the wounds of war and return to the bustling prosperity that had characterized the last years of the antebellum decade. But the Civil War had unleashed forces of social change that went far beyond the expectations of all but a few Americans in 1860. The war was, in the words of Charles and Mary Beard, a "Second American Revolution."[2] Four million black Americans were now free, and they were eager to play a role in restructuring the defeated society of the postwar South. For a brief instant some leaders in the North were willing to make an effort to give them that role, but those efforts fell short. Radical Reconstruction was a bold experiment that failed. As W. E. B. DuBois so eloquently put it, "the slave went free; stood a brief moment in the sun; then moved back again toward slavery."[3]

Notwithstanding the shortcomings of Reconstruction, we have seen that the economic and social structure of the South was profoundly changed by the impact of emancipation and the Civil War. What about the rest of the country? Clearly the events of 1860–5 had an impact in the North as well. Unlike the South, where the presence of slavery meant

---

1 Louis M. Hacker, *The Triumph of American Capitalism* (Columbia University Press, 1940), p. 340 (emphasis in original).
2 Charles Beard and Mary Beard, *The Rise of American Civilization* (Macmillan, 1927). Perhaps the best statement of this argument, which is often referred to as the "Hacker–Beard thesis," is in Hacker's *The Triumph of American Capitalism*.
3 Cited in Eric Foner, *Reconstruction: America's Unfinished Revolution* (Harper and Row, 1988), p. 602.

that effects of its abolition were direct and very large, the effects in the North were more diffuse.

Before the war Northerners had complained about the obstructionist tactics used by the infamous "slave power" to stymie the economic and political interests of "free" labor and capital in the North. The abolition of slavery removed these obstacles and presumably paved the way for the political economy of the Republican party to become the determining force in shaping economic policy. That economic policy was shaped not by the radicals who were preoccupied by Reconstruction of the South, but rather by the conservative wing of the party. These men, as Louis Hacker observed, were less interested in civil rights for free blacks than in enacting an economic program based on a political economy that had its roots in the views of northern Whigs before the war.[4] This program included, among other things, a nationally regulated banking system, a higher tariff, federal support of transportation to the West, and free land. Beginning with the war effort itself, and extending on into the postwar period, the Republican party reshaped the economic environment in the postwar United States.

Was this a "revolution" as the Beards and Hacker claimed? Given the strong elements of continuity in history, revolutions are always difficult to identify. Yet one thing is clear: The war unleashed (or at the very least greatly accelerated) political and economic forces that fundamentally altered the economic structure of the United States after 1860. Sometime between the beginning of the nineteenth century and the beginning of the twentieth century, the United States was transformed from an economy that was dominated by agricultural production into an economy that was dominated by industrial production. Whether or not one accepts their interpretation of the motives behind the political economy of the conservative Republicans, the issues raised by Hacker and the Beards are fundamental to an understanding of the economic development that came after the war.

The problem of assessing the impact of the Civil War on the North is complicated by several factors. First is the obvious fact that the war had a very different effect on the economic system of the North than it did on the southern economy, and at the national level these two effects tend to cancel each other. Thus, for example, the stagnation of agriculture in the South offset the expansion of agriculture in the North. A second problem is that some of the effects of the war on the economy were quite subtle, working in ways that are not easily recognized. Finally, as Louis Hacker

---

4 For an excellent analysis of the evolution of postwar Republican economic philosophy and that of the Whig party before the war, see Louis Hartz, "Government–Business Relations," in *Economic Change in the Civil War Era*, eds. David T. Gilchrist and W. David Lewis (Eleutherian Mills–Hagley Foundation, 1965).

reminds us, the most profound economic changes may have stemmed from institutional changes brought about by the overwhelming political dominance of the Republican party in the two decades after 1860. We shall therefore divide our examination of the impact of the war in the North into three parts. First, we shall look at the most direct effects: the impact of the war on output and the labor force. Next we shall analyze some more subtle economic changes brought about by emancipation and wartime finance. Finally, we shall tackle the question of whether the triumph of the Republican party after 1860 fundamentally altered the pattern of economic development in the last third of the nineteenth century.

We begin with the most obvious question: Did the wartime activity directly accelerate economic growth?

Direct Effects of the War: Industry and Agriculture in the North

At first glance one might ask how the war could do anything but stimulate production in the North. The war was fought almost entirely in the South, so there was no destruction of northern property. The war effort, as we have seen, involved an intense mobilization effort that required the production of a large array of armaments. This effort was so successful that, by the time of Lee's surrender, the Union possessed one of the largest, best-equipped, military machines in the world. And by 1865 it was American industry that was filling the demands of that machine. At the very least, one might argue that the war provided a stimulus to industrial expansion.

Appealing though such an argument may seem, it is not supported by what we know about economic growth during the Civil War decade. The most comprehensive measure of economic activity is gross national product (GNP), which measures the total value of goods and services produced in the economy for a given year. Table 8.1 presents two estimates of GNP; one using "current prices," the other using the prices of goods and services in 1860.[5] Figure 8.1 plots the annual growth rate of GNP per capita for each decade from 1839 to 1899.

5   The estimate of GNP computed with constant prices is called *real* GNP. The GNP deflator presented in Table 8.1 is the implicit index of prices for the goods and services measured in GNP. These GNP estimates differ from those of Robert Gallman and Simon Kuznets in that they include estimated flows of income from the annual increase in the value of the slave stock in the antebellum years, and the flow of rent from consumer durables for all years. For a more complete discussion, see Roger L. Ransom and Richard Sutch, "Domestic Saving as an Active Constraint on Capital Formation in the American Economy, 1839–1928: A Provisional Theory," *Working Papers on the History of Saving*, no. 1 (Institute for Business and Economic Research, University of California, Berkeley, December 1984).

Table 8.1. *Real and per capita gross national product of the United States in current and 1860 prices by decade averages, 1839–99*

	GNP		Annual growth in GNP		
Year	Current prices	1860 prices	Current prices	1860 prices	GNP deflator
Total GNP					
1839	1,519	1,620			94
1849	2,278	2,392	4.14	3.98	95
1859	4,120	4,074	6.10	5.47	101
1869	7,636	4,798	6.36	1.65	159
1879	9,316	8,223	2.01	5.54	113
1889	14,104	14,472	4.23	5.82	97
1899	19,089	20,331	3.07	3.46	94
GNP per capita					
1839	91	97			
1849	101	106	1.01	0.86	
1859	134	133	2.92	2.30	
1869	195	123	3.83	−0.77	
1879	189	167	−0.32	3.12	
1889	228	234	1.89	3.44	
1899	255	272	1.12	1.50	

Sources: Estimates of aggregate gross national product (GNP) in current prices are from Roger Ransom and Richard Sutch, "Domestic Saving as an Active Constraint on Capital Formation in the American Economy, 1839–1928: A Provisional Theory," *Working Papers on the History of Saving* 1 (December 1984), table 7, p. 57. The estimates include the value of consumer durables and the increase in value of the slave stock before 1859. GNP deflator is from Roger Ransom and Richard Sutch, "A System of Life-Cycle National Accounts: Provisional Estimates, 1839–1938," *Working Papers on the History of Saving* 2 (December 1984), table A-3; the value for 1860 has been interpolated using the Warren Pearson price index. Population is from U.S. Bureau of the Census, *Historical Statistics of the United States from Colonial Times to 1970* (U.S. Government Printing Office, 1975), part 1, series A-2.

These data suggest three very interesting conclusions. First, it obviously makes a big difference whether the value of output is measured with current prices, or with a fixed set of prices. The increase in prices during the war, as well as the subsequent deflation afterward, had a dramatic effect on the level of nominal GNP. Second, although the growth rates in both aggregate and per capita GNP support the observation that output expanded very rapidly *after* the war, output was also expanding rapidly *before* the war, suggesting that the trend of economic

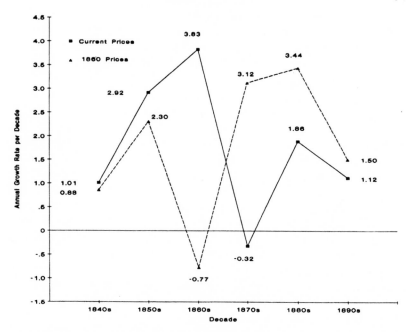

Figure 8.1. Annual growth of gross national product per capita by decade,
1839–99 (current and 1860 dollars)

growth was already firmly planted. Finally, the immediate impact of the
war was most certainly not an acceleration of GNP measured in real
terms. In aggregate terms, real GNP grew at a rate of only 1.7 percent per
year in the 1860s, by far the lowest of any decade for which we have
estimates (Table 8.1). This growth was so slight that *per capita* GNP
actually declined by almost 1 percent per annum during the 1860s (Figure 8.1).

The trends in real GNP evident in Figure 8.1 have led a number of
economic historians to argue that, far from accelerating economic
growth, the war actually interrupted growth.[6] Yet this sense of the wartime period was not held by many contemporaries. Measured in prices
prevailing at the time, the value of goods and services increased substan-

6 The initial presentation of this argument was by Thomas C. Cochran, "Did the Civil
War Retard Industrialization?" *Mississippi Valley Historical Review* 48 (September
1961). Cochran's argument is supported and expanded in Stanley L. Engerman, "The
Economic Impact of the Civil War," *Explorations in Entrepreneurial History* 2d ser. 3
(Spring 1966).

tially both in aggregate and per capita terms during the 1860s. The reason for this rapid increase in value is clear enough. Between 1859 and 1869 the prices of goods and services rose by 70 percent. This divergence of real and nominal levels of GNP in the 1860s and 1870s produced an illusion of expanding economic activity that was highly misleading. Thus, for example, the very high growth rate measured in current dollars for the 1860s gives an impression of economic growth and prosperity during the war. The value of output was expanding at a rate – 6.4 percent per year for aggregate GNP and 3.8 percent in per capita terms – that was substantially above even the prosperity of the 1850s. Looking back after the war, the wartime expansion seemed all the more impressive when compared with the slow growth of nominal GNP in the 1870s. In terms of current prices, Figure 8.1 portrays a wartime boom followed by a postwar depression; however, in terms of "real" growth, the war decade was stagnant and the 1870s showed a very respectable growth in output. Although they were certainly aware of the wartime inflation and the deflation of the 1870s, it was natural for contemporaries as well as many historians to conclude that the war had been a boon to economic growth.

Price inflation was not the only way in which wartime production created a false impression of industrial growth. We stressed in Chapter 7 that both the North and the South were called upon to divert a significant share of their production to the production of goods and services for the military. Inflation is common during modern wars precisely because the mobilization effort diverts production away from consumer goods at the same time that it places money in the hands of workers who then want to spend their income on goods and services that are no longer being produced. The increase in prices amounts to a flat "tax" levied on all commodities. This problem became so severe in the Confederacy toward the end of the war that the economy finally collapsed.

A final way in which wartime production distorts the pattern of economic growth is that increased production is partly the result of patriotic exhortation to defeat the enemy. The increased effort – most commonly in the form of greater labor-force participation – that occurs during the war is seldom sustained once the war is over. Although "demobilization" may create a temporary bulge in the labor force as the soldiers return to peacetime jobs, the labor force will eventually move back to its prewar level as the normal work routines are resumed.

Once the war ended, these illusions of growth disappeared and the true cost of the war became more apparent. Despite the increased level of military activity, the overall performance of the American economy in the 1860s was distinctly below par. "The Civil War decade," concludes

Robert Gallman in his 1960 study of commodity output in the United States, "was one of very small advance for agriculture, manufacturing, and aggregate commodity output."[7] These data on GNP are not alone in supporting this conclusion; the low rate of productivity during the Civil War decade is corroborated by a considerable body of evidence for individual sectors and industries.[8]

In addition to the evidence on the value of total output, we have data on employment and labor force participation in the United States during the nineteenth century, presented in Table 8.2 and Figure 8.2 according to sector of employment. The most obvious conclusion from these data is the sharp decline in the fraction of the labor force in agriculture from 1820 to the end of the century. In 1820 four out of five Americans worked in agriculture; by the end of the century this fraction had been cut in half.

Obviously, this long-term decline in agricultural employment was accompanied by a rise in other sectors, particularly manufacturing. Employment in manufacturing grew in this period from insignificant levels in 1820 to 20 percent of the labor force in 1900. Moreover, employment in manufacturing exhibited a marked increase – from 14 to 19 percent of total employment – over the Civil War decade, suggesting that the war accelerated manufacturing activity. One must view this jump over the course of the war decade with some caution, however. The increase in manufacturing during the 1860s stands out so clearly in part because that sector's share of employment fell in the 1850s. If the war did provide a spur to manufacturing employment, the impetus was not sustained in subsequent decades. The share of manufacturing employment increased only slightly after 1870. Nor do the periods of rapid exodus from agriculture coincide with wartime activity. Between 1850 and 1880, the share of employment in agriculture fell by only 3 percentage points. In fact, were it not for the withdrawal of black labor that accompanied emancipation, the share of employment in agriculture would have been almost constant.

The stability of agricultural employment during a period of very rapid growth in the labor force recalls a fact that is often overlooked in the discussion of the postwar economy. While southern cotton farmers found themselves cut off from their markets by the Union blockade during the war, and struggled with reorganization after the war, northern

---

7 Robert E. Gallman, "Commodity Output, 1839–1899," in National Bureau of Economic Research, *Trends in the American Economy in the Nineteenth Century,* Studies in Income and Wealth (Princeton University Press, 1960), 24: 42.
8 See, for example, the data on value added by industry in Engerman, "The Economic Impact of the Civil War."

Table 8.2. *Labor force by sector of employment, 1820–1900 (thousands)*

Year	Total	Free	Slave	% of labor force in Agriculture	Manufacturing	Trade	Labor force participation rate
1820	3,135	2,185	950	78.8	—	—	32.5
1830	4,200	3,020	1,180	70.6	—	—	32.6
1840	5,660	4,180	1,480	63.1	8.8	6.2	33.2
1850	8,250	6,280	1,970	54.8	14.5	6.4	35.6
1860	11,110	8,770	2,340	52.9	13.8	8.0	35.3
1870	12,930	12,930	—	52.5	19.1	10.1	32.5
1880	17,390	17,390	—	51.3	18.9	11.1	34.7
1890	23,320	23,320	—	42.7	18.8	12.7	37.0
1900	29,070	29,070	—	40.2	20.3	13.7	38.3

Source: Stanley Lebergot, "Labor Force and Employment, 1800–1960," *Conference on Research in Income and Wealth Output, Employment, and Productivity in the United States after 1800*, National Bureau of Economic Research, Studies in Income and Wealth, vol. 30, (Princeton University Press, 1966), table 1, p. 118.

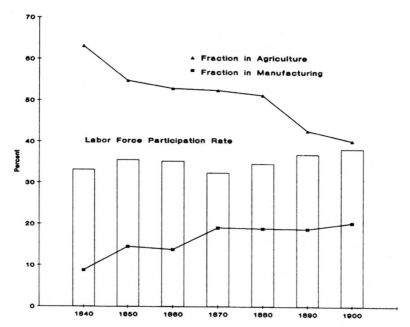

Figure 8.2. Labor force participation rate and the share of employment in agriculture and manufacturing, 1840–1900

farmers were experiencing an unprecedented boom.[9] One reason for this agricultural prosperity is immediately apparent: The inflation of prices that hurt consumers was a boon to farmers. Figure 8.3 presents data on the prices of farm products between 1850 and 1880, together with the exports of wheat for those years.[10] Prices more than doubled between 1861 and 1865, and wheat exports similarly show a large jump during the war. After 1865 farm prices fell dramatically (as did the prices of other commodities) but the value of wheat exports quickly recovered from its postwar slump and began a sharp upward movement. The high

9   The fall in production of southern farms accounts, in large measure, for the low rates of growth in aggregate farm output observed by Robert Gallman in his estimates of GNP at the national level.

10 Statistics on agricultural prices and production that span the period 1850 to 1880 are extremely limited. Comprehensive data for the United States begin, for the most part, with the 1866–7 crop year, when the U.S. Department of Agriculture began to publish systematic figures. To maintain continuity over the period, Figure 8.3 presents the Warren–Pearson index of farm products.

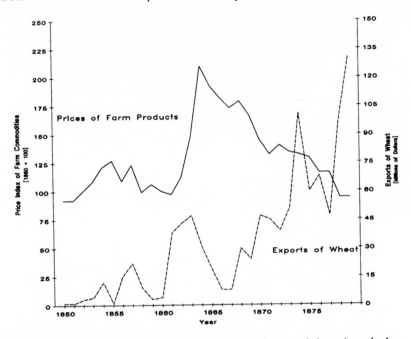

Figure 8.3. Index of wholesale prices of farm products and the value of wheat exports, 1850–79

wartime prices helped to trigger a boom in agricultural exports that continued until the 1890s.

This expansion of agricultural production was not limited to markets abroad; the domestic market for foodstuffs continued to expand as well. The Union Army had a voracious appetite for food and animal feed. And unlike the demand for armaments, which required a redirection of peace-time industrial efforts, the army's demands for food and feed crops called for the same farm products as those produced in "normal" times. There were, to be sure, problems because so much male labor had left to serve in the army. But the labor problems on northern farms were far less severe than on nonslave farms in the South. Food crops were less labor intensive than crops such as tobacco, sugar, or cotton, and farm machinery had already begun to lessen the labor requirements on many northern farms. That, together with the increased efforts of female labor on the farm, enabled northern farms to continue to operate at high levels of output.

The introduction of several improvements in marketing of agricultural products greatly facilitated the ease with which American farmers could sell their products not only in the United States, but throughout the world. The telegraph, introduced in the 1850s, allowed the use of more sophisticated marketing techniques, such as the development of futures markets, to expand greatly the geographical scope of agricultural markets. The completion of trunk-line railroads was soon accompanied by the introduction of bills of lading that expedited through shipment of grains, and the use of grain elevators to store commodities further simplified the market processes. By the end of the 1860s, when the telegraph reached across the Atlantic, these improvements had established American farmers as major suppliers not only in Britain but throughout Europe. While cotton exports from the South struggled to regain their power levels, the world market for grains, meats, and dairy products from the West continued to expand rapidly throughout the 1870s. That boom in agricultural output played a pivotal role in stimulating economic activity in other sectors.[11]

Expansion of farm output in the North, therefore, proceeded at much the same pace as it had prior to the war. This growth helps to explain why the share of employment in agriculture, which had fallen sharply in the years before the war, fell only slightly in the 1860s and 1870s. Figure 8.4, which presents the value of farmland and buildings, provides another view of farm prosperity outside the South at this time. The effect of the drastic fall in farm values in the South is immediately apparent. In the North, by contrast, the aggregate value of farmland and buildings grew at a steady rate throughout the entire period 1850 to 1880. Finally, we should note in connection with the economic position of farmers that wartime inflation meant that the real value of debt was declining during the war. Many farmers were able to pay off the mortgages on their farms and farm machinery at a time when the value of money was only half what it had been a few years before.[12]

The quantitative evidence on economic activity during the Civil War

11   For an excellent account of the expansion of international markets in the postwar era, see Morton Rothstein, "America in the International Rivalry for the British Wheat Market, 1860–1914," *The Mississippi Valley Historical Review* 47 (December 1960); and idem, "The International Market for Agricultural Commodities, 1850–1873," in *Economic Change in the Civil War Era*, eds. David T. Gilchrist and W. David Lewis (Eleutherian Mills–Hagley Foundation, 1965). On the role of agriculture in stimulating other sectors of the economy in the 1870s, see Jeffrey G. Williamson, "Greasing the Wheels of Sputtering Export Engines: Midwestern Grains and American Growth," *Explorations in Economic History* 17 (July 1980).

12   The other side of this equation of prices and the value of debt became apparent shortly after the war. As prices fell in the 1870s the real value of farm debt *rose*, and farmers found that the debt incurred at Civil War prices was becoming increasingly more burdensome each year.

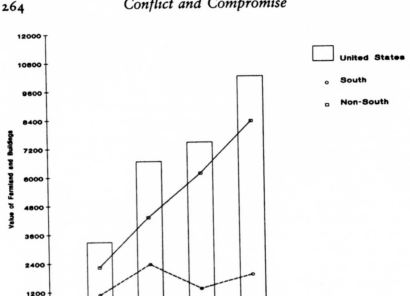

Figure 8.4. Value of farmland and buildings by region,
1850–80 (thousands of dollars)

decade presents a somewhat mixed picture. The balance of scholarly opinion is that, taken at the broadest level, the direct economic impact of the war was to *retard* economic growth in the industrial sector, but probably to *stimulate* growth of agriculture outside the South. If we include the South, the net gain in agriculture was far less, and perhaps disappears altogether. The answer to our first query does not lend support to the argument that the immediate effect of the war was to stimulate economic growth.

Indirect Effects of the War: Saving and Investment

There is one area where a break with past trends seems clearly evident in the quantitative data. The rate of gross capital formation – what is commonly called gross investment – experienced a considerable jump between 1859 and 1869. Over the decade prior to the war, gross investment, as a fraction of GNP, averaged just over 16 percent of GNP. In the decade after the war, this rate averaged over 19 percent of GNP and continued to increase slowly until the end of the century. This anomalous

jump in the rate of investment has been confirmed by several investigators, but it has never been adequately explained.[13] Could developments
associated with the Civil War have been responsible for this jump in the
rate of capital formation? At least two arguments have been put forward
suggesting that it did. The first possibility is that the impact of emancipation created a significant change in the rate of saving; the second is that
the retirement of wartime debt in the years after 1865 may have had a
significant impact on investment.

To understand how emancipation might affect the rate of saving, we
must consider the way people react to changes in the level of their wealth.
One explanation of saving, first developed by economist Franco Modigliani, is called the life cycle theory of saving. Modigliani's theory postu-
lates that the basic reason people save is to accumulate a stock of assets
that can provide income for their old age.[14] An important implication of
this model is that the relationship between the level of assets held by
investors in an economy and the flow of income they receive, what
economists call the wealth–income ratio, will remain relatively stable
over time. If this is so, an unexpected fall in wealth should cause people
to increase their rate of saving in order to reestablish the target wealth–
income ratio.[15]

The emancipation of slaves at the end of the Civil War produced just
such an unexpected shock. Slaves, as we emphasized in Chapter 3, were
regarded by their owners as economic assets producing a stream of income over time. In 1860, the total value of the slave stock represented
roughly half the total stock of wealth in the cotton states, and about 15
percent of the total value of assets in the United States.[16] Slaveholders

13 The percentages given in the text are those reported by Ransom and Sutch, "Domestic
Savings," Table 2, p. 10. Robert E. Gallman first pointed to the jump in gross capital
formation, and his estimates of the components of GNP showed a jump of at least 6
percentage points over the Civil War decade; see "Gross National Product in the
United States, 1834–1909," in National Bureau of Economic Research, *Output, Employment, and Productivity in the United States after 1800*, Studies in Income and
Wealth (Princeton University Press, 1966), 30: table 3, p. 11. Gallman and Lance E.
Davis noted that the shift in savings "draws attention to the possibility that the events
of the Civil War had an important bearing" on the fraction of income that went into
gross investment; see Davis and Gallman, "The Share of Savings and Investment in
Gross National Product during the 19th Century in the U.S.A.," in *Fourth International Conference of Economic History, Bloomington, 1968* (Mouton, 1973), pp.
440–1.
14 See Franco Modigliani, "The Life Cycle Hypothesis of Saving, the Demand for Wealth
and the Supply of Capital," *Social Research* 33 (Summer 1966); and idem, "Life
Cycle, Individual Thrift, and the Wealth of Nations," *American Economic Review* 76
(June 1986).
15 For a discussion of the life-cycle model in the context of the present argument, see
Ransom and Sutch, "Domestic Saving," and idem, "Capitalists without Capital: The
Burden of Slavery and the Impact of Emancipation," *Agricultural History* (Fall 1988).
16 Ransom and Sutch, "Capitalists without Capital," table 1.

should have reacted to the sharp decline in their wealth by increasing their rate of saving. Given the enormous magnitude of the capital loss from emancipation, such a reaction might account for much of the jump observed in the national savings rate.[17] A similar though much smaller effect on saving and investment could have resulted from the wartime destruction of property.[18] Unfortunately for the South, whatever increased savings was produced by a reaction to emancipation appears to have left the region and financed investment elsewhere in the United States.[19]

Uncompensated emancipation should have promoted an upward shift in saving by former slaveholders. The manner in which the war was financed could also have produced a significant effect on the rates of saving and investment after the war. Between 1861 and 1865, the Union government issued just over $2 billion of interest-bearing debt.[20] These government bonds were viewed as wealth–assets comparable with the stocks and bonds issued by private firms for the purpose of capital investment. The life-cycle model of saving implies that the increase in private wealth represented by these government bonds could only be absorbed by private investors if they held fewer private assets. In the jargon of twentieth-century economics, the issuance of Civil War bonds should have "crowded out" private investment during the war.[21] Put another

17 A tentative estimate of order of magnitude of such an effect is presented in Ransom and Sutch, "Capitalists without Capital."
18 It should be noted in this regard that increased rates of investment and saving have frequently been associated with the economic recovery of countries after a major war. See the analysis in Donald F. Gordon and Gary M. Walton, "A Theory of Regenerative Growth and the Experience of Post World War II West Germany," in *Explorations in Economic History: Essays in Honor of Douglass C. North*, eds. Roger L. Ransom, Richard Sutch, and Gary M. Walton (Academic Press, 1982).
19 We have little direct evidence that savings by former planters flowed out of the South after 1865. Evidence on interregional flows of capital in the United States during the nineteenth century supports the notion that capital flowed out of the South in the period after the Civil War. See Richard A. Easterlin, "Regional Growth of Income: Long Term Tendencies, 1880–1950," in *Population Redistribution and Economic Growth, United States, 1870–1950*, vol. 2; *Analysis of Economic Change*, eds. Simon Kuznets and Dorothy Swaine Thomas (American Philosophical Society, 1957), table 4.25, p. 180.
20 See the discussion of financing the Civil War in Chapter 6. In addition to the issuance of bonds by the federal government, there was also a significant expansion of government debt on the part of states during the war, for which no reliable estimates exist.
21 The "crowding-out" phenomenon is familiar to students of contemporary public finance, because of the massive deficits by governments that have produced increases in the national debt on a scale far exceeding that of the Civil War era. On the theoretical basis for crowding out, see Franco Modigliani, "Long-run Implications of Alternative Fiscal Policies and the Burden of the National Debt," *Economic Journal* 71 (December 1961); and Peter A. Diamond, "National Debt in a Neoclassical Growth Model," *American Economic Review* 55 (December 1965). For a historical analysis,

way, the purchase of war bonds represented private savings that were diverted away from productive capital formation in the economy. Consequently, even though the rate of saving may have remained the same, the rate of private investment surely declined. "The North," claims Jeffrey Williamson, "could hardly have achieved significant rates of capital formation [during the Civil War], burdened as she was with war financing."[22]

After the war, the federal government committed itself to the retirement of the large war debt. This policy was pursued with particular vigor between 1866 and 1878, when the outstanding interest-bearing debt of the federal government fell from $2.3 billion to $1.8 billion; by 1893, the total had fallen to only $587 million.[23] Just as the issuance of debt crowds out private investment and lowers the rate of capital formation, so will the retirement of debt tend to "crowd in" private investment and raise the rate of capital formation.[24] How large an effect did debt retirement have on capital formation after the Civil War? Jeffrey Williamson estimates that "perhaps as much as half of the rise [in the rate of capital formation] can be attributed to debt retirement and the redistributive impact of interest payments on the debt."[25] Richard Sutch and I suggest that the "crowding-in" effect was more modest, but still significant.[26] These estimates are, of course, highly conjectural. Nevertheless, their order of magnitude is sufficient to lend strong support to the argument that the financing of the Civil War and the policy of debt retirement after

see Jeffrey G. Williamson, "Watersheds and Turning Points: Conjectures on the Long-Term Impact of Civil War Financing," *Journal of Economic History* 34 (September 1974); and Ransom and Sutch, "Domestic Saving."

22 Williamson, "Watersheds and Turning Points," p. 648. We have only limited quantitative estimates of capital formation to document this fall. However, as Williamson points out, the Gallman estimates of GNP support the argument that capital formation during the 1860s was disappointing.

23 Williamson, "Watersheds and Turning Points." Williamson's estimates of the interest-bearing debt and the annual retirement of debt are reproduced in Table A.8.3.

24 This is because the retirement of government debt exchanges an income-earning asset in private portfolios with cash. Investors would then seek new assets to replace the bonds redeemed by the government. Although the rate of *saving* remains unchanged by this swap of assets, the rate of private *capital formation* will be increased.

25 Williamson, "Watersheds and Turning Points," p. 651. In addition to the crowding-in effect, Williamson and others have noted that, because the bonds were held predominately by the wealthy, the interest payments on the debt represented a redistribution of income in favor of the rich. This would also tend to increase the rate of investment if, as is commonly believed, the rich save a higher fraction of marginal income than the poor.

26 Williamson did not take into account the fact that, while the federal government was retiring debt, state and local governments were issuing more debt. Sutch and I suggest that about one-fourth of the decline of federal debt was offset by an increase in state and local debt. See Ransom and Sutch, "Domestic Savings," p. 45.

the war had a major impact on the rate of investment in the postwar years.

To summarize the argument to this point, we have concluded that the quantitative evidence leaves little doubt that the most direct effect of the Civil War on the economy of the North was to divert production away from production for home consumption, retard the rate of capital formation, and lessen the rate of industrial growth during the war years. At the same time, there was a strong stimulus to northern agriculture during the war that continued into the postwar years. After the war, there seems to have been a major shift in the rate of capital formation that can be at least partially explained as a reaction to the effects of emancipation and war financing. We must remember, however, that the quantitative evidence on economic growth does not tell the full story of economic change during the Civil War era. We must turn now to the third part of our story: the *structural* changes brought about by the Republicans after their political triumph in 1860.

The Legislative Legacy: Tariffs, Banks, and the West

When the Beards spoke of a "Second American Revolution" they were referring to the changes that were produced, in their view, by the sudden emergence of the Republican party as the dominant political party in the United States. Facing little or no opposition in Congress, the Republicans wasted no time in putting their economic program into place. "The second session of the 37th Congress (1861–62)," claims James McPherson, "was one of the most productive in American history."[27] He supports this statement with an enumeration of the legislation passed by the Congress: an increased tariff; a bill chartering a company to build the transcontinental railroad; establishment of land-grant universities and the creation of a Department of Agriculture; and the "Homestead Act" offering land to anyone who was willing to settle on it. These acts were followed by legislation in the next session that drastically restructured the banking system of the United States. All of these measures had been held up in Congress because of the sectional friction between slave and free states. The removal of the "slave power" offered the Republicans an opportunity to create an economic policy that would favor the northern industrial and commercial interests in the years after the war. As Louis Hacker claimed:

27 James M. McPherson, *Battle Cry of Freedom: The Civil War Era* (Oxford University Press, 1988), p. 450.

The industrialist capitalists, through their political spokesmen, the Republicans, had succeeded in capturing the state and using it as an instrument to strengthen their economic position. It was no accident, therefore, that while the war was waged on the field and through Negro emancipation, in Congress' halls the victory was made secure by the passage of tariff, banking, public land, railroad and contract-labor legislation.[28]

Let us take a closer look at several of these laws.

The Tariff

High tariffs had always been dear to the heart of Whigs, and in the late 1850s the Republicans took up the banner for a protective tariff. Launching a campaign in 1858 that went beyond the narrow interests of producers, they demanded "that American laborers shall be protected against the pauper labor of Europe."[29] During the congressional session of 1859–60, they succeeded in passing a bill with substantially higher import duties. But the tariff had always been anathema to the agricultural interests of the South, and thanks to the weight of southern representation in the Senate, Democrats were able to block the measure.[30] Rising costs of the war soon created pressures for added revenues, and with the Southern bloc removed from Congress, Republican leaders gained speedy approval for a sharp increase in tariff rates in early 1861. This process was repeated every year to the point where customs revenues had doubled by 1865. Figure 8.5 presents data on the revenue collected from customs duties between 1850 and 1893.

There can be little doubt that the sharp increase in tariff rates was a victory for those favoring protectionism in the Republican party. Yet it is easy to exaggerate the extent to which this represents a major shift in economic policy by the federal government. Revenues from customs had always been the principal source of tax revenues for the federal government, and with increased expenditures, Congress naturally turned to a familiar source of tax revenues to help pay for a costly war. Viewed in this light, the increased tariff revenues during the war that are so evident in Figure 8.5 are hardly extraordinary. In fact, they barely kept pace with inflation during the war. It was fiscal considerations, not protectionism, that dictated the decision to raise tariffs during the war.

28 Hacker, *Triumph of American Capitalism*, p. 373.
29 Quoted in McPherson, *Battle Cry of Freedom*, p. 192.
30 Recall the furor in the South over the tariff during the 1830s. Western agricultural interests also tended to oppose the tariff; however, their opposition was moderated by the growing presence of urban industrialization in the 1850s.

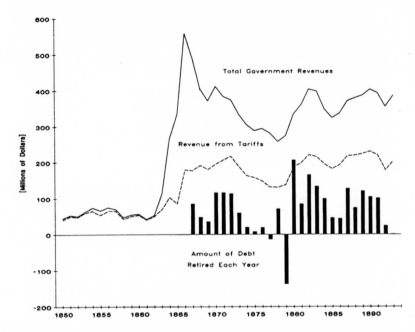

Figure 8.5. Total revenues of the federal government, revenues from tariffs, and federal debt retired, 1850–93

But what of the period after 1865? The high wartime schedules were not rescinded, and as Jeffrey Williamson has observed, "Civil War tariffs were enormously high by any standard."[31] Does this mean protectionist interests had gained the upper hand in the determination of economic policy? Again, the answer is not so clear. Before we attribute the higher duties to a victory of the protectionist lobby, we should note that fiscal pressures for tariff revenues remained strong; government outlays after 1865 remained at a level approximately three times that experienced before the war.[32] The administration's determination to retire the war debt as quickly as possible created an added need for revenues. This was hardly a time to abandon the most lucrative source of tax revenues available.

Whether or not high tariff rates could be defended on the grounds of

31 Williamson, "Watersheds and Turning Points," pp. 656–7.
32 By the 1870s, pension expenditures alone were approaching the level of government outlays in the late antebellum period. See Table A.8.3 for data on total federal government expenditures.

sound fiscal policy, the fact remains that such protection obviously helped the interests it protected. But did it also stimulate economic growth? Williamson suggests that it did. He argues that, because the burden of the tariff fell largely on consumer goods rather than on intermediate products used in the production of capital goods, the most important effect of protectionism was to lower the price of durable goods and thereby spur capital formation.[33] The Republican policy favoring high tariffs therefore spurred economic growth in two ways: It enabled the government to pursue its policy of debt retirement, and it stimulated investment by lowering the costs of capital goods relative to consumer goods.

The political economy of the tariff after 1870 involved more than a simple response to protectionist pressures. One of the few studies dealing with the "effectiveness" of the tariff in protecting American industries concluded that "there was much less increase in the protection given to U.S. industries between 1879 and 1904 than is commonly believed."[34] As the data of Figure 8.5 demonstrate, the big shift in tariff revenues came during and just after the war; revenues did not continue to grow thereafter. Tariffs remained an important source of revenue after the war, and fiscal considerations surely played an important role in the decision to maintain high duties. Yet the imposition of a high tariff did not represent the change in tax policy; what was new was the introduction of excise taxes on alcoholic beverages and tobacco. Throughout the postwar era these excise taxes provided almost as much revenue as the tariff. Both the tariff and the excise taxes were regressive taxes – that is, they were taxes that placed a larger burden on the poor than on the rich. What was being "protected" by this fiscal policy was the income of wealthier Americans, who had successfully lobbied for an end to the income-tax experiment tried during the war.

Banks

Apart from slavery, no issue generated more heated debate in national elections than the question of banks and a "sound" monetary system. The bitter fight over the rechartering of the Bank of the United States in

33 Williamson's analysis involves a rather complicated general equilibrium model of the economy. He summarizes his findings on the tariff issue by saying that Hacker and the Beards "were on the right track" when they claimed the higher postwar tariff had an impact on economic development after the war (Williamson, "Watersheds and Turning Points," p. 658).

34 Guy Hawke, "The United States Tariff and Industrial Protection in the Late Nineteenth Century," *Economic History Review* 28 (February 1975): 98; see his analysis on pp. 94–98.

the 1820s and 1830s left deep divisions that remained long after the bank itself had disappeared. Although they persisted in efforts to reform the banking system thereafter, advocates of a more tightly regulated banking system never succeeded in implementing major changes. With the demise of the Whig political organization in the 1850s, those favoring revisions in the banking system managed to get banking reform placed on the Republican agenda in the late 1850s.

Southern Democrats had viewed the imposition of any federal regulations on banking as an effort to resurrect the "money monopoly" enjoyed by the Bank of the United States. The departure of southern congressmen offered proponents of banking reform an opportunity to act, and early in 1863 they saw their chance. The Lincoln administration was having difficulty selling its latest issue of war bonds to the public. With the support of Secretary of the Treasury Salmon Chase, Senator John Sherman of Ohio introduced a bill that would, in his words, "establish a uniform national currency, based on the public credit."[35] A key provision of Sherman's bill was that the newly chartered national banks must purchase government securities as backing for their issuance of bank notes. Thus, passage of the act would create an instant market for government securities. Sherman made pointed reference to the need for such action. "It must be remembered," he pointed out to his colleagues, "that this bill is taken up when our financial condition is not the most favorable. . . . We are in the midst of a war, when the necessities of the Government require us to have large sums of money."[36] Despite Sherman's appeals to the needs of the war effort, his bill passed the Senate by the narrow margin of 23 to 21, and the House by only 78 to 63. In each case there was substantial opposition from Republican members of Congress, as well as the Democrats. Despite this resistance to the idea, a national banking system was now a reality.[37]

The National Banking Acts of 1863 and 1864 had several key provisions that represented a sharp change from past banking practices. Most significant was the creation of a federally chartered banking system with provisions that were considerably more restrictive than regulations exist-

35 "Senator Sherman on the National Banking Act of February 10, 1863," reproduced in *Major Documents in American Economic History,* ed. Louis M. Hacker (Van Nostrand, 1961), 1: 94.

36 Ibid., p. 95.

37 Amendments to the 1863 law were passed in June 1864 to facilitate the process of converting from a state-chartered to a federally chartered bank. The most detailed account of the formation of the national banking system is Andrew M. Davis, *The Origins of the National Banking System* (U.S. Government Printing Office, 1910). For an excellent summary of the legislation, see Robert P. Sharkey, *Money, Class, and Party: An Economic Study of Civil War and Reconstruction* (Johns Hopkins University Press, 1959), chap. 6.

ing in most states. National banks were required to have an initial capital investment of between $50,000 to $100,000 depending on the size of the town in which the bank was located, and they were required to hold government bonds as backing for banknotes in circulation. National banks were also prohibited from making loans on real estate. Because of these stringent requirements, there was hardly a stampede to sign up with the new system. Sixteen months after passage of the initial act, only 450 banks had taken out national charters.[38] In March 1865, Congress responded to this lack of enthusiasm by placing a 10 percent tax on notes issued by state or private banks. That did the trick; by 1870 there were over 1,600 national banks, while the number of state-chartered banks had fallen to just over 250.[39] As the 1870s began, the new banking system was firmly in place.

The pressures of wartime finance were obviously an important element behind the creation of the National Banking System. Indeed, one observer has noted that "it seems highly doubtful if the act could have passed Congress without the war emergency as an excuse, for that body was neither anxious to legislate on banking nor conscious of the full significance of their action when they did legislate."[40] The short-term objective from the creation of a new banking system was the creation of an instant market for government securities and Treasury Secretary Chase wasted no time in selling war bonds to the newly chartered national banks. The long-term effects of the restructuring of the banking system are less obvious, and have been the subject of considerably more discussion.[41]

A principal aim of those pressing for a national banking system was creation of a more stable "national" currency and the imposition of some restrictions on the operation of banks. In this they were successful for a time, thanks to the restrictive terms of the national bank charter and the effects of the tax on state bank notes. However, "money" can prove to be a very elusive thing. By the time of the Civil War the use of banknotes as

---

38 John A. James, *Money and Capital Markets in Postbellum America* (Princeton University Press, 1978), p. 27.
39 This number compares with a situation in December 1865, when there had been 1,146 state banks and 702 national banks. See Roger L. Ransom and Richard Sutch, "Debt Peonage in the Cotton South after the Civil War," *Journal of Economic History* 32 (September 1972): appendix table 1, p. 666.
40 Margaret G. Myers, *The New York Money Market*, vol. 1, *Origins and Development* (Columbia University Press, 1931), p. 218.
41 Economic historians have examined the impact of the national banking system with some care. Among the studies that provide particularly useful summaries of the early years are Richard E. Sylla's essay, "The United States, 1863–1913," in *Banking and Economic Development*, ed. Rondo Cameron (Oxford University Press, 1972); and James, *Money and Capital Markets*, chaps. 1 and 2.

a form of money was already declining as banks and businesses increasingly turned to the use of deposit checking. It soon became apparent to those interested in operating a state-chartered bank that they could avoid the tax on banknotes by concentrating on deposit banking. Beginning in the early 1880s, there was a veritable explosion of banks chartered by the state and open for business. By the end of the century there were more state banks than national banks, and deposits represented almost 90 percent of the total stock of money in circulation.[42]

One of the most significant features of the national banking system was that it strongly discriminated against rural areas. The minimum investment required for a charter made it difficult for more than one bank to operate in smaller cities, which produced two effects. First, it brought back the old antagonisms associated with the monopoly position of the Bank of the United States by seeming to favor the position of large-city banks. Critics protested that the new banking laws had been "conceived in infamy and . . . for no other purpose but to rob the many for the benefit of the few."[43] Second, the restrictive nature of national bank charters gave banks in rural areas considerable monopoly power. This monopoly power, combined with the prohibition against mortgage lending, meant that agriculture felt poorly served by the new banking arrangements, particularly in the South.[44] As a result of this perceived discrimination, farmers in virtually every region of the country persistently lobbied for changes in the law.

One very positive contribution of the national banking system was to establish a national market for "loanable" funds. Although its initial aim was simply to generate a demand for wartime government securities, the system of reserves mandated by the act also produced a very active market for funds that were transferred between banks. All national banks were required to set aside "reserves" against the bank's deposits, and a portion of these reserves could be left on deposit with another national bank.[45] These accounts, called bankers' balances, could earn

42 On the expansion of deposits and the effect on state banks, see James, *Money and Capital Markets*, chap. 2.
43 Quoted in Sylla, "The United States," p. 247.
44 For the impact of the national bank system in the South, where very few national banks had been established even as late as 1880, see Ransom and Sutch, "Debt Peonage in the Cotton South." A more general analysis of the monopoly position of rural national banks can be found in Richard E. Sylla, "Federal Policy, Banking Market Structure, and Capital Mobilization in the United States, 1863–1913," *Journal of Economic History* 29 (December 1969).
45 The National Banking Act of 1864 designated New York and eighteen other cities as "reserve cities." Banks outside a reserve city were required to maintain 15 percent of their assets as reserves, three-fifths (i.e., 9 percent) of which could be in the form of cash on deposit with a reserve-city correspondent bank. Reserve-city banks were required to hold 25 percent reserves, up to half of which could be deposited in a bank in New York City. See James, *Money and Capital Markets*.

interest, which meant that country banks could earn income on funds that otherwise would have remained idle. The result was a large outflow of funds from rural to reserve city banks, a development that produced a large concentration of funds on deposit with urban banks. These banks were then able to use the bankers' balances as a base for expanding industrial and commercial loans. By encouraging this transfer of funds from rural to urban areas, the national bank system facilitated the development of a national capital market in the United States.[46]

Finally, we should note that on one important issue of the time – the provision of liquidity to meet the needs of financial crises – the new banking system proved woefully inadequate. The regulations on reserve deposits produced a "pyramiding" of reserves that left the system vulnerable to any sudden demand for cash on the part of depositors. In the event that depositors demanded cash, rural bankers immediately withdrew their bankers' balances from their correspondent banks in reserve cities. These banks in turn withdrew their reserves from correspondent banks in New York City. Isolated cases of banks needing liquidity could be handled in this way. If, however, there was a general loss of confidence in the banking system, there was no "lender of last resort" to provide cash reserves for the New York City banks. Unable to meet the demand for funds, the New York banks would then "suspend payments," and other banks would have to follow suit. The result would be a liquidity crisis throughout the entire banking system. These intermittent "panics" produced interruptions of business activity that ranged from relatively minor dislocations within a region to systemwide collapses such as those in 1873 and 1893.

The helter-skelter world of antebellum banking had produced pressures for some sort of reform even before the war, and the need for an organized market for government securities provided added encouragement for the organization of a nationwide network of federally chartered banks. The result was the National Banking Acts of 1863 and 1864. Even with the benefit of hindsight, it is not an easy matter to judge who benefited or lost from the change in banking regulations after the Civil War. The rise of deposit banking rendered one of the major concerns of those who founded the national banking system – a unified national currency – a moot point. The most significant impact of the new banking system, the creation of a national market for bankers' balances and the

---

46 For an explanation of this rather complicated network of interbank transfers of reserves and securities, see Sylla, "The United States," pp. 249–55. A more complete analysis of the system of correspondent banks is in James, *Money and Capital Markets*, chap. 4. On the emergence of a capital market and the role of banks in facilitating the integration of regional capital markets, see Lance E. Davis, "The Investment Market, 1870–1914: The Evolution of a National Market," *Journal of Economic History* 25 (September 1965); and James, *Money and Capital Markets*, chap. 6.

development of an integrated capital market, came about more as a side effect from the system of reserves held in urban centers than as a consequence of any carefully worked out plan. And the failure to deal with the problem of liquidity meant that periodic crises continued to plague the economic system despite the attempt to create a "sound" currency. Richard Sylla summarizes the complexities well when he notes that the national banking system "promoted industrial development and growth with a ruthless efficiency."[47] One thing is certain: The reorganization of the banking system during the Civil War did nothing to diminish the arguments over "hard" and "easy" money that had characterized monetary debates before the war. The only difference was that the "hard money" Republicans had supplanted the Jacksonian "easy money" Democrats as the group in control of monetary arrangements in the United States.[48]

Railroads and the West

By the middle of the nineteenth century Americans had reached the edge of the "Great American Desert," a vast expanse of arid prairies and high mountains stretching from just west of the Mississippi River to the valleys of the Pacific Coast. Everyone agreed that the obvious means of getting across this desert was to construct a "transcontinental" railroad, and everyone conceded that the federal government would have to assist in the project. Disagreement arose over the route that the railroad project would follow to the West Coast. The stakes were high, and everyone wanted the railroad to go through their backyard, a situation that was the cause of much sectional bickering in the mid-1850s. It was, we should recall, Stephen Douglas's desire to organize a company to construct a transcontinental railroad through the Kansas–Nebraska Territory that prompted his disastrous proposal to organize that territory in 1853–4. The issue of the railroad was lost amid the ensuing dispute over slavery in Kansas, and the question of a transcontinental railroad was quietly shelved.

47 Sylla, "The United States," p. 258. In making this judgment, Sylla largely discounts any disruptive effects of panics on the economy.
48 The term "hard money" has been widely used to describe a policy favoring stringent monetary control. Because there was no central bank in the United States before 1913, such a policy had to rely on indirect controls on money and credit. In the context of our discussion, the terms "hard money" or "sound banking" refer to advocates of stricter banking regulations and policies by the Treasury that would curtail the monetary base of the United States. For a general discussion of the debates on "hard" versus "easy" money after the war, see Walter T. K. Nugent, *The Money Question during Reconstruction* (W. W. Norton, 1967).

Once the slave interests were no longer in Congress, the proponents of a transcontinental railroad were able to agree on a route and a means of financing construction. In July 1862, Congress passed the Pacific Railway Act, which empowered the Union Pacific Railroad and Telegraph Company to "lay out, locate, construct, furnish, maintain, and enjoy a continuous railroad and telegraph," from a point not far from Omaha, Nebraska, to the western boundary of the Nevada Territory.[49] At the same time that the newly formed company was building west, the act empowered the Central Pacific Railroad Company of California to build east from the California border. To encourage construction of the railroad, Congress offered subsidies for each mile constructed, and the companies were granted alternate sections of land along the route of the road.[50]

There were delays in getting construction under way at both ends, and the building of the railway did not really get into high gear until after the war. Financial crises and scandals posed problems almost as formidable as the rugged terrain of the West. Still, excitement mounted as construction crews from both directions raced to complete one of the most impressive engineering feats of the time. On May 10, 1869, officials from the Union Pacific and Central Pacific railroads gathered at Promontory Point, Utah, to drive the symbolic gold spike that completed the nation's first transcontinental railroad.

Building transcontinental railroads was not the only encouragement offered to those interested in western settlement. Barely a month before Congress approved authorization of a railroad that would "open" the West, an act was passed stating that "any person who is head of a family, or who has arrived at the age of twenty-one years, and is a citizen of the United States . . . [shall] be entitled to enter one quarter section or a less quantity of unappropriated public lands, upon which said person may have filed a preemption claim."[51] In plain English, the Homestead Act

49 "The Pacific Railway Act of July 1, 1862," in Hacker, *Major Documents in American Economic History,* 1: 89.
50 An interesting feature of the formula worked out by the Pacific Railway Act is that it involved no cash outlay by the federal government. The subsidies were in the form of bonds issued by the company and backed by the United States Treasury, and the grants of land were a subsidy "in kind." If the project proved to be a financial success, the railroad would sell this land at some future date and reap the capital gains. By retaining alternate sections along the route, the government ensured that it, too, would reap gains from increased land values. In fact, the minimum price on these lands was set at twice that on other land in the public domain. For an excellent discussion of the economics of the land grant policy, see Stanley L. Engerman, "Some Economic Issues Relating to Railroad Subsidies and the Evaluation of Land Grants," *Journal of Economic History* 32 (June 1972).
51 "The Homestead Act of May 20, 1862," in Hacker, *Major Documents in American Economic History,* 1: 85.

said that anyone who settled on a parcel of up to 160 acres of public domain could claim title to that land.

The offer was not, to be sure, quite as generous as at first seemed. The most desirable farmland in the unsettled regions of the West was the area adjacent to the railroads, and that was reserved for sale at twice the normal minimum price for government land. Nevertheless, "free land" was now a reality in the United States, and thousands headed west to take up the government's offer. Few of them met with instant success. Obtaining a land grant proved to be only the first step in establishing a farm. Costs of breaking and clearing the land, building a house and barn, and obtaining the necessary tools for farming in the relatively arid areas of the great plains placed a heavy burden on the frontier sodbusters. One group in particular who might have benefited from the availability of land – the freed blacks in the South – found themselves largely unable to take advantage of the opportunity to "homestead." In addition to the problem of obtaining credit for the start-up costs of farming, most blacks lacked the background and experience for farming in the great plains. Consequently, only a few freedmen tried homesteading; most remained in the cotton agriculture with which they had grown up.

Both the Homestead Act and the Pacific Railway Act were hailed as landmark pieces of legislation in their day. Yet neither was really much of a departure from antebellum policy on transportation and the settlement of the public domain. The principle of government promotion of inter-regional transportation projects dated back to the beginning of the century, when the state of New York constructed the Erie Canal. Nor was the use of land grants to encourage construction new; in 1850 the government had chartered the Illinois Central Railroad, and provided land as an inducement for construction of that project.[52] The Homestead Act was the culmination of a series of laws that made the public domain more and more accessible. The most important of these, the Preemption Act of 1843, had established the right of "squatters" to purchase land they occupied at the minimum price. The Homestead Act simply lowered that price to the ten dollar filing fee.[53]

It is difficult to attribute very much importance to the Civil War as a

---

52 On the evolution of a system of "national" subsidy for transportation, see Carter Goodrich, *Government Promotion of American Canals and Railroads* (Columbia University Press, 1960).

53 The standard historical work on the evolution of land policy is still Benjamin Horace Hibbard, *A History of The Public Land Policies* (Macmillan, 1924; reprint, University of Wisconsin Press, 1965); also see the selection of articles in part 3 of Vernon L. Carstensen, ed., *The Public Lands: Studies in the History of the Public Domain* (University of Wisconsin Press, 1963), particularly the article on "The Homestead Act in an Incongruous Land System," by Paul Gates.

factor in getting either the Homestead Act or the Pacific Railway Act enacted into law. Southern Democrats had, it is true, quibbled over approval of a route for the first railroad, and slave interests expressed little enthusiasm for a homestead law that would encourage small family farms in the unsettled regions of the West. Thus, the elimination of southern interests in Congress probably facilitated speedy passage of these acts. Still, given the trend of legislation in the 1850s, it is likely that even with the slave interests present, homesteading and the transcontinental railroad would have come into their own in the 1860s. If anything, the effect of the wartime disruption was to delay the impact of the legislation when it finally got through Congress.

We have examined four of the most important pieces of legislation to assess their significance as part of the legislative package introduced by the Republicans during and after the Civil War. What we found was that each of the acts had a perceptible impact on the course of subsequent economic development. But we also found that each had strong roots in past proposals and legislation. Only the National Banking Act could be described as a truly novel experiment, and it should be kept in mind that the banking reforms were the only measures that faced serious opposition from *within* the Republican party. This is hardly the stuff of which revolutions are made.

Postwar Political Economy: The Triumph of Industrial Capitalism

One of the basic theorems of mathematics is that "the sum of the parts cannot be greater than the whole." Our analysis thus far suggests that, if we sum together the "parts" of the Republican legislative program enacted during the war, the "whole" does not add up to anything approaching a "revolution." But economic and social phenomena do not necessarily conform to the laws of mathematics; in a market society interactions between economic phenomena can produce a total impact that is greater than the sum of the individual effects of particular actions. To see this, one must look at the larger picture of the political economy of Republican leaders after 1860. That picture, according to the Hacker–Beard view, was shaped by the vision and interests of a relatively new political group: the industrial capitalist.

We have already encountered evidence that the economic interests of industrial capitalism played a role in the enactment of protectionist tariffs and more restrictive banking regulations, though industrial interests by themselves could not account for those legislative changes. However, the influence of those advocating policies favoring industrial interests extended beyond the banking reforms. One of the most obvious evidences of this influence can be seen in the determination of "hard money" advocates to return the United States to the "gold standard" after the war. "Resumption," as the policy was called, was one of the dominating forces behind Republican fiscal policy in the period 1865 to 1879.

The problem confronting the United States in international financial markets after the war was a complicated one. Prior to 1861, the United States government stood ready to exchange any note of the U.S. Treasury for gold bullion of comparable value. In so doing, the government tied the value of the U.S. currency to the price of gold in the international marketplace. Early in the war, the Union government decided to abandon this policy of having notes "redeemable" in gold. This allowed the treasury to pay for the costs of the war by issuing notes, called "greenbacks," that were declared to be legal tender but could not be redeemed for gold.[54] As prices in the United States continued to rise throughout the war, the value of the greenbacks in terms of gold declined. This produced what was termed a "gold premium" – a sum equal to the difference between the value of something when paid for with specie (or a gold-backed note), and the value when paid for in greenbacks or national bank notes.

Within the United States, all of this made little difference; people were obliged to accept the greenbacks because they were legal tender. But in the international marketplace, the gold premium created considerable confusion, because there were, in effect, two sets of prices that could be quoted. The problem was particularly acute in the case of securities that were traded internationally, where the issuer had to specify whether the premium would be paid "in gold." Quite apart from the inconvenience involved, the return to gold involved, in the eyes of some, a moral commitment on the part of the United States. In a speech given in October 1865, Hugh McCulloch, the secretary of the Treasury, announced that he belonged "to that class of persons who . . . look upon an irredeemable currency as an evil which circumstances may for a time render a necessity, but which is never to be sustained as a policy. By common consent of the nations, gold and silver are the only true measure of

54 The government was forced to make this decision because, as inflationary pressures mounted, the value of the dollar fell, and people sought to convert their currency into gold. To avoid losing all its bullion reserves, the treasury suspended payments of gold until further notice. The issue was further confused when Congress also authorized issuance of interest-bearing notes that were designated as "legal tender." For a discussion of the economic implications of this, see James K. Kindahl, "Economic Factors in Specie Resumption: The United States, 1865–79," *Journal of Political Economy* 49 (February 1961).

value."[55] However, before the United States government could offer to redeem its currency at the 1860 price of gold, there would either have to be a significant fall in the price level in the United States, or a significant increase in the price of gold abroad.[56]

The international price of gold did not change, and consequently the policy of resumption necessitated a severe deflation in the United States. By 1879 the price level in the United States had declined to a point where the gold premium on greenbacks had reached a point where the Treasury could announce that it would once again redeem notes for gold at the international price of gold.[57] The details of how resumption was accomplished, together with the rather considerable clamor raised by those opposed to the policy, are beyond the scope of the present study.[58] What is significant about this episode of economic policy is that it reveals that the sharp divisions over "hard" and "easy" money that had characterized antebellum political economy were not yet settled. Now it was the "hard money" men, represented by men such as McCulloch, who were in the driver's seat. Together with the policy of debt retirement and regressive taxation, the decision to return to the gold standard reflected a marked shift in the underlying philosophy of economic policy in the United States.

There was more to this change in philosophy than tariffs, resumption, and national banks. The Republicans, according to historian Louis Hartz, had "advanced the spirit of Adam Smith on the American Scene." "But," he goes on, "they did more than this. They turned the old Jacksonian symbolism against itself, producing in favor of corporate power one of the grand confusions in all of American thought. . . . The state itself becomes the soulless monster, the corporation the splendid human per-

---

55 McCulloch, quoted in Sharkey, *Money, Class, and Party*, pp. 59–60.
56 In theory, there was a third option. The United States could have accepted the inflationary price increase at home and agreed to return to the gold standard at a higher price of gold. Such an action – what today we term a *devaluation* of the dollar – was not acceptable to the hard-money men in the U.S. Treasury.
57 See the data on prices in Table 8.1. Technically, the United States did not officially return to the gold standard until 1900. Between 1879 and 1900 the Treasury stood willing to redeem currency in *either* gold or silver. However, because the price established by the Treasury for silver was below the market price, what was in theory a bimetallic standard operated as a de facto gold standard.
58 Initial fears that the deflation could only be accomplished through a highly contractionary fiscal policy proved unfounded. In fact, the government pursued monetary contraction only in the first three years after the war. As James Kindahl explains, "The deflation which permitted resumption was brought about largely by the growth of the economy in the years following the Civil War"; see Kindahl, "Economic Factors in Specie Resumption," p. 48, an article in which Kindahl provides an excellent analysis of this period. For an account of the politics behind resumption, see Sharkey, *Money, Class, and Party*.

sonality."[59] Joint stock companies, the forerunners of business corporations today, had been around for as long as the Republic itself. For most
of that time, the privilege of obtaining a corporate charter had been
limited to the granting of charters to a relatively few enterprises, most of
which were banks or transportation companies. But the advantages of
the corporate structure, both from the standpoint of finance as well as
the efficiency of operation, were becoming increasingly obvious to entrepreneurs by the middle of the nineteenth century.[60] As charters became easier to obtain from states anxious to attract business enterprises,
corporations became more prominent in the economic landscape.

Even before the war, it had been fairly well established that the corporation was a legal entity. But how far did legal rights of a corporation
extend with regard to its relationship with the state? According to Republican political economy, corporations were entitled to the same rights
as any other citizen, and the more avid champions of corporate "rights"
pursued this point with extraordinary zeal. Consider, for example, the
interpretation they placed on the Fourteenth Amendment to the Constitution. That amendment, which was passed at the height of outrages
against free blacks in the South, included a clause guaranteeing every
"individual" due process before the law. According to one member of the
congressional committee that framed the text, the word "individual" was
carefully chosen so that corporations, as well as individual people, could
benefit from the protection of "due process" offered by the amendment.[61] The actual intent of the authors will never be known, and in one
sense makes little difference, because the legislators could hardly guarantee that the courts would interpret the amendment the way they intended
when they wrote it. Yet the fact remains that the "due process clause" of
the Fourteenth Amendment eventually did far more to protect corporate

59 Louis Hartz, "Government–Business Relations," in Gilchrist and Lewis, *Economic
    Change in the Civil War Era*, p. 88.
60 On the growing importance of the corporation in the middle of the century, see Alfred
    D. Chandler, Jr., *The Visible Hand: The Managerial Revolution in American Business*
    (The Belknap Press, 1977).
61 The claim was made by Roscoe Conkling of New York twenty years after the fact.
    Conkling argued that because "individuals and joint stock companies were appealing
    for congressional and administrative protection against individuals and discriminating
    state and local taxes," it was important that corporations receive protection; quoted in
    Bernard Schwartz, *From Confederation to Nation: The American Constitution, 1835–
    1877* (Johns Hopkins Press, 1973), p. 201. Also see Hartz, "Government–Business
    Relations," pp. 89–90. Both Schwartz and Hartz discount Conkling's claim that the
    committee was so cynical in its intent. Louis Hacker gives greater credence to such a
    view, arguing that the men who wrote the Fourteenth Amendment were more preoc-
    cupied with the protection of business interests than with the rights of blacks in the
    South. See Hacker, *Triumph of American Capitalism*, pp. 387–92.

rights than it did to protect the rights of southern blacks. Surely that tells us something about the extent to which the political climate in the years after the war had come to accept the corporate structure as an integral part of the economic system.

The Civil War did not spawn this corporate view of political economy but it did provide an opportunity for change to be introduced into the economic and social system. It did this in two ways. Politically, the war not only destroyed slavery; it catapulted the Republican party to a political dominance by a single party that had not been seen since the days of Thomas Jefferson. For almost two decades, Republican leaders in Congress could obtain virtually any piece of legislation they sought, and the economic policies of Republican leaders went through Congress relatively unchallenged. The dominance of a single party allowed the industrial interests within that party to have a major impact in shaping the changes we have been discussing.

The second effect of the war was to create a crisis atmosphere that provided a rallying point for those seeking legislative reform. We have already seen the role of the war in rallying support for what was otherwise an unpopular action – the emancipation of black slaves in the South. To a lesser degree, the same is true of the economic changes enacted by the wartime Congress. All of the path-breaking legislation was passed during the war. Although Republican leaders did not hesitate to appeal to patriotism and support of the war effort, their success in bringing about reform reflected a more subtle effect of wartime crisis as well. The Civil War was, in Allan Nevins's phrase, an "organized war." Mobilizing for war, as we saw in chapter 6, required a willingness to try out new methods of organization in both the military and the private sector. The Republican program of political economy was able to take advantage of the confusion and excitement of the war to introduce changes in many areas that had little or nothing to do with the war effort.

Once the war was ended, that excitement quickly ebbed. However, the economic changes proved surprisingly durable. Indeed the conservative economic agenda was able to push aside the more radical social agenda of reconstruction and reform in the South. As we have seen, the heyday of radical Republicanism was extremely brief. Barely a decade after Lee's surrender at Appomattox, questions of tariff, greenbacks and "resumption," and the latest proposals for transcontinental railroads were more pressing issues in the minds of most voters in the North than was the issue of whether troops should remain in the conquered South. Rutherford B. Hayes's offer to "compromise" with southern conservatives in order to keep Republican control of the White House secure for another term seemed reasonable enough.

Did the centennial celebration of independence mark the "triumph" of industrial capitalist interests in the United States? Clearly, to some extent, it did. But the triumph was fashioned by a much broader spectrum of American life than the phrase "industrial capitalist" suggests. Robert Sharkey points out that the decision to retire the debt and the commitment to resumption of gold were not seriously challenged at the time they were introduced.[62] The same could be said about the concern over corporate rights. The Republicans had succeeded in making the corporation, once a symbol of economic power, a symbol of business success. In doing so, they gained the support of that large number of Americans who, in the words of Louis Hartz, "cherished the dream of business success, of bourgeois redemption, as it were."[63] These people – capitalist farmers as well as capitalist entrepreneurs of commerce and industry – were the groups that shaped the postwar economic environment of postwar America. The war had, to some degree, given them the opportunity to enhance their political stature and they seized that opportunity.

The great tragedy of the decade following the Civil War was that, in seizing one opportunity, the Republicans let another, far more significant opportunity, slip away. Reconstruction, as we have seen, remained an aborted revolution in the South.

Epilogue: The Second Reconstruction

The Civil War removed the contradiction of slavery in a free society that had plagued the first four generations of Americans. In so doing, it preserved the Union. In its wake, however, the war left that union still deeply divided between North and South. Indeed, the division may have been as deep as and more enduring than ever. Three-quarters of a century after the fighting ended, W. J. Cash observed that "there exists among us . . . a profound conviction that the South is another land, sharply differentiated from the rest of the American nation."[64] The "mind" of the South, according to Cash,

---

62 "Imbued with a conviction derived from readings in American history that farmers are usually debtors and *ipso facto* inflationists," notes Sharkey, "I confidently expected to uncover a wealth of information confirming the preconceived notion that the farmer would be naturally violently opposed to McCulloch's policy of currency contraction." Yet, he concluded, "it seems safe to say that . . . farmers were the least concerned of all economic groups" about McCulloch's policy. Sharkey, *Money, Class and Party*, pp. 135 and 140.

63 Hartz, "Government–Business Relations," p. 84.

64 W. J. Cash, *The Mind of the South* (Vintage Books, 1941), p. vii.

is continuous with the past. And its primary form is determined not nearly so much by industry as by the purely agricultural conditions of that past. So far from being modernized, in many ways it has actually always marched away, as to this day it continues to do, from the present toward the past.[65]

The failure of the South to keep pace with the rest of the United States in the years that followed the Civil War is well documented. At the root of that failure, I have argued, was something much deeper than an unyielding commitment to agriculture or a refusal to industrialize. What crippled southern development was the legacy of 250 years of racial slavery – a legacy that was to poison both the economic and social climates of the region for another century.

The agreement reached in 1876 to remove federal troops from the South was the last in a long string of compromises on the question of race and slavery. Southerners had lacked the will to carry on military resistance once slavery had been effectively destroyed, but they refused to bend on the issue of equal rights for blacks in the "New South." This time, it was the northern will that gave way, and returned political power to those who had lost the war. The race question was once again an issue "peculiar" to the South.

It would remain so until the blacks took things into their own hands. By abandoning their masters during the war, slaves had helped force the hand of Union officials reluctant to give them freedom. As the twentieth century dawned blacks decided once again to abandon their masters, this time leaving a system that had offered them only a poor substitute for slavery, for the promise of a better life in northern cities. In a migration that continued for the next four decades, blacks left the South by the thousands and traveled North. Reluctantly, white Americans were forced to concede that the race problem was no longer simply a "southern problem."

We have seen that equality for black Americans has always been difficult for white Americans to accept. The efforts at Reconstruction between 1865 and 1876 made little progress beyond removing the shackles of slavery. It would be another century before Americans – white and black – would once again take up the task of completing what the Civil War had begun. The civil rights movement of the early 1960s began a "Second Reconstruction." It has been a long time in coming, but perhaps the United States will finally realize the promise that Lincoln had prayed for in his address at Gettysburg – *that this nation, under God, shall have a new birth of freedom.*

65 Ibid., p. x.

Appendix Tables

Table A.8.1. *Index of wholesale prices and the value of wheat exports, 1850–80*

Year	Warren–Pearson index [1860 = 100] All goods	Farm products	Value of wheat exports (mill. $)	Quantity of wheat exports (mill. bu)
1850	90	92	1	1
1851	89	92	1	1
1852	95	100	3	3
1853	104	108	4	4
1854	116	121	12	8
1855	118	127	1	1
1856	113	109	15	8
1857	119	123	22	15
1858	100	99	9	9
1859	102	106	3	3
1860	100	100	4	4
1861	96	97	38	31
1862	112	112	43	37
1863	143	147	47	36
1864	208	210	31	24
1865	199	192	19	10
1866	187	182	8	6
1867	174	173	8	6
1868	170	179	30	16
1869	162	166	24	18
1870	145	145	47	37
1871	140	132	45	34
1872	146	140	39	26
1873	143	134	51	39
1874	135	132	101	71
1875	127	129	60	53
1876	118	116	68	55
1877	114	116	47	40
1878	98	94	97	72
1879	97	94	131	122
1880	108	104	191	153

Note: The Warren–Pearson price index has been adjusted to a base year of 1860 = 100; wheat is measured in sixty-pound bushels.
Source: United States Bureau of the Census, *Historical Statistics of the United States, Colonial Times to 1970* (U.S. Government Printing Office, 1975), p. 201, series E-52–3; p. 899, series U-279–80.

Table A.8.2. *Total value of land and buildings in agriculture by region, 1850–80 (millions of dollars)*

Year	United States	Northeast	North Central	South	Non-South
1850	3,272	1,056	1,455	752	2,216
1860	6,645	2,323	2,122	2,130	4,322
1870	7,444	1,289	2,527	3,452	6,155
1880	10,197	1,873	2,803	5,129	8,324

Source: United States Bureau of the Census, *Historical Statistics of the United States, Colonial Times to 1970* (U.S. Government Printing Office, 1975), p. 462, series K-17–81.

Table A.8.3. *Total outlays and revenues, customs revenues, and interest-bearing debt of the federal government, 1850–93 (millions of dollars)*

Year	Total outlays	Total revenue	Customs revenues	Total interest-bearing debt	Debt retired or issued
1850	39.5	43.6	39.7	—	
1851	47.7	52.6	49.1	—	—
1852	44.2	49.8	47.3	—	—
1853	48.2	61.6	58.9	—	—
1854	58.0	73.8	64.2	—	—
1855	59.7	65.4	53.0	—	—
1856	69.6	74.1	64.0	—	—
1857	67.8	69.0	63.9	—	—
1858	74.2	46.7	41.8	44.9	—
1859	69.1	53.5	49.6	58.5	(13.6)
1860	63.1	56.1	53.2	64.8	(6.3)
1861	66.5	41.5	39.6	90.6	(25.8)
1862	474.8	52.0	49.1	365.6	(275.0)
1863	714.7	112.7	69.1	708.0	(342.4)
1864	865.3	264.6	102.3	1,360.4	(652.4)
1865	1,297.6	333.7	84.3	2,219.8	(859.4)
1866	520.8	558.0	179.0	2,326.6	(106.8)
1867	357.5	490.6	176.4	2,240.7	85.9
1868	377.3	405.4	191.1	2,192.5	48.2
1869	322.9	370.9	180.0	2,156.6	35.9
1870	309.7	411.3	194.5	2,039.5	117.1
1871	292.2	383.3	206.3	1,922.7	116.8
1872	277.5	374.1	216.4	1,808.7	114.0
1873	290.3	333.7	188.1	1,748.4	60.3

(*continued*)

Table A.8.3. (*cont.*)

Year	Total outlays	Total revenue	Customs revenues	Total interest-bearing debt	Debt retired or issued
1874	302.6	305.0	163.1	1,728.1	20.3
1875	274.6	288.0	157.2	1,720.1	8.0
1876	265.1	294.1	148.1	1,700.5	19.6
1877	241.3	281.4	131.0	1,714.6	(14.1)
1878	237.0	257.8	130.2	1,786.3	71.7
1879	266.9	273.8	137.3	1,924.7	(138.4)
1880	267.7	333.5	186.5	1,717.6	207.1
1881	260.7	360.8	198.2	1,632.3	85.3
1882	258.0	403.5	220.4	1,466.1	166.2
1883	265.4	389.3	214.7	1,332.1	134.0
1884	244.1	348.5	195.1	1,232.2	99.9
1885	260.2	323.7	181.5	1,186.3	45.9
1886	242.5	336.4	192.9	1,141.8	44.5
1887	267.9	371.4	217.3	1,013.8	128.0
1888	267.9	379.3	219.1	939.0	74.8
1889	299.3	387.1	223.8	817.8	121.2
1890	318.0	403.1	229.7	713.1	104.7
1891	365.8	392.6	219.5	612.1	101.0
1892	345.0	354.9	177.5	587.8	24.3
1893	383.5	385.8	203.4	587.1	0.7

Sources: For revenues and outlays: United States Bureau of the Census, *Historical Statistics of the United States, Colonial Times to 1970* (U.S. Government Printing Office, 1975), p. 1104, series Y-335–6; for interest-bearing debt: Jeffrey Williamson, "Watersheds and Turning Points: Conjectures on the Long-Term Impact of Civil War Financing," *Journal of Economic History* 34 (December 1974), table 2, p. 642.

Bibliography

Abbott, Martin. "Free Land, Free Labor, and the Freedman's Bureau." *Agricultural History* 30 (October 1956): 150–6.

Aitken, Hugh G. J., ed. *Did Slavery Pay? Readings in the Economics of Black Slavery in the United States.* Houghton Mifflin, 1971.

Andreano, Ralph, ed. *The Economic Impact of the American Civil War.* Schenkman, 1967.

Andrews, Sidney. *The South since the War as Shown by Fourteen Weeks of Travel in Georgia and the Carolinas.* 1866. Reprint. Houghton-Mifflin, 1970.

Atack, Jeremy, and Fred Bateman. *To Their Own Soil: Agriculture in the Antebellum North.* Iowa State University Press, 1987.

"Yankee Farming in Settlement in the Old Northwest: A Comparative Analysis." In *Essays on The Economy of the Old Northwest,* edited by David C. Klingaman and Richard K. Vedder, pp. 77–102. Ohio University Press, 1987.

Atherton, Lewis E. *The Southern Country Store, 1800–1860.* Louisiana State University Press, 1949.

Bailyn, Bernard. *The Ideological Origins of the American Revolution.* Harvard University Press, 1967.

Bateman, Fred, and Thomas Weiss. *A Deplorable Scarcity: The Failure of Industrialization in the Slave Economy.* University of North Carolina Press, 1981.

Batty, Peter, and Peter Parrish. *The Divided Union: The Story of the Great American War, 1861–1865.* Salem House Publishers, 1987.

Bauer, K. Jack. *Zachary Taylor: Soldier, Planter, Statesman of the Old Southwest.* Southern Biography Series. Louisiana State University Press, 1985.

Beard, Charles. *An "Economic" Interpretation of the Constitution of the United States.* Macmillan, 1913.

Beard, Charles, and Mary Beard. *The Rise of American Civilization.* Macmillan, 1927.

Bensen, Lee, ed. *Turner and Beard: American Historical Writing Reconsidered.* Free Press, 1969.

Bergeron, Paul H. *The Presidency of James K. Polk.* University Press of Kansas, 1987.

Beringer, Richard E., Herman Hattaway, Archer Jones, and William N. Still, Jr. *Why the South Lost the War.* University of Georgia Press, 1986.

Berwanger, Eugene. *The Frontier against Slavery: Western Anti-Negro Prejudice and the Slavery Extension Controversy.* University of Illinois Press, 1967.

Billington, Ray Allen. *The Origins of Nativism in the United States, 1800–1844.* Arno Press, 1974.

Birney, William. *James G. Birney and His Times: The Genesis of the Republican Party with Some Account of Abolition Movements in the South before 1828.* D. Appleton and Company, 1890.

Boyd, Julian P., ed. *The Papers of Thomas Jefferson.* 20 volumes. Princeton University Press, 1952.

Brown, Richard D. "The Missouri Crisis, Slavery, and the Politics of Jacksonianism." *South Atlantic Quarterly* 65 (Winter 1966): 55–72.

Modernization: The Transformation of American Life, 1600–1865. Hill and Wang, 1976.

Brown, Robert. *Charles Beard and the Constitution.* Princeton University Press, 1956.

Bullock, Henry A. *A History of Negro Education in the South from 1619 to the Present.* Harvard University Press, 1967.

Burns, John T. *Annual Report of the Comptroller General of the State of Georgia . . . October 16, 1866.* J. W. Burke and Company, 1866.

Busey, Samuel C. *Immigration, Its Evils and Consequences.* Dewitt and Davenport, Publishers, 1856. Reprint. Arno Press and the New York Times, 1969.

Cairnes, J. E. *The Slave Power: It's Character, Career, and Probable Designs: Being an Attempt to Explain the Real Issues Involved in the American Contest.* 1862. Reprint. Harper and Row, 1969.

Carstensen, Vernon, L., ed. *The Public Lands: Studies in the History of the Public Domain.* University of Wisconsin Press, 1963.

Cash, W. J. *The Mind of the South.* Vintage Books, 1941.

Chandler, Alfred D., Jr. *The Visible Hand: The Managerial Revolution in American Business.* The Belknap Press, 1977.

Cochran, Thomas C. "Did the Civil War Retard Industrialization?" *Mississippi Valley Historical Review* 48 (September 1961): 197–210.

Coddington, Edward B. *The Gettysburg Campaign: A Study in Command.* Scribners, 1984.

Cole, Arthur H. "Cyclical and Sectional Variations in the Sale of Public Lands, 1816–60." *Review of Economic Statistics* 9 (January 1927): 41–53.

Connelly, Thomas L., and Archer Jones. *The Politics of Command: Factions and Ideas in Confederate Strategy.* Louisiana State University Press, 1973.

Conrad, Alfred H., and John R. Meyer. "The Economics of Slavery in the Ante Bellum South." *Journal of Political Economy* 66 (April 1958): 93–130.

Conrad, Alfred H., et al. "Slavery as an Obstacle to Economic Growth in the United States: A Panel Discussion." *Journal of Economic History* 27 (December 1967): 518–60.

Cook, Adrian. *The Armies of the Streets: The New York City Draft Riots of 1863.* University of Kentucky Press, 1974.

Cooling, Benjamin Franklin. *Forts Henry and Donelson: The Key to the Confederate Heartland.* University of Tennessee Press, 1987.

Cooper, William J., Jr. *The South and the Politics of Slavery: 1828–1856.* Louisiana State University Press, 1978.

Liberty and Slavery: Southern Politics to 1860. Alfred A. Knopf, 1983.

Cornish, Dudley Taylor. *The Sable Arm: Black Troops in the Union Army, 1861–1865.* 1956. Reprint. University Press of Kansas, 1987, with a foreword by Herman Hattaway.

Cox, Lawanda. "Promise of Land for the Freedmen." *Mississippi Valley Historical Review* 45 (December 1958): 413–40.

Lincoln and Black Freedom: A Study in Presidential Leadership. University of South Carolina Press, 1981.

Cox, Lawanda, and John H. Cox. *Reconstruction, the Negro, and the New South.* University of South Carolina Press, 1973.

Coxe, Tench. *A View of the United States of America.* William Hall and Wrigley and Berriman, 1794. Reprint. Augustus Kelly, 1965.

Cunliffe, Marcus. *American Presidents and the Presidency.* 2d edition. McGraw-Hill, 1973.

Cunningham, Noble E., Jr. *In Pursuit of Reason: The Life of Thomas Jefferson.* Louisiana State University Press, 1987.

Current, Richard N. *Those Terrible Carpetbaggers: A Reinterpretation.* Oxford University Press, 1988.

David, Paul, Herbert Gutman, Richard Sutch, Peter Teinin, and Gavin Wright. *Reckoning with Slavery: A Critical Study in the Quantitative History of American Negro Slavery.* Oxford University Press 1976.

Davis, Andrew M. *The Origins of the National Banking System.* U.S. Government Printing Office, 1910.

Davis, David Brion. *The Problem of Slavery in the Age of Revolution, 1770–1823.* Cornell University Press, 1975.

Slavery and Human Progress. Oxford University Press, 1984.

Davis, Lance E. "The Investment Market, 1870–1914: The Evolution of a National Market." *Journal of Economic History* 25 (September 1965): 355–99.

Davis, Lance E. and Robert E. Gallman. "The Share of Savings and Investment in Gross National Product during the 19th Century in the U.S.A." In *Fourth International Conference of Economic History, Bloomington, 1968,* pp. 437–66. Mouton, 1973.

Davis, Lance E., and John Legler. "The Government in the American Economy, 1815–1902: A Quantitative Study." *Journal of Economic History* 26 (December 1966): 514–52.

Davis, William C. *Battle at Bull Run: A History of the First Major Campaign of the Civil War.* Louisiana State University Press, 1977.

Debow, James D. B. "The Future of the South." *Debow's Review* 1 (January 1866): 6–16.

Deforest, John W. *A Union Officer in the Reconstruction.* 1867. Reprint. Yale University Press, 1948.

Dennett, John Richard. *The South As It Is: 1865–66.* 1867. Reprint. Viking Press, 1967.

Detweiler, Philip F. "Congressional Debate on Slavery and the Declaration of Independence, 1819–1821." *American Historical Review* 63 (April 1958): 598–616.

Diamond, Peter A. "National Debt in a Neoclassical Growth Model." *American Economic Review* 55 (December 1965): 1126–50.

Donald, David H. *Lincoln Reconsidered: Essays on the Civil War Era.* 2d edition, enlarged. Vintage Books, 1961.

Liberty and Union. D. C. Heath, 1978.

Donald, David H., ed. *Why The North Won the Civil War.* Collier Books, 1960.

Donald, David H., and James G. Randall. *The Civil War and Reconstruction.* 2d edition. D. C. Heath, 1961.

Donaldson, Thomas. *The Public Domain: Its History, with Statistics.* U.S. Government Printing Office, 1884.

Dowd, Douglas. "A Comparative Analysis of Economic Development in the American West and South." *Journal of Economic History* 16 (December 1956): 558–74.

Easterlin, Richard A. "Regional Growth of Income: Long Term Tendencies, 1880–1950." In *Population Redistribution and Economic Growth, United States, 1870–1950.* vol. 2, *Analysis of Economic Change,* edited by Simon Kuznets and Dorothy Swaine Thomas, pp. 141–288. American Philosophical Society, 1957.

"Interregional Differences in Per Capita Income, Population, and Total Income: 1840–1950." In *Trends in the American Economy in the Nineteenth Century.* Conference on Research in Income and Wealth. National Bureau of Economic Research, Studies in Income and Wealth, 24: 73–140. Princeton University Press, 1960.

"Regional Income Trends, 1840–1950." In *American Economic History,* edited by Seymour E. Harris, pp. 525–47. McGraw-Hill, 1961.

Engerman, Stanley L. "The Economic Impact of the Civil War." *Explorations in Entrepreneurial History,* 2d ser. 3 (Spring 1966): 176–99.

"Some Economic Factors in Southern Backwardness in the Nineteenth Century." In *Essays in Regional Economics,* edited by John F. Kain and John R. Meyer. Harvard University Press, 1971.

"Some Economic Issues Relating to Railroad Subsidies and the Evaluation of Land Grants." *Journal of Economic History* 32 (June 1972): 443–63.

Engerman, Stanley L., and Robert E. Gallman, eds. *Long-term Factors in American Economic Growth.* National Bureau of Economic Research, Studies in Income and Wealth, vol. 51. University of Chicago Press, 1986.

Escott, Paul D. *After Secession: Jefferson Davis and the Failure of Confederate Nationalism.* Louisiana State University Press, 1978.

Evans, Robert, Jr. "The Economics of American Negro Slavery." In Universities-National Bureau Committee for Economic Research, *Aspects of Labor Economics.* Princeton University Press, 1962.

Farrand, Max, ed. *The Records of the Federal Convention of 1787.* Yale University Press, 1911.

Fehrenbacher, Donald E. *Slavery, Law, and Politics: The Dred Scott Case in Historical Perspective.* Oxford University Press, 1981.

Fields, Barbara J. "Ideology and Race in American History." In *Region, Race and Reconstruction: Essays in Honor of C. Vann Woodward,* edited by J. Morgan Kousser and James M. McPherson. Oxford University Press, 1982.

Slavery and Freedom on the Middle Ground: Maryland during the Nineteenth Century. Yale University Press, 1985.

Fishlow, Albert. "Antebellum Interregional Trade Reconsidered." *American Economic Review* 54 (May 1964): 352–64.

Fogel, Robert W. *The Union Pacific Railroad: A Case in Premature Enterprise.* Johns Hopkins University Press, 1960.

Fogel, Robert W., and Stanley L. Engerman, eds. *The Reinterpretation of American Economic History.* Harper and Row, 1971.

"The Economics of Slavery." In *The Reinterpretation of American Economic History,* edited by Robert William Fogel and Stanley L. Engerman, pp. 311–41. Harper and Row, 1971.

Time on the Cross. 2 vols. Little, Brown, 1974.

Foner, Eric. "The Wilmot Proviso Revisited." *Journal of American History* 61 (September 1969): 262–79.

Free Soil, Free Men and Free Labor: The Ideology of the Republican Party before the Civil War. Oxford University Press, 1970.

"Politics, Ideology and the Origins of the American Civil War." In *A Nation Divided,* edited by George M. Fredrickson. Burgess, 1975.

Politics and Ideology in the Age of the Civil War. Oxford University Press, 1980.

Nothing But Freedom: Emancipation and Its Legacy. Louisiana State University Press, 1983.

Reconstruction: America's Unfinished Revolution. Harper and Row, 1988.

Ford, Paul Leicester, ed. *The Writings of Thomas Jefferson.* Vol. 2: *1776–1781.* G. P. Putnam's and Sons, 1893.

Formisano, Roland P. *The Birth of Mass Political Parties: Michigan, 1827–1861.* Princeton University Press, 1971.

Foust, James, and Dale Swan. "Productivity and Profitability of Antebellum Slave Labor: A Micro Approach." *Agricultural History* 44 (January 1970): 39–62.

Freehling, William. *Prelude to Civil War: The Nullification Crisis in South Carolina: 1816–1836.* Harper and Row, 1965.

"Nullification, Blackmail, and the Crisis of Majority Rule." In *A Nation Divided,* edited by George M. Fredrickson. Burgess, 1975.

Gallman, Robert E. "Commodity Output, 1839–1899." In National Bureau of Economic Research, *Trends in the American Economy in the Nineteenth Century.* Studies in Income and Wealth, 24: 13–67. Princeton University Press, 1960.

"Gross National Product in the United States, 1834–1909." In National Bureau of Economic Research, *Output, Employment, and Productivity in the United States after 1800.* Studies in Income and Wealth, 30: 3–90. Princeton University Press, 1966.

"Trends in the Size Distribution of Wealth in the Nineteenth Century: Some Speculations." In National Bureau of Economic Research, *Six Papers on the Size Distribution of Wealth and Income.* Studies in Income and Wealth, 33: 1–30. Princeton University Press, 1969.

"The United States Capital Stock During the Nineteenth Century." In *Long-*

Term Factors in American Economic Growth, edited by Robert E. Gallman and Stanley L. Engerman. National Bureau of Economic Research, Studies in Income and Wealth, vol. 51. University of Chicago Press, 1986.

Gara, Larry. "Slavery and the Slave Power: A Crucial Distinction." *Civil War History* 15 (March 1969): 5–18.

Gates, Paul Wallace. "The Homestead Act in an Incongruous Land System." In *The Public Lands: Studies in the History of the Public Domain*, edited by Vernon L. Carstensen, pp. 315–48. University of Wisconsin, 1962.

Genovese, Eugene D. *The Political Economy of Slavery: Studies in the Economy and Society of the Slave South*. Vintage Books, 1965.

   "The Origins of Slavery Expansionism." In *The Political Economy of Slavery: Studies in the Economy and Society of the Slave South*, edited by Eugene D. Genovese, pp. 243–74. Vintage Books, 1965.

   Roll, Jordan, Roll: The World the Slaves Made. Pantheon, 1974.

Gibbon, John. "The Council of War on the Second Day." In *Battles and Leaders of the Civil War*, Grant–Lee edition, edited by Robert U. Johnson and Clarence C. Buel, 3: 313–14. The Century Company, 1884.

Gienapp, William E. "The Crime against Sumner: The Caning of Charles Sumner and the Rise of the Republican Party." *Civil War History* 25 (September 1979): 218–45.

   The Origins of the Republican Party, 1852–1856. Oxford University Press, 1987.

Gilchrist, David T., and W. David Lewis, eds. *Economic Change in the Civil War Era*. Eleutherian Mills–Hagley Foundation, 1965.

Gillette, William. *Retreat from Reconstruction, 1869–1879*. Louisiana State University Press, 1979.

Glatthaar, Joseph T. *The March to the Sea and Beyond: Sherman's Troops in the Savannah and Carolinas Campaigns*. New York University Press, 1985.

Godwin, Parke. *Political Essays*. Dix Edwards, 1856.

Goldin, Claudia Dale. "The Economics of Emancipation." *Journal of Economic History* 33 (March 1973): 66–85.

   Urban Slavery in the American South, 1820–1860: A Quantitative History. University of Chicago Press, 1976.

Goldin, Claudia Dale, and Frank Lewis. "The Economic Costs of the American Civil War: Estimates and Implications." *Journal of Economic History* 35 (June 1975): 299–326.

Goodrich, Carter. *Government Promotion of American Canals and Railroads*. Columbia University Press, 1960.

Gordon, Donald F., and Gary M. Walton. "A Theory of Regenerative Growth and the Experience of Post World War II West Germany." In *Explorations in Economic History: Essays in Honor of Douglass C. North*, edited by Roger L. Ransom, Richard Sutch, and Gary M. Walton, pp. 169–92. Academic Press, 1982.

Govan, Thomas. "Was Plantation Slavery Profitable?" *Journal of Southern History* 8 (November 1942): 513–35. Reprinted in *Slavery and the Southern Economy: Sources and Readings*, edited by Harold D. Woodman. Harcourt, Brace and World, 1966.

Grady, Henry W. "Cotton and Its Kingdom." *Harper's New Monthly Magazine* 63 (October 1881): 719–34.

Gray, Lewis Cecil. *History of Agriculture in the Southern United States to 1860.* 2 vols. Carnegie Institution, 1933. Reprint. Peter Smith, 1958.

Grayson, Benson Lee. *The Unknown President: The Administration of President Millard Fillmore.* University Press of America, 1981.

Gunderson, Gerald. "Southern Ante-Bellum Income Reconsidered." *Explorations in Economic History* 10 (Winter 1973): 151–76.

"The Origin of the American Civil War." *Journal of Economic History* 34 (1974): 915–50.

"Southern Income Reconsidered: A Reply." *Explorations in Economic History* 12 (January 1975): 101–2.

Hacker, Louis M. *The Triumph of American Capitalism.* Columbia University Press, 1940.

ed. *Major Documents in American Economic History.* 2 vols. Van Nostrand, 1961.

Hagerman, Edward. "The Tactical Thought of R. E. Lee and the Origins of Trench Warfare in the American Civil War, 1861–1862." *The Historian* 38 (November 1975): 21–38.

Hahn, Steven. *The Roots of Southern Populism: Yeoman Farmers and the Transformation of the Georgia Upcountry, 1850–1860.* Oxford University Press, 1983.

Hamilton, Holman. *Prologue to Conflict: The Crisis and Compromise of 1850.* Norton, 1964.

Hartz, Louis. *Economic Policy and Democratic Thought: Pennsylvania, 1776–1860.* Harvard University Press, 1948.

"Government–Business Relations." In *Economic Change in the Civil War Era,* edited by David T. Gilchrist and W. David Lewis, pp. 83–92. Eleutherian Mills–Hagley Foundation, 1965.

Hattaway, Herman and Archer Jones. "Lincoln as Military Strategist." *Civil War History* 26 (December 1980): 293–303.

How the North Won: A Military History of the Civil War. University of Illinois Press, 1983.

Hawke, Guy. "The United States Tariff and Industrial Protection in the Late Nineteenth Century." *Economic History Review* 28 (February 1975): 84–99.

Helper, Hinton R. *The Impending Crisis of the South: How to Meet It.* A. B. Burdick, 1860.

Hibbard, Benjamin Horace. *A History of the Public Land Policies.* Macmillan, 1924. Reprint. University of Wisconsin Press, 1965.

Higgs, Robert. *Competition and Coercion: Blacks in the American Economy, 1865–1914.* Cambridge University Press, 1977.

Holt, Michael. *Forging a Majority: The Formation of the Republican Party in Pittsburgh, 1848–1860.* Yale University Press, 1969.

"The Politics of Impatience: The Origins of Know-Nothingism." *Journal of American History* 60 (1973): 309–31.

The Political Crisis of the 1850's. W. W. Norton, 1978.

Hughes, Jonathan R. T. "The Great Land Ordinances: Colonial America's Thumbprint on History." In *Essays on the Old Northwest,* edited by David C. Klingaman and Richard C. Vedder, pp. 1–18. Ohio University Press, 1987.

James, John A. *Money and Capital Markets in Postbellum America.* Princeton University Press, 1978.

Johnson, Robert U., and Clarence C. Buel, eds. *Battles and Leaders of the Civil War.* Grant–Lee edition, 4 vols. The Century Company, 1884.

Jordan, Winthrop. *White over Black: American Attitudes toward the Negro: 1550–1812.* University of North Carolina Press, 1968.

Julian, George W. *Political Recollections, 1840 to 1872.* Chicago, Jansen, McClung and Co., 1884.

Kessel, Rueben A., and Armen A. Alchian. "Real Wages in the North during the Civil War: Mitchell's Data Reinterpreted." In *The Economic Impact of the American Civil War,* edited by Ralph Andreano. Schenkman Publishing Company, 1967.

Kindahl, James K. "Economic Factors in Specie Resumption: The United States, 1865–79." *Journal of Political Economy* 49 (February 1961): 30–48.

King, Charles R., ed. *The Life and Correspondence of Rufus King.* 6 vols. G. P. Putnam's Sons, The Knickerbocker Press, 1894. Reprint. Da Capo Press, 1971.

Klein, Herbert S. *Slavery in the Americas: A Comparative Study of Virginia and Cuba.* University of Chicago Press, 1967.

Klingaman, David C., and Richard C. Vedder, eds. *Essays on the Economy of the Old Northwest.* Ohio University Press, 1987.

Kolchin, Peter. *First Freedom: The Response of Alabama's Blacks to Emancipation and Reconstruction.* Greenwood Press, 1972.

Kotlikoff, Laurence J., and Sebastian E. Pinera. "The Old South's Stake in the Inter-Regional Movement of Slaves." *Journal of Economic History* 37 (June 1977): 434–50.

Kousser, J. Morgan, and James M. McPherson, eds. *Region, Race and Reconstruction: Essays in Honor of C. Vann Woodward.* Oxford University Press, 1982.

Kruman, Marc W. *Parties and Politics in North Carolina, 1836–1865.* Louisiana State University Press, 1983.

Latner, Richard B. "The Nullification Crisis and Southern Subversion." *Journal of Southern History* 43 (1977): 19–33.

Lebergott, Stanley. "Labor Force and Employment, 1800–1960." Conference on Research in Income and Wealth, *Output, Employment, and Productivity in the United States after 1800.* National Bureau of Economic Research, Studies in Income and Wealth, 30: 117–204. Princeton University Press, 1966.

Lee, Susan Previant. *The Westward Movement of the Cotton Economy, 1840–1860: Perceived Interests and Economic Interests.* Ph.D. Dissertation, Columbia University, 1975. Reprint. Arno Press, 1977.

"Antebellum Land Expansion." *Agricultural History* 52 (October 1978): 488–502.

Lee, Susan Previant, and Peter Passell. *A New Economic View of American History*. W. W. Norton, 1979.

Lerner, Eugene M. "The Monetary and Fiscal Programs of the Confederate Government, 1861–65." *Journal of Political Economy* 62 (December 1954): 506–22.

"Money, Prices and Wages in the Confederacy, 1861–65." *Journal of Political Economy* 62 (October 1955): 20–40.

Litwack, Leon F. *North of Slavery: The Negro in the Free States, 1790–1860.* University of Chicago Press, 1971.

Been in the Storm So Long: The Aftermath of Slavery, Vintage Books, 1979.

Livermore, Thomas L. *Numbers and Losses in the Civil War in America 1861–1865.* Houghton-Mifflin, 1901.

Longstreet, James. "The Invasion of Maryland." In *Battles and Leaders of the Civil War*, Grant–Lee edition, edited by Robert U. Johnson and Clarence C. Buel, 2: 663–74. The Century Company, 1884.

"Lee's Invasion of Maryland." In *Battles and Leaders of the Civil War*, Grant–Lee edition, edited by Robert U. Johnson and Clarence C. Buel, 3: 244–51. The Century Company, 1884.

Luraghi, Ramondo. "The American Civil War and the Modernization of American Society: Social Structure and Industrial Revolution in the Old South before and during the War." *Civil War History* 18 (September 1972): 230–50.

Lynd, Staughton. "On Turner, Beard, and Slavery." *Journal of Negro History* 48 (1963): 235–50.

"The Compromise of 1787." *Political Science Quarterly* 81 (1966): 225–50.

Class Conflict, Slavery and the United States Constitution. Bobbs-Merrill, 1967.

McClelland, Peter D., and Richard J. Zeckhauser. *Demographic Dimensions of the New Republic: American Interregional Migration, Vital Statistics, and Manumissions, 1800–1860*. Cambridge University Press, 1982.

McCormick, Richard P. *The Second American Party System: Party Formation in the Jacksonian Era*. University of North Carolina, 1966.

The Presidential Game: The Origins of American Presidential Politics. Oxford University Press, 1982.

McDonald, Forrest. *We the People: The Economic Origins of the Constitution*. University of Chicago Press, 1958.

E Pluribus Unum: The Formulation of the American Republic, 1776–1790. Houghton-Mifflin, 1965.

McDonough, James Lee. *Shiloh – In Hell before Night*. University of Tennessee Press, 1977.

Chattanooga: A Death Grip on the Confederacy. University of Tennessee Press, 1984.

McFeely, William S. *Grant: A Biography*. W. W. Norton, 1981.

McGuire, Robert A. "Constitution Making: A Rational Choice Model of the Federal Convention of 1787." *American Journal of Political Science* 32 (May 1988): 483–522.

McGuire, Robert A., and Robert L. Ohsfeldt. "Economic Interests and the American Constitution: A Quantitative Rehabilitation of Charles A. Beard." *Journal of Economic History* 44 (June 1984): 509–20.

"An Economic Model of Voting Behavior over Specific Issues at the Constitutional Convention of 1787." *Journal of Economic History* 66 (March 1986): 79–111.

McPherson, James M. *Ordeal by Fire: The Civil War and Reconstruction.* Alfred Knopf, 1982.

Lincoln and the Strategy of Unconditional Surrender. Twenty-Third Annual Robert Fortenbaugh Memorial Lecture. Gettysburg College, 1984.

Battle Cry of Freedom: The Civil War Era. Oxford University Press, 1988.

McWhiney, Grady, and Perry D. Jamieson. *Attack and Die: Civil War Military Tactics and the Southern Heritage.* University of Alabama Press, 1982.

Mercer, Lloyd. "The Antebellum Interregional Trade Hypothesis: A Reexamination of Theory and Evidence." In *Explorations in the New Economic History: Essays in Honor of Douglass C. North,* edited by Roger L. Ransom, Richard Sutch, and Gary M. Walton. Academic Press, 1982.

Merk, Frederick. *Manifest Destiny and Mission in American History.* Vintage, 1963.

Slavery and the Annexation of Texas. Alfred Knopf, 1972.

Millett, Alan R., and Peter Maslowski. *For the Common Defense: A Military History of the United States of America.* Free Press, 1984.

Modigliani, Franco. "Long-run Implications of Alternative Fiscal Policies and the Burden of the National Debt." *Economic Journal* 71 (December 1961): 730–55.

"The Life Cycle Hypothesis of Saving, the Demand for Wealth and the Supply of Capital." *Social Research* 33 (Summer 1966): 160–217.

"Life Cycle, Individual Thrift, and the Wealth of Nations." *American Economic Review* 76 (June 1986): 297–313.

Mohr, Clarence L. *On the Threshold of Freedom: Masters and Slaves in Civil War Georgia.* University of Georgia Press, 1986.

Moore, Glover B. *The Missouri Controversy, 1819–1821.* University of Kentucky Press, 1953.

Murfin, James V. *The Gleam of Bayonets: The Battle of Antietam and the Maryland Campaign of 1862.* 1965. Paperback edition. Louisiana State University Press, 1982.

Myers, Margaret G. *The New York Money Market,* vol. 1, *Origins and Development.* Columbia University Press, 1931.

Nevins, Allan. *Ordeal of the Union.* 8 vols. Charles Scribners and Sons, 1947–61.

Nichols, Roy F. *Franklin Pierce: Young Hickory of the Granite Hills.* 2d edition. University of Pennsylvania Press, 1958.

Niven, John. *Martin Van Buren: The Romantic Age of American Politics.* Oxford University Press, 1983.

North, Douglass C. *The Economic Growth of the United States, 1790–1860.* Prentice-Hall, 1961.

North, Douglass C., and Andrew R. Rutten. "The Northwest Ordinance in Historical Perspective." In *Essays on the Economy of the Old Northwest*, edited by David C. Klingaman and Richard C. Vedder, pp. 19–35. Ohio University Press, 1987.

Nugent, Walter T. K. *The Money Question during Reconstruction.* W. W. Norton, 1967.

Oakes, James. "From Republicanism to Liberalism: Ideological Change and the Crisis in the Old South," *American Quarterly* 37 (Fall 1985): 551–71.

Ohline, Howard A. "Republicanism and Slavery: Origins of the Three-Fifths Clause in the United States Constitution." *William and Mary Quarterly* 28 (October 1971): 563–84.

Olmsted, Frederick Law. *A Journey in the Seaboard Slave States.* Dix and Edwards, 1856.

A Journey through Texas. Dix and Edwards, 1857.

A Journey in the Back Country. Mason Brothers, 1860.

The Cotton Kingdom. 1861. Edited with an introduction by Arthur Schlesinger. Alfred A. Knopf, 1953.

Onuf, Peter S. "Liberty, Development and Union: Visions of the West in the 1780s." *William and Mary Quarterly* 43 (April 1986): 179–213.

Owsley, Frank L. *Plain Folk of the Old South.* Louisiana State University Press, 1949.

King Cotton Diplomacy: Foreign Relations of the Confederate States of America. 2d edition. Revised by Harriet C. Owsley. University of Chicago Press, 1959.

Parker, William N. ed. *The Structure of the Cotton Economy of the Antebellum South.* University of North Carolina Press, 1970.

Parrish, Peter J. *The American Civil War.* Holmes and Meir, 1975.

Passell, Peter. "The Impact of Cotton Land Distribution on the Antebellum Economy." *Journal of Economic History* 31 (December 1971): 917–37.

Passell, Peter, and Gavin Wright. "The Effects of Pre-Civil War Territorial Expansion on the Price of Slaves." *Journal of Political Economy* 80 (November–December 1972): 1188–202.

Paxson, Frederick L. "The Railroads of the Old Northwest before the Civil War." *Wisconsin Academy of Science, Arts, and Letters* 15, part 1 (1914).

Perman, Michael. *Reunion without Compromise: The South and Reconstruction 1865–1868.* Cambridge University Press, 1973.

Emancipation and Reconstruction, 1862–1879. Harian Davidson, 1987.

Pessen, Edward. *Jacksonian America: Society, Personality and Politics.* Dorsey Press, 1969.

Phillips, Ulrich Bonnell. "The Economic Cost of Slaveholding in the Cotton Belt." *Political Science Quarterly* 20 (June 1905): 257–75.

American Negro Slavery: A Survey of the Supply, Employment, and Control of Negro Labor, as Determined by the Plantation Regime. D. Appleton, 1918.

Life and Labor in the Old South. Little, Brown, 1929.

Potter, David M. "Jefferson Davis and the Political Factors in Confederate Defeat." In *Why the North Won the Civil War,* edited by David Donald. Collier Books, 1962.

The Impending Crisis: 1848–1861. Harper Torchbooks, 1976.

Pressly, Thomas J. *Americans Interpret Their Civil War.* Princeton University Press, 1954.

Ramsdell, Charles W. "The Natural Limits of Slavery Expansion." *Mississippi Valley Historical Review* 16 (September 1929): 151–71.

Ransom, Roger L. "Government Investment in Canals: A Study of the Ohio Canal, 1825–1860." Ph.D. dissertation, University of Washington, Seattle, 1962.

"Social Returns from Public Transport Investment: A Case Study of the Ohio Canal." *Journal of Political Economy* 78 (September–October 1970): 1041–60.

Ransom, Roger L., and Kerry Ann Odell. "Land and Credit: Some Historical Parallels between Mexico and the American South." *Agricultural History* 60 (Winter 1986): 4–31.

Ransom, Roger L., and Richard Sutch. "Tenancy, Farm Size, Self-Sufficiency, and Racism: Four Problems in the Economic History of Southern Agriculture, 1865–1880." *Southern Economic History Project Working Paper Series,* no. 8. Institute for Business and Economic Research, University of California, Berkeley, April 1970.

"Economic Regions of the South in 1880." *Southern Economic History Project Working Paper Series,* no. 3. Institute for Business and Economic Research, University of California, Berkeley, March 1971.

"Debt Peonage in the Cotton South after the Civil War." *Journal of Economic History* 32 (September 1972): 641–69.

"The Ex-Slave in the Postbellum South: A Study of the Economic Impact of Racism in a Market Environment." *Journal of Economic History* 33 (March 1973): 131–47.

"The Impact of the Civil War and of Emancipation on Southern Agriculture." *Explorations in Economic History* 12 (January 1975): 1–28.

One Kind of Freedom: The Economic Consequences of Emancipation. Cambridge University Press, 1977.

"Sharecropping: Market Response or Mechanism of Race Control?" In *What Was Freedom's Price?* edited by David S. Sansing, pp. 51–69. University Press of Mississippi, 1978.

"Growth and Welfare in the American South in the Nineteenth Century." *Explorations in Economic History* 16 (April 1979): 207–35.

"Credit Merchandising in the Post-Emancipation South: Structure, Conduct, and Performance." *Explorations in Economic History* 16 (January 1979): 64–89.

"Domestic Saving as an Active Constraint on Capital Formation in the American Economy, 1839–1928: A Provisional Theory." *Working Papers on the History of Saving,* no. 1. Institute for Business and Economic Research, University of California, Berkeley, December 1984.

"A System of Life-Cycle National Accounts: Provisional Estimates, 1839–

1938." *Working Papers on the History of Saving,* no. 2. Institute for Business and Economic Research, University of California, Berkeley, December 1984.

"Capitalists without Capital: The Burden of Slavery and the Impact of Emancipation." *Agricultural History* (Fall 1988): 119–47.

Rawley, James A. *Race and Politics: "Bleeding" Kansas and the Coming of Civil War.* J. B. Lippincott, 1969.

Reid, Whitelaw. *After the War: A Tour of the Southern States, 1865–1866.* 1866. Reprint. Harper and Row, 1965.

Remini, Robert V. *Andrew Jackson and the Bank War: A Study in the Growth of Presidential Power.* W. W. Norton, 1966.

Roark, James L. *Masters without Slaves: Southern Planters in the Civil War and Reconstruction.* W. W. Norton, 1977.

Robertson, James I. *General A. P. Hill: The Story of a Confederate Warrior.* Random House, 1987.

Robinson, Donald L. *Slavery in the Structure of American Politics, 1765–1820.* Harcourt Brace Jovanovich, 1971.

Rockoff, Hugh. "Money, Prices, and Banks in the Jacksonian Era." In *The Reinterpretation of American Economic History,* edited by Robert Fogel and Stanley Engerman, pp. 448–58. Harper and Row, 1971.

Rose, Willie Lee. *Rehearsal for Reconstruction: The Port Royal Experiment.* Alfred A. Knopf, 1964.

Rothstein, Morton. "America in the International Rivalry for the British Wheat Market, 1860–1914." *The Mississippi Valley Historical Review* 47 (December 1960): 401–18.

"The International Market for Agricultural Commodities, 1850–1873." In *Economic Change in the Civil War Era,* edited by David T. Gilchrist and W. David Lewis, pp. 62–72. Eleutherian Mills–Hagley Foundation, 1965.

Russel, Robert R. "The General Effects of Slavery upon Southern Economic Progress." *Journal of Southern History* 4 (February 1938): 34–54.

"The Effects of Slavery on Nonslaveholders in the Ante-Bellum South." *Agricultural History* 15 (April 1941): 112–26.

"Constitutional Doctrines with Regard to Slavery in the Territories." *Journal of Southern History* 32 (November 1966): 466–86.

Salinger, Sharon V. *"To Serve Well and Faithfully": Labor and Indentured Servants in Pennsylvania, 1682–1800.* Cambridge University Press, 1987.

Schlesinger, Arthur M. Jr. *The Imperial Presidency.* Houghton-Mifflin, 1973.

Schmitz, Mark, and Donald Schaefer. "Paradox Lost: Westward Expansion and Slave Prices before the Civil War." *Journal of Economic History* 41 (June 1981): 402–7.

Schurz, Carl. "Report of Carl Schurz on the States of South Carolina, Georgia, Alabama, Mississippi, and Louisiana." In *Message of the President of the United States, Communicating . . . Information in Relation to the States . . . Lately in Rebellion (December 19, 1865).* Senate Executive Document no. 2, 39th Congress, 1st Session. U.S. Government Printing Office, 1865.

Schwartz, Bernard. *From Confederation to Nation: The American Constitution, 1835–1877.* Johns Hopkins Press, 1973.

Sears, Stephen W. *Landscape Turned Red: The Battle of Antietam.* Ticknor and Fields, 1983.

George B. McClellan: The Young Napoleon. Ticknor and Fields, 1988.

Sewell, Richard H. *A House Divided: Sectionalism and Civil War, 1848–1865.* Johns Hopkins University Press, 1988.

Shalhope, Robert E. "Race, Class, Slavery and the Antebellum Southern Mind." *Journal of Southern History* 37 (November 1971): 557–74.

Sharkey, Robert P. *Money, Class, and Party: An Economic Study of Civil War and Reconstruction.* Johns Hopkins University Press, 1959.

Shelton, Cynthia J. *The Mills of Manayunk: Industrialization and Social Conflict in the Philadelphia Region, 1787–1837.* Johns Hopkins University Press, 1986.

Shugg, Roger W. "The Survival of the Plantation System in Louisiana." *Journal of Southern History* 3 (August 1937): 311–25.

Origins of Class Struggle in Louisiana: A Social History of White Farmers and Laborers during Slavery and After, 1840–1875. Louisiana State University Press, 1939.

Silbey, Joel. *The Partisan Imperative: The Dynamics of American Politics before the Civil War.* Oxford University Press, 1985.

Silbey, Joel, ed. *The Transformation of American Politics, 1840–1860.* Prentice-Hall, 1967.

Silversmit, Arthur. *The First Emancipation: The Abolition of Slavery in the North.* University of Chicago Press, 1967.

Simpson, Albert F. "The Political Significance of Slave Representation, 1787–1821." *Journal of Southern History* 7 (August 1941): 315–42.

Slocum, Henry W. "Sherman's March from Savannah to Bentonville." In *Battles and Leaders of the Civil War,* Grant–Lee edition, edited by Robert U. Johnson and Clarence C. Buel, 4: 681–95. The Century Company, 1887.

Smith, Elbert B. *The Presidency of James Buchanan.* University Press of Kansas, 1975.

Somers, Robert. *The Southern States since the War: 1870–1.* Macmillan, 1871.

Stampp, Kenneth. *The Peculiar Institution: Slavery in the Antebellum South.* Alfred Knopf, 1956.

The Era of Reconstruction, 1865–1877. Vintage Press, 1965.

Stegmaier, Mark J. "Zachary Taylor versus the Old South." *Civil War History* 33 (September 1987): 219–41.

Sutch, Richard. "The Profitability of Slavery – Revisited." *Southern Economic Journal* 31 (April 1965): 365–77.

"Slavery as an Obstacle to Growth in the United States: A Panel Discussion." *Journal of Economic History* 27 (December 1967): 518–60.

"The Breeding of Slaves for Sale and the Westward Expansion of Slavery, 1850–1860." In *Race and Slavery in the Western Hemisphere: Quantitative Studies,* edited by Stanley Engerman and Eugene Genovese. Princeton University Press, 1975.

"Douglass North and the New Economic History." In *Explorations in the New Economic History: Essays in Honor of Douglass C. North,* edited by Roger L. Ransom, Richard Sutch, and Gary M. Walton. Academic Press, 1982.

Sutch, Richard, Roger Ransom, and George Boutin. "A Sample of Southern Farms in 1880: Sampling Procedure." *Southern Economic History Project Working Paper Series,* no. 2. Institute for Business and Economic Research, University of California, Berkeley, September 1969.

Sylla, Richard E. "Federal Policy, Banking Market Structure, and Capital Mobilization in the United States, 1863–1913." *Journal of Economic History* 29 (December 1969): 657–86.

"American Banking and Growth in the Nineteenth Century: A Partial View of the Terrain." *Explorations in Economic History* 9 (Winter 1971–72): 197–227.

"The United States, 1863–1913." In *Banking and Economic Development,* edited by Rondo Cameron, pp. 232–62. Oxford University Press, 1972.

The American Capital Market, 1846–1914. Arno Press, 1975.

Symonds, Craig L. *A Battlefield Atlas of the Civil War.* 2d edition. The Nautical and Aviation Publishing Company of America, 1983.

Taylor, George Rogers. *The Transportation Revolution, 1815–1860.* Holt, Rinehart and Winston, 1951.

Taylor, Tim. *The Book of Presidents.* Arno Press, 1972.

Temin, Peter. *The Jacksonian Economy.* W. W. Norton, 1979.

Thomas, Emory M. *The Confederate Nation: 1861–1865.* Harper Torchbooks, 1979.

Bold Dragoon: The Life of J. E. B. Stuart Harper and Row, 1986.

Thorton, J. Mills, III. *Politics and Power in a Slave Society: Alabama, 1800–1860.* Louisiana State University Press, 1978.

Trefousse, Hans L. *The Radical Republicans: Lincoln's Vanguard for Racial Justice.* Louisiana State University Press, 1968.

Tunnell, Ted. *Crucible of Reconstruction: War, Radicalism and Race in Louisiana, 1862–1877.* Louisiana State University Press, 1984.

Turner, Frederick Jackson. "The Significance of the Frontier in American History." *American Historical Association Annual Report* (1893): 199–227.

United States Bureau of the Census. *Historical Statistics of the United States, Colonial Times to 1970.* 2 parts. U.S. Government Printing Office, 1975.

United States Census Office, Eighth Census. *Population of the United States in 1860.* U.S. Government Printing Office, 1864.

Agriculture in the United States in 1860, Compiled from the Original Returns of the Eighth Census. U.S. Government Printing Office, 1864.

United States Congress, Senate Committee on Agriculture and Forestry. "Present Conditions of Cotton-Growers of the United States Compared with Previous Years." In *Senate Report Number 986,* 53rd Congress, 3d Session, 2 vols. U.S. Government Printing Office, 1895.

Vandiver, Frank E. "Editor's Introduction," In *Confederate Blockade Running through Bermuda, 1861–1865,* edited by Frank E. Vandiver. University of Texas Press, 1947.

Ploughshares into Swords: Josiah Gorgas and Confederate Ordnance. University of Texas Press, 1952.

Vartanian, Pershing. "The Cochran Thesis: A Critique in Statistical Analysis." *Journal of American History* 51 (June 1964): 77–89.

Voegeli, V. Jacque. *Free But Not Equal: The Midwest and the Negro during the Civil War.* University of Chicago Press, 1967.

Walton, Gary M., and James F. Shepherd, eds. *Market Institutions and Economic Progress in the New South, 1865–1900: Essays Stimulated by One Kind of Freedom.* Academic Press, 1981.

Wiener, Jonathan M. "Planter Persistence and Social Change in Alabama, 1850–1871." *Journal of Interdisciplinary History* 7 (Autumn 1976): 235–60.

Social Origins of the New South: Alabama, 1865–1885. Louisiana State University Press, 1978.

Wilentz, Sean. "On Class and Politics in Jacksonian America." *Reviews in American History* 10 (December 1982): 45–63.

Wiley, Bell Irwin. *The Road to Appomattox.* Memphis State University Press, 1956.

Williamson, Jeffrey G. *Late Nineteenth Century Development: A General Equilibrium History.* Cambridge University Press, 1974.

"Watersheds and Turning Points: Conjectures on the Long-Term Impact of Civil War Financing." *Journal of Economic History* 34 (September 1974): 636–61.

"Greasing the Wheels of Sputtering Export Engines: Midwestern Grains and American Growth." *Explorations in Economic History* 17 (July 1980): 189–217.

Wilson, Major L. *The Presidency of Martin Van Buren.* University Press of Kansas, 1984.

Woodman, Harold D. *King Cotton and His Retainers: Financing and Marketing the Cotton Crop of the South, 1800–1925.* University of Kentucky Press, 1968.

Woodward, C. Vann, ed. *Mary Chesnut's Civil War.* Yale University Press, 1981.

Wright, Gavin, "'Economic Democracy' and the Concentration of Agricultural Wealth in the Cotton South." *Agricultural History* 44 (January 1970): 63–93.

"New and Old Views on the Economics of Slavery." *Journal of Economic History* 33 (June 1973): 452–66.

The Political Economy of the Cotton South: Households, Markets, and Wealth in the Nineteenth Century. W. W. Norton, 1978.

Old South, New South: Revolutions in the Southern Economy since the Civil War. Basic Books, 1986.

"Capitalism and Slavery on the Islands: A Lesson from the Mainland." *Journal of Interdisciplinary History* 17 (Spring 1987): 851–70.

Zeichner, Oscar. "Transition from Slave to Free Agricultural Labor in the Southern States." *Agricultural History* 13 (January 1939): 22–32.

Index

Printed in the United States
132994LV00005B/1/A

9 780521 311670